ISSUES IN CONTEMPORARY ECONOMICS
Volume 2: Macroeconomics and Econometrics

This is IEA conference volume no. 99

ISSUES IN CONTEMPORARY ECONOMICS

Issues in Contemporary Economics

Proceedings of the Ninth World Congress of the
International Economic Association, Athens, Greece

Volume 2
MACROECONOMICS AND ECONOMETRICS

Edited by
Marc Nerlove

NEW YORK UNIVERSITY PRESS
Washington Square, New York

© International Economic Association, 1991

First published in the U.S.A. in 1991 by
NEW YORK UNIVERSITY PRESS
Washington Square
New York, N.Y. 10003

Library of Congress Cataloging-in-Publication Data
International Economic Association. World Congress (9th: 1989:
  Athens, Greece)
    Issues in contemporary economics: proceedings of the Ninth World
  Congress of the International Economic Association, Athens, Greece,
  August 18, 1989.
      p. cm.
  ISBN 0–8147–5767–7
    Contents: v. 1   v. 2 Macroeconomics and econometrics
  /edited by Marc Nerlove.
      1. Economics—Congresses.   2. Nerlove, Marc. 1933–   .
  II. Title.
  HB21.I65   1991
  330—dc20   90–6578
                                                            CIP

Contents

Preface

Amartya Sen

'Reading maketh a full man', according to Francis Bacon, and 'conference a ready man'. Those who missed the Ninth World Congress of the International Economic Association, held at Athens during August–September 1989, may no longer have the chance of being 'ready' (for whatever), but these proceedings offer them an opportunity of reading the papers presented there, and thus achieving 'fullness' (presumably, a solid, if somewhat obscure, virtue). Less immodestly, we at the International Economic Association are happy to be able to make a selection of the many interesting and productive papers presented at the Ninth World Congress available in book form (in five volumes).

Each of the previous World Congresses of the International Economic Association had one 'unifying' theme (the last one had the theme 'The Balance between Industry and Agriculture in Economic Development'[1]). The Ninth Congress had no such unique theme. Instead papers were invited and contributions sought in a number of different theme areas, covering different parts of the discipline of economics. The purpose of choosing a plurality of themes was to make it possible for economists all over the world to participate in this World Congress despite wide variations in their specialisation. To some extent this had been implicitly permitted in previous conferences too by taking a rather liberal view of the allegedly unifying theme – and by practising what I can only describe as 'diversity in unity'.

The Ninth Congress went a good deal further in making the conference open to economists of different interests and expertise. Since these conferences are three-yearly phenomena, it seems unreasonable to make economists of particular specialisation wait many multiples of three years for their turn to come up. We were rewarded in the Ninth Congress by the attendance of economists of widely different fields and practice. As the variety of papers in these volumes indicate, the range of economic issues covered was quite remarkable.

The programme consisted of twenty-two sections – fifteen sections for presentation of invited and contributed papers and seven sections for panel discussion. The conference was planned by a Programme Committee, which I was privileged to chair. Each member of the committee took particular responsibility for inviting and selecting papers for one session.

Paper Sections

1. *General microeconomics* (Takashi Negishi)
2. *General macroeconomics* (Jean-Paul Fitoussi)
3. *Welfare and social choice* (Kenneth Arrow)
4. *Econometrics* (Marc Nerlove)
5. *Centrally Planned Economies* (Béla Csikós-Nagy)
6. *Economic History* (Marcello de Cecco)
7. *International Economics* (Elhanan Helpman)
8. *Economic Development* (Victor Urquidi)
9. *Labour Economics* (Richard Layard)
10. *Public Economics* (Lawrence Summers)
11. *Industrial Economics* (Jean Gabszewicz)
12. *Agricultural Economics* (Glenn Johnson)
13. *Food and Nutrition* (Amartya Sen)
14. *Theory of Policy* (Heraklis Polemarchakis)
15. *Economics of Integration* (George Kottis)

Panel Sections

P.1. *Women's and Men's Role in the Economy of the Future* (Barbara Bergmann)
P.2. *The Greek Economy Today* (Thanos Skouros)
P.3. *Game Theory and Economics* (Partha Dasgupta)
P.4. *Rational Expectations after the Event* (Frank Hahn)
P.5. *Neo-Marxian Perspectives on Production Relations and Property Rights* (Stephen Marglin)
P.6. *What Remains of Development Economics?* (Louis Lefeber)
P.7. *Social Justice and Quality of Life* (Zdzislaw Sadowski)

The Programme Committee refereed the papers proposed for presentation, and the final programme was drawn up on that basis. I take this opportunity of thanking the members of the Programme Committee for their immense help in making the Ninth World Congress a success. Not only did they select, severally or jointly, the invited paper writers and assess the contributed papers, but they were also responsible for the selection and appropriate revision of the invited papers for inclusion in these proceedings.

Neither the discussants' comments, nor any reports of the general deliberation in the sessions, are being published. Instead, the paper writers were encouraged to take note of the comments and suggestions made in the sessions, with appropriate acknowledgement.

There were also five invited plenary lectures (in addition to the presidential address), and we were lucky enough to have as plenary speakers: Abel G. Aganbegyan ('Economic Restructuring of the USSR and International Economic Relations'); A. B. Atkinson ('Basic Income Schemes and the Lessons from Public Economics'); Zsuzsa Ferge ('Mechanisms of Social Integration: the Role of the Market'); Frank Hahn ('History and Economic Theory'); and Mahar Mangahas ('Monitoring the Economic and Social Weather in the Philippines').

The proceedings of the congress are being published in five volumes, edited respectively by: Kenneth J. Arrow (vol. 1: *Markets and Welfare*); Marc Nerlove (vol. 2: *Macroeconomics and Econometrics*); Partha Dasgupta (vol. 3: *Policy and Development*); Nancy Folbre, Barbara Bergmann, Bina Agarwal and Maria Floro (vol. 4: *Women's Work in the World Economy*); Thanos S. Skouras (vol. 5: *The Greek Economy: Economic Policy for the 1990s*).

Each editor has his or her own 'Introduction' to the respective volume, and so I need not go into substantive contents of the volumes in this general Preface. I take this chance of thanking the volume editors for their tremendous help in producing these proceedings.

One of the new things in the Ninth Congress was a very active working session – spread over two full days – on 'women's and men's roles in the economy of the future', organised by Barbara Bergmann. This is the first time the International Economic Association has had a special session on gender issues in economics, and the idea met with remarkably active and positive response. There were so many contributions in this field that a special volume is devoted to the papers presented at this session (volume 4).

There was also a full day meeting on the Greek economy. This too had many participants, with presentation of different interpretations and approaches, and the papers from this session are being published also in a separate volume edited by Thanos Skouras.

I should like to put on record our great debt to our Greek hosts.

We are most grateful for the cooperation of the respective Greek governments and the Bank of Greece, and for the superb work done by the Local Organising Committee, under the leadership of Maria Constantopoulos (the others on the committee were Panayotis Korliras, George Kottis and Thanos Skouras). The Local Advisory Board was chaired by George Kottis.

I would also like to thank Patricia Hillebrandt, Rita Maurice and Maureen Hadfield for looking after the editorial arrangements for these proceedings. Without their efficient help, my task as general editor of these volumes would have been impossibly hard. I am also most grateful to Michael Kaser, the Editor, and Jean-Paul Fitoussi, the Secretary General, of the International Economic Association for their constant help in organising the congress and in the publication of these proceedings. I would also like to acknowledge my debt to Kenneth Arrow, the preceding President of the IEA, whose wise counsel I have had to seek on many occasions.

Note

1. The proceedings of that conference were published in five volumes (*The Balance between Industry and Agriculture in Economic Development*, London, Macmillan, 1988), edited respectively by Kenneth J. Arrow (the last President of the IEA), Jeffrey G. Williamson and Vadiraj R. Panchamukhi, Sukhamoy Chakravarty, Irma Adelman and Sylvia Lane, and Nurul Islam.

The International Economic Association

A non-profit organisation with purely scientific aims, the International Economic Association (IEA) was founded in 1950. It is in fact a federation of national economic associations and presently includes fifty-eight such professional organisations from all parts of the world. Its basic purpose is the development of economics as an intellectual discipline. Its approach recognises a diversity of problems, systems and values in the world and also takes note of methodological diversities.

The IEA has, since its creation, tried to fulfil that purpose by promoting mutual understanding of economists from the West and the East, as well as from the North and the South, through the organisation of scientific meetings and common research programmes, and by means of publications on problems of current importance. During its thirty-nine years of existence, it has organised eighty-six round-table conferences for specialists on topics ranging from fundamental theories to methods and tools of analysis and major problems of the present-day world. Nine triennial World Congresses have also been held, which have regularly attracted the participation of a great many economists from all over the world.

The Association is governed by a Council, composed of representatives of all member associations, and by a fifteen-member Executive Committee which is elected by the Council. The present Executive Committee (1989–92) is composed as follows:

President	:	Professor Anthony B. Atkinson, UK
Vice-President	:	Professor Luo Yuanzheng, China
Treasurer	:	Professor Alexandre Lamfalussy, Belgium
Past President	:	Professor Amartya Sen, India
Other Members	:	Professor Abel Aganbegyan, USSR
		Professor Kenneth J. Arrow, USA
		Professor Edmar Lisboa Bacha, Brazil
		Professor B. R. Brahmananda, India
		Professor Wolfgang Heinrichs, GDR
		Professor Edmond Malinvaud, France
		Professor Takashi Negishi, Japan

	Professor Don Patinkin, Israel
	Professor Agnar Sandmo, Norway
	Professor Erich Streissler, Austria
	Professor Stefano Zamagni, Italy
Advisers :	Professor Mohammed Germouni, Morocco
	Professor Oleg T. Bogomolov, USSR
Secretary-General :	Professor Jean-Paul Fitoussi, France
General Editor :	Mr Michael Kaser, UK
Advisor to General	
Editor :	Professor Sir Austin Robinson, UK
Conference Editor :	Dr Patricia M. Hillebrandt, UK

The Association has also been fortunate in having secured the following outstanding economists to serve as President:

Gottfried Haberler (1950–53), Howard S. Ellis (1953–56), Erik Lindahl (1956–59), E. A. G. Robinson (1959–62), G. Ugo Papi (1962–65), Paul A. Samuelson (1965–68), Erik Lundberg (1968–71), Fritz Machlup (1971–74), Edmond Malinvaud (1974–77), Shigeto Tsuru (1977–80), Victor L. Urquidi (1980–83), Kenneth J. Arrow (1983–86), Amartya Sen (1986–89).

The activities of the Association are mainly funded from the subscriptions of members and grants from a number of organisations, including continuing support from UNESCO.

Acknowledgements

The hosts for the Ninth World Congress of the International Economic Association were the Hellenic Economic Association and the Athens School of Economics and Business Science. We are grateful to them for the organisation of the Congress, for a stimulating social programme with generous hospitality and for the welcome given to economists from all over the world. The task was daunting but the execution ensured a successful Congress. The International Economic Association wishes to express its thanks on behalf of all participants.

The Congress would not have been possible without the financial help from the Greek Government and the Bank of Greece. The International Economic Association and the Greek host organisations express their appreciation for this support.

The members of the IEA Programme Committee and the Local Organising Committee and Advisory Board are listed overleaf. Our special thanks go to Professor Maria Constantopoulos, the Managing Chairman of the Local Organising Committee, who gave unstintingly of her time and energy to make the Congress a success.

This volume is published by the International Economic Association under the auspices of ISSC and with the financial assistance of UNESCO.

The IEA Programme Committee

Kenneth J. Arrow
Barbara Bergmann
Marcello de Cecco
Béla Csikós-Nagy
Partha Dasgupta
Jean-Paul Fitoussi
J. J. Gabszewicz
Frank Hahn
Elhanan Helpman
Glenn L. Johnson
George Kottis
Richard Layard
Louis Lefeber
Stephen Marglin
Takashi Negishi
Marc Nerlove
Heraklis Polemarchakis
Amartya Sen
Thanos Skouras
Lawrence Summers
Victor L. Urquidi

Local Organising Committee

Panayotis Korliras (Chairman)
Maria Constantopoulos (Managing Chairman)
George Kottis
Thanos Skouras

Local Advisory Board
George Kottis (Chairman)
Angelos Angelopoulos
Dimitris Chalikias
Nickolas Consolas
Constantine Drakatos
George Drakos
Rossetos Fakiolas
Argyris Fatouros
Constantine Kyriazis
Maria Negreponti-Delivanis
George Oekonomou
Stylianos Panagopoulos
Alexandros Yanniotis
Xenophon Zolotas

List of Contributors and Section Leaders

Contributors

Dr Steve Alpern, Department of Mathematics, London School of Economics and Political Science, UK.

Professor Olivier Blanchard, Department of Economics, Massachusetts Institute of Technology, Cambridge, Massachusetts, USA.

Professor Angus Deaton, Woodrow Wilson School of Public and International Affairs, Princeton University, New Jersey, USA.

Dr Paul J. Gertler, Department of Economics and Statistics, The Rand Corporation, Santa Monica, California, USA.

Professor Lawrence Katz, Department of Economics, Harvard University, Cambridge, Massachusetts, USA.

Professor Edward Leamer, Department of Economics, University of California, Los Angeles, USA.

Professor Assar Lindbeck, Institute for International Economic Studies, Stockholm University, Sweden.

Professor G. S. Maddala, Center for Econometrics and Decision Sciences, University of Florida, Gainesville, Florida, USA.

Dr Rainer Masera, Istituto Mobiliare Italiano, Rome, Italy.

Professor Bruce Meyer, Department of Economics, Northwestern University, Evanston, Illinois, USA.

Dr John L. Newman, Welfare and Human Resources Division, The World Bank, Washington, District of Columbia, USA.

Professor Edmund S. Phelps, Department of Economics, Columbia University, New York, USA.

Professor Manuel C. L. Porto, Facultade de Direito, University of Coimbra, Coimbra, Portugal.

Professor Dennis J. Snower, Department of Economics, Birkbeck College, University of London, UK.

Professor Larry Summers, Department of Economics, Harvard University, Cambridge, Massachusetts, USA.

Section Leaders

Professor Jean-Paul Fitoussi, International Economic Association, Paris, France.

Professor Elhanan Helpman, Department of Economics, Tel Aviv University, Israel.

Professor George C. Kottis, Athens School of Economics and Business Science, Greece.

Professor Richard Layard, London School of Economics and Political Science, UK.

Professor Marc Nerlove, Department of Economics, University of Pennsylvania, Philadelphia, Pennsylvania, USA.

Professor Larry Summers, Department of Economics, Harvard University, Cambridge, Massachusetts, USA.

Abbreviations and Acronyms

AEA	American Economic Association
ARCH	Autoregressive conditional heteroscedasticity
ASA	American Statistical Association
BCFF	Blue Chip Financial Forecasts
BIS	Bank for International Settlements
CCR	Comissões de Coordenação Regionais (Regional Coordinating Commissions) Portugal
CCRC	Comissão de Coordenação da Região Centro (Coordinating Commission for the Centre Region) Portugal
CWBH	Continuous wage and benefit history
DGDR	Direccăo Geral do Desenvolvimento Regional (General Directorate for Regional Development) Portugal
EAGGF	European Agricultural Guidance and Guarantee Fund
EC	European Community
ECU	European Currency Unit
EDC	Entrant demand curve
EFTA	European Free Trade Area
EIB	European Investment Bank
EMS	European Monetary System
ERDF	European Regional Development Fund
ESF	European Social Fund
FEF	Fundo de Equilibrio Financeiro (Financial Equilibrium Fund) Portugal
GATT	General Agreement on Tariffs and Trade
GDP	Gross domestic product
GMM	Generalised method of moments
GNP	Gross national product
GOP	Grandes Opções do Plano (Broad Planning Guidelines)
H–O	Heckscher–Ohlin
H–O–V	Heckscher–Ohlin–Vanek

IDC	Insider demand curve
IFADAP	Instituto Financeiro de Aprio ao Desenvolvimento da Agricultura Portuguesa (Financial Institute for the Promotion of the Development of Portuguese Agriculture)
IFO	Ifo-Institut für Wirtschaftsforschung, Munich, West Germany
i.i.d.	independently and identically distributed
IMI	Istituto Mobiliare Italiano, Rome
INE	Instituto Nacional de Estadistica, Peru
INE	Instituto Nacional de Estatistica, Portugal
INSEAD	European Institute of Business Administration
INSEE	Institut Nationale de la Statistique et des Études Économiques, Paris, France
IPD	Implicit price deflator
IS-LM	Investment Saving-Liquidity Money
ISTAT	Istituto Statistico, Italy
JCIF	Japan Centre for International Finance
LDC	Less developed country
MIMIC	Multiple indicator – multiple cause
MIT	Massachusetts Institute of Technology, USA
MMS	Money Market Services
MRP	Marginal revenue product
NAIRU	Non-accelerating inflation rate of unemployment
NBER	National Bureau of Economic Research, USA
OECD	Organisation for Economic Cooperation and Development, Paris, France
OEEC	Organisation for European Economic Cooperation
OLS	Ordinary least squares
PDR	Programa de Desenvolvimento Regional (Regional Development Programme), Portugal
PEDAP	Programa Especifico de Desenvolvimento da Agricultura Portuguesa (Special Programme for the Development of Portuguese Agriculture)
PLSS	Peruvian Living Standards Survey
PPP	Purchasing power parity
PNICIAP	Programa Nacional de Interesse Comunitário de Incentivo à Actividade Productiva (National Programme of Community Interest for Incentives to Production)

PSID	Panel study for income dynamics
R&D	Research and development
RPC	Relative profitability constraint
SEBR	Sistema de Estímulos de Base Regional (System for the Valuation of the Regional Base)
SIBR	Sistema de Incentivos de Base Regional (Regional Base Incentive System)
SIFIT	Sistema de Incentivos Financeiros ao Investimento no Turismo (System of Financial Incentives for Investment in Tourism), Portugal
SINPEDIP	Sistema de Incentivos do Programa Espesifico para o Desenvolvimento da Indústria Portuguesa (Incentive System of the Special Programme for the Development of Portuguese Industry), Portugal
SIPE	Sistema de Incentivos ao Potencial Endógeno (System of Incentives for Indigenous Potential)
STICERD	Suntory–Toyota International Centre for Economics and Related Disciplines
UI	Unemployment insurance

Introduction

Marc Nerlove

The twelve papers in this volume deal with a number of general issues in macroeconomics as well as with the most important issues arising in the analysis of unemployment, consumption decisions, and aspects of economic integration and international monetary relations bearing on macroeconomic equilibrium and on macroeconomic fluctuations.

The first paper by L. H. Summers, 'Should Keynesian Economics Dispense with the Phillips Curve?' deals with the alleged relationship between the rate of unemployment and the rate of price and wage inflation. Discussions of macroeconomic policy assign a prime role to the concept of a non-accelerating inflation rate of unemployment and debate its level. Keynesian economists generally argue that the stability of the so-called Phillips curve relating the rate of inflation and the rate of unemployment is a central relationship in explaining macroeconomic equilibrium and fluctuations. Summers argues that models containing a standard relationship of this sort, known as the Phillips curve, which characterises the sluggish adjustment of prices are fatally flawed as depictions of Keynes's vision of the economy. He argues instead that models allowing for hysteresis effects – models in which equilibria are fragile and history-dependent – offer the best prospect for redeeming the promise of Keynesian macroeconomics.

The paper by Edmund S. Phelps, 'Testing Keynesian Unemployment Theory against Structuralist Theory: Global Evidence of the Past Two Decades', also deals with the issue of unemployment in Keynesian theory and contrasts the Keynesian position with a non-monetary theory built on real wage rigidity, which stems from contractual considerations, and which has the real rate of interest at the centre of its transmission mechanism. This theory is called 'structuralist' by Phelps. Phelps's paper discusses a series of tests designed to distinguish between these two alternative theories of unemployment. His finding is, in general, that the Keynesian theory is dubious for other than very short-term analysis.

In 'Unemployment Through "Learning From Experience"', by Steve Alpern and Dennis J. Snower, the authors analyse how workers' wage claims can serve as a learning tool and thus provide

xxi

some further detail with respect to the kind of labour market assumed in the structuralist theory of unemployment, contrasted with the Keynesian theory in the previous essay by Phelps. They construct a model of wage determination in which the central problem is one of asymmetric information; workers are assumed to have less information than their employers about their own marginal-revenue products and are able to acquire this information from their employers only by making wage claims and observing the resulting job offers; also, it might be added, facing unemployment in the process.

In the next paper, 'Unemployment and Labour Market Imperfections', Assar Lindbeck takes a closer look at the institutional setting in which labour-market decisions are made and which determine unemployment. Lindbeck is particularly concerned to explain the *persistence* of unemployment, that is, the fact that the unemployment rate in the current year is positively correlated with that of the previous year, and perhaps also, with the rate in one or two years before that. His analysis looks at the role of various types of labour market imperfections in the performance of aggregate employment and unemployment over time and in the light of the persistence experienced. Lindbeck distinguishes between factors which have their impact mainly on the demand for labour, that is to say the willingness of firms to hire workers, and factors which have their direct impact mainly on the supply of labour, that is the willingness of workers to look for jobs, or to accept job offers.

In 'Two Tools for Analysing Unemployment', Olivier Jean Blanchard develops some general analytical apparatus for dealing with the functioning of markets with large flows. Labour markets in developed economies are, in fact, characterised by large flows of workers, continual job creation, and continual job destruction. Unemployment tends to average only a tiny fraction of employment and the labour force. The two tools which he has found useful in the analysis of labour market phenomena in developing countries are the so-called Beveridge curve and the Phillips curve. Blanchard develops a conceptual framework in which one can interpret both relationships and then applies the resulting analytical apparatus to the analysis of unemployment in the USA, UK and in the Federal Republic of Germany over the past twenty years.

In the next paper, Lawrence F. Katz and Bruce D. Meyer take a look at the potential duration of unemployment benefits and the duration of unemployment. In this paper, they analyse data from a number of European countries with relatively generous unemployment insurance systems, such as Belgium, France, Germany, the Netherlands and the UK, which have suffered larger, more persistent increases in unemployment in the 1980s than has the USA with its less generous unemployment insurance system. They present new empirical evidence on the impact of the level and potential duration of benefits on the duration of unemployment. They analyse unemployment spells of a large sample of household heads in the USA and compare the distributions for those receiving unemployment insurance benefits and those not receiving such unemployment insurance benefits. A second aspect of their empirical work looks at the impact of the level and length of unemployment insurance benefits on the escape rate from unemployment for a large sample also in the USA. The evidence which they present indicates that the potential duration of unemployment insurance benefits has a strong impact on the duration of the unemployment spells of such recipients in the USA. Substantial increases in both the recall rate and the new-job-finding rate are apparent for such recipients around the time when benefits are likely to lapse.

Part II of the volume contains two papers on international aspects of macroeconomic fluctuations and macroeconomic equilibrium. In 'The European Monetary System Ten Years On: The System's Architecture, Problems and Perspectives', Rainer Masera discusses operational experience with the European Monetary System and argues the case that a system of fixed exchange rates that can be adjusted discretely will be difficult to maintain under conditions of complete capital mobility even with unlimited short-term reciprocal lines of credit. Masera thus throws light on the question of how to arrange an orderly process of financial and monetary unification in Europe in coming years in such a way that financial and fiscal regulations for the control of macroeconomic activity can be appropriately harmonised.

In the next paper, Manuel Porto looks at the effects of EC regional aid on the economic development of Portugal. He is particularly concerned to analyse the effects of European integration on regional imbalances within Portugal.

Finally, the group of papers in Part III deals with econometric issues and particularly with the use of survey data and microeconomic theory to analyse decisions important to the understanding of macroeconomic fluctuations and expectation formation.

In the first paper in this Part, 'The Interplay of Theory and Data in the Study of International Trade', Edward Leamer focuses on two questions: the role empirical work plays in understanding trade between countries and the role empirical work should play. Leamer looks at a number of theories about aggregate international commodity flows in this light and finds that empirical work has generally had only a minor influence on the development of the theory of such flows in part because such empirical work has only a fuzzy foundation in economic theory and because hypotheses are rarely phrased in such a way that the theory is genuinely at risk.

The paper by Angus Deaton on 'Price Elasticities from Survey Data: Extensions and Indonesian Results', shows how survey data can be used to analyse how consumers change their expenditures on goods in response to changes in prices. He applies a methodology which he has developed for using household survey data to detect spatial variation in prices and to estimate price elasticities by comparing spatial price variation with spatial demand pattern.

In 'Family Consumption and Labour Supply Decisions in Developing Countries: Farm and Off-farm Work in Peru', Paul J. Gertler and John L. Newman look at family allocation of labour in response to on-farm and off-farm opportunities.

In the final paper in the volume, G. S. Maddala looks at what we have learned from survey data on expectations. Expectations play a major role in all economic activity and they are, above all, central in the study of macroeconomic fluctuations and equilibrium. Maddala surveys the entire literature on expectation information and asks what we can learn and what we have learned, from various surveys of expectations about their formation and the role which they play in determining decisions at the household and firm levels, decisions which have an important impact on macroeconomic equilibrium.

Part I

Macroeconomic Aspects of Unemployment

1 Should Keynesian Economics Dispense with the Phillips Curve?

Lawrence H. Summers
HARVARD UNIVERSITY and NBER

1 INTRODUCTION

My title should surprise the reader. That is certainly its intent. The presence of some sort of Phillips curve describing the process of sluggish price adjustment is often regarded as a defining characteristic of Keynesian models. Leading Keynesian macroeconomics textbooks all assign a central role to wage and price rigidity and to 'natural rate' Phillips curves describing the adjustment of wages and prices. On both sides of the Atlantic, discussions of macroeconomic policy assign a prime role to the concept of the non-accelerating inflation rate of unemployment (NAIRU) and debate its level. Keynesian economists in the USA point to the stability of the Phillips curve in recent years as decisive evidence upholding their position and refuting the views of new-classical economists. In Britain, Keynesians dolefully track the NAIRU as it continues its upward march into double digits, while remaining resolute in their devotion to the Keynesian paradigm.

In these remarks I shall try to make the case that models containing standard Phillips curves depicting the sluggish adjustment of prices are fatally flawed as depictions of Keynes's vision of the economy or of reality. More fundamentally, I will argue that the premise common to both Keynesian and classical macroeconomic models, that a downwards sloping aggregate demand schedule and an upwards sloping aggregate supply schedule intersect to determine uniquely and sharply the level of output and prices is untenable. Instead, I believe that models allowing for hysteresis effects – models in which equilibria are fragile and history-dependent – offer the best prospect for redeeming the promise of Keynesian macroeconomics.

I believe that accounting for hysteresis effects will require

3

revolutionary and not merely evolutionary changes in the way Keynesian (and classical) macroeconomists view the world. If this judgement is correct, there is nothing to be gained from my pretending that only minor modifications in textbook treatments are necessary, or that the points made here are already widely appreciated. On the other hand, if my judgements are wrong, there is little cost to my stating them in as vivid and bold a way as I can. These remarks, therefore highlight the flaws in conventional models and the promise of new approaches, but do not provide balance by stressing the scientific successes that have led sticky price models to be enshrined in textbooks.

Before proceeding further I want to stress one set of considerations that greatly reinforces my convictions. Even its friends must acknowledge that the textbook Keynesian view of aggregate supply possesses many of the attributes that Thomas Kuhn has ascribed to dying scientific paradigms. Two aspects are most obvious – its proponents maintain a wholly defensive posture and it is subject to regular and substantial amendment. I comment on these two points in turn.

Empirical work within successful scientific paradigms is outward-looking. It articulates the paradigm by resolving anomalies, or by demonstrating the paradigm's application to new phenomena. Keynesian empirical work on issues relating to wages and prices is usually inward- if not backward-looking. Many studies have been directed at defending the fundamental premise that wages and prices are rigid, at demonstrating the continued validity of an equation estimated several years earlier, or more frequently at finding out why an equation estimated several years earlier went off track. While words like menu costs, and overlapping contracts are often heard, little if any empirical work has demonstrated any connection between the extent of these problems and the pattern of cyclical fluctuations. Nor have these concepts been successfully related to phenomena other than cyclical fluctuations. It is difficult to think of any anomalies that Keynesian research in the 'nominal rigidities' tradition has resolved, or of any new phenomena that it has rendered comprehensible.

More striking evidence of the barrenness of the textbook Keynesian paradigm comes from scientific statesmen's overviews of the state of the science. It is difficult to find one in the Keynesian tradition that is constructive in charting past triumphs and pointing towards future challenges. Rather, prominent Keynesians' evaluations of the state of the field are destructive – being primarily comprised of attacks on the doctrines of the New Classical or monetarist schools. I think of the AEA Presidential addresses of James Tobin (1982), and Franco Modigliani (1977) or of Alan Blinder's recent evaluation of Keynes's contributions (1988). Similar overviews by economists of the New Classical school, notably Robert Lucas and Thomas Sargent (1981) have a much more constructive and confident tone. This does not guarantee that New Classical economists are right, and indeed they are not. But Keynesian economics should aspire to more than Churchill's defence of democracy as the best of bad alternatives.

Frequent *ad hoc* adjustments to account for embarrassing realities were a hallmark of Ptolemaic astronomy. It is sad but true that the half-life of various Keynesian views about the aggregate supply curve has been little more than a decade. In *The General Theory* (1947) Keynes proposed that the aggregate supply curve drawn in unemployment-price space was L-shaped. This view was falsified by the coincidence of inflation and less than full employment in the late 1940s and 1950s. By the early 1960s, a derivative was slipped and Keynes's view had given way to the Phillips curve vision of a stable downward-sloping relationship between unemployment and the rate of inflation. This view remained popular for not much more than a decade. The stagflation of the 1970s led to the slipping of another derivative and the widespread acceptance of the view that there existed a natural rate of unemployment, which was the only rate at which inflation could remain stable. On this 'expectations augmented' Phillips curve view, there is a trade-off not between current inflation and current unemployment but between permanent inflation and current unemployment.

A decade has now passed since the natural-rate hypothesis came to be widely accepted. In what follows, I will argue that it is again time for a major change in Keynesian conceptions. Secion 2 of this paper lays out the arguments on normative, logical and empirical grounds against the sticky price Phillips curve approach to economic fluctuations. Section 3 briefly makes it clear why New Classical theories are hopeless as descriptions of real world economic fluctuations, especially in Europe. It then demonstrates how hysteresis models can resolve the problems with sticky price formulations and at the same time account for the empirical observations that motivate the Keynesian approach to macroeconomics. Section 4 concludes the paper by discussing some policy implications of hysteresis models.

2   THE KEYNESIAN ORTHODOXY

The orthodox Keynesian view of economic fluctuations goes something like this. Real factors uniquely determine an equilibrium level of output and employment in an economy. However wages and prices are sticky because of long-term contracts and sluggish expectations and so can temporarily diverge from their equilibrium values. As a consequence of price stickiness, changes in aggregate demand, typified by an increase in the money stock, affect the quantity of output and employment in the short run. In the long run, purely nominal changes do not have real effects.

The proposition that changes in nominal magnitudes do not have real effects in the long run implies that the long run Phillips curve trade-off is vertical. Increases in the permanent anticipated rate of inflation do not affect the level of unemployment or output. In the short run, however, because wages and prices are inertial, there is a trade-off between inflation and unemployment represented by the short run Phillips curve. This view implies that when disinflationary policies are pursued, as they were at the beginning of the 1980s in both the USA and the UK, output falls and the rate of inflation slowly declines. Conversely, expansionary policies can temporarily but not permanently increase output. The extent and magnitude of nominal effects on output and employment will depend on the importance of the factors leading wages and prices to be rigid.

These orthodox views are flawed in three important respects. First, they are dispiriting and discouraging. If they were valid, there would be very little scope for macroeconomic policy to increase (or reduce) economic welfare. Second, they are logically deficient in failing to consider seriously the implications of wage and price rigidities for choices about quantities. Third, they are empirically refuted by the great persistence of unemployment and output fluctuations, and by the very substantial variability of output even in settings where wages and prices are highly flexible. Let me develop each of these points.

2.1   The Natural Rate Hypothesis is Dispiriting

Contemporary Keynesian views about the inflation–output trade-off are well captured by the slightly stylised Phillips curve relation:

$$P_t = b^*GAP + P_{t-1} \tag{1}$$

where GAP represents the difference between output or employment and some natural or equilibrium value consistent with steady inflation. This equation holds that the rate of change of inflation depends on the output gap. Similar expressions may be found in leading Keynesian textbooks like those of Dornbusch and Fischer (1984), Gordon (1987), and Hall and Taylor (1988). Its striking implication for the efficacy of stabilisation policies may be seen by summing it over time and rearranging:

$$GAP = (P_T - P_0)/bT \qquad (2)$$

Equation (2) holds that over any interval, the average value of GAP is proportional to the change from beginning to end in the rate of inflation. Over any period when the rate of inflation does not change, the average value of the output gap must equal zero. Macroeconomic policies which do not raise the long-run inflation rate cannot affect the average level of output and employment in the economy. Put differently, stabilisation policies can only mitigate recessions to the same extent that they also limit expansions. Perhaps more strikingly, bad macroeconomic policies cannot raise the average level of unemployment in an economy over any interval as long as the rate of inflation at the end of the interval is no less than the rate of inflation at the beginning.

This result is very general. It should be obvious that adding lagged values of GAP in order to capture persistence or rate of change effects, or allowing for a more elaborate lag structure on inflation would affect it. Some economists prefer to replace lagged inflation in (1) by expected inflation, or by a lag distribution of expected inflation as of various points in time. In these cases, it is easy to demonstrate that policy cannot affect the average level of the output gap over any interval sufficiently long that surprises average zero. The conclusion that policy cannot affect average output is likely to be a feature of any model that postulates a unique equilibrium level of output around which output fluctuates.

If the natural rate Phillips curve (1) is accepted as a description of reality, it seems as if Keynesians are fighting for the low ground in their running battles with classical economists. If increasing output in one period requires acceptance of an equal output reduction in another, it is hard to see why it matters very much whether policy can increase output for one period, as in the classical model, or for several periods as in the Keynesian model. Remember that no one really knows how much calendar time corresponds to one of a model's periods.

The natural rate Phillips curve hypothesis also implies that the social gains from macroeconomic stabilisation policies are not very large. Even assuming that the marginal utility of income diminishes very rapidly, Robert Lucas (1981) has shown that the social gains from stabilising consumption around a fixed mean are likely to be very small. Thinking about other aspects of fluctuations, it is far from obvious that having 8 million workers unemployed for 1 year is worse than having 4 million workers unemployed for 2 years. Certainly, the burden of unemployment is likely to be borne more broadly in the former case than in the latter. Stabilisation policies have costs. If they really could do nothing to increase the average level of output, it is doubtful that they could make much contribution to social welfare.

While many Keynesian economists accept equation (1) at least as a first approximation, they shrink from its normative implication that policy cannot affect the average level of output over long periods of time. Instead they regularly write and speak as if it were possible to fill in troughs without shaving peaks or accepting ever-accelerating inflation. Certainly this was how Keynes saw the proper objective of macroeconomic policy. Since Keynes wrote, criticism of avoidable recessions has been far more common than criticism of inappropriate expansions. Indeed, while American Keynesians condemn the 'three Eisenhower recessions', and the recessions of 1975 and 1982, as the result of excessively contractionary policies, there is no peacetime period when any consensus regarded policy as too expansionary.

Keynesian, and for that matter monetarist, tracts invariably leave the impression that the Depression was avoidable, and that avoiding it would not have saddled current generations with a higher permanent rate of inflation. As I discuss below, I think these convictions are correct. But they cannot be defended within the context of the current mainstream Keynesian model.[1] Justifying activist policy will necessitate looking elsewhere.

2.2　The Logic of Wage and Price Rigidity

Keynesian discussions of the Phillips curve assign a pivotal role to the sluggish adjustment of wages and prices. The idea is that because of wage contracts, menu costs or slowly adapting expectations, wages and prices remain stuck for a time at disequilibrium levels. As a consequence, the argument goes, employment and output are determined not by the intersection of demand and supply curves but by demand alone along the predetermined level of wages and prices. This story makes sense as a depiction of contractions caused by unexpected decreases in demand. In the short run, output falls as suppliers of labour are constrained by the sticky downwards wage.

But the mainstream Keynesian model has no coherent explanation at all for booms. Suppose an economy with rigid wages but flexible prices is initially in equilibrium and then the money supply unexpectedly increases.[2] Then the notional demand for labour will exceed the notional supply. Economists concerned with rationing in markets that do not clear worked out the solution to this problem long ago. One would expect to observe the level of employment generated by the supply curve and realised real wage – a level that must be below the equilibrium level. This of course is not what we observe. We observe that monetary expansions raise employment, contradicting what the standard analysis of markets where prices are rigid would predict. The mainstream Keynesian model passes over this difficulty by simply assuming that output is always determined by demand.

The rationale for this assumption is rarely provided. Sometimes vague reference is made to contracts entitling employers to force their workers to work overtime. This cannot be important. Apart from the difficulty of enforcing contracts that call for people to work against their will, there is the prominent fact that most cyclical employment gains take the form of more people working, not people working more hours. Another suggestion is that employment gains come because workers are somehow fooled and do not realise that real wages are lower. This suggestion has more of a classical than a Keynesian flavour. More importantly, observation suggests that booms cause few regrets. Somehow there are few complaints after cyclical expansions by people who wish that they had not been tricked into working. Perhaps the Keynesian position can be defended by some sort of argument suggesting that demand expansions reduce frictional unemployment – unemployment that is notably absent from the aggregate supply–demand diagrams found in the textbooks.

I am not aware of any convincing answer that those who ascribe cycles to nominal rigidities can give to the problem of explaining booms. This difficulty is really symptomatic of a general problem plaguing all attempts to explain fluctuations in terms of wage and price rigidities. Any serious thought about the rigidities leads one to despair of using standard supply and demand curves along with disequilibrium prices to determine the level of output. Suppose, for example, that firms and workers agree to long-term contracts fixing nominal wages and that there is no possibility of renegotiating them while they are in force. Is there any reason to expect firms to operate along their labour demand curves? If agreements about employment can be negotiated, then one certainly would not expect them simply to allow firms to move regularly along their demand curve. Even if they cannot be negotiated, firms are likely to set employment recognising that their choices will affect subsequent wage bargains in a variety of ways.

Take another example. It is often noted that firms raise prices infrequently for fear of alienating customers and that this makes the price level more sticky. Grant for a moment that this is an important aspect of firm pricing policies. Does it make sense to suppose that their customers always operate along a Walrasian demand curve that makes no allowance for the alienating effects of price changes? Probably not.

These examples could be multiplied. It think it will usually be found that whatever logic explains wage or price rigidity also undercuts the use of standard supply and demand curves to determine quantities. In every other part of economics price rigidities lead to too little being bought or sold. Only in Keynesian macroeconomics do wage and price rigidities lead half the time to quantities in excess of their equilibrium level.

2.3 Nominal Rigidities and the Real World

In addition to the logical arguments, there are important empirical problems with the nominal rigidities model as an explanation of economic fluctuations. First, the nominal rigidities explanation is less plausible in the current era of secular inflation than it might have been at an earlier time. The original Phillips curve could be thought of as capturing *tâtonnement* effects – more demand pressure meant more rapidly rising prices. The pattern of high unemployment and high inflation observed during the 1970s made it clear that prices could rise rapidly even in the absence of abnormally strong demand conditions. This renders the whole idea of sluggish price adjustment to demand conditions less plausible, and suggests instead that inflation is better thought of as generating a sequence of equilibrium price levels.

Second, there is even at this late date no concrete empirical evidence linking the extent of nominal rigidities and the extent of cyclical fluctuations. A number of less than satisfactorily controlled comparisons point in the opposite direction. Countries with high inflation where wages and prices change extremely frequently, have especially volatile economies. The decline in cyclical variability in the USA after the Second World War coincided with the introduction of three-year union contracts and other institutions often thought to generate nominal rigidities. Employment is most variable among secondary workers, whose wages are not set by contract and are subject to wide variations. Across a sample of OECD countries Sushil Wadwhani and I (1988) recently found a positive association between wage flexibility and output variability.

Third, an essential feature of the mainstream view is the idea that economic fluctuations represent transitory movements away from equilibrium. This idea receives little empirical support. While evidence of very substantial persistence in output can be explained by arguing that technical progress today suggests greater growth in the future, it is much more difficult for the mainstream view to account for great persistence in unemployment. Yet Olivier Blanchard and I (1986) find that in recent years unemployment in a number of European countries has followed a process very close to a random walk. Over the past century, the first autocorrelation of unemployment for both the USA and the UK is over 0.9. I am aware of no other evidence suggesting a tendency for output or employment in any country to demonstrate a strong equilibrium-reverting tendency.

These empirical considerations as well as the logical difficulties with nominal rigidity theories and their disquieting normative implications lead me to conclude that macroeconomists should look elsewhere in trying to account for economic fluctuations. *A fortiori*, classical approaches are not the way to go. This point as well as the profound problems with the mainstream Keynesian model is driven home by recent British experience.

The most resolute and right-wing government in Britain since the Second World War has been in power for a decade, during which time it has launched major attacks on trade unions and on market imperfections generally. Its commitment to disinflation is not in doubt. Yet more man-years of unemployment have been suffered during the Thatcher years than were experienced over the whole of the period after the Second World War and prior to 1979. In Britain today, about 60 per cent of all unemployment is composed of persons in the midst of spells lasting two years or more. Can anyone seriously maintain that this outcome is the result of intertemporal substitution, misperceptions, or efficient search? For that matter, what microeconomic factors could possibly have doubled the NAIRU since 1979? Certainly continuing wage inflation belies the idea that unemployment is currently held far above its equilibrium level by rigid nominal wages.

These phenomena suggest the need to look beyond the mainstream Keynesian and classical models. I take up this challenge in the next section.

3 FRAGILE EQUILIBRIA AND HYSTERESIS

One of Keynes's distinctive contributions to the study of economic fluctuations was his stress on the possibility that they were caused by 'animal spirits', fluctuations in businessmen's and financiers' expectations about future prosperity unrelated to real events. His suggestion was that exogenous conditions determined the level of output with a degree of arbitrariness. As a result, there was scope for expectations about future output to be self-fulfilling. More recently the question of whether anticipated purely nominal changes have real effects has been treated as a litmus test for determining whether a model is 'Keynesian'. And Keynesian economists have produced evidence demonstrating that anticipated nominal changes matter empirically. In a sense these two ideas are closely related. The relevance of animal spirits and of purely nominal changes for the determination of output is difficult to understand in an environment where exogenous conditions sharply determine equilibrium. Were multiple equilibria possible, and so the level of output is in some sense arbitrary, it would be much easier to understand how extrinsic variables like the money stock or animal spirits could affect the level of output.

3.1 The Daylight Savings Time Example

My point is well made by example. Consider the problem of the way in which we measure time. Any competent economics graduate student would have no difficulty proving the following proposition: *The numbers attached by convention to moments when the sun is at different levels in the sky have no effect on an economy's real allo-*

cations. More informally, the time standard is a purely nominal variable that should have no effect on real outcomes. The proof mimics the standard demonstration that doubling the stock of nominal money should have no effect on the level of real output. A unique equilibrium may not exist. But to each equilibrium under time standard A, there will correspond an equilibrium under time standard B, in which all real variables (like the time at which things open relative to the time when the sun is highest in the sky) take on the same values. In theorists' language, altering the units in which we measure time does not change the set of equilibrium allocations that the price system can support.

There is one important thing to understand about this proposition. It is false as an empirical statement. Every spring we see daylight savings time imposed, and then observe people getting an extra hour of sunlight after they get home from work. Is there anyone who believes that if daylight savings time did not exist, somehow all opening and closing times in the economy would simultaneously be altered? Over the years, thousands of pages of Congressional testimony have been taken arguing the merits of daylight savings time. Considerations relating to energy conservation, school buses, and the safety and convenience of farm workers have all played a prominent role in these debates. I doubt very much that it has ever been argued that the choice of a time standard is of no consequence, because it is a purely nominal variable.

The reasons why the choice of a time standard has real effects are instructive. Imagine a store in a shopping centre. Its owner may care about how much time s/he gets in the sun after work. But s/he cares far more about opening and closing the shop at the same time as the other stores. As a consequence, many real equilibria in which all firms open and close at the same time are possible. While all store-owners might prefer to open and close an hour earlier in the summer time, it would be very difficult to coordinate this outcome in the absence of a change in the time standard. Any one store that changed its hours of operation would regret it, even though all would be better off if all changed. In this setting, daylight savings time is a constructive innovation that yields benefits by shifting the economy from less to more favourable equilibria.

Note several features of this argument. First, the efficacy of daylight savings time depends on whether people care more about their relative time of opening than their absolute time of opening. In a community of hermits, there would be a unique equilibrium in which

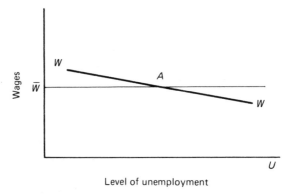

Figure 1.1 The determination of wages paid by a firm when other firms' wages are the dominant influence

everyone woke up at the time they most preferred, and daylight savings time would have no real effects. The impact of a purely nominal value – the time standard – is dependent on the fact that multiple real equilibria are possible. Second, sufficiently large changes in the time standard would cause firms to alter their stated opening and closing times. If the USA were put on Greenwich time, people would not find themselves leaving work before the sun had reached its highest point in the sky. Opening and closing times would adjust, and it is impossible to predict just what real equilibrium would be selected. Third, the efficacy of daylight savings time is related to the coordination problem arising because people care about relative rather than absolute time, not any nominal rigidity in opening and closing times. Stores open and close at different times on different days of the week and in different parts of the year. The costs of posting a sign with opening and closing times have nothing to do with the efficacy of daylight savings time.

3.2   Fragile Macroeconomic Equilibria

What does all this have to do with economic fluctuations generally or hysteresis specifically? I believe there is a very close analogy. In developing it, I will focus on the labour market and on the determination of wages and unemployment. Parallel arguments stressing product market considerations could probably be developed. Figures 1.1, 1.2 and 1.3 provide a plausible description of the way a given firm sets wages. Concerned about turnover, the problem of motivat-

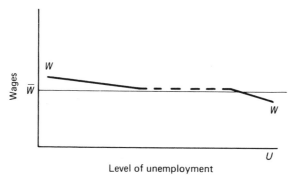

Figure 1.2   The determination of wages paid by a firm when all firms wish to pay similar wages

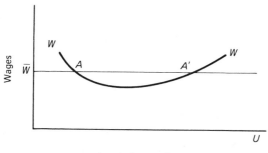

Level of unemployment

Figure 1.3   The determination of wages paid by a firm when extrinsic factors affect the relationship between wages and unemployment

ing its workers, the need to fill vacancies and so forth, it uses other firms' wages as a benchmark ($\bar{W}$) in setting its own wage. If unemployment is low, the firm is likely to decide to pay higher than prevailing wages. If unemployment is high it will decide to pay lower than prevailing wages. If all firms are symmetric, equilibrium is determined at point A, where each firm is happy to pay the average wage. As long as the typical firm would prefer to pay supra-normal wages in a hypothetical situation where unemployment is zero, unemployment will be observed in equilibrium.

The slope of the WW schedule in Figure 1.1 will depend on the relative importance firms attach to other firms' wages and unemployment in setting their own wages. If, as is plausible, other firms' wages have the dominant influence, the *WW* schedule will be very flat, as in the figure. While in this case there is a unique equilibrium unemployment rate, it will be extremely sensitive to anything that moves the *WW* schedule. Moreover, it should be clear there will be a large number of 'near equilibrium' unemployment rates where the wages which firms actually pay differ only trivially from those they would optimally pay. In such a setting, very small expectational errors are likely to have large effects. In the limit, where firms always want to pay the same wage as other firms over some range of unemployment rates, a multiplicity of equilibria are possible, as in Figure 1.2, and so unemployment is arbitrary. Just as in the case of the time standard, when firms care a great deal about conformity, it will be possible for extrinsic variables to have important real effects.

It is probably a mistake to distinguish too sharply the cases depicted in Figures 1.1 and 1.2. Situations with multiple equilibria, and with very weakly determined but unique equilibria are not likely to be observationally different. Think about hemlines. Their determination could be analysed using Figures 1.1–1.3 by replacing unemployment with the average hemline and representing the preferred relative hemline on the vertical axis. When hem lengths are long, the average woman prefers to wear shorter than average skirts and when they are short the average woman prefers a longer than average hemline. Equilibrium is attained at that hemline where the average woman desires to have the average hemline. Whether there are literally multiple equilibria or not is unclear. It is obvious that extrinsic variables matter and that instability is likely.

There are other possibilities as well, besides those depicted in Figures 1.1 and 1.2. Suppose that increases in unemployment are associated with more generous unemployment benefits as society recognises that long-term unemployment may not be the fault of the unemployed, or that they reduce the stigma associated with losing a job, or that, as Olivier Blanchard and I argue (1986) increases in unemployment lead unions to set a lower employment target as they bargain over wages. In any of these cases, the *WW* schedule might look like that depicted in Figure 1.3. There will be two equilibrium unemployment rates. Extrinsic variables can move the economy between them.

So far, my argument has been that if firms care a great deal about their relative wage, an economy's equilibrium unemployment rate may be very sensitive to small changes in conditions, or that an economy may actually possess many equilibrium unemployment rates. In such settings, it is natural to expect that extrinsic variables could have real effects in moving the economy between equilibria. It is also plausible that unemployment would be unstable because of the possibility of movements between multiple equilibria as well as movements in equilibrium values. Finally, small changes in its determinants may lead to very large movements in equilibrium values. Think of a change in union power that lifted slightly the *WW* schedule in Figures 1.1–1.3. Fragile equilibria of this type seem to me to correspond much more closely to what is observed in the world than the unique well-defined equilibrium displayed in textbook supply and demand or *IS–LM* diagrams.

While I have been brief, I am confident that it is possible to provide detailed microeconomic justifications for a variety of shapes of the *WW* locus in Figures 1.1–1.3. The real challenge at this point is to provide some indication of how an equilibrium is selected, and how changes in extrinsic variables alter real equilibria. This is where the idea of hysteresis comes in. Surely history is what determines the equilibrium an economy selects. It is history that conditions the wages that firms expect other firms to pay, and expect workers to expect other firms to pay. Once an economy is in an equilibrium state, it may be reasonable for agents to form expectations that it will remain there. These expectations may prove to be self-fulfilling.

Unfortunately, there is only one conclusion of which I am confident at this stage. There is no reason to expect market forces automatically to select the best of many equilibria. Saying more will require us to develop a deeper understanding of hysteresis effects than we have at present.

3.3 Resolving the Problems with Keynesian Models

Let me conclude this section by making clear how models of multiple equilibria and hysteresis can resolve the problems with the mainstream Keynesian model that I stressed in the first section of this paper. From the perspective of these models, the economy does not fluctuate around a unique equilibrium. Instead, it is capable of settling at many different equilibria, one of which is best. Policies that improve today's outcome need not compel the selection of an inferior equilibrium tomorrow. We do not talk about cycles around a fixed mean in people's health. Instead, we talk about them being healthy or getting sick. The multiple equilibrium approach to fluctuations takes a similar view of periods of high and low employment.

It should be obvious from the perspective advocated here that booms are no mystery. They simply represent the attainment of desirable equilibria. Since there is chronic involuntary unemployment in the model sketched here, no one regrets the extra work done in a boom. Since the perspective taken here is that the economy is always in equilibrium, no problems of describing quantity choices in the presence of disequilibrium prices need to be faced.

Models of multiple equilibria do not suffer the empirical defects of models emphasising nominal rigidities. They do not predict that systematic inflation should have systematic real effects, or that there should be a relationship between the costs of changing wages and prices and the extent of output variability. Most importantly, they do not carry any implication that economies should exhibit equilibrium reverting behaviour. As in any other social situation where individuals value conformity highly, the model sketched here suggests that outcomes should be both volatile and persistent.

Continuing inflation, rapid GNP growth, the fact that redundancy and short-time rates are low by historical standards, and the fact that overtime work is abnormally common by historical standards all suggest that it is not fruitful to think of the contemporary British economy as being far out of equilibrium. It is neither plausible nor bearable to think of this equilibrium as being unique. This too compels consideration of models with many equilibria.

4 CONCLUSIONS

Robert Lucas (1981) in his celebrated critique of econometric policy evaluation charged that 'it is only recently that the proposition that inflation and output are positively correlated and therefore more inflation is good has been elevated from obvious fallacy to the cornerstone of economic policy'. He was right. It is, however, equally fallacious to suppose, as do Lucas and mainstream Keynesians, that because steady inflation does not affect the average level of unemployment, nothing else can do so either. Purging this fallacious view will require us to eliminate the natural-rate Phillips curve from our models.

My daylight savings time example supports these conclusions. It is easy to imagine time policies that would be undone by the private sector and so have no real effects. Think of a policy of changing the clocks by three hours every week. Presumably under such a regime, people would find ways of setting opening and closing times that do not lead to stores being open only before dawn. This proves only that there are limits to the equilibria that policy can impose on the economy, not that all policy is ineffective. And it shows that no simple equation can explain the process by which opening and closing hours are determined. But it hardly demonstrates the impossibility of government policies that help to solve the coordination problem involved in time setting.

The difficulty, of course, is in designing policies that can work. This will require improved hysteresis theories describing how history determines an economy's equilibrium. But a little bit can be said at a high level of generality. From the perspective of the view of cyclical fluctuations considered here, the problem of economic policy is very much like that of winning at poker. To succeed at poker one has to guess the endowments, intentions, and the guesses of others. A poker player can insure an average outcome by following a simple policy rule – not betting. This is what he will do if he assumes the universal rationality of expectations and decision-making that modern macroeconomists so blithely postulate. Many poker players do much better than breaking even. Likewise shrewd policy makers who, like successful poker players, make case-by-case judgements and do not shrink from bold actions will do much better than those who passively follow fixed rules. Improved theories of economic hysteresis will help them out.

Notes

1. One possible defence would stress non-linearities in the relation between GAP and changes in inflation. I am not aware of strong evidence demonstrating the existence of such non-linearities. While an asymmetry between upward and downward adjustment of prices is plausible, the idea of an asymmetry between upward and downward adjustment of the rate of inflation seems less compelling.
2. Similar arguments can be carried out assuming that prices are less than fully flexible and allowing for some flexibility in wages.

References

Blanchard, O. J. and Summers, L. H. (1986) 'Hysteresis and the European Unemployment Problem', *NBER Macroeconomics Annual*, vol. 1, pp. 15–78.

Blinder, A. S. (1988) 'The Challenge of High Unemployment', *American Economic Review*, vol. 78, pp. 1–15.

Dornbusch, R. and Fischer, S. (1984) *Macroeconomics*, 3rd edn (New York: McGraw-Hill).

Gordon, R. J. (1987) *Macroeconomics*, 4th edn (Boston: Little, Brown).

Hall, R. E. and Taylor, J. B. (1988) *Macroeconomics: Theory, Performance and Policy*, 2nd edn (New York: Norton).

Keynes, J. M. (1947) *The General Theory of Employment, Interest and Money* (London: Macmillan).

Lucas, R. E. and Sargent, T. J. (1981) (eds.) *Rational Expectations and Econometric Practice* (London: George Allen & Unwin).

Modigliani, F. (1977) 'The Monetarist Controversy or, Should We Forsake Stabilization Policies?', *American Economic Review*, vol. 67, pp. 1–19.

Summers, L. H. and Wadhwani, S. B. (1988) 'Some International Evidence on Labour Cost Flexibility and Output Variability', unpublished mimeo, Harvard University, Cambridge, Mass.

Tobin, J. (1982) 'Inflation and Unemployment', *American Economic Review*, vol. 62, pp. 1–18.

2 Testing Keynesian Unemployment Theory against Structuralist Theory: Global Evidence of the Past Two Decades

Edmund S. Phelps[1]
COLUMBIA UNIVERSITY

1 INTRODUCTION

The theory of unemployment accorded the status of orthodoxy in Western macroeconomics – the theory expounded in the textbooks – is, in a word, Keynesian. It derives from (among others) Keynes, Hicks, Tobin, Patinkin, the 'natural rate', and either a 'new micro-economics' apparatus without rational expectations or a New Keynesian apparatus compatible with rational expectations in order to generate inappropriate responses or inertia in nominal wages or prices. Some would allow hysteresis making the natural rate of unemployment 'path-dependent'. The monetarists use the same theory, though with different emphases, and in a sense the New Classical theory is a special (and more fully elaborated) case of it. So entrenched has it become in conventional economic thinking that people who know no economics at all have learned, like Samuelson's parrot, to say 'weaker demand' or 'supply shock' with every slump no matter how prolonged it is or how obscure its source or sources.

Until fairly recently the only alternative to this continually re-newed Keynesian theory has been neoclassical economics – the homely parables of Pigou and Ramsey and latter-day contributors on to the 'real' stochastic ('neo-neoclassical') models coming out of the Minnesota–Pittsburgh–Rochester axis. But this theory has been short of ideas to illuminate the present times, and seems not to want to do so. The same narrowness that caused it to lose its title to the Keynesian theory in the historic match-up of the 1930s appears to prevent it from winning back the title in subsequent rematches. For years, if a critic suggested that Keynesian theory was poor a defender could reply, 'Compared with what?'

Now, looking back on the past two decades, one can see two notable developments that threaten the supremacy of the Keynesian approach to unemployment fluctuations. Over the past decade the clear and distinct ideas of a new paradigm have been taking shape, a paradigm with enough explanatory power to be the first contender to pose a serious challenge to Keynesian thinking. In its non-monetary version, it is a theory built on real wage rigidity or real wage stickiness, which are in turn founded on employee-incentive or contractual considerations, and having the real interest rate at the centre of its transmission mechanism; some monetary considerations may strengthen rather than weaken the argument. I have labelled it the 'structuralist' theory.

Second, the past decade has seen another problematic perform-ance by Keynesian theory. Most countries suffered in the 1980s from what may come to be called the Second World Depression of this century, a depression from which the majority have now recovered to an important degree. Although some defenders of the orthodox theory have maintained that the 1980s slump in most countries can typically be attributed to increased fiscal austerity and temporarily tighter money, some sceptics have seen these as weak reeds – if they are there at all – on which to rest an explanation of such steep and sustained increases of unemployment. Further, no one has so far shown how to reconcile the Keynesian hypothesis of weak aggregate demand in the 1980s with the historic highs reached by the real interest rates around the world in the same decade.

This paper will discuss a series of tests, some of the author's own devising and some representing the work of others, of the Keynesian explanation of the past two decades, tests in which the 'alternative hypothesis' is the contending structuralist theory. No reader, I sup-pose, will find any of these tests, which are generally rather informal and preliminary, to be conclusive or even very persuasive. This paper aims only to consolidate and to communicate the research reviewed here with a view to calling the attention of a large audience to the central issue and to stimulating wider discussion and fresh research on the matter.

Let me end this introduction with the personal remark that, although this paper will cast doubts on the serviceability of the Keyne-sian theory for other than very short-term analysis at least, I feel a close attachment to Keynesian theory, having worked for most of my years as an economist on micro-foundations for its supply side. So I am not writing out of some surprising and new-found enmity toward that theory. However, by now, having worked a few years on it, I also have some vested interest in the alternative theory! So I can no longer play the dedicated defender of the Keynesian approach.

2 'KEYNESIAN' THEORY VERSUS 'STRUCTURALIST' THEORY

Keynesian theory needs no summary, but it may be useful to define terms. Current employment is determined by *aggregate* demand and *aggregate* supply corresponding to the current parameters (tax rates, etc.) and the 'state' of the economy (average nominal wage, capital stock, etc.). Demand and supply are conveniently depicted by intersecting curves in the employment–price level plane, (N, P). The demand curve corresponding to the given money supply measures the nominal 'demand' price for the amount of output producible by the specified employment level; it is derivable from the *IS–LM* equations of Hicks. The supply curve corresponding to a given nominal wage level measures the nominal supply price of the associated output; it is essentially marginal cost plus any mark-up. Finally, the natural rate together with the labour force – the amount of labour supplied at the equilibrium real wage – yields a 'natural employment curve' that is vertical in the (N, P) plane provided we take as negligible any real cash balance effects upon labour supply. When current employment differs from the natural level, the nominal wage and price dynamics will be moving the aggregate supply curve up or down so as to bring its intersection with the demand curve – and hence the current employment level – into equality with the natural level. When actual and natural rates of unemployment are equal, the associated path of the economy will sometimes be described as the equilibrium path.

Real shocks as well as nominal ones – *IS* shocks as well as *LM* shocks – disturb aggregate demand. There results a *stimulatory* effect upon demand – a well-known multiplier effect on demand – from the various Keynesian 'fiscal stimuli': from increases in public spending of all types, from income tax cuts, and from excise tax cuts.[2] (The latter in addition stimulate aggregate supply.) A stimulus to demand has an *expansionary* effect on employment, given aggregate supply. The expansion will be gradually counteracted by nominal supply price increases resulting from upward nominal wage or price pressure until the economy is again on the path of the natural rate, u^* (t). The *IS*-type demand stimuli are expansionary because, in driving real, and hence nominal, interest rates to higher levels, they induce an increased velocity of money.

Many practising macroeconomists have now moved significantly away from the Keynesian conceptualisation in the way they rationalise their still largely Keynesian-looking models. Perhaps the work of Malinvaud and of Sachs in the late 1970s marks the sea-change. *Real wage rigidity* is the cry now – generalised from a flat line to a possibly upward sloping 'real wage curve' (or labour market equilibrium locus) in the employment–real wage plane, say (N, v). That rigidity is invoked to argue that *supply* shocks contract the *natural* employment level by lowering the real wage and thus (if the wage curve is sloping) to raise u^* (t). Those who wish to keep the natural rate invariant have taken to postulating that the real wage slides down only gradually, in feedback response to the actuality of an abnormal volume of unemployment, until it has declined by enough to accommodate the drop in the real demand price of labour; this is a case of what may be labelled *real-wage stickiness*. These two distinct concepts of real wage behaviour are illustrated in Figures 2.1 and 2.2.

Yet the practising macroeconomists of whom I am speaking, while altering radically the premiss set, have steadfastly retained a characteristic feature of Keynesian theory with regard to real *demand* shocks. Some econometric models assume that the Keynesian fiscal stimuli have *no effect* on the *natural* rate, so the expansion they produce is vanishing, hysteresis excluded.[3] Some other models virtually abandon all appeal to nominal wage-price mistakes and inertia but tacitly assume that 'government demand' serves to elasticise product demand, thus to raise the real demand price of labour at given employment and hence to boost the *natural* employment level.[4]

Real wage rigidity first appeared as a theoretical construct in the early contract models, Azariadis (1975) and the rest, in some recent union-wage-setting models, such as Solow (1979), and finally in some recent elaborations of the theory of incentive pay, or 'efficiency wages', such as Shapiro and Stiglitz (1984). These citations are, I imagine, far from complete. It was comparatively recently that I realised that there may exist an entire *locus* of *potential* natural rate points in the employment-real wage plane, a locus on which the natural rate of Phelps (1968) is a *point* – a point corresponding to real conditions (with respect to productivity and other real parameters)

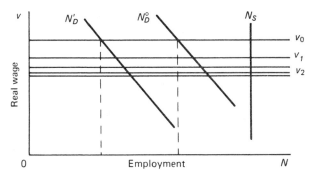

Figure 2.1 The determination of real wages: stickiness

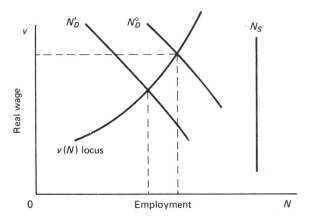

Figure 2.2 The determination of real wages: generalised rigidity

taken as given.[5] Note, however, that such a locus is a partial equilibrium construction in the sense that a general equilibrium analysis is required to determine the point of *actual* equilibrium.

What needs developing, then, is a theory with which to conduct a general equilibrium analysis of the natural rate in order to see how it will change (or may change) with demand stimuli as well as supply stimuli. This is the function, or the main task, of structuralist theory – to endogenise the natural rate in a general way, paying democratic attention to demand stimuli as well as supply impulses. The term structuralist is appropriate since it aims to explain the natural rate by appeal to the *real* forces in the economy on both the demand and supply side, and also since it proceeds to make distinctions where necessary among the components of demand – the structure of aggregate demand.

2.1 Structuralist Theory

As noted above, the early attention of structuralists was drawn to the supply side. Bruno and Sachs did extensive work on the contractionary effects of oil shocks; see their 1985 summary work. Malinvaud (1979), Drèze and Modigliani (1981) and Kouri (1982) among many others modelled the effects of real wage shocks. With regard to productivity shocks, a number of structuralist investigators have suggested that increased unemployment results in the manner of a rear-end highway collision when ever-growing productivity slows down too rapidly and too suddenly for ever-rising real wages to slow down in tandem. There is the further point, made in too many structuralist contributions to cite, that once a slump occurs, the decline of the capital stock thereby set in motion serves to deepen the downswing, either deepening the permanent slump (the case if real wages are rigid) or adding to the task of recovery (the case if real wages are merely sticky).

The demand side has been the object of structuralist attention throughout the second half of this past decade. By 1986 the sharp elevation of the world real interest rate became the focus of many discussions. Lal and van Wijnbergen (1985) argued in a wide-ranging paper that the world slump of the decade was tied to the effect of government deficits on the world real interest rate. Sinn (1985) and Phelps (1985) suggested that the fiscal incentives to investment enacted in the USA in 1981 were accounting for the elevation of real interest rates and damaging the rest of the world in the process. Fitoussi and I then developed formal arguments, using models circulated in the spring of 1986 but not yet published, that in a two-country world a fiscal stimulus in 'America' drives up the real interest rate in 'Europa' with the theoretically unorthodox result that the latter contracts; see Fitoussi and Phelps (1986, 1988).

My recent efforts to introduce the demand side into a non-monetary version of structuralist theory draw importantly on two of the models in Fitoussi–Phelps (1988, for details). I will discuss here only my work on the closed economy, just as the evidence to be examined later will be largely 'global' rather than national or cross-country.

One kind of model of this type starts from the two sector model of capital theory with the following feature: capital in the consumer-good-producing sector is at each moment wholly predetermined since either capital is not *ex post* shiftable (in Arrow–Kurz terminology) from the capital-good sector to the consumer-good sector (and vice-versa) or there is no capital used in the capital-good-producing sector. Then increased consumption demand, whether spontaneous or induced by income tax cuts, is mischievous for it cannot elicit an increase in the amount of the consumer good supplied because that output would be increased only if the real wage fell or the marginal productivity of labour rose, neither of which consumer demand is capable of causing; but this market has to clear, which implies that wealth must drop and the real interest rate must rise – these are the same thing in the simplest settings – and these effects in turn drive down the real demand price of the capital good and thus bring about a decrease in capital-good output and employment. For further details see my paper for the Kaldor conference volume (Phelps, 1988a) and my paper for a Hicks conference volume (Phelps, 1988b). These papers postulate real wage stickiness, which adds further dynamics; real wage rigidity would have delivered the main point more easily.

The second kind of model of the non-monetary closed economy I have developed starts from the customer-market model analysed in Phelps and Winter (1970). Here there is no capital good, but consumer good output can be sold by a firm only to its existing 'customers' or to the government in so far as there is a public demand. Here increased aggregate consumption demand is again a hopeless failure at eliciting an increase in the amount of the goods supplied because no price-elasticising of demand results. On the contrary, the drop of wealth and jump of real interest that must result for the market again to clear has the counter-productive side effect of inducing producers to contract the amount of output supplied since they will be led to discount the benefits of a marginal future customer more heavily. (In effect, they manage to raise their mark-ups closer to the textbook $MC=MR$ level only by reducing the real wage which means sliding down the wage curve to lower employment.) See Phelps (1989).

In a nutshell, consumer-good demand, in driving up the real interest rate, reduces the willingness of producers to 'invest' in the broad sense of the term – invest in new capital or invest in new customers (or to try to, that being impossible in the aggregate for a closed economy) – and this effect has *contractionary* consequences

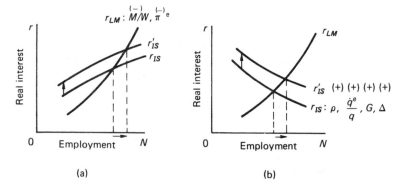

Figure 2.3 The Keynesian relationship between the real interest rate and the level of employment: an increase of the public debt, Δ, government expenditure, G, the expected appreciation in the real price of capital goods, $\dot{q}^e/q$, or the rate of time preference, ρ, all shift up r_{IS}, thus raising r and N

for employment, not the expansionary effects seen by the Keynesian theory as a result of the fillip to the velocity of money. I am afraid, in fact, that these papers represent a considerable effort at a proposition that is entirely obvious from first principles: if consumers drive up the real interest rate, the real wage must fall but under real wage stickiness it cannot, so employment must fall; and under real wage rigidity it cannot at the pre-existing level of employment (since the real wage is a rigid function of employment) so here too employment must fall.

Every theory needs its ideogram. Keynesian theory has its *IS–LM* diagram, as in Figure 2.3 to which a vertical line at the natural employment level is now generally added. Structuralist theory presents quite a different picture in this Hicksian employment–real interest plane, (N, r) as shown in Figure 2.4. The structuralist picture has a familiar element to it: an increase in time preference or a helicopter drop of public debt, in boosting the level of consumer demand, drives up a negatively sloped curve – a curve which we are tempted to call the *IS* curve, though the assignment of labels to curves is not so easy – so the rate of interest must rise at any given level of employment. But the other curve, which tells us how much output and employment producers are willing to provide at a specified real interest rate, is negatively sloped! It is not positively sloped like Hicks's *LM* curve so we are not going to move upward and to the

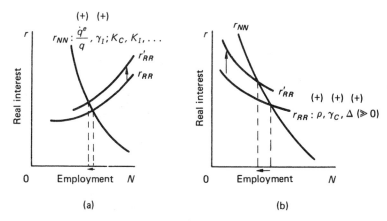

Figure 2.4 The structuralist relationship between the real interest rate and the level of employment: an increase of Δ, ρ, or government expenditure on output of consumer-good industries, γ_c, shift up r_{RR}, thus raising r and contracting N

right along this companion curve. One can say that, under conditions necessary for uniqueness of the economy's trajectory, the former curve cuts this latter curve from below; that implies that the former curve, if negatively sloped, is not as steep as the latter. Hence the economy will move upward and to the left along the latter curve to a higher real interest rate and a lower level of employment. Figure 2.4 portrays the two structuralist cases in which an upward shift of a curve labelled *RR* (in one case upward-sloping and in the other case sloping downward) causes a leftward movement along the negatively sloped curve labelled *NN*.

What about government demand? In the customer-market model, it is also true that increased government demand, either for output of the firms or labour services by the households, will decrease aggregate employment if and only if it raises the real interest rate, which it tends to do in all but very special cases. The same is also obviously true of increased public purchases of the consumer good in the two-sector model; wealth must fall and real interest rise to clear the market. But there is some hope that it will be possible to show that, say, a *decrease* of government demand for the capital good, such as a truck, may have the Keynesian effect of decreasing employment in the capital-goods sector and in the aggregate while at the same time actually increasing the real rate of interest. (But this is still a conjecture at the time of writing.)[6]

The real world is monetary, of course. So one has to have in mind a monetary model in which, when increased demand occurs, real outside money is driven down, which takes some of the burden off the stock and bond market; but the real interest rate at the original employment level must still be increased since the reductions of real cash balances also serve to raise the real interest rate since they raise the nominal rate. Yet it is helpful when thinking about natural rate determination at first to hold money out of the picture.

Let me try now to picture structuralist theory from a somewhat wider perspective. The insider–outsider theory of real wage and unemployment determination offers a third way of treating real wages; it generates a variant of real wage rigidity in which, paradoxically, a slump from whatever cause, if temporary, might cause real wages actually to increase and hence cause persistence in the unemployment rate. I would be willing to call this hysteresis even if there is no implication that the unemployment rate will lie non-vanishingly above its original path for all time. Lindbeck and Snower (1988) is the most extensive treatment.

There are also all the 'classic' sources of hysteresis, many of which were discussed in my 1972 book where the term was first used in this context. An econometric investigation of the hysteresis phenomenon can be found in Blanchard and Summers (1986). A particularly interesting innovation in this area is the recent suggestion by Lindbeck and Snower (1987) that a residue of a boom is an increase in the number of firms, which has the salutary effect of increasing the competitiveness of the product market and thus driving up the equilibrium real wage and the natural level of employment. That effect could be but one example from a collection of such hysteretic influences. For example, a boom might serve to enfranchise workers who would not otherwise have achieved a full-time orientation and attachment to the labour force; quit-rates might decline and firms would respond by reducing the premium of wages over the reservation level, thus reducing unemployment again.

Unfortunately these enrichments of the structuralist theory inject an unwelcome ambiguity into the implications of the approach. Now the theoretical possibility must be admitted that an increase in the level of consumer demand – even a sustained one such as we have been considering – may very well have two opposing effects on the natural level of employment. It may be that the early effect of the demand increase is expansionary on balance as the initial effect of the higher interest rates on the velocity of money outweighs the immediate employment effect of the desire of producers to push up their mark-ups at the deliberate expense of sales. (Notwithstanding that, if the enriched theory is right there will undoubtedly be uses for it.)

The last element in the structuralist theory to put in place is what may be called the structuralist model of the demand for money. Several years ago I suggested that money demand should be regarded as a function of after-tax income, not before-tax income, so that a tax increase might be expansionary; see Phelps (1982) for example. The idea goes back at least as far as Hall and Tobin (1954) and is surely implicit in Hicks's view of money holding as the quasi-involuntary response to the fact that our periodic payments come in money form and there are transactions costs. I remember that a colleague tested this hypothesis (Taylor in an unpublished memorandum) and found that the expansionary effect of the so-called Burns tax refund of 1975, if not negligible, was vastly smaller than traditional Keynesian theory led us to expect. By the same logic, a balanced-budget increase of government expenditure (i.e. increased tax-financed purchases of goods and services as distinct from transfer payments) might be vastly more expansionary than the traditional Keynesian model implies.

A variation on this theme was subsequently heard from Mankiw and Summers, in part in a joint paper (1985). Their assumption is that the government does not need money to purchase goods – its holdings of cash are not in the definition, after all – and firms do not need much, but households need money balances in order to be ready to pay for their expenditures; households do not hold appreciable cash in reserve against the arrival of possible portfolio placement opportunities. Hence, as in the previous model of cash holding, a tax increase may be expansionary since it reduces the consumption expenditure volume associated with any given output level and thereby shifts outward the Hicksian *LM* curve – possibly by enough to outweigh the downward shift of the *IS* curve and thus cause employment to increase. An increase of government expenditure, by crowding-out consumption at any given aggregate output level, will have a doubly expansionary effect. A balanced-budget increase of public expenditure will again have the extra *LM* effect that is not present in the traditional Keynesian model. As I suggested might be the result when increased public expenditure takes the form of capital-goods purchases, the effect on the interest rate might be negative while the employment effect is positive. For some evidence, see Penati (1984).

I submit that enough structuralist theory has accumulated to make it interesting to confront it with data. Let us then move on to the empirical section of this paper.

3   RECENT ANALYSES OF THE GLOBAL TIME SERIES

I had thought when planning this paper that I would survey not just the 'global' evidence on the 'world' economy, which will in fact be my focus here, but in addition the several international studies – cross-country analyses, typically using national time-series data from many countries – that bear on the adequacy of Keynesian theory for understanding the past two decades. I would have discussed the early work of Bean, Layard and Nickell (1986) and Tullio (1987a and b) as well as informal reports of unpublished work, such as that by Richard Freeman. I realised, however, that an analysis of empirical results of this work would require me to expound the extension of the structur-alist closed-economy theory to the case of two or more open econ-omies. This would have pulled the present paper in too many directions, I think, and, moreover, the international case – even the two-country case! – is too complex to fit into a small space. Suffice it to say that, if my understanding of the cross-country work is not mistaken, the evidence suggests that the international pattern of the Keynesian fiscal variables – government expenditure and so forth – provides little or no statistical explanation for the international pattern with respect to the growth of employment. However, it will be clear to the reader that this question is very different from the questions about the world aggregates for which, let us hope, the above discussion of the closed economy has to some degree prepared us.

It will help to organise the global evidence by first taking up the approach that seeks to explain world employment (and unemploy-ment) by reference to the world real-interest rate and then, in a separate step, to explain the world real-interest rate by reference to global exogenous variables such as world fiscal stimuli. Subsequently I will take up approaches that directly estimate an explanatory equation for the world unemployment rate. It happens that the former approach was the first to develop, so this is also the chrono-logical order.

3.1 Causes and Employment Effects of the World Real Interest Rate

The year 1987 marked another milestone in the development of the structuralist explanation of employment. In that year Newell and Symons circulated from University College, London, a working paper on the inter-war period, with an added section on the post-war period, that was identical in spirit to the general theme of the three two-country models in the chapters which Fitoussi and I had circulated in the spring of 1986 from the European University Institute. (The same motif, it will be recalled, had been sounded in Lal and van Wijnbergen.) In a terse discussion of a sentence or two they suggested that a rise of world real interest rates would be contractionary for Britain as it would reduce the real prices of goods emerging earlier in the roundabout process from raw trees to finished lumber or, I take it, from ovens to bread, and hence induce a contraction in jobs offered and the aggregate production supplied at a given real wage (in terms of finished consumer goods). Someone else had evidently read some capital theory! Yet there were signs of cognitive dissonance on other pages where the authors deny that their enterprise is anything other than orthodox Keynesian theory, so even now I cannot be sure that the authors would agree to my structuralist interpretation of their ground-breaking work.

Turning to their econometric work on their 'world' series, for both the inter-war and the post-war periods, Newell and Symons essentially sought to explain the employment level, normalised by the capital stock, I believe, by appeal to the level of the real wage – I shall take this to mean the wage in terms of consumption goods (which are finished goods, of course) and to the level of the real rate of interest. If one is using a pure real wage rigidity model, in which there exists a positively sloped locus relating the real wage to the level of employment, there would appear to be some statistical difficulty here: there would be that upward-sloping curve and alongside it the downward-sloping curve representing employment demand by firms; it would be hard to understand an equation explaining employment by the real wage and some exogenous variable (here the real interest rate) in that case. But the difficulty dissipates if one invokes instead the real wage stickiness model, in which case one can treat the real wage as exogenous from an econometric standpoint, since it is then a predetermined variable like the capital stock or the stock of customers or any other slowly adjusting variable of state. I will adopt the stickiness interpretation of the Newell–Symons work.

Newell and Symons find that both the real wage and the real interest rate are significant and negative determinants of the employment level; the capital stock is a positive determinant. I believe these findings were true of both the eras studied, and that there was much less in the way of disparity in the estimates of the coefficients between the two periods than might have been imagined. As far as I know, the authors did not investigate the possibility that some or all types of government expenditure might have a direct impact upon employment besides the (un-Keynesian) effect that goes through the real interest rate.

It was then simply a matter of waiting for the other shoe to drop. The next order of business was to estimate an equation for the world real interest rate.

A study that was enormously important for my own confidence in the structuralist theory was the econometric model of the world real interest rate developed by Dirk Morris (1988). (This was a doctoral dissertation at the Geneva Institute in 1987, and I am indebted to Hans Genscher for bringing this research to my attention.) In this work there are some real demand forces and some monetary forces among the explanatory variables used. The latter include the expected rate of inflation, an average over the twenty-odd countries comprising the 'world' aggregate; this appears with a negative coefficient, as the Mundell–Tobin treatment predicted, though it is barely statistically significant. The other monetary force is the stock of money normalised, apparently by the actual nominal gross product for the world (not the potential), so it is perhaps another indicator of the velocity of money; this variable also showed a negative coefficient and was strongly significant.

The real variables included the real public debt (normalised in some way). The main finding of the study by Morris, in my view, is that the public debt was found to have a large and strongly significant positive effect upon the real interest rate. Such a finding had escaped investigators of national time series perhaps because most countries most of the time will not engineer an increase of their national debt large enough to drive up noticeably the world real interest rate, and even when they do, much of the effect is diffused over the rest of the world via a real appreciation in the country originating the increased debt, so the effect is not great per real dollar; by contrast, when there is an increase of a dollar in real debt per country we are talking 'real money' and when the rise in the average of the world's real interest rates is measured we are capturing the global effect, not just the remaining national effect after diffusion.

In some work I did aimed at imitating Morris's work and producing some variations on it I found that public expenditure, reasonably normalised, also had an effect. But, strikingly, the effect on the real interest rate had the 'wrong' sign: it was negative, though only borderline significant or, in the case of moving averages, insignificant. Clearly this is bad news for traditional Keynesian theory. It is good news, taken alone, from the point of view of the monetary part of structuralist theory, discussed above, according to which increased government expenditure, by crowding out other consumer expenditure at given output, must shift inward the demand for money and thus shift outward the Hicksian *LM*, driving down the real rate of interest. It is also good news from the point of view of the non-monetary chapter of structuralist theory if, and only if, the increased public purchase is for capital goods, so that the expenditure drives up the real price of capital goods and drives down the rate of return on them. But for this to be good news, all things considered, it must also be the case that the increased public expenditure increased employment. Did it? That question awaits the next section.

Another model of the world real interest rate has been developed by Michael Beenstock at the Central Bank of Israel. However I have not had the opportunity so far to discuss with him how his model differs from the foregoing and whether his findings are importantly different from those of Morris and myself.

I should point out that if we take the real wage to be a predetermined variable in the employment equation we should also include it among the explanatory variables in the real interest rate equation. But perhaps the statistical properties of some of the variables of the problem make that an infeasible course.

Let me close this section with the acknowledgement that a better model of the world real interest rate could easily be written down. The obstacle standing in the way of the development and implementation of such models is the costliness of gathering the world time series that those models will require. It is unfortunate that the large research departments of the international organisations, while doing so much useful data gathering as well as statistical work, have not organised themselves to produce extensive world aggregates on wealth, capital, debt, consumption, investment, and so forth on a regular basis so that private economists with modest research budgets can begin to make progress in understanding the world rate of unemployment.

3.2   Effects of Fiscal and Other Influences on World Unemployment

Here I will discuss first an equation of the reduced-form type with which to explain the world rate of unemployment. In some work undertaken during 1988 but not written up I wanted to see how the explanatory variables used by Morris to explain the world real interest rate would fare as explanations of world unemployment. For this exercise I did not have a capital stock series with which to normalise employment and hence used as the dependent variable the very variable of ultimate concern, the world unemployment rate, or actually the world employment rate, $1 - u$. I looked at both a simple equation in annual data without any lags and the corresponding equation in which the variables appear as three-year moving averages.

For this work I did not (and do not yet) have a real wage series. So I am compelled therefore to take up friendly relations with the real wage rigidity view according to which the real wage is codetermined along with the unemployment rate as the economy's shocks drive it up and down its equilibrium labour-market locus.

The 'world' series here are those from the collection of OECD countries with a few quantitatively minor exclusions for reasons of data availability. The time period is approximately 1971 to 1987.

Among the monetary variables, the money stock variable performed powerfully, as expected, especially in the moving average case. I do not know whether the lag is variable, but evidently Milton Friedman is right that the lag is long. Oddly, the expected inflation rate is insignificant or, in the moving average equation, negative, which is the wrong side from the viewpoint of Mundell–Tobin plus Hicks. If higher inflation expectations reduce the real interest rate, they ought to slide the economy down its *IS* curve to higher employment. This was an unexpected and unsought mishap for Keynesian theory, a sort of unforced error to turn from boxing to tennis.

What now of the real demand impulses, the Keynesian fiscal stimuli? Will they come bouncing back from their defeat in the real interest rate equation?

The Keynesian theory implies that public debt is expansionary, as readers already knew, and the structuralist theory, it will be recalled, implies that the debt is contractionary. In fact, the coefficient is in every case negative – the employment rate falls when the beginning-of-year real public debt, suitably normalised, is increased. But the effect is never remotely significant. So perhaps a statistician would say that we cannot reject with confidence the hypothesis of Keynesian theory that the coefficiency is truly positive. I incline more to the inference that the empirical finding here puts the Keynesian theory in further trouble.

For Keynesian theory, I should think, getting a positive coefficient for government expenditure is almost a must-win game. Even a structuralist would not be unhappy to find it if he takes seriously the finding, cited above, that increased public expenditure tends to lower the real interest rate. The equation without lags in fact gave a negative coefficient that was quite significant; the equation with lags also showed a negative coefficient though with only borderline significance.

Perhaps these findings about the fiscal variables have another explanation. I am sorry to have to report that the fiscal variables were normalised by actual gross product rather than potential gross product. Hence the fiscal variables in the regression equation will go up whenever there is an unexplained drop of gross product and employment; an oil shock is a rather bad example since the fall of output may be counterbalanced by the fall in output per manhour, leaving the unemployment rate unchanged, but a drop in the 'marginal efficiency of investment' is a good example. When these variables go up and the employment rate goes down for this reason, there results a bias toward a negative coefficient. But I am doubtful that the output and employment fluctuations from such extraneous sources are important enough to change the signs of the coefficients if otherwise they would be positive and significant.

Recent econometric research by Annalisa Cristini (1989) at Cambridge has produced somewhat different findings on the influence of demand upon employment. In effect, demand 'instrumented' by some sort of lagged public expenditure variable is found to have a positive effect. Perhaps this is the positive effect of public expenditure that both Keynesian and structuralists must wish for if they cannot shake the finding of a negative effect on the real interest rate. The point I would make, however, is that by representing the whole 'structure' – the entire panoply of demands by households, firms, and the various governmental entities – by a single variable (or possibly even by two variables) when the monetary variables by themselves cannot explain nearly all the variation to be explained, one makes it almost inevitable that that heroic real variable will be strongly significant; but with another data set, possibly for a different time period, the coefficient having to do so much work might flip over to the opposite sign. The question is, what are the respective effects of each of a considerable assortment of demand stimuli? The emerging 'structuralism' should warn us not to expect that all the traditional demand stimuli will prove to have positive coefficients or all negative coefficients. The world is not so simply constructed.

Despite some reservations about the proto-model with which Cristini has started out, it is clear to me that the higher econometric level at which she is proceeding is essential if we are to arrive at findings in which we can have confidence. And I do believe that the explanation of the global time series will hold many lessons for us. As will be obvious to anyone who has studied international economics, a global collection of national studies that use only national data, no world data, will not tell us anything reliable about the global effects of global disturbances, nominal and real.

4   CONCLUDING COMMENTS

This paper will have performed well in relation to its objectives if it has persuaded readers that there now exists an interesting and plausible alternative to Keynesian theory, which has so long monopolised the market for macrotheory, and that the global evidence is surprisingly unsupportive of Keynesian theory when tested against the alternative hypotheses of the new theory, which I have labelled structuralist.

The paper has not established a strong set of empirical findings that would convince us of the structuralist alternative. It would be naive in any case to imagine that a handful of regression estimates might cause the mantle of orthodoxy to be passed to the new structuralist challenger.

Yet the findings do lend appreciable support, tentatively and provisionally, to the structuralist perspective. After all, it has scored a much higher number of right signs than the Keynesian theory. It should perhaps be recalled in this connection that the early Keynesian models did not have clear econometric sailing until an enormous effort was made by the profession in the 1950s.

The next step is to turn over this econometric research to the professional econometricians. I will be looking forward to following that research as it proceeds and, if possible, to interacting on occasion in its design.

Notes

1. This paper was written without complete acccss to my own files so the report of the statistical results was left somewhat imprecise but, I think, not inaccurate. My thanks to Alan Malz for computations and to a number of economists for 'leads' in the search for evidence, including Annalisa Cristini, Dennis Snower, and Giuseppe Tullio. A grant from the US National Science Foundation is gratefully acknowledged.
2. This stimulus would be absent under so-called 'Ricardian equivalence' but the Keynesian tradition excludes that special case.
3. An admirably clear example is the model in Dimsdale, Nickell, and Horsewood (1989) p. 273: 'Demand side factors', as they put it, 'have no effect on the real equilibrium [meaning, at the natural rate]. Thus the model has the standard natural rate property despite the fact that we have made no assumption about clearing markets.' The reader might demand to know what is noteworthy about that. How does this assumption differ from all models in the spirit of the Microeconomic Foundations volume of twenty years ago? The subtle difference is simply that the latter volume was silent, if not oblivious, about supply-side as well as real demand-side influences upon the natural rate; we focused on nominal demand-side shocks presumed to be Hume–Patinkin neutral. So my point in the text is only that the recent development in macroeconomic thinking, and exemplified in the paper just cited, is one-sided in recognising only supply-side influences.
4. Again selecting an example somewhat at random, there is Malinvaud (1989) in which 'demand' is an elixir the powers of which are unexplained and, to me at least, mysterious, at least in the limiting case of a closed economy.
5. For a time I thought this locus must be nearly vertical, as Summers (1989) has argued, appealing to the implications of secular productivity growth in the contrary case, or worse, that the locus may be backward-bending, thus lacking *a priori* predictive power though none the less useful for explanatory purposes. However I am now persuaded that, as a short run relation, an upward-sloping locus is highly plausible, especially insofar as it is based on the shirking model of Calvo/Bowles rather than the quitting model of Phelps/Stiglitz/Salop. So I will have the shirking model in mind as a foundation when, as I will frequently do, I want to use real wage rigidity rather than real wage stickiness.
6. I believe it would be quite interesting to integrate into this survey of emerging structuralist theory the intriguing paper on consumer durables by Mankiw (1985). However this must await further work on this subject.

References

Azariadis, C. (1975) 'Implicit Contracts and Underemployment Equilibrium', *Journal of Political Economy*, vol. 83, no 6, pp. 1183–202.

Bean, C., Layard, R. and Nickell, S. (1986) 'The Rise of Unemployment: A Multi-country Study', *Economica*, vol. 53, pp. 1–22.

Blanchard, O. J. and Summers, L. K. (1986) 'Hysteresis in Unemployment', *European Economic Review*, vol. 30.

Bruno, M. and Sachs, J. D. (1985) *Economics of Worldwide Stagflation* (Cambridge, Massachusetts: Harvard University Press).

Cristini, A. (1989) Unpublished doctoral dissertation, University of Cambridge, Cambridge, UK.

Dimsdale, N. H., Nickell, S. J. and Horsewood, N. (1989) 'Real Wages and Unemployment in Britain in the 1930s', *Economic Journal*, vol. 99, no 2, pp. 271–92.

Drèze, J. and Modigliani, F. (1981) 'The Trade-off between Real Wages and Employment in an Open Economy', *European Economic Review*, vol. 25, January–February, pp. 1–40.

Fitoussi, J.-P. and Phelps, E. (1986) 'Causes of the 1980s Slump in Europe', *Brookings Papers on Economic Activity*, vol. 16, no 2, pp. 487–520.

Fitoussi, J.-P. and Phelps, E. (1988) *The Slump in Europe: Open Economy Macroeconomics Reconstructed* (Oxford: Basil Blackwell).

Hall, C. A. Jr and Tobin, J. (1954) 'Income Taxation, Output and Prices', *Economica Internazionale*, vol. 8, August and November, pp. 522–9, 751–5.

Hicks, J. (1973) *The Crisis in Keynesian Economics* (Oxford: Basil Blackwell).

Kouri, P. J. K. (1982) 'Profitability and Growth', *Scandinavian Journal of Economics*, vol. 84, pp. 317–39.

Lal, D. and van Wijnbergen, S. (1985) 'Government Deficits, the Real Interest Rate and LDC Debt', *European Economic Review*, vol. 29, November–December, pp. 157–91.

Lindbeck, A. and Snower, D. (1987) 'Transmission Mechanisms from the Product to the Labor Market', Seminar Paper no 403, Institute for International Economic Studies, University of Stockholm, Stockholm, Sweden.

Lindbeck, A. and Snower, D. (1988) *The Insider–Outsider Theory of Employment and Unemployment* (Cambridge, Massachusetts: MIT Press).

Malinvaud, E. (1979) *Profitability and Unemployment* (Cambridge, UK: Cambridge University Press).

Malinvaud, E. (1989) 'The Role of High Real Wages', unpublished paper, proceedings of the conference on 'Competing Explanations of High Unemployment' International School of Economic Research, University of Siena, Siena.

Mankiw, N. G. (1985) 'Consumer Durables and the Real Interest Rate', *Journal of Political Economy*, vol. 93, May, pp. 353–62.

Mankiw, N. G. and Summers, L. K. (1985) 'Are Tax Increases Expansionary?', mimeograph, Harvard University, Cambridge, Massachusetts.

Morris, D. (1988) *A Model of the World Real Interest Rate* (London: Pinter).

Newell, A. and Symons, J. (1987) 'Wages and Employment between the

Wars', Discussion Paper no 87–02, Department of Economics, University College, London.

Penati, A. (1984) 'Money, Business Cycles and the Real Rate of Interest in the United States', doctoral dissertation, University of Chicago, Chicago.

Phelps, E. S. (1968) 'Money Wage Dynamics and Labor-Market Equilibrium', *Journal of Political Economy*, vol. 76, no 4, part 2, pp. 678–711.

Phelps, E. S. (1972) *Inflation Policy and Unemployment Theory* (New York: W. W. Norton).

Phelps, E. S. (1982) 'Cracks on the Demand Side', *American Economic Review*, Papers and Proceedings, vol. 72, no 3, pp. 378–81.

Phelps, E. S. (1985) 'Appraising the American Fiscal Stance', Temi di Discussione, Research Department, Bank of Italy, Rome.

Phelps, E. S. (1988a) 'A Working Model of Slump and Recovery from Disturbances to Capital-Goods Demand in a Closed Non-Monetary Economy', Working Paper 88/82, Research Department, International Monetary Fund, Washington, DC, in Nell, E. J. and Semmler, W. (eds) (1991) *Nicholas Kaldor and Mainstream Economics* (London: Macmillan).

Phelps, E. S. (1988b) 'An Extended Working Model of Slump and Recovery from Disturbances to Capital-Goods Prices in an Overlapping-Generations Closed Economy: IS–LM without Money' September; to appear in Heyn-Johnson, C. (ed.) (forthcoming) *IS–LM after Fifty Years*.

Phelps, E. S. (1989) 'Aggregate Demand in a Non-Monetary Model of Labor-Market and Product-Market Equilibrium', mimeograph, Columbia University, New York, revised June 1989 (original, November 1988).

Phelps, E. S. and Winter, S. G. Jr (1970) 'Optimal Price Policy under Atomistic Competition', in Phelps *et al.* (1970), pp. 309–37.

Phelps, E. S. *et al.* (1970) *Microeconomic Foundations of Employment and Inflation Theory* (New York: W. W. Norton).

Sachs, J. D. (1979) 'Wages, Profits and Macroeconomic Adjustment: A Comparative Study', *Brookings Papers on Economic Activity*, vol. 9, no 2, Autumn.

Shapiro, C. and Stiglitz, J. E. (1984) 'Equilibrium Unemployment as a Worker Discipline Device', *American Economic Review*, vol. 74, no 3, pp. 433–44.

Sinn, H.-W. (1985) 'Why Taxes Matter: Reagan's Accelerated Cost Recovery System', *Economic Policy*, November.

Solow, R. M. (1979) 'Another Possible Source of Wage Stickiness', *Journal of Macroeconomics*, vol. 1, no 2, pp. 79–82.

Summers, L. K. (1989) *Unemployment* (Cambridge, Massachusetts: MIT Press).

Tullio, G. (1987a) 'Inflation Adjusted Government Budget Deficits and their Impact on the Business Cycle: Empirical Evidence for Eight Industrial Countries', Bank of Italy, October.

Tullio, G. (1987b) 'Long-term Growth, Money and Inflation in Germany, 1880–1979: Historical Overview' in Sommariva, A. and Tullio, G. (1987) *German Macroeconomic History, 1880–1979* (London: Macmillan), pp. 1–79.

3 Unemployment Through Learning from Experience

Steve Alpern
LONDON SCHOOL OF ECONOMICS

and

Dennis J. Snower
BIRKBECK COLLEGE
UNIVERSITY OF LONDON

1 INTRODUCTION

This paper analyses how workers' wage claims can serve as a learning tool. We argue that when workers have some market power and face substantial uncertainty in the labour market, it may be in their interests to formulate their wage claims with a view to the information thereby revealed, in order to make more informed wage claims in the future. This learning behaviour can have an important by-product: unemployment. Our analysis shows how the process of information acquisition through wage claims generates:

(a) rates of youth unemployment and long-term unemployment that are *higher*;
(b) dismissal probabilities for incumbent workers that are *lower* than would otherwise be the case.

We construct a model of wage-setting in which the central problem is one of asymmetric information. Workers are assumed to have less information than their employers about their marginal revenue products (MRPs), and are able to acquire MRP information from their employers by making wage claims and observing the resulting job offers.

In this context, a worker has the incentive to gain MRP information through his wage claims if his actual MRPs (about which he has imperfect information) are correlated through time. This implies that when the worker acquires information about his current MRP, he thereby also gains information about his future MRP. Examples of situations in which workers face uncertain and autocorrelated MRPs are easy to come by. A new entrant to the labour force may have little knowledge of his future MRPs at any particular job but he may expect them to be autocorrelated, since his MRP depends on his ability and on the technologies associated with the job, both of which change only gradually through time. Moreover, when an economy experiences a 'permanent' macroeconomic shock (i.e. a shock that persists through time), workers may be uncertain about their new, post-shock MRPs, but they have reason to expect that these MRPs will be related to their future MRPs.

Our model has two important general features:

1. Information acquisition is not conducted independently of wage decisions. In particular, agents gain information by observing the consequences of their wage claims. This may be called 'learning from experience'.
2. The information that is acquired in this way tends to be qualitative rather than quantitative. For example, a worker who receives no job offer can infer that his wage claim was 'too high' (say, greater than his MRP), whereas a worker who is hired can infer that his wage claim was 'too low' or 'just right' (say, less than or equal to his MRP).

Different wage claims generate different types of information and these, in turn, are not all of the same value to the worker. In our model, for example, a worker gains more information from a high wage claim that elicits a job offer than from a low wage claim that also elicits that job offer.[1] It is because different wage decisions have different information contents that agents have an incentive to make these decisions with a view to the quality of information thereby revealed. The process of acquiring high–low information through wage-setting is an example of 'high–low search', which has been surveyed in Alpern and Snower (1988).

We argue that our analysis may help to illuminate the labour-market experience of various European countries in the wake of the oil-price shocks in the mid- and late-1970s. An important open question is why European real wages remained as high as they did in the face of substantial uncertainty. Why did workers not take wage cuts in order to reduce their chances of unemployment? Although we do not dispute the various answers that this question has received in the recent labour-market literature (e.g. in the insider–outsider and efficiency–wage theories), we wish to argue here that workers 'learning by experience' may have had a role to play as well.

The oil-price shocks of the mid- and late-1970s were quite persistent and initiated prolonged periods of uncertainty regarding firms' sales prospects, factor substitution, and labour productivity. In the aftermath, many workers are likely to have perceived themselves to be facing uncertain but autocorrelated MRPs. We suggest that under these conditions – which are consonant with the spirit of our analysis – those groups of European workers with sufficient market power may have had an incentive to use their wage claims as a learning tool. Our analysis shows how the information motive underlying wage claims may give rise to youth unemployment and make it more difficult for senior unemployed workers to get jobs.

However, the potential purview of our analysis extends well beyond these historical periods. In the 'formal' sectors – where jobs are associated with significant labour turnover costs – employees generally exercise some market power in the wage-bargaining process (regardless of whether they are unionised).[2] Furthermore, these employees are generally able to gain information about their current MRPs by observing whether they are offered jobs at the negotiated wages. In so far as the determinants of the MRPs (e.g. the employees' abilities, the firms' technologies) remain reasonably stable through time, the employees are able to learn about their future MRPs by observing their current job offers.

The paper is organised as follows. Section 2 clarifies the relation of our contribution to the relevant literature and explains some underlying concepts. Section 3 presents our model of wage-setting as a learning tool and examines how unemployment can arise as result. Section 4 explores the effect of learning on unemployment by examining wage formation under alternative learning scenarios. Finally, Section 5 outlines some practical implications.

2   RELATED LITERATURE AND UNDERLYING CONCEPTS

Some current theories of labour market behaviour have implications for the relation between uncertainty and unemployment. For example, in the search theories of Diamond (1982), Mortensen (1970), Pissarides (1985) a rise in uncertainty may be associated with a rise in 'mismatch', which leads to a rise in unemployment (*ceteris paribus*). In the theory of employment adjustment costs (e.g. Bertola, 1990; Bentolila and Bertola, 1988; Nickell, 1978, 1986), and the insider–outsider theory (e.g. Lindbeck and Snower, 1989), a rise in uncertainty implies a rise in firms' average hiring, training and firing costs required at any given level of employment and therefore leads to a drop in employment. In the context of efficiency wage theory (e.g. Shapiro and Stiglitz, 1984; Weiss, 1980), a rise in uncertainty may weaken the incentive effect of wages on productivity and may thereby induce firms to raise their wage offers and generate more unemployment.[3]

However, the formal implications of these theories for the ways in which uncertainty affects unemployment remain largely unexplored. Moreover, the theories mentioned are not concerned with the way in which learning under uncertainty affects unemployment.

Conventional micro- and macro-economic theory tends to portray information acquisition and price–quantity decisions as independent activities. In particular, economic agents are generally seen to make their decisions in two stages: first, they acquire their information; then, on the basis of this information, prices and quantities are set. For example, in the New Classical macroeconomics, the public formulates its price expectations, given its information set; and given the discrepancy between these expectations and actual prices, the levels of production and employment may be determined. We are not told what the public does to acquire its current information set and there is an implicit presumption that its information acquisition activities have no significant macroeconomic implications.

Although we do not deny that learning activities and price-quantity decisions are sometimes conducted independently of one another, we wish to argue that the conventional theories tend to leave out an important feature of everyday economic activity, namely, that price-quantity decisions may be used as learning tools.

It is useful to distinguish between two different types of learning:

1. 'passive learning', whereby agents acquire information merely by passively observing their environment;
2. 'active learning', whereby agents' market decisions are made with a view to acquiring information.

In practice, the participants in the labour market engage in both types of learning. Learning is passive whenever information acquisition is not the result of market participation, as when workers and firms gain labour-market information from the news media and friends, and these activities generally do not require them to make price-quantity decisions. Yet active learning also has an important role to play – and not only with regard to wage-setting (analysed here), but also regarding a wide variety of market activities. For example, firms that do not produce exclusively to order often gain information about the product demands they face by putting specified quantities of output up for sale at specified prices and observing how much is sold. This may be a major source of information when customer surveys are inaccurate or very costly. Other examples include strikes called by unions in order to gain information about firms' profits, or lock-outs called by firms in order to gain information about unions' fall-back positions.

Economic theory has something to say about passive learning, but surprisingly little about active learning. The main paradigm for analysing decision-making under uncertainty consists of optimisation subject to constraints that include error terms whose distribution is known. For example, the monopoly union model generally portrays the union as maximising its objective function (which depends, say, on the real wage and employment) subject to a labour-demand function which may have an additive or multiplicative error term whose distribution the union is assumed to know. The union is not portrayed as making its decisions with a view to acquiring more information.

Although the principal-agent literature involves market activities (such as advertising, screening and monitoring) that reveal information (e.g. the efficiency-wage models of Calvo and Wellisz, 1978; Shapiro and Stiglitz, 1984; and Weiss, 1980), the focus of attention is the provision of incentives rather than the acquisition of new information. In the traditional job-search literature (e.g. Mortensen, 1970; Phelps, 1970), agents engage in market activities (e.g. bearing the costs of search) in order to elicit wage offers, but the search activity takes the form of sampling from a known distribution. The search decisions are not made with a view to discovering what the distribution is.

The work on Bayesian learning (e.g. Bray and Savin, 1986) also tends to be about passive learning. Although agents are assumed to update their subjective distributions by observing the consequences of their actions, the updating is a passive by-product of past search activities; it does not provide a *motive* for these activities.

Our models of active learning are based on the mathematical theory of high–low search, developed by Baston and Bostock (1985) and Alpern (1985). It has been used to analyse firms' pricing decisions (Aghion, *et al.*, 1987; Lazear, 1986), the demand for inventories (Alpern and Snower, 1987a), and the supply of goods (Alpern and Snower, 1987b; Reyniers, 1990).

This paper analyses a process of active learning that involves the following sequence of decisions:

1. making a wage claim under uncertain market conditions;
2. observing the employment repercussions;
3. using these observations to make inferences about the market conditions, which (in turn) are used to make subsequent wage decisions.

The wage decision is based on given information, but it is made with a view to providing employment observations that reveal an optimal amount of new information. In short, the wage-setter seeks to 'learn' from the employment 'experience' generated by the wage decision.

3 WAGE-SETTING AS A LEARNING TOOL

We use a simple two-period model to show how workers' wage claims can reveal information about their MRP. In particular, let each worker have a working life of two periods, so that he may be called 'young' in the first and 'senior' in the second. If he finds a vacancy as a young worker, he makes a wage claim w_y (where the subscript, y, stands for 'young'). Should he get a job in response to his wage claim, he becomes an 'incumbent' in the second period of his working life. As such, he makes another wage claim, w_i (where the subscript, i, stands for 'incumbent').

However, should he fail to get a job as a young worker, he joins the ranks of the youth unemployed and receives the transfer payment, t, (say, an unemployment benefit). In the second period, he then becomes a 'senior outsider'. If this senior job-seeker finds a vacancy, he makes a wage claim, w_s (where the subscript, s, stands for 'senior' unemployed).

In what follows, we first describe the MRP uncertainty faced by the young and the senior workers, then we derive their optimal wage claims, and finally we analyse the resulting levels of unemployment.

3.1   MRP Uncertainty

A worker's MRP at a particular job depends both on the characteristics of that worker (such as his ability and motivation) and on the characteristics of the job (such as the technologies and cooperating factors associated with the job and the prospects of selling the output). Whereas the worker may be expected to know more about the former characteristics than his employer, the employer may be expected to know more about the latter characteristics. Since our aim is to show how a worker's wage claim can reveal information about his MRP, we start by assuming that the employer has the informational advantage and we then examine how the worker can use his wage claim as a tool to gain some of the information available to his employer.

To put this idea into sharp focus, let the actual value of the worker's MRP (net of any labour turnover costs) at a particular job, b^a, be known to the firm but unknown to the worker. The worker's actual MRPs at different jobs are assumed to be i.i.d. Each young worker is assumed to have a prior (subjective) notion of the density of his MRP at any vacant job. For simplicity, we take this density to be uniform over the 'uncertainty interval' $[(\underline{b}-v), (\underline{b}+v)]$, where $\underline{b}$ and v are positive constants and $(\underline{b} - v) > 0$. We assume that jobs are 'idiosyncratic', so that the worker cannot gain information about his own MRP by observing the wage claims and employment outcomes of other workers. The transfer payment t is assumed to be such that $t < (\underline{b}-v)$.

The young worker makes his wage claim w_y taking into account this transfer payment and the subjective MRP density, and the firm responds by making or withholding a job offer. If $b^a \geq w_y$, the worker gets the vacant job; if $b^a < w_y$, he is rejected. By implication, the worker will set his wage claim w_y within the MRP uncertainty interval $[(\underline{b}-v), (\underline{b}+v)]$. The firm's employment decisions reveal information

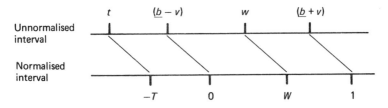

Figure 3.1 The normalisation

to the worker: a job offer implies that the worker's MRP is greater than or equal to his wage claim; and a rejection implies that his MRP falls short of his wage claim.

As noted in Section 1, if the worker's MRP when he is young is correlated with his MRP when he is senior, then the MRP information he gains in the first period may be of value to him in formulating his second-period wage claim. To fix ideas, let the worker's actual MRP, b^a, be constant over his working life. Then, if he gets a job as a young worker at wage w_y, his MRP uncertainty interval in the second period of his working life becomes $[w_y, (\underline{b}+v)]$. Here, the size of the second-period uncertainty interval depends on the magnitude of the first-period wage claim (w_y). Under these circumstances, we show that the young worker has an incentive to make his wage claim with a view to gaining MRP information.

On the other hand, if the young worker does not get a job and thus remains unemployed, he seeks a vacancy at a new job in the next period.[4] Given that he knows his MRPs at different jobs to be i.i.d., his MRP uncertainty interval is the same as that of a young worker: $[(\underline{b}-v), (\underline{b}+v)]$. In short, whereas a young worker who receives a job offer gains MRP information that he can use in formulating his second-period wage demand, a young worker who receives no offer does not acquire such information.

To derive the optimal wage claims, it is convenient to normalise the young worker's MRP uncertainty interval to $[0, 1]$, as shown in Figure 3.1. Accordingly, any unnormalised wage claim, w, corresponds to the following position W in the normalised uncertainty interval:

$$W = (w - \underline{b} + v)/(2 \cdot v), \tag{1a}$$

any unnormalised MRP value, b, corresponds to the normalised value, B:

$$B = (b - \underline{b} + v)/(2 \cdot v),$$ (1b)

and the unnormalised transfer payment t corresponds to the normalised value T:

$$T = (\underline{b} - v - t)/(2 \cdot v)$$ (1c)

The parameter T has an important role to play in our subsequent analysis; it may be interpreted as follows. $2 \cdot v$ is the magnitude of the MRP uncertainty interval; and $(v - t - \underline{b})$ is the difference between the minimum MRP $(\underline{b} - v)$ and the transfer payment (t), which we may call the minimum 'penalty' associated with unemployment. Thus, T may be called the 'penalty–uncertainty ratio'. Note that a fall in the penalty–uncertainty ratio may be due to:

- an increase in uncertainty (viz, a rise in v);
- a rise in the transfer payment (t); or
- a fall in the average MRP level $(\underline{b})$.

3.2   Wage Claim of the Senior Workers

Our analysis of the optimal wage claims begins with the decision problems of the senior workers, whom we have divided into 'senior outsiders' and 'incumbents'. Each senior outsider makes a wage claim W_s so as to maximise his current expected income,[5] given his MRP uncertainty interval of $[0, 1]$, pictured in Figure 3.2. For any given wage claim W_s, his prior probability of getting the job (pictured by the shaded area to the right of W_s in Figure 3.2) is

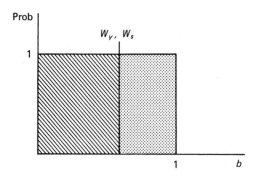

Figure 3.2   The wage decisions of a young worker and a senior outsider

$$\text{Prob } (B \geq W_s) = 1 - W_s \tag{2a}$$

and his prior probability of being rejected (pictured by the shaded area to the left of W_s) is:

$$\text{Prob } (B < W_s) = W_s \tag{2b}$$

The senior outsider's problem is to make a wage claim W_s that maximises his expected income, $Y(0)$:[6]

$$\text{Max } Y(0) = (1 - W_s) \cdot W_s - W_s \cdot T \tag{3}$$
$$W_s$$

The optimal wage claim is

$$W_s^* = \text{max } \{[(1 - T)/2], 0\} \tag{4a}$$

We call this the 'myopic wage', since it is optimal for a worker with a one-period time horizon. Let us assume that $0 < T < 1$, which has the plausible implication that the senior worker makes a wage claim associated with a positive probability of unemployment.[7] Thus:

$$W_s^* = (1 - T)/2 \tag{4b}$$

The corresponding level of expected income is:

$$Y(0)^* = \left(\frac{1 - T}{2}\right)^2 \tag{5}$$

Now turn to the incumbent's decision problem. Having received a job offer in response to his wage claim W_y in the previous period, he infers that his MRP uncertainty interval is $(W_y, 1)$ (under the normalisation above). Consequently, his prior probability of getting the job (pictured by the shaded area to the right of W_i in Figure 3.3) is

$$\text{Prob } (B \geq W_i) = (1 - W_i)/(1 - W_y) \tag{6a}$$

and his prior probability of being rejected (pictured by the shaded area to the left of W_i) is:

$$\text{Prob } (B < W_i) = (W_i - W_y)/(1 - W_y) \tag{6b}$$

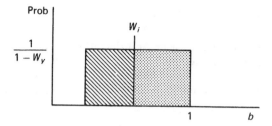

Figure 3.3 The wage decision of an incumbent

If the incumbent gets a job offer, his income is W_i; and if he does not, it is $-T$. He makes his wage claim W_i so as to maximise his expected income, $Y(W_y)$, given his MRP uncertainty interval:

$$\underset{W_i}{\text{Max }} Y(W_y) = [(1 - W_i)/(1 - W_y)] \cdot W_i$$

$$- [(W_i - W_y)/(1 - W_y)] \cdot T \qquad (7)$$

It is easy to show that the optimal wage claim is:

$$W_i^* = \max \{[(1 - T)/2], W_y\} \qquad (8)$$

The corresponding level of expected income is

$$Y(W_y)^* = \left(\frac{1}{1 - W_y}\right) \cdot \left[\left(\frac{1 - T}{2}\right)^2 + T \cdot W_y\right]$$

$$\text{if } W_y \leqslant (1 - T)/2$$

$$Y(W_y)^* = W_y \qquad \text{if } W_y \geqslant (1 - T)/2 \qquad (9)$$

Observe that if the young worker's wage claim (W_y) is less than the myopic wage $((1 - T)/2)$, then the incumbent's optimal wage is associated with a positive probability of dismissal. On the other hand, if the young worker's wage claim exceeds the myopic wage, then the incumbent's optimal wage is equal to the young worker's wage. In the latter event, the incumbent is certain to be retained, since his experience as a young worker indicates that the firm finds it profitable to employ him at W_y.

3.3 Wage Claim of the Young Workers

For any wage claim W_y that a young worker makes, his prior probability of receiving a rejection is Prob $(B < W_y) = W_y$ (given by the shaded area to the left of W_y in Figure 3.2) and the probability of receiving a job offer is Prob $(B \geq W_y) = 1 - W_y$ (given by the shaded area to the right of W_y in Figure 3.2). We consider each of these cases in turn.

What happens when the young worker fails to get a job is pictured in the left-hand side of Figure 3.4. In his youth he receives $-T$. In the next period he searches for a new job as a senior outsider,[8] and has a probability $(1 - \rho)$ of finding no vacancy and a probability of ρ of finding one (where ρ is assumed to be an exogenously given constant between zero and unity). In the absence of a vacancy, he again receives $-T$. Yet if he finds a vacancy, he makes another wage claim, W_s^* (in Equation 4b), which is associated with the expected income $Y(0)^*$ (in Equation 5). Thus, the present value of the worker's expected income if he receives no job offer in the first period is:

$$A = -T + \delta \cdot [\rho \cdot Y^*(0) - (1 - \rho) \cdot T] \tag{10}$$

where δ is the worker's time discount factor.

The right-hand side of Figure 3.4 shows what happens if the young worker receives a job offer in response to his wage claim W_y, so that he becomes an incumbent in the next period. As we have seen, an incumbent's optimal wage claim is W_i^* (in Equation 8 and his expected income is $Y(W_y)^*$ (in Equation 9). Incumbents are assumed to face more favourable employment opportunities than senior outsiders. Specifically, we assume that each incumbent has the opportunity to reapply for his previous job; thus his probability of finding a vacancy is unity (whereas the corresponding probability of a senior outsider is ρ, which may be less than unity).[9] By implication, the present value of a worker's expected income if he receives a job offer in the first period is $[W_y + \delta \cdot Y(W_y)^*]$.

In sum, the present value of a worker's lifetime income, given optimal second-period wage claims, is:

$$V = \text{Prob } (B \geq W_y) \cdot [W_y + \delta \cdot Y^*(W_y)] + \text{Prob } (B < W_y) \cdot A$$
$$= (1 - W_y) \cdot [W_y + \delta \cdot Y^*(W_y)] + W_y \cdot A \tag{11}$$

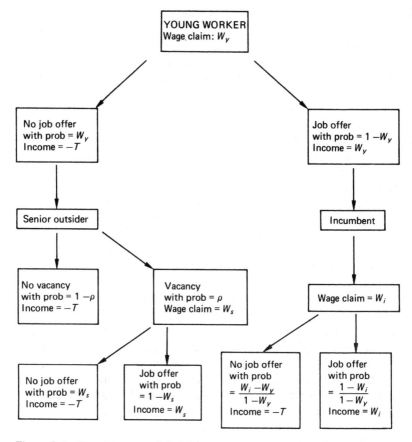

Figure 3.4 The sequence of decisions

The young worker seeks to set his wage claim W_y so as to maximise this present value V. It can be shown that the optimal wage claim is:

$$W_y^* = \left(\frac{1-T}{2}\right) + \left(\frac{\delta \cdot \rho \cdot (1+T)^2}{8 \cdot (1+\delta)}\right) \tag{12}$$

Observe that the young worker's wage claim (W_y^*) exceeds the myopic wage $((1-T)/2)$, and thus – by Equation (9) – the optimal wage claim of the incumbent is equal to that of the young worker:

$$W_i^* = W_y^* = \left(\frac{1-T}{2}\right) + \left(\frac{\delta \cdot \rho \cdot (1+T)}{8 \cdot (1+\delta)}\right)^2 \tag{8'}$$

To gain an intuitive understanding of these results, observe that a young worker faces the following trade-off when formulating his wage claim:

(a) On the one hand, a rise in his wage claim W_y reduces his probability of getting a job in the current period and this reduces his expected lifetime income, because (i) the young worker's current income when unemployed $(-T < 0)$ is less than his current income from employment $(W_y \geq 0)$ and (ii) if he is unemployed in his youth, he has a smaller chance of finding future employment than if he is employed in his youth.

(b) On the other hand, a rise in the wage claim W_y raises his expected lifetime income if he does manage to receive a job offer in his youth, because the greater his wage claim W_y, (i) the greater the young worker's current income, and (ii) the smaller his MRP uncertainty interval if he becomes incumbent and thus the greater the incumbent's optimal wage claim.

The last element – b (ii) – of this trade-off indicates the role of information acquisition in the formulation of the wage claim W_y. Observe that if the young worker does not get a job at W_y, he gains no information of value, since he seeks a new job in the next period. On the other hand, if he receives a job at W_y, he gains valuable information, since he can infer that his next period's MRP uncertainty interval is $[W_y, 1]$. Clearly, the value of this latter information depends on the initial wage claim W_y. Thus we see that when the young worker raises his wage claim W_y, he not only raises the probability of gaining no information of value, but also raises the value of the information that he does gain in the event of getting a job.

4 UNEMPLOYMENT

We are now in a position to evaluate how this use of wage claims as a learning tool affects the level of unemployment. Moving from the micro- to the macroeconomic level, consider a labour market with n workers. The actual MRPs of each of these workers across all jobs are assumed to be uniformly distributed over the normalised interval $[0, 1]$. (This distribution is identical to each worker's prior in the first period.) Workers are assumed to apply randomly for the available jobs.

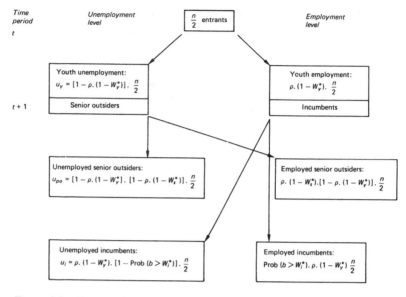

Figure 3.5 Unemployment

In accordance with our two-period analytical framework, we assume that the labour market contains two generations of workers: In any period, there are $n/2$ 'young' workers and $n/2$ 'senior' workers. All workers looking for new jobs (that is, the young workers and the senior outsiders) face the same probability ρ of finding a vacancy. Each young worker who finds a vacancy makes a wage claim of W_y^*, each senior outsider who finds a vacancy claims W_s^*, and each incumbent claims W_i^*.

The levels of unemployment among these workers are summarised in Figure 3.5. The top of the figure shows $(n/2)$ young workers entering the labour force in a particular period of time, t. Each of these workers faces a probability $\rho \cdot \mathrm{Prob}\,(B \geq W_y^*) = \rho \cdot (1 - W_y^*)$ of finding employment, given the MRP uncertainty interval of $[0, 1]$. When n is a large number, the level of youth employment (in the top right of Figure 3.5) may be approximated by $\rho \cdot (1 - W_y^*) \cdot (n/2)$. Similarly, the probability that a young worker will remain unemployed is approximately equal to the youth unemployment rate, which is

$$u_y = [1 - \rho \cdot (1 - W_y^*)] \tag{13}$$

(where the time subscript is suppressed for simplicity). $u_y \cdot (n/2)$ is the level of youth unemployment.

These unemployed young workers in period t turn into senior outsiders in period $t + 1$, each facing a probability of

$$\rho \cdot \text{Prob } (B \geq W_s^*) = \rho \cdot (1 - W_s^*)$$

of finding employment, given the MRP uncertainty interval of $[0, 1]$. Thus, the number of employed senior outsiders is

$$\rho \cdot [1 - \rho \cdot (1 - W_y^*)] \cdot (1 - W_s^*) \cdot (n/2).$$

Thus, the unemployment rate among the senior outsiders is:

$$u_s = [1 - \rho \cdot (1 - W_y^*)] \cdot [1 - \rho \cdot (1 - W_s^*)] \tag{14}$$

and $u_s \cdot (n/2)$ is the number of unemployed senior outsiders.

Finally, each incumbent faces a probability of Prob $(b > W_i^*)$ of gaining employment. Thus, the number of employed incumbents is Prob $(B > W_i^*) \cdot \rho \cdot (1 - W_y^*) \cdot (n/2)$. Obversely, the unemployment probability of each incumbent is $[1 - \text{Prob } (B > W_i^*)]$, and thus the unemployment rate among incumbents is:

$$u_i = [1 - \text{Prob } (B > W_i^*)] \cdot \rho \cdot (1 - W_y^*) \tag{15a}$$

and $u_i \cdot (n/2)$ is the number of unemployed incumbents.

Since the employment probability of an incumbent is

$$\text{Prob } (B \geq W_i^*) = [1 - W_i^*]/[1 - W_y^*]$$

the number of employed incumbents is $\rho \cdot [1 - W_i^*] \cdot (n/2)$. Moreover, the probability that an incumbent will lose his job is

$$\text{Prob } (B < W_i^*) = [W_i^* - W_y^*]/[1 - W_y^*],$$

so that the unemployment rate among incumbents is:

$$u_i = \rho \cdot [W_i^* - W_y^*] = 0 \tag{15b}$$

since $W_i^* = W_y^*$ (by Equations 8′ and 12).

Observe that when the vacancy probability ρ is positive, the youth unemployment rate in our model exceeds that of the senior outsiders. The reason does not lie merely in the positive vacancy probability, implying that some of the workers who were unemployed in their youth do find vacancies once they become senior outsiders. Beyond that, young workers set their wage claims higher than the senior outsiders, because the former have an incentive to gain information through their wage claims while the latter do not. Consequently each young worker runs a greater risk of having his wage claim rejected than a senior worker does.

Also observe that the youth unemployment rate exceeds that of the incumbents.[10] Because of the information acquisition motive, workers find it worthwhile to make wage claims over their working lifetimes so as to bear greater risk of becoming unemployed when they are young (and wage claims can reveal MRP information) than when they are incumbents. As incumbents, they take advantage of previously gained MRP information partly through higher wages and partly through greater job security than they achieve in the absence of learning.

Furthermore, note that the unemployment rate among senior outsiders exceeds that among incumbents. This is not merely because of differences in these workers' vacancy probabilities (i.e. each incumbent is sure to find a vacancy, whereas each senior outsider finds a vacancy only with probability ρ). Even if the senior outsiders' vacancy probability is $\rho = 1$ in our model (so that the senior outsider and the incumbents have the same chance of finding a vacancy) some senior outsiders remain unemployed whereas incumbents do not. The reason is that incumbents have more information about their MRPs than the senior outsiders do, and thus the incumbents can afford to make wage claims that expose them to less risk of rejection than the wage claims of the senior outsiders.

The above results may be summarised by the following proposition:

Proposition 1: *In the context of the model above, in which young workers make wage claims with a view to acquiring MRP information, the youth unemployment rate exceeds the unemployment rate among senior outsiders which, in turn, exceeds the incumbents' unemployment rate.*

Figures 3.6 to 3.9 illustrate the effects of exogenous parameter changes on the rates of youth unemployment, u_y and senior unemployment, u_s. Figures 3.6 and 3.7 indicate that both unemployment

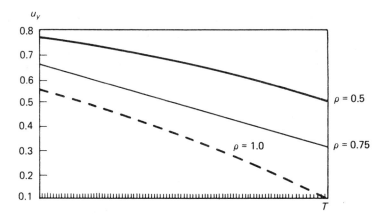

Figure 3.6   Youth unemployment as a function of penalty/uncertainty

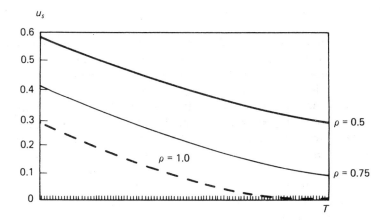

Figure 3.7   Senior unemployment as a function of penalty/uncertainty

---

rates are declining functions of the penalty-uncertainty ratio, T. This means that a mean-preserving increase in the MRP uncertainty interval $(2 \cdot v)$, a rise in the transfer payment (t), and a fall in the average MRP $(\underline{b})$ – all of which are associated with a fall in T (by Equation 1b) – will raise the rates of youth and senior unemployment.

Figures 3.8 and 3.9 show that these unemployment rates are declining functions of the vacancy probability, ρ. Thus, although a rise in the vacancy probability, ρ, leads young workers to raise their

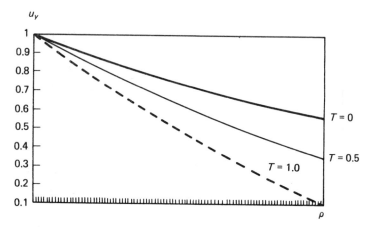

Figure 3.8   Youth unemployment as a function of vacancy probability

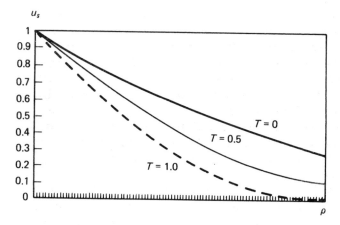

Figure 3.9   Senior unemployment as a function of vacancy probability

wage claim, w_y, this wage claim does not rise sufficiently to keep the unemployment rates from falling.

The aggregate level of unemployment is $[u_y + u_s + u_i] \cdot (n/2)$, and thus the aggregate unemployment rate is

$$u = u_y + u_s + u_i \tag{16}$$

where $u_i = 0$. Figure 3.10 pictures this aggregate unemployment rate

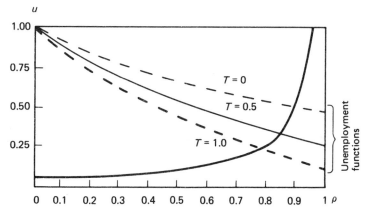

Figure 3.10 The equilibrium unemployment rate (N = 0.95; δ = 0.9)

as a function of the vacancy probability (ρ) for $T = 0.0, 0.5, 1.0$. We call this relation the 'unemployment function', for short.

To find the equilibrium unemployment rate for the labour market above, we endogenise the vacancy probability ρ. In general, this vacancy probability depends on (i) the ratio of vacancies to job-searchers and (ii) the degree of 'mismatch' (that is information imperfections which prevent vacant jobs from being filled by job-searchers). For simplicity, let us assume that that there is no mismatch in our labour market and that all jobs-searchers have an equal chance of finding a vacancy. Then the vacancy probability must equal the ratio of the number of vacancies to the number of unemployed workers, provided that this ratio does not exceed unity.

Let m be the aggregate number of available job slots. Since the aggregate number of employed workers is $(1 - u) \cdot n$, the aggregate number of vacancies is $m - (1 - u) \cdot n$. Thus, the ratio of vacancies to unemployment is

$$\frac{m - (1 - u) \cdot n}{u \cdot n} = 1 - \frac{1 - N}{u} \tag{17a}$$

and $N = (m/n)$, the ratio of job slots to workers, which we take to be exogenously given. Consequently, the vacancy probability is

$$\rho = \min \left[\left(1 - \frac{1 - N}{u} \right), \ 1 \right] \tag{17b}$$

Note that when $N < 1$ (so that $\rho < 1$), the vacancy probability (ρ) depends positively on the unemployment rate (u). The reason is that if the number of vacancies is less than the number of unemployed workers, an equal rise in the number of unemployed workers and the number of vacancies raises the ratio of vacancies to unemployed workers.[11] The relation between the vacancy probability and the unemployment rate we call the 'vacancy function', for short.

The equilibrium unemployment rate, u^*, and the equilibrium vacancy probability, ρ^*, lie at the intersection of the unemployment function (16) and the vacancy function (17a). This is pictured in Figure 3.10 for three different values of the penalty-uncertainty ratio: $T = 0, 0.5, 1.0$.

Recall that an expansion of the MRP uncertainty interval ($2 \cdot v$), a rise in the transfer payment to unemployment workers (t), and a fall in the average MRP level ($\underline{b}$) are all associated with a fall in the penalty-uncertainty ratio, T. As Figure 3.10 illustrates, a fall in T shifts the unemployment function upwards in (ρ, u) space and thereby raises the equilibrium unemployment rate. In short, a rise in uncertainty, a rise in unemployment benefits, or a fall in average MRPs all lead to a rise in unemployment.

5 WAGES AND UNEMPLOYMENT IN DIFFERENT LEARNING SCENARIOS

In order to explore the role that 'active learning from experience' plays in generating unemployment, let us compare our model above with two alternative models, which are the same in all respects except with regard to workers' learning behaviour. The two alternative models have the following salient features:

1. In the *Passive Learning Model*, workers face the same conditions of uncertainty as in our model above (in particular, each worker's MRP at any job is uncertain and constant through time), but their wage claims are based only on 'passive learning', that is, the wage claims make use of the workers' available information but are not formulated with a view to revealing information. It is clear that such passive learning does not generate optimal wage claims for the workers, for we have shown in Section 3 that it is in the workers' interests to use their wage claims as tools for acquiring MRP information. Nevertheless it is instructive to compare the

wage and unemployment outcomes of active and passive learning, since the distinctive contribution of our analysis to the standard Bayesian updating models lies in the role which wage decisions play in information acquisition.

2. In the *No-Learning Model*, workers face the same conditions as in our model above, except that each worker's MRP at any particular job is assumed to be statistically independent through time. Consequently, a worker's employment observations in one time period yield no information about his MRP in subsequent time periods. In short, the worker has *no* opportunity to 'learn from experience' about his MRP by observing the employment responses to his wage claims.

Now consider wage-formation in the Passive Learning Model. For the senior workers, the nature of their decision problem is the same as in the Active Learning Model. Each senior outsider makes a wage claim $(W_s(PL))$ so as to maximise his expected current income, given an MRP uncertainty interval of $[0, 1]$. As in the Active Learning Model, his optimal wage claim is the myopic wage:

$$W_s^*(PL) = (1 - T)/2 \qquad (18)$$

by Equation (4b) the corresponding level of expected income is $Y(0)^*$, given by Equation (5).

Each incumbent's wage claim $(W_i(PL))$ maximises his expected income, given the uncertainty interval $[W_y(PL), 1)$. By Equation (8), his optimal wage claim is:

$$W_i(PL)^* = \max [((1 - T)/2), W_y(PL)^*] \qquad (19)$$

and his excepted income, $Y[W_y(PL)]^*$, is given by Equation (9), for $W_y = W_y(PL)^*$.

The difference between the Passive and Active Learning Models lies in the behaviour of the young workers. Whereas a young active learner makes his wage claim with a view to the information he will thereby acquire, a young passive learner does not take such information into account. Thus, the decision problem of the young passive learner may be summarised as follows. For any given wage claim $W_y(PL)$, he faces the probability Prob $[B \geq W_y(PL)] = 1 - W_y(PL)$ of receiving a job offer. In that case, his current income is $W_y(PL)$, and his expected future income – given that he does not take account of information revealed by the wage claim $W_y(PL)$ – is $Y^*(0)$. His probability of receiving no job offer is Prob $[B < W_y(PL)]$, in which case his current income is T and his expected future income is $(\rho \cdot Y^*(0) + (1 - \rho) \cdot T)$.

The young worker's problem is to make a wage claim $W_y(PL)$ that maximises the present value $V(PL)$ of his expected income over both periods:

$$
\begin{aligned}
\text{Max } V(PL) &= \text{Prob } [b \geq W_y(PL)] \cdot [W_y(PL) + \delta \cdot Y^*(0)] \\
&\quad + \text{Prob } [b < W_y(PL)] \\
&\quad \cdot \{-T + \delta \cdot [\rho \cdot Y^*(0) - (1 - \rho) \cdot T]\} \\
&= [1 - W_y(PL)] \cdot [W_y(PL) + \delta \cdot [(1 + T)/2]^2 \\
&\quad + W_y(PL) \cdot \{-T + \delta \cdot \rho \cdot [(1 + T)/2]^2 \\
&\quad - (1 - \rho) \cdot T]\}
\end{aligned}
\tag{20}
$$

by Equation (5). Solving this problem, it can be shown that the young worker's optimal wage claim under Passive Learning is:

$$
W_y^*(PL) = \max \left\{ 0, \left(\frac{1 - T}{2} \right) - \left(\frac{\delta \cdot (1 - \rho) \cdot (1 + T)^2}{8} \right) \right\} \tag{21}
$$

From Equations (19) and (21), it is clear that the optimal wage of an incumbent under Passive Learning is the myopic wage:

$$
W_i(PL)^* = (1 - T)/2 \tag{19'}
$$

Observe that young workers make lower wage claims than senior workers (both incumbents and senior outsiders) in the No Learning Model. The intuitive reason is that finding a job in the first period of the worker's lifetime gives him an advantage in the second period, for an incumbent is assumed certain to find a vacancy (at his previous job) whereas a senior outsider finds such a vacancy only with probability ρ. Thus, it is in the young worker's interest to make a comparatively low wage claim so as to raise his chances of getting this advantage. As the vacancy probability ρ approaches unity, or as the worker's time discount factor δ approaches zero (so that the worker becomes progressively more myopic) the young workers' optimal wage claim $(W_y(PL)^*)$ rises to the level of senior workers' optimal wage claim $(W_s(PL)^*$ and $(W_i(PL))$, by Equations (8), (19), and (20).

Now consider the No Learning Model. The difference between the MRP uncertainty intervals under Active Learning and No Learning arises because of the difference in the assumed behaviour of workers' MRPs through time. In the Active Learning Model, as we have seen, workers face job-specific MRPs that are unknown but constant through time, as in the aftermath of a long-lasting macroeconomic shock that workers had not anticipated. It is the stability of the MRPs through time that permits incumbents to infer their MRPs from previous employment observations. Yet in the No Learning Model, workers' job-specific MRPs are subject to temporary shocks, as in the course of transient cycles which workers do not anticipate. Here, a young worker who receives a job offer in response to his wage claim $W_y(NL)$ can infer that his current MRP must lie in the interval $[W_y(NL), 1]$, but this information is not useful in formulating subsequent wage claims since his current and future MRPs are statistically independent. Hence, the incumbent's MRP uncertainty interval – like that of the young worker – is $[0, 1]$.

Clearly, the decision problems of the senior outsiders is the same as in the Passive Learning Model, so that their optimal wage claim is:

$$W_s(NL)^* = W_s(PL)^* \tag{22}$$

Since incumbents in the No Learning Model do not have superior MRP information to senior outsiders, their optimal wage claim is the same as that above. Thus,[12]

$$W_i(NL)^* = W_s(NL)^* \tag{23}$$

The young workers' decision problem is also the same in the Passive Learning and No Learning Models. To see this, observe that the young worker's current MRP uncertainty interval is $[0, 1]$ in both models, and those that turn into senior outsiders will clearly face the same uncertainty interval. Furthermore, those that turn into incumbents also face this uncertainty interval, but for different reasons in the two models. In the Passive Learning Model it is because the young worker does not make his wage claim with a view to reducing his future MRP uncertainty interval, whereas in the No Learning

Table 3.1   Optimal wage claims

The Active Learning Model	
Young workers:	$W_y(AL)^* = \left(\dfrac{1-T}{2}\right) + \left(\dfrac{\delta \cdot \rho \cdot (1+T)^2}{8 \cdot (1+\delta)}\right)$
Senior outsiders:	$W_s(AL)^* = (1-T)/2$
Incumbents:	$W_i(AL)^* = \left(\dfrac{1-T}{2}\right) + \left(\dfrac{\delta \cdot \rho \cdot (1+T)^2}{8 \cdot (1+\delta)}\right)$
The Passive Learning and No Learning Models	
Young workers:	$W_y(PL)^* = W_y(NL)^* = \left(\dfrac{1-T}{2}\right) + \left(\dfrac{\delta \cdot (1-\rho) \cdot (1+T)^2}{8}\right)$
Senior outsiders:	$W_s(PL)^* = W_s(NL)^* = (1-T)/2$
Incumbents:	$W_i(PL)^* = W_i(NL)^* = (1-T)/2$

Model it is because the worker's MRP in one period is not related to his MRP in the next. Hence, the young worker's optimal wage claim in the No Learning Model is[13]

$$W_y(NL)^* = W_y(PL)^* \tag{24}$$

The optimal wage claims in the Active, Passive, and No Learning Models are summarised in Table 3.1.

Observe that the optimal wage claims in the Active Learning Model exceed those in the Passive Learning and No Learning Models: the incentive to learn induces the young workers to make greater wage claims than they otherwise would, and given that this learning has taken place, the incumbents find it worthwhile to make greater wage claims than they otherwise would. The intuitive reason for this result emerges straightforwardly when we compare workers' expected incomes in the different models. The present value of a young worker's income in the Active Learning Model is:

$$V(AL) = \text{Prob}\,[B \geq W_y(AL)] \cdot [W_y(AL) + \delta \cdot Y^*\,(W_y(AL))]$$
$$+ \text{Prob}\,[B < W_y(AL)] \cdot A \tag{25}$$

(by Equation 11), and the corresponding present value in the Passive and No Learning Models is:

$$V(J) = \text{Prob } [B \geq W_y(j)] \cdot [W_y(AL) + \delta \cdot Y^*(0))]$$
$$+ \text{Prob } [B < W_y(j)] \cdot A \qquad j = PL, NL \qquad (26)$$

(by Equation 20). Note that these two present values differ only in terms of the incumbent's expected income (which is $Y^*(W_y(AL))$ in the Active Learning Model and $Y^*(0)$ in the Passive and No Learning Models).

Starting from any particular wage claim $W_y = \bar{W}_y$ in all three models, a rise in W_y has a different effect on the incumbent's expected income in the two sets of models. In the Passive and No Learning Models, a rise in W_y clearly has no influence on the incumbent's income $Y^*(0)$ $((\partial Y^*(0)/\partial W_y) = 0)$, since the first period MRP information revealed by W_y is irrelevant to his second period MRP. However, in the Active Learning Model, a rise in W_y does affect the incumbent's income $Y^*(W_y)$, because here the first period MRP information can be used in formulating the second period wage claim. The greater the first period wage claim (W_y), the smaller the incumbent's MRP uncertainty interval $[W_y, 1]$, and the greater the incumbent's wage claim can be $[(\partial Y^*(W_y)/\partial W_y)] = 1$, by Equations (9) and (12). Thus, a rise in the young worker's wage claim W_y is associated with a greater pay-off in the Active Learning Model than in the Passive and No Learning Models, and consequently the optimal wage claim of the young worker is greater in the Active Learning Model than in the Passive and No Learning Models.

The implications of these wage comparisons for the unemployment rate are straightforward. By Equation (13), the youth unemployment rate (u_y) is positively related to the young workers' wage claim (W_y) and thus the youth unemployment rate is greater under Active Learning than under Passive or No Learning.

As for the senior outsiders, recall that their wage claim is the same in all three models, since their past failure to get job offers does not reveal information about their MRPs at the new jobs for which they are applying. By implication, in all three models the same fraction of the young unemployed in one period remain unemployed in the next period. However, since the youth unemployment rate is greater under active learning than under passive and no learning, the unemployment rate among senior outsiders is greater under active learning.

Finally, it can be shown that the unemployment rate among incumbents is *smaller* under active learning than under passive or no learning. To see this, recall that under active learning the incumbents' MRP uncertainty interval is $[W_y(AL), 1]$, and the incumbents set their wage claim at the lower bound of this interval. Consequently no incumbents become unemployed. By contrast, the incumbents' MRP uncertainty interval under no learning is [0, 1], and under passive learning is $[W_y(PL), 1]$, and the incumbents' wage claims lie above the lower bounds of these intervals (that is, $W_i(NL) = W_i(PL) > W_y(PL) \geq 0$). This means that some incumbents lose their jobs under no learning and passive learning.

Specifically, under no learning the probability that a young worker will gain employment is $\rho \cdot (1 - W_y(NL)^*)$ and the probability that an incumbent will lose his job is Prob $(B < W_i(NL)) = W_i(NL)^*$. Thus, the incumbents' unemployment rate is

$$u_i(NL) = \rho \cdot [1 - W_y^*(NL)] \cdot W_i(NL)^* \qquad (27a)$$

Under passive learning, an incumbent's probability of job loss is Prob $(B < W_i(PL) = [W_i(PL) - W_y(PL)]/[1 - W_y(PL)]$. Thus, the incumbents' unemployment rate is

$$u_i(PL) = \rho \cdot (1 - W_y^*(PL)) \cdot [(W_i(PL) - W_y(PL))/(1 - W_y(PL))]. \qquad (27b)$$

The results above may be summarised in the following proposition:

Proposition 2: *In the analytical context above, (a) the unemployment rate among the youth and the senior outsiders is higher, and (b) the unemployment rate among the incumbents is lower, for any given vacancy probability ρ, when workers use their wage claims as an instrument of 'active learning' than when they engage in passive learning or no learning.*

6 IMPLICATIONS

Of the three models considered above, the Passive Learning Model is a 'straw man' while the Active Learning and No Learning Models have straightforward practical interpretations.

As noted, conventional economic theory on learning deals primarily with passive learning: agents are portrayed as gaining information (generally through Bayesian updating) and using this information in making their market decisions, but not as making their market decisions with a view to the information they can thereby acquire. We have shown, however, that such passive learning may be suboptimal; in our model of learning, workers have an incentive to use their wage claims as learning instruments. It is for this reason that the Passive Learning Model is merely a 'straw man' against which the impact of active learning on wage formation and unemployment may be assessed.

As we have seen, the Active Learning and No Learning Models differ only with regard to the assumed behaviour about workers' MRPs: in the Active Learning Model a worker's MRPs at a particular job are perfectly correlated through time,[14] whereas in the No Learning Model these MRPs are taken to be statistically independent. In practice, workers' MRPs at given jobs tend to be correlated, but not perfectly correlated. In this sense, workers' potential opportunities for gaining information through wage claims may be expected to lie somewhere between the two extremes represented by the Active Learning and No Learning Models.

On an economy-wide level, the behaviour of MRPs in the Active Learning Model may be viewed as relevant to 'persistent' macroeconomic shocks, in particular, shocks that are unanticipated by the workers and which may be expected to last for a prolonged span of time. Such shocks may lead workers to view their MRPs as uncertain but stable through time. By contrast, the behaviour of MRPs in the No Learning Model may be viewed as relevant to 'transient' sectoral shocks, in particular, short-lived sectoral changes that are unanticipated by the workers. These shocks may leave workers' average MRPs across all sectors unchanged, but may lead them to view their MRPs in a particular sector as uncertain and unstable through time.

Our main focus of attention has been on the Active Learning Model. This model shows how active learning can generate youth unemployment (that is, unemployment among new entrants to the labour force) and long-term unemployment (that is, unemployment among senior workers who were unemployed in their youth). It also indicates how active learning may help to explain why unemployment among these groups tends to be greater than that among incumbent workers.

Specifically, a marginal wage increase (*ceteris paribus*) has a greater pay-off for a young worker under active learning than under no learning, because under active learning this wage increase means that the worker can demand a higher wage if he becomes an incumbent. For this reason, young workers have an incentive to make higher wage claims – and consequently face a higher incidence of unemployment – when there are opportunities for active learning than when there are none. The incumbent takes advantage of his prior MRP information by reaping both higher wages and greater job security than he could otherwise have achieved. Consequently, the incumbents' unemployment rate falls short of the youth unemployment rate. Moreover, the senior outsiders' unemployment rate lies between these two extremes, for the senior outsiders (in contrast to the young workers) have no incentive to use their wage claims as learning instruments, and (in contrast to the incumbents) cannot take advantage of prior MRP information.

In the context of the Active Learning Model, we have shown that an increase in MRP uncertainty (represented by a mean-preserving increase in the MRP uncertainty interval) raises the equilibrium aggregate unemployment rate. It does so, moreover, by increasing the unemployment rates among the young workers and the senior outsiders, rather than among the incumbents.

It is important to emphasise that workers have the opportunity to use their wage claims as learning instruments, along the lines described by our analysis, only when workers (i) view their marginal revenue products as uncertain but correlated through time, (ii) have less information about their MRPs than their employers do, and (iii) are able to exercise market power in the wage determination process. On these three counts, we may expect our analysis to be relevant to European labour markets in the aftermath of 'persistent' macroeconomic shocks, such as the supply side shocks of the mid- and late-1970s.

Many European labour markets are characterised by high rates of unionisation, pervasive job security legislation, and established bargaining procedures, and consequently workers wield substantial market power in the wage determination process. Furthermore, as we have argued above, 'persistent' macroeconomic shocks may lead workers to view their MRPs as uncertain but stable through time. These shocks – whether of the demand side or supply side variety – may be expected to have MRP effects that are more widely known to firms than to their employees, since firms tend to be more intimately acquainted with changes in factor prices, factor supplies, and sales prospects.

The adverse supply side shocks that initiated the European recessions starting in the mid- and late-1970s undoubtedly brought in their wake periods of persistent uncertainty regarding workers' marginal revenue products. The underlying causes were diverse. First, the supply side shocks induced firms to employ new, raw-material-saving technologies which made marginal products of labour more difficult to predict than heretofore. Second, the magnitude of the business downturns may be expected to have led some European firms to shed labour that would have been hoarded in milder recessions. By implication, there would be greater MRP uncertainty once the recession was over and a new business upturn was beginning, since it is more difficult to predict the marginal products of new recruits than of hoarded labour. Third, a precipitate fall in aggregate product demand – such as the one initiated by the comparatively contractionary monetary and fiscal policies in many European countries in the early 1980s – must have led to greater uncertainty regarding firms' sales prospects and thereby generated MRP uncertainty.

Our model of active learning also implies that a rise in uncertainty leads to a fall in the *outflow rate* from the unemployment pool (that is, a fall in the employment probabilities of the young workers and the senior outsiders) rather than a rise in the *inflow rate* to the unemployment pool (that is, increased firing of incumbents).

The conclusions above – particularly those concerning youth unemployment and long-term unemployment, as well as the effect of uncertainty on unemployment – are broadly in consonance with the European unemployment experience in the mid-1970s and early 1980s.[15]

Of course, our model is far too simple and too single-mindedly learning-oriented to be of use as a predictive instrument on its own. Our analysis merely serves to suggest that workers' use of wage claims as a learning instrument may contribute to unemployment.

Notes

1. Assuming that the worker knows his marginal product to lie within a fixed interval, each observation allows him to infer a lower bound of his marginal revenue product. But this lower bound is higher in the former case than in the latter.
2. See, for example, Lindbeck and Snower (1989).
3. For example, in the Shapiro–Stiglitz model, a rise in uncertainty may lead to a decline in the effectiveness of monitoring and thereby to a rise in the wage that discourages shirking. In the 'gift exchange' model of Akerlof (1982) and Akerlof and Yellen (1988), a rise in uncertainty may

make it more expensive for firms to offer 'fair' wages and thus may lead to a fall in employment and a rise in unemployment.

4. We discuss below why it is not in his interest to seek a vacancy at the old job.

5. In other words, the worker's utility is assumed to be equal to the income he receives.

6. The variable in brackets denotes the lower bound of the MRP uncertainty interval.

7. Clearly, if $T \geq 1$, then $W_s = 0$, and thus the worker is certain to receive a job offer.

8. It is easy to see why the worker has an incentive to seek a new job rather than to reapply to the old one, provided that he faces the same probability of finding a second period vacancy in the old job as in the new one. The reason is that his uncertainty interval at the old firm is $[0, W_s]$, where $W_s < 1$, whereas his uncertainty interval at a new firm is $[0, 1]$. Thus, if he found a vacancy at the old firm, his expected income resulting from a second-period wage claim W_s would be $Y(W_y) = \text{Prob} (b \geq W_s) \cdot W_s - \text{Prob} (b < W_s) \cdot T = [(W_y - W_s)/W_y] \cdot W_s - (W_s/W_y) \cdot T$. Maximising this with respect to W_s, we obtain the optimal second-period wage claim: $W_s^* = (W_y - T)/2$ and the associated level of second-period expected income is $Y_s^* = (W_y - T)^2/(4 \cdot W_y)$. From Equation (5) it is clear that this expected income is identical to the expected income from applying for a new job when $W_y = 1$. Since $W_y^* < 1$ and $(\partial Y_s^*/\partial W_y) > 0$, the expected income from applying to a new job is greater than that from applying to the old one.

9. The incumbents' preferential employment opportunities may be rationalised through the insider–outsider theory (see, for example, Lindbeck and Snower, 1989). If the firm faces labour turnover costs, it may have an incentive to give the incumbents (last period's 'insiders') preference over the 'outsiders' in occupying the available job slots.

10. It is worth noting that our extreme result of zero unemployment among incumbents is an artifact of our two-period framework of analysis. For long time horizons it can be shown that incumbents make wage claims associated with a positive probability of dismissal.

11. To take an extreme example, if one vacancy is available to 100 unemployed applicants, then a unit increase in both the number of vacancies (to 2) and the number of applicants (to 101) raises the ratio of vacancies to unemployed applicants.

12. This result is an artifact of the two-period framework of our analysis. Over longer time horizons, incumbents in the passive learning model do gain MRP information even though their wage claims are not formulated with a view to eliciting such information.

13. Our conclusion that $W_y(PL)^* = W_y(NL)^*$ is an artifact of the two-period time horizon, because young workers with a longer time horizon would anticipate a shrinking of their MRP uncertainty interval in the Passive Learning Model, for reasons given in note 12.

14. For expositional simplicity, we assumed that these MRPs are constant through time, but this is not an assumption of substance. The critical feature of the Learning Model is that the information which a worker

gains about his MRP at a particular job in one time period continues to apply in the next time period. For this purpose, the worker's MRPs at that job must be perfectly correlated.

15. Note that some of these predictions are similar to those of the insider–outsider theory (Lindbeck and Snower, 1989), but the underlying rationale is quite different. Our theory examines how unemployment can arise through the use of wage claims as tools of active learning, whereas the insider–outsider theory describes the unemployment generated through labour turnover costs and insider power.

References

Akerlof, G. (1982) 'Labor Contracts as Partial Gift Exchange', *Quarterly Journal of Economics*, vol. 97, pp. 543–69.

Akerlof, G. and Yellen, J. L. (1988) 'Fairness and Unemployment', *American Economic Review*, Papers and Proceedings, May, vol. 78, pp. 44–9.

Aghion, P., Bolton, P. and Jullien, B. (1987) 'Learning through Price Experimentation by a Monopolist facing Unknown Demand', Working Paper no 8748, University of California, Berkeley.

Alpern, S. (1985) 'Search for a Point in an Interval, with High–Low Feedback', *Mathematical Proceedings Cambridge Philosophical Society*, vol. 98, pp. 569–78.

Alpern, S. and Snower, D. J. (1987a) 'Inventories as an Information-Gathering Device', STICERD Discussion Paper no 87/151, London School of Economics, London.

Alpern, S. and Snower, D. J. (1987b) 'Production Decisions under Demand Uncertainty: the High–Low Search Approach', Discussion Paper no 223, Centre for Economic Policy Research, London.

Alpern, S. and Snower, D. J. (1988) ' "High–Low Search" in Product and Labor Markets', *American Economic Review*, May, vol. 78(2) pp. 356–62.

Baston, V. J. and Bostock, F. A. (1985) 'A High–Low Search Game on the Unit Interval', *Mathematical Proceedings Cambridge Philosophical Society*, vol. 97, pp. 345–8.

Bentolila, S. and Bertola, G. (1988) 'Firing Costs and Labor Demand: How Bad is Eurosclerosis?', unpublished mimeograph, Harvard University.

Bertola, G. (1990) 'Job Security, Employment and Wages', *European Economic Review*, vol. 34, pp. 851–86.

Bray, M. M. and Savin, M. E. (1986) 'Rational Expectations Equilibria, Learning, and Model Specification, *Econometrica*, vol. 54, pp. 1129–60.

Calvo, G. and Wellisz, S. (1978) 'Supervision, Loss of Control and the Optimum Size of the Firm', *Journal of Political Economy*, vol. 86, pp. 943–52.

Diamond, P. (1982) 'Aggregate Demand Management in Search Equilibrium', *Journal of Political Economy*, vol. 86, pp. 943–52.

Lazear, E. P. (1986) 'Retail Pricing and Clearance Sales', *American Economic Review*, vol. 76, pp. 4–32.

Lindbeck, A. and Snower, D. J. (1989) *The Insider–Outsider Theory of*

Employment and Unemployment (Cambridge, Massachusetts: MIT Press).

Mortensen, D. T. (1970) 'A Theory of Wage and Employment Dynamics', in Phelps *et al.* (1970), pp. 167–211.

Nickell, S. J. (1978) 'Fixed Costs, Employment and Labour Demand over the Cycle', *Economica*, vol. 45, pp. 329–45.

Nickell, S. J. (1986) 'Dynamic Models of Labor Demand', in Ashenfelter, O. and Layard, R. (eds) *Handbook of Labor Economics* (Amsterdam: North Holland).

Phelps, E. S. (1970) 'Money Wage Dynamics and Labor Market Equilibrium', in Phelps, E. S. *et al.* (1970).

Phelps, E. S. *et al.* (1970) *Microeconomic Foundations of Employment and Inflation Theory* (New York: W. W. Norton).

Pissarides, C. A. (1985) 'Short-run Equilibrium Dynamics of Unemployment, Vacancies and Real Wages', *American Economic Review*, vol. 75, pp. 676–90.

Reyniers, D. (1990) 'High–Low Search Algorithm for a Newsboy Problem with Delayed Information Feedback', *Operations Research*, vol. 38, no. 5, September.

Shapiro, C. and Stiglitz, J. E. (1984) 'Equilibrium Unemployment as a Worker Discipline Device', *American Economic Review*, vol. 74, no 3, pp. 433–44.

Weiss, A. (1980) 'Job Queues and Layoffs in Labor Markets with Flexible Wages', *Journal of Political Economy*, vol. 88, pp. 526–38.

4 Unemployment and Labour Market Imperfections

Assar Lindbeck

INSTITUTE FOR INTERNATIONAL
ECONOMIC STUDIES,
UNIVERSITY OF STOCKHOLM, SWEDEN

1 INTRODUCTION

Time series of unemployment rates for various countries look like stochastic processes with high probabilities of small disturbances and low probabilities of large disturbances. While the former may be interpreted as standard business cycles the latter usually (or perhaps even always) seem to be related to easily identifiable, dramatic 'historic events'. Examples of the latter are the deflationary monetary and exchange rate policy in some countries, such as the UK, in the early 1920s (when these countries went back to the gold standard at the old parity), the world-wide Depression in the early 1930s, and the well-known macroeconomic shocks in most developed countries around 1974–5 and, again, around 1979–81. Developments in various countries are illustrated in Figures 4.1–4.4.

Another pronounced feature of time series of unemployment rates is the absence of a time trend in the very long run, that is, over several decades. The number of employed workers has basically developed in parallel with the labour force over the very long run – in spite of considerable variations in the (upward) long-run trend of both productivity and population size. This observation is perhaps the strongest empirical evidence available today for the view that in the long run there is a 'natural' rate of unemployment towards which real world economies tend to move (a kind of 'Say's Law' in the long run), though new disturbances all the time tend to shift the actual unemployment rate around. In most countries, this 'natural' rate seems, according to 'eye-ball econometrics', to be around 3–6 per cent.

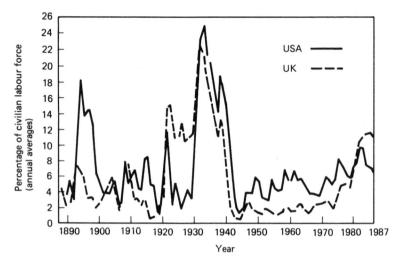

Sources: (for this figure and Figures 4.2, 4.3 and 4.4)
USA: *Historical Statistics of the US, Colonial Times to 1970*, US Dept. of
         Commerce, Bureau of the Census, Tables D85–86 (1890–1970);
         and OECD, *Economic Outlook*, no 44, December 1988, Table
         R.18 (1971–87).
Europe: B. R. Mitchell, *European Historical Statistics, 1750–1975*, 2nd
         revised edn (London: Macmillan, 1980); Sijthoff and Noordhoff
         Facts on File (from starting-points indicated in the figures to 1970,
         except for Norway, from starting-point indicated in Figure 4.3 to
         1967); OECD, *Economic Outlook*, no 44, December 1988, Table
         R.18 (1971–87, except for Norway, 1968–87).

Figure 4.1 Unemployment percentages in USA, 1890–1987 and UK,
1888–1987

Time series of unemployment also suggest some 'unemployment
persistence' phenomena, in the sense that the unemployment rate in
year t is positively correlated with the rate in year $t - 1$, and perhaps
also with the rate in one or a few previous years. However, the
empirical evidence hardly makes it reasonable to argue that the
economy tends to be 'stuck' at extreme unemployment rates. It
seems that the *speed* by which the unemployment rate moves towards
the natural rate is at least as fast when starting from an extreme level
as when starting from a less extreme level, though it takes, of course,
a longer time to return to the 'natural' rate in the former case simply
because the unemployment rate has a longer distance to 'travel'.
   A good macroeconomic theory of unemployment should be able to

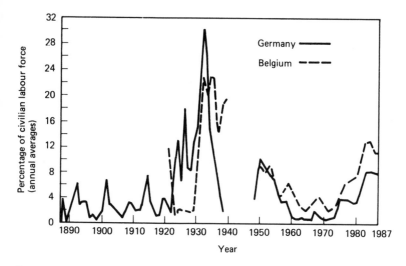

Sources: As given for European countries, Figure 4.1.

Figure 4.2 Unemployment percentages in Germany, 1887–1987, and Belgium, 1921–87

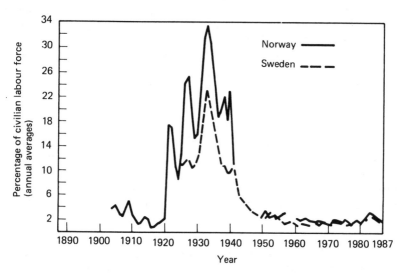

Sources: As given for European countries, Figure 4.1.

Figure 4.3 Unemployment percentages in Norway, 1904–87, and Sweden, 1925–87

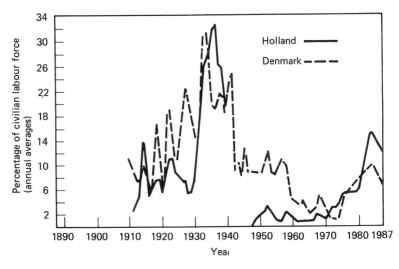

Sources: As given for European countries, Figure 4.1.

Figure 4.4 Unemployment percentages in Holland, 1911–87, and Denmark, 1910–87

explain empirical generalisations like these. However, it should ideally also be able to explain the pronounced differences actually observed between countries. For instance, there were two marked differences between the employment performance in the USA and Western Europe (subsequently referred to as Europe, for short) during the first twenty-five years after the Second World War, more specifically during the period 1950–75:

(i) the general *level* of measured unemployment was considerably higher in the USA – usually 4–6 per cent as compared with 2½–4 per cent in Europe;[1]

(ii) the short-term (cyclical) *fluctuations* in both employment and unemployment were larger in the USA than in Europe.

The latter observation holds also when fluctuations in unemployment are measured relative to the fluctuations in aggregate output: that is, the USA was characterised by a lower 'Okun coefficient' – expressing the percentage change in output per percentage point change in the unemployment rate – than Europe. The employment performance of Japan in this period was closer to the European pattern than to the

US pattern in terms of both the level of employment and unemployment and the amplitude of the fluctuations in these variables.

In view of these empirical observations, it was often argued in the 1950s and 1960s that the labour market in Europe and Japan functioned better than in the USA. Labour market specialists and politicians from the USA travelled to Europe and Japan to learn about the wonders of the labour markets in those parts of the world!

While the aggregate employment performance in Japan has continued to be impressive since the mid-1970s, the relative performance of the USA and Europe, as we know, largely reversed. The cyclical recovery of unemployment from the recessions in the mid-1970s and early 1980s was much stronger in the USA than in Europe. Indeed, during the 1980s the USA operated on a generally lower level of unemployment than did Europe. Moreover, the trend of labour force participation rates was downward in several European countries from the mid-1970s to the late 1980s, while the corresponding rate in the USA, which has traditionally been lower than in Europe, showed no such downward trend.

These experiences in the 1980s have profoundly influenced the views among economists on how the labour markets in the USA and Europe actually operate. Moreover, and more importantly, they have changed the general conception of the types of features that are 'desirable' and 'undesirable', in labour markets. Generally speaking, while large cyclical fluctuations in employment and unemployment were earlier regarded as signs of deplorable 'labour-market instability', the same phenomena have tended in the 1980s to be regarded rather as signs of 'labour-market flexibility', reflecting an ability of employment to bounce back rapidly after downturns, rather than being stuck in prolonged periods of unemployment. However, when drawing on empirical experience, it is also important to note, and if possible explain, the wide differences among European countries, as illustrated by the relatively low unemployment rates during the 1970s and 1980s in some small European countries, such as Austria, Norway, Sweden, Switzerland, and perhaps also Finland.

The basic purpose of this paper is to look at the role of various types of *labour-market imperfections* in the performance of aggregate employment and unemployment, in the light of the experiences mentioned above. It is useful to organise the analysis around the conventional distinction between factors that have their direct impact mainly on the *demand* for labour – that is, the willingness of firms to hire workers (Section 2) – and factors that have their direct impact mainly on the *supply* of labour – that is, the willingness of workers to look for jobs or to accept job offers (Section 3). However, it is also useful to consider various imperfections in *the interaction* between labour demand and labour supply, such as distortions of relative wages and the related issue of mismatches between demand and supply for labour between industries, geographical regions, skills and occupations (Section 4). By contrast, the paper does not deal much with firings, lay-offs and quits of labour. The reason is simply that both periods of cyclically increased unemployment and periods of persistently high unemployment, at least after the Second World War, seem to be characterised by low hiring of labour rather than by large-scale firing, lay-offs or quits (Flanagan, 1989). Moreover, as the paper deals with the role of labour-market imperfections, various macroeconomic factors that influence employment performance, such as aggregate product demand and exchange rates, will not be much considered.

2   LABOUR DEMAND FACTORS[2]

Among features of the labour market that may influence the demand for labour this paper emphasises one, namely various labour-turnover costs. These take many different forms. Hiring and training costs, including the costs of advertising, screening and training of labour are perhaps the most obvious ones. As these costs constitute unavoidable resource costs, they should not, by themselves, be regarded as labour-market imperfections, though as we shall see they may result in wage behaviour that can be characterised in that way. The situation is quite different for the costs of firing labour, which have largely been created by political decisions or bargaining agreements for the purpose of enhancing job and/or income security among employees; these costs are not unavoidable resource costs but rather obligatory transfer payments. There are also more 'sophisticated' types of labour turnover costs. Some of these reflect the negative consequences for the profitability of a firm when incumbent workers refuse to cooperate with potential entrants who try to get a job by way of 'wage underbidding'. Other types of labour turnover costs may arise in connection with deterioration in the working morale if incumbent workers are regularly fired and replaced by underbidding outsiders; more specifically, work effort in a firm may be harmed by a high rate of labour turnover as the expected future return to work effort today becomes small in firms that often fire workers.

Each of these various types of labour turnover costs helps to explain why workers without employment in the formal sector of the economy (defined as firms with high turnover costs for labour) – so called 'outsiders' – do not succeed in getting jobs in the formal sector of the economy by way of wage underbidding, even though their reservation wage may be lower than the going wage of incumbent workers, so called 'insiders'. Outsiders may also be prevented from 'underbidding' by insiders threatening to treat potential underbidders harshly, that is to 'harass' them, and hence to push up the reservation wage of potential entrants and as a result raise the wage costs of these for firms.

Obviously some of these turnover costs are not exogenous but rather created, or at least accentuated, by the activities of the insiders themselves. This is the case not only for threats to withdraw cooperation with entrants, which tend to reduce the productivity of the latter, and for threats to 'harass' underbidding outsiders, hence raising the reservation wage of potential entrants. Insiders also have incentives to lobby politically for legislated firing costs. (For detailed discussions of these various types of labour turnover costs, see Lindbeck and Snower, 1986b and 1988.)

Analytically, a basic implication of the existence of non-infinitesimal turnover costs for labour is that they generate two different demand curves for labour – one for insiders and one for outsiders.[3] It is easy to show formally that the labour demand curve for insiders in such a situation is the *sum* of (the capital value of) the traditional marginal value product curve and the marginal firing costs for labour: the firm is willing to pay the marginal incumbent worker more than (the capital value of) his marginal value product by an amount equal to the costs of firing him. By contrast, the labour demand curve for outsiders, or more precisely for entrants to the firm, is equal to (the capital value of) the marginal value product of labour *minus* the marginal hiring and training costs for labour, since this difference expresses the *net* contribution to the firm of a marginal entrant.

The issue is illustrated in Figure 4.5, with *IDC* denoting the 'insider demand curve' and *EDC* 'the entrant demand curve'. The figure assumes perfect competition in the product market, but the curves look the same, in principle, in the case of monopolistic competition.[4] The analysis to be pursued below does *not*, in fact, depend in any

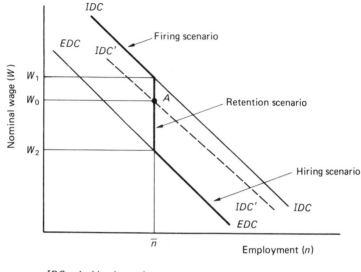

IDC = Insider demand curve
EDC = Entrant demand curve

Figure 4.5 Labour demand with turnover costs

---

crucial way on the assumption of perfect competition in the product market, mainly because it is not the purpose of the paper to discuss how disturbances in the product market are transmitted to the labour market.

In Figure 4.5 I have chosen to depict the labour demand curve with the nominal wage, W, on the vertical axis, rather than the product wage rate, W/P (the wage expressed in terms of the price, P, of the product produced by the firm); n denotes employment. To begin with, let us assume that entrants and insiders are paid the same wage, W, and also that the size of the incumbent labour force initially is $\bar{n}$. Let us also assume that this wage rate is the outcome of some bargaining process between the firm and its insiders, or their union, and that neither the firm nor the insiders have complete market power. (Complete market powers of the insiders would imply a wage rate of W_1, while complete market power of the firm would imply a wage rate of W_2.)

We may now distinguish between three segments of the relevant labour demand curve. If the wage is high, more specifically above a certain critical value W_1, we are in a 'firing scenario': the firm wants to reduce the labour force and hence fire some insiders and move along the insider labour demand curve, *IDC*, to the left of the employment level $\bar{n}$. By contrast, if the wage is low, more specifically below a critical value W_2, we are in a 'hiring scenario': not only will all insiders be kept, the firm also wants to add to its labour force by hiring some entrants and move along the entrant demand curve, *EDC*, to the right of the employment level $\bar{n}$. In an interval in between W_1 and W_2, we are in what may be called a 'retention scenario', where the firm chooses to keep its labour force unchanged even though the product wage may vary within that interval. Thus, with (non-infinitesimal) turnover costs we get *a discontinuous* labour demand curve, depicted by the thick lines in Figure 4.5 (see Lindbeck and Snower, 1986b and 1989; Bentolila and Bertola, 1988). It is obvious from this analysis that the existence of (non-infinitesimal) labour turnover costs tends to stabilise the employment level for an individual firm in the case of exogenous fluctuations in the wage rate, provided these fluctuations are kept within a certain vertical 'corridor', $W_1 \leqslant W \leqslant W_2$. On an *aggregate* level of analysis, the consequences of variations in the wage rate for labour demand will then depend on the *distribution* of firms among the three scenarios – as well as on the magnitude of the variations in the wage rate.

The analysis also suggests that (non-infinitesimal) labour turnover costs tend to stabilise employment when there are fluctuations in the marginal value product curve for labour. For instance, suppose that the insider demand curve is originally *IDC*, and that the number of incumbent workers is $\underline{n}$. Suppose further that the wage rate initially is W_0, so that the firm is in the 'retention scenario'. Let us then assume that the insider labour demand curve suddenly shifts down *at most* to *IDC′* due to a sudden fall in labour productivity with a corresponding shift also of the entrants demand curve (a shift that is not depicted in the figure). The consequence for the labour demand curve is basically the same in the case of an increase in the relative price of an intermediary input good, or wider tax wedges associated with higher taxes on labour or non-actuarial pay-roll fees.[5] In this simple setting, the firm has no incentive to fire any insiders, as the net marginal value product, measured at the initial employment level $\bar{n}$, is still (at least) as high as the wage rate W_0. A later return of the insider demand curve to the initial position, that is, to *IDC*, would also leave the desired level of employment at $\bar{n}$. Of course, if the initial wage rate had been higher than W_0, or if the negative shift of the labour demand curve had been larger, incentives to fire workers would have existed, provided the wage rate did not adjust downward as a result of the shift of the labour demand curve.

For a given distribution of firms between the three scenarios, a society with larger labour turnover costs than another society would then, in the case of (limited) fluctuations in either the wage rate or the marginal value product of labour, be characterised by a more stable time-path of aggregate employment and unemployment. In Figure 4.6 this is illustrated by the solid curve for a country with high turnover costs, and the broken curve for a country with low turnover costs: hiring would be smaller in booms and firing would be smaller in recessions in the country with the higher turnover costs. Labour would be 'hoarded' in recession, as it would often not be profitable for the firm to fire and later rehire labour when hiring and firing costs are high. We may say that the solid curve in the figure illustrates the situation in Europe and the broken curve the situation in the USA in the 1950s and 1960s. Thus, the differences in labour turnover costs may provide at least part of the explanation for the earlier-mentioned smaller cyclical instability of aggregate employment in Europe than in the USA during that period, when the macroeconomy was characterised by rather mild macroeconomic fluctuations.

Let us then instead look at the situation after a long period of economic stagnation and high unemployment. Both a country with high and a country with low turnover costs would now experience rather low levels of employment, as firms in both types of countries would not only have fired workers but also avoided labour hiring to compensate for attrition via quits and retirement. The basic point then is that the employment level in the country with high turnover costs would be expected to show a slower recovery than the country with low turnover costs. As a result, the unemployment spells of workers may therefore be particularly long in the former type of country – as illustrated in Figure 4.7, again with the solid curve depicting a country (such as a typical European country) with high turnover costs and the broken curve a country (such as the USA) with low turnover costs.

This tendency may be particularly pronounced if there is also *great uncertainty* about the sustainability of an ensuing business upswing, as firms in countries with high turnover costs would be particularly reluctant to hire workers when the firms are very uncertain whether they need the workers in the future. We would expect that small firms in particular would hesitate to hire labour in situations of great

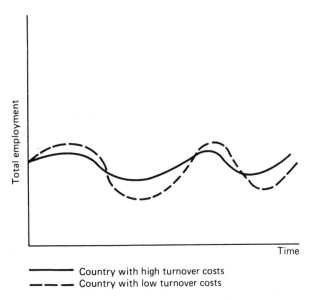

Figure 4.6   Variations in total employment during ordinary cycles

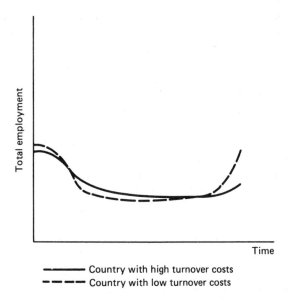

Figure 4.7   Variations in total employment during long recessions and great uncertainty

uncertainty in countries with high hiring and firing costs. One reason
is that small firms often do not have a reasonably even distribution of
workers in different age groups, which means that the firms cannot
easily adjust their labour force downwards by way of retirement. It is,
therefore, particularly dangerous for small firms to hire labour in
societies with high firing costs when there is great uncertainty
whether the firms will or will not need the workers in the future.

This discussion illustrates the well-known fact that labour turnover
costs have an ambiguous effect on the aggregate employment level,
because such costs discourage both the hiring and the firing of labour.
However, the discussion also illustrates the somewhat more profound
point that the consequences depend on the type of economic instability that prevails. While high turnover costs tend to stabilise *employment* during 'regular' business cycles, high turnover costs rather
tend to stabilise *unemployment* after prolonged recessions, in particular if the uncertainty about future business conditions is substantial. Thus, differences in labour turnover costs may help to explain
the earlier-mentioned differences in the employment performance
between Europe and the USA not only in the period 1950–75 with a
'regular' business cycle, when the European employment performance was more impressive, but also in the period 1975–89 with two
prolonged recessions, after which employment recovered much faster
and more strongly in the USA.

So far the wage rate has been taken as *exogenous*. However, the
role of labour turnover costs in the behaviour of employment and
unemployment can be further clarified by recognising that such costs
give market power to the 'insiders', and that this market power may
be exploited to push the wages of insiders above the reservation wage
of 'outsiders', without the insiders losing their jobs. Indeed, this
mechanism is the essence of the so called 'insider–outsider theory' of
the labour market (Lindbeck and Snower, 1986a and 1988), which is
basically designed to explain why the market power of incumbent
workers prevents unemployment from being automatically removed
by way of 'underbiddings' of existing wages. More specifically, the
turnover costs of labour explain *from where* the market powers of
incumbent workers arise. (In the efficiency wage theory, by contrast,
wages are kept above the reservation wage of unemployed workers
due to the market powers of *firms* in combination with the efficiency-
promoting effects of wages.) This insider–outsider theory is certainly
consistent with conventional labour union models, if these are
amended by the assumption that the union is more concerned with

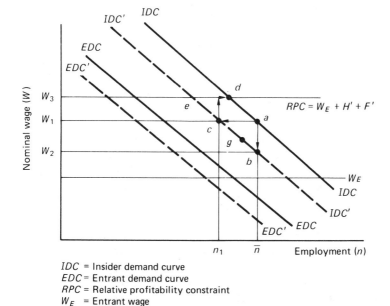

Figure 4.8 Insider market power

IDC = Insider demand curve
EDC = Entrant demand curve
RPC = Relative profitability constraint
W_E = Entrant wage
H' = Marginal hiring costs
F' = Marginal firing costs

the welfare of employed workers than unemployed workers. (Such amendments of the conventional labour union model have been made by Blanchard and Summers, 1986, and Gottfries and Horn, 1987.) However, the insider–outsider theory goes *beyond* the union models by explaining where the powers of incumbent workers come from, and why unemployed workers may be unable to get jobs in the formal sector of the economy by offering to work for less than the wages of incumbent workers, that is, by underbidding them.

To carry this approach further, let us drop the previous assumption that entrants are paid the same wage as insiders. The analysis may then be pursued with the help of Figure 4.8 which is simply an elaboration of Figure 4.5. As compared with Figure 4.5, two extra lines have been introduced. The horizontal line, W_E, denotes the entrant wage; for simplicity we may assume that this is equal to the reservation wage of the outsiders, or we may assume that it is higher than that due to the influence of unions on the entrant wage. The upper horizontal line is the sum of the entrant wage *and* the marginal hiring and firing costs for labour; it expresses the maximum wage that insiders may acquire without being replaced by outsiders. It will therefore be called the 'relative profitability constraint', *RPC*.

As in Figure 4.5, let us assume that the insider work force initially is $\bar{n}$. However, in contrast to the situation in Figure 4.5, suppose, to begin with, that the insiders have been able to push up their wage rate to the maximum level that is consistent with continuing employment for all the insiders; that is, the wage rate is W_1 ('complete' market power of insiders), and the wage/employment point is *a*. In spite of this 'high' wage rate, the outsiders are unable to get jobs. The simple reason is that the marginal value product of entrants, net of hiring costs, is less than their reservation wage, because of the various turnover costs for labour which were discussed above. (The *EDC* line is below the W_E line at the employment level $\bar{n}$.) Thus, the presence of labour turnover costs helps to explain the absence of the hiring of unemployed workers in spite of the fact that the insider wage is higher than the reservation wage of the unemployed workers. In other words, the insider–outsider model goes some way to explain *the existence* of unemployment. It also spells out some factors that determine the *size* of unemployment: the magnitude of the labour turnover costs, the relative bargaining power of workers and firms, the reservation wage of potential entrants and the influence of the insiders on the wage of entrants.

In contrast to the *descriptive* (statistical) terms 'employed' and 'unemployed', the terms 'insiders' and 'outsiders' are used in this analysis as an analytical distinction which highlights the asymmetric positions of incumbent workers and unemployed workers, and the market powers of the latter. Workers who are employed in the 'informal' sector of the economy may be included among the 'outsiders'.

A more complete analysis of unemployment also requires an explanation why some workers who are unable to get jobs in the formal sector of the economy, where there are substantial turnover costs, are unwilling or unable to get jobs in the informal sector, where the turnover costs are lower and hence insider market power weaker, or even (approximately) absent. In other words, we would have to explain not only why outsiders are unable to get jobs in the formal sector in spite of the fact that their reservation wages are *below* the insider wage, but also why that reservation wage is *higher* than the wage rate in the informal sector. However, that issue will not be discussed in this paper.

Let us now assume that a negative labour demand shift occurs, from *IDC* to *IDC'* in Figure 4.8. The consequences for the wage rate and the employment level now depend crucially on how wage formation responds. It is useful to tie the analysis of this issue to two extreme alternatives. In the first alternative, the insiders are anxious that all of them keep their jobs. As a consequence, they would accept a reduction in the wage rate to W_2, implying that we move from point *a* to point *b* in Figure 4.8. This may be expected to occur if, for instance, there is no seniority system, so that every insider has the same probability of being fired if the wage rate is not cut. It may also occur if there is a special kind of profit sharing system, so that the remuneration of labour is automatically reduced by the same amount as the fall in the marginal value product of labour.

The other extreme alternative is that insiders want, and are able, to keep their wages unchanged and then have to accept an ensuing reduction in employment. The firm then winds up at point *c* in the figure, with employment n_1. This is a particularly likely outcome if there is a 'complete' seniority system, in the sense that everybody knows his seniority ranking *and* the high-seniority workers (possibly a majority of all the incumbents) do not care (much) about the employment status of the fired workers. If then the laid-off workers try to keep their jobs by offering to work for a lower wage, the remaining insiders could prevent this form of underbidding by threatening not to cooperate with them and/or to treat them badly (that is to harass them). In this sense, the 'cooperation and harassment' version of the insider–outsider model explains not only the existence of unemployment but also *the tendency for lay-offs* in the case of adverse business shocks – that is, it explains the inability of the laid-off workers to keep their jobs by way of underbidding.

The new lower level of employment in the over-simplified framework presented so far, will persist as long as the negative demand shift is not reversed. This type of *persistent unemployment*, which would be the consequence of the absence of 'wage underbidding', is in turn, a combined effect of:

(i)   the existence of labour turnover costs;
(ii) the market power of insiders that is created by these turnover costs;
(iii) the willingness and ability of the insiders to exploit this market power in wage formation without (much) concern for the interest of the outsiders.

An alternative explanation of unemployment persistence is a gradual deterioration of the stock of physical capital, which may then, after a while, not be large enough to employ the entire labour force (see Snessens and Drèze, 1986; and Malinvaud, 1984). However, this explanation is not complete. We would have to add the assumption that the wage rate does not adjust downwards sufficiently to make it profitable for firms *either* to employ the labour force at the existing capital stock, *or* to induce enough new investment. Moreover, the quantitative importance of this 'capital shortage' explanation may be questioned in view of the rapid employment expansion in the USA both at the end of the 1930s and in the early 1940s (even before the US entry into the war), and indeed also in Europe after the Second World War.

Attempts to explain unemployment persistence by way of a deterioration in the stock of human capital of the long-term unemployed workers have the same kind of limitations, as a sufficiently large reduction in wage rates could, in principle, compensate for this. A stronger explanation of unemployment persistence is probably the hypothesis, developed by Layard and Nickell (1985) that long-term unemployed workers stop searching, and hence become 'discouraged workers'.

As pointed out in the introduction to the paper, realistic theories of unemployment have to include mechanisms that sooner or later bring back the economy towards 'normal' rates of unemployment, even though unemployment is *path-dependent* in the sense that unemployment in period t depends on unemployment in period $t-1$. Indeed in extended versions of insider–outsider models there are alternative mechanisms of gradually coming out of situations of *complete* unemployment persistence; such complete persistence has recently been called 'hysteresis' (Blanchard and Summers, 1986). One such mechanism builds on the willingness of outsiders to reduce their wage demands (a fall in their reservation wage) when *aggregate* unemployment goes up. Another mechanism focuses on the willingness of insiders to modify their wage demands at higher levels of unemployment, if there is uncertainty about the future position of the labour demand curve, since the expected income in the case of job loss falls when unemployment goes up. Both mechanisms may then, after some time, help to put an end to a period of prolonged unemployment, even if the original negative shift of the labour demand curve was a permanent one. In other words, insider–outsider theories, in contrast to 'pure' insider theories, do *not* predict 'hysteresis' as defined above, though they do predict 'persistence'.

This discussion relates to the case of *permanent* shifts in the labour demand curve. However, let us also look at the case when the initial negative shift is *transitory* in the sense that there is a later return of the labour demand curve to the initial position, that is to *IDC* in Figure 4.8. What happens after the return shift depends on the extent to which the new, smaller group of insiders (n_1) are willing and able to exploit the higher labour demand curve to push up their wages rather than to allow a return to the initial employment level at an unchanged wage rate. If the insiders follow the first strategy, they could, in principle, push up the wage rate to W_3 and the firm would then choose point *d*, with only a rather modest amount of hiring of new entrants. (Insiders cannot push up the wage rate above the *RPC* curve without being replaced by outsiders.) Thus, in spite of the fact that the labour demand curves have returned to the initial positions (to *IDC* and *EDC*, respectively), the employment level has not. This is an example of persistent effects of a temporary shift, or 'asymmetric persistence' for short, as equally large negative and positive labour demand shocks have quantitatively different effects on wages and employment. As a consequence, a succession of equally large downward and upward shifts of the labour demand curve may yield a wage-employment ratchet, characterised by an upward trend in wages and a downward trend in employment.

It may be argued that this type of ratchet is more likely to occur if the subsequent positive shift in the labour demand curve is *unexpected* than when it is expected. Moreover, the longer the period for which the labour demand curve is assumed to stay at its lower position (when it is expected to shift back later on), the more likely it is that such a ratchet will arise, as the number of fired workers would be a rising function of the length of the period of unfavourable business conditions.

It is important to realise that such an asymmetry does not mean that we should predict ever higher unemployment over time! One reason is that in the real world, we would expect a rising trend in labour productivity, with a corresponding trend of the labour demand curve to drift to the right, in spite of occasional temporary leftward shifts. Another reason is that the relative profitability constraint (*RPC*) sets a limit to how much the wage rate can be raised, and hence how much employment can fall. To be more specific, let us assume that the relative profitability constraint has been reached, and that the economy starts from point *d* in the figure when a leftward shift of the insider demand curve occurs from *IDC* to *IDC'*, moving the employment point from *d* to *e*. A later shift back of the labour demand to the initial position, at *IDC*, would now return employment to point *d*. Thus, when the wage rate reaches the *RPC* line, the wage-employment ratchet referred to above, arising from the shifts back and forth of the labour demand curve, would disappear.

This analysis may help to explain some of the previously mentioned differences in the unemployment experience of various nations. For instance, the analysis suggests an additional explanation why the USA recovered much better than did most of Europe from the last two recessions. Not only the relatively low labour-turnover costs *per se* in the USA, but also the limited market powers which this gives to incumbent workers would imply only a modest tendency for wages to increase as a result of positive labour demand shifts in the USA. Moreover, as unions give a leverage to insider market powers, the fact that unions in the USA are weaker than in Europe would accentuate this factor. The same considerations may help to explain the apparent tendency to more wage concessions in cyclical downturns in the USA than in most European countries.

Moreover, in some countries, and in some geographical regions within a country, unions may feel greater solidarity with their unemployed fellow workers than in other countries or regions. This may help to explain the apparent willingness of Japanese workers to make wage concessions in cyclical downturns without much actual increase in aggregate unemployment and in spite of the pronounced seniority system in Japan. It could possibly also be argued that 'group solidarity' among workers in Sweden and Norway helps to explain why unions have accepted real wage reductions by way of devaluations during recessions, in spite of high market powers due to high hiring and firing costs and strong unions.[6]

These considerations suggest that we should modify the assumption in the model discussed above that insiders do not care *at all* about outsiders. To the extent that insiders do care about fellow workers who are threatened with loss of their jobs, it is likely that the wage/employment point, originally at *a*, would move 'south-west', rather than 'west', after a downward shift of the labour demand curve from *IDC* to *IDC'*. The firm may then wind up at a point like *g* rather than point *c*. Moreover, after the labour demand curve has shifted back to *IDC*, we would predict a move north-east rather than north, for instance to a point between *a* and *d* rather than to point *d*.

A further modification of the model is to assume that the longer period of time that fired workers have been unemployed, the less willing the remaining insiders would be to take them back at an unchanged wage rate in a later business upswing, instead of exploiting the upswing to push up their own wage rates. Here we may have an alternative to the attempted explanation by Layard and Nickell (1985) as to why long-term unemployed workers seem to exert a weaker influence on wage formation than do the short-term unemployed. While Layard and Nickell hypothesise that the long-term unemployed exert very little influence on wages because self-confidence gradually deteriorates when a person is unemployed for a long time, the insider–outsider explanation of the same phenomenon would be that the long-term unemployed simply are *more* 'outsiders' in the process of wage formation than are the short-term unemployed, and hence that the insiders feel less concern for the former than for the latter.

3 LABOUR SUPPLY FACTORS

So far, I have emphasised labour market imperfections which influence the *demand side* of the labour market. However, it is often argued that the large increases in unemployment in developed countries is the 1970s and 1980s also reflect reduced willingness of workers to search for jobs, or accept job offers. So let us look also at imperfections on the *supply side* of the labour market.

The level of *unemployment benefits* has, in particular, been singled out in this context. Indeed, most 'respectable' theories of labour supply and search predict that higher unemployment benefits stimulate longer periods of search and leisure, and hence result in more 'voluntary' unemployment. This assertion assumes then, quite reasonably, a *given* level of labour demand; thus, it is explicitly or implicitly assumed that the effects of higher unemployment benefits on aggregate product demand are either negligible, or that these effects are removed by other elements of demand management policies.

However, it is important to emphasise that not only the benefit level, but also the *administration* of the unemployment benefit system is relevant to its employment effects. For instance, in the USA the benefit level is low and the duration period short, so that unemployed workers have a strong interest, not to say compulsion, to look for jobs and to accept job offers after short periods of unemployment. The system in Norway and Sweden is different: while the duration period, as in the USA, is a limited one (though considerably longer than in the USA) the benefit level is high. However, the system is strictly administered in the sense that workers lose unemployment benefits if they repeatedly turn down both job offers and offers of retraining. The most unemployment-prone benefit systems are probably the continental European and British systems, according to which the benefits are quite high, the duration period very long, and the administration also very 'slack' in the sense that workers who repeatedly refuse offers of jobs and retraining can still stay on benefit. Such systems are doomed to raise the level of unemployment more than do both the US system and the Norwegian–Swedish system, at a given level of labour demand.

As the benefit levels were raised considerably in several European countries during the 1970s, this factor may be responsible for part of the increased unemployment during that decade. There have been some heroic attempts to quantify its influence.[7] Here is then a mechanism on the labour *supply* side by which high levels of long-term unemployment may breed future unemployment, and hence contribute to *path-dependence* of unemployment, that is unemployment in period *t* being a function of unemployment in earlier periods. However, as benefit levels were not generally increased in the 1980s – rather the reverse in several countries – we can hardly make the same point for that period. It may be argued, however, that the more liberal *administration* of the benefit system may have contributed to higher unemployment also in the 1980s. A more speculative point is that the high level and liberal administration of the unemployment benefits in the 1980s have increased the unemployment leverage of negative macroeconomic shocks, in the sense of not only helping finance longer periods of unemployment, but also making life 'on the dole' more socially acceptable.

4   INTERACTION OF LABOUR DEMAND AND LABOUR SUPPLY: RELATIVE WAGES AND 'MISMATCHES'

Let us turn to some aspects of the *interaction* between demand and supply for labour, namely relative wage formation, and the composition of the demand and supply for labour, as well as the related issue of mismatches between them.

It is fairly generally agreed that a 'high' *average* wage level – sustained by strong labour unions, efficiency wage considerations by firms or insider–outsider powers – may contribute to unemployment. It should then be equally easy to agree that 'distortions' of the *structure of relative wages* can do the same, as compared with a hypothetical structure that would be more in conformity with relative demand and supply of labour – even if the average wage level is regarded as 'appropriate'. Aggregate unemployment would then tend to be high because of 'mismatches' between demand and supply for labour in various sectors of the economy: there would be a 'high' unemployment figure for each level of vacancies. The so-called Beveridge curve, depicting the relationship between vacancies and unemployment, would in this case be far to the right.

While this argument is usually put forward for the wage relationships between industries, regions, firms and occupations, wage distortions *within* individual firms, for one and the same occupation, may also contribute to unemployment. For instance Flanagan (1989) has argued that a flat wage-ladder within firms mitigates the operation of the mechanisms of 'self-selection' of good workers, as only workers who are anxious to prove themselves 'good' are willing to start with low wage rates, in the hope of qualifying for higher wages later on. An enforced flattening of the wage schedule, for instance by way of minimum wage legislation or egalitarian wage policies of unions, may therefore induce firms to rely more on 'pre-employment screening' rather than self-selection. As a consequence, firms would be expected to be more cautious when hiring workers. In principle, this may help to prolong aggregate unemployment.

The *quantitative* importance of relative wage distortions for aggregate unemployment depends, of course, also on the speed at which people 'swim' from sectors with excess supply of labour, that is from the 'unemployment island', to sectors with excess demand, that is to 'vacancy islands'. This would be expected to depend both on institutions and incentives in the labour market. For instance, an elaborate system of nation-wide labour market exchange and efficiently organised systems of retraining of labour, such as seem to exist in some Nordic countries, may mitigate the unemployment-creating effects of distorted relative wage rates, though such policies also, of course, give rise to administrative costs to the national economy. By contrast, high marginal tax rates, rent control, public or 'council' housing would be expected to accentuate the unemployment effects of enforced reductions in relative wages.

So does reference to relative wage distortions help to explain the wide differences in the unemployment experience of various countries during the 1970s and 1980s? For instance, is there any evidence that relative wage rates have been less 'market-oriented' (that is, less adjusted to demand and supply for labour) in Europe than in the USA during this period? One piece of circumstantial evidence pointing in this direction is that labour unions are much stronger in several European countries than in the USA, and that their strength has fallen much more in the USA than in most countries in Europe. An underlying assumption behind this argument is, of course, that unions often try to reduce wage differentials *against* the signals coming from the interplay between demand and supply for labour. Another piece of circumstantial evidence is that while the wage differentials seem to have widened in the USA during the 1970s (and indeed also during the 1980s), they seem broadly to have been compressed in most European countries in the 1970s, and have probably not widened again in the 1980s (except mainly in the UK). The view that relative wage compression contributed to higher unemployment in Europe during the 1970s and early 1980s is supported by the way in which this relative wage compression took place, namely by way of increased union militancy, more ambitious minimum wage legislation and government-imposed rules of price-indexation of wages in favour of low wage groups (Flanagan, 1989, pp. 12–15). For instance, while minimum wage rates fell in the USA in the 1970s they usually rose in Europe.

However, this various circumstantial evidence is certainly far from conclusive. To feel confident that wage compression in Europe, relative to the USA, contributed to the different performance of unemployment in the two areas in the 1970s and 1980s, we would need more direct evidence on whether the widening of wage differentials in the USA was in fact 'market-oriented', and whether the compression of wage differentials in Europe was in fact in conflict with market forces – or if it was instead just the reverse.

Conceptually, one way to answer that question would be to investigate whether relative wage changes have been positively correlated with changes in *ex ante* excess demand (supply) for labour in different sectors of the economy. However, as *ex ante* excess demand (or supply) is difficult to measure, actual studies have instead investigated whether there have, in fact, been reductions in the relative wage rates in sectors (occupations) with relatively large (or rapidly rising) unemployment relative to the number of vacancies – as compared with sectors (or occupations) with lower (or more modestly rising) unemployment relative to the number of vacancies. However, to the best of my knowledge there are still no *reliable* empirical studies on this subject.

The upshot of all this is that we have to wait for the verdict on whether relative wage distortions help to explain the rise and persistence of unemployment in Europe, and/or the diverging paths of unemployment in various countries, such as between the USA and most of the European countries. Until then, we can at most suspect that this is the case, in view of the circumstantial evidence mentioned above.

Enforced compressions of the distribution of relative wages, of course, are only one conceivable explanation for the apparent increase in mismatches in the labour market, in the sense of the earlier-mentioned rightward shifts of the Beveridge curve. An increased rate of 'structural change' in the economy, as manifested in larger dispersions of excess demand and excess supply of labour between different sectors of production is an alternative hypothesis – with the implicit (or explicit) additional assumption that relative wage rates have not adjusted fully to these structural changes. In the case of individual countries, some evidence has been found in support of this hypothesis – in some cases between industries, in other cases between regions, occupations or skill groups. However, the overall evidence of a more rapid rate of structural change and related increases in the dispersion of excess supply for labour between sectors is not very strong (Jackman and Roper, 1987). For the time being, explanations of increased mismatches, in the sense of rightward shifts of the Beveridge curve, cannot be based on the hypothesis of increased structural shifts. The hypotheses of distortions of relative wages, or of consequences for labour market mismatches of the unemployment benefit system, seem today more plausible explanations.

5 POLICY IMPLICATIONS

Against the background of the discussion in this paper, what can governments do to make the functioning of the labour market more

conducive to full employment? Beside aggregate demand management in the product market, which is not discussed in this paper, the
most straightforward policy measure to stimulate the *demand* for
labour is perhaps for the government to demand more labour itself,
for instance to produce services for the citizen. Of course, it may be
extremely costly for society to expand public sector employment just
to reduce unemployment, especially in the long run, as a rapid
increase in public sector employment may reduce the efficiency in the
allocation of labour in the economy.

How then can private sector labour demand be enhanced by labour
market policies? One type of policy is explicitly designed to limit the
preferential treatment of 'insiders' by diminishing their market
power; we may talk about *power-reducing policies* for short. Such
policies can take many forms. On the one hand, they may involve
dismantling some existing job-security legislation, for instance by
way of reduced severance pay or simplified firing procedures, either
for all workers or for special groups such as young workers. On the
other hand, they may cover legislation to reduce union power, such
as by way of legal restrictions on strikes and picketing. Of course, as
labour unions fulfil social and political functions other than influenc-
ing wages and employment, a case for or against power-reducing
policies of unions also has to take account of these other considerations.

Another type of labour market policy to stimulate the private
demand for labour may be called *enfranchising policies*. It aims at
bringing more workers into the 'employment pool' and thereby
giving more people a voice in future wage negotiations. One example
is profit-sharing schemes of labour remuneration, whereby workers
receive part of their pay as a share of firms' profits. Another example
is apprenticeship systems. Whereas profit-sharing schemes aim to
enfranchise outsiders by reducing the marginal cost of hiring, apprenticeship systems may achieve such enfranchising by giving firms a
longer span of time in which to take advantage of the differential
between insiders' and entrants' wage claims.

Job-sharing programmes during recessions is another example of
methods of enfranchising workers in the wage negotiation process, as
then insider status is given to more workers, all of whom have a
vested interest in negotiating their wages with their own job security
in mind. Finally, reducing barriers to the entry of new firms may be a
particularly effective way of enfranchising outsiders, as new firms
generally have no insiders whose activities can contribute to perpetu-

ating unemployment. Indications that entry barriers are often higher in Europe than in the USA may help to explain why Europe has been less successful than the USA in creating new jobs in the 1970s and 1980s.

Turning to employment-promoting policies operating on *the supply side* of the labour market, such measures consist mainly of attempts to stimulate unemployed workers to look for jobs and to accept job offers – forgetting about policies that induce people to withdraw from the labour force, such as by way of early retirement. For instance, the discussion above of the unemployment benefit systems suggests that the basic choice, if we want to stimulate workers to search and to accept job offers, is between a US-type system with low benefits and short benefit duration and a Norwegian–Swedish type system with strict eligibility requirements and a strictly limited period of benefits, though with quite a high benefit level. Scandinavian experience also suggests that there are some gains from integrating the unemployment benefit system with both the labour market exchange system and the labour retraining system at least in the sense of coordinating information about these three systems, so that workers who refuse both job offers and retraining can easily be cut off from further benefits.

It is also rather clear that a lowering of minimum wages, or at least a postponement of future increases, may help to remove mismatches in the labour market and mitigate unemployment of unskilled labour in some countries, in particular perhaps among the young, immigrants and women. Other obvious actions to improve the functioning of the labour market are policies that improve the functioning of the housing market. If there are 'artificial' – for example, policy induced – obstacles to geographical labour mobility, there may also be a second best policy case for subsidising the movement of labour from one sector to another (such as partial government financing of removal costs).

However, perhaps the most important policy conclusion of the discussion in this paper is the following: as certain mechanisms in the labour market tend to create persistence of unemployment once it has occurred, it is important *to avoid long periods of unemployment developing in the first place*. Indeed, the countries most successful on employment issues during the 1970s and 1980s seem to be exactly those that have either avoided heavy unemployment developing in the first place (such as Austria, Japan, Norway, Switzerland and Sweden) or countries where macroeconomic policies have, at an early stage, reversed an initially heavy increase in unemployment (such as the USA). In Austria, Japan and Switzerland a large increase in unemployment seems to have been avoided partly by way of wage moderation, partly by the withdrawal of some workers to the household sector (and in the case of Switzerland to other countries), while in Norway and Sweden the same result was achieved mainly by way of devaluation and increased public sector employment. In the USA, a rapid reversal of the huge increase in unemployment in the early 1980s seems to have been facilitated by having a 'supply-side president' pursue a Keynesian-type demand management policy in the product market in the first half of the 1980s! However, that is another story, which is not to be told here.

Notes

1. The figures refer to the period 1960–74; OECD, *Labour Force Statistics.*
2. This section draws on joint work with Dennis J. Snower, Birkbeck College, University of London.
3. By 'non-infinitesimal' turnover costs I mean that labour turnover costs do not fall to zero when the number of hired or fired workers approaches zero.
4. In the latter case the curves are, of course, 'semi-reduced forms' rather than labour demand curves proper, and the curves will shift if the elasticity of product demand changes. See, for instance, Lindbeck and Snower (1987 and 1989).
5. A non-actuarial pay-roll fee is one larger than the expected social security benefit that is supposed to be financed by the fee.
6. We may also ask a more technical question concerning the model: why did a negative productivity shock, at a constant product wage, reduce the employment level in the context of Figure 4.8 in contrast to the conclusion from the analysis in the context of Figure 4.5? The simple reason is, of course, that the insider wage in Figure 4.8, as pointed out earlier, was initially assumed to be at the maximum level that is consistent with continued employment by all insiders; that is, it was assumed to be at point *a* in Figure 4.8 but at point *A* in Figure 4.5. If this assumption is modified in Figure 4.8 so that insiders do not have full market powers, there is, in this analysis, too, *an interval* within which fluctuations in the labour demand curve(s) do not change the employment level, as in the discussion in the context of Figure 4.5.
7. Layard and Nickell (1985) estimate that about 0.5 per cent of the unemployment increase in the UK in the 1970s could possibly be explained by higher levels of benefits.

References

Bentolila, S. and Bertola, G. (1988) 'Firing Costs and Labor Demand: How Bad is Eurosclerosis?' unpublished mimeograph, Harvard University, June.

Blanchard, O. J. and Summers, L. H. (1986) 'Hysteresis and the European Unemployment Problem', *National Bureau of Economic Research Macroeconomics Annual 1986*, vol. 1, pp. 15–78.

Flanagan, R. J. (1989) 'Unemployment as a Hiring Problem', unpublished mimeograph, Graduate School of Business, Stanford University.

Gottfries, N. and Horn, H. (1987) 'Wage Formation and the Persistence of Unemployment', *Economic Journal*, vol. 97, pp. 877–84.

Jackman, R. and Roper, D. (1987) 'Structural Unemployment', *Oxford Bulletin of Economics and Statistics*, vol. 49.

Layard, R. and Nickell, S. J. (1985) 'The Causes of British Unemployment', *National Institute Economic Review*, vol. III, pp. 62–85.

Lindbeck, A. and Snower, D. J. (1986a) 'Wage Rigidity, Union Activity and Unemployment', in Beckerman, W. (ed.) *Wage Rigidity and Unemployment* (London: Duckworth) pp. 97–125.

Lindbeck, A. and Snower, D. J. (1986b) 'Wage Setting, Unemployment, and Insider–Outsider Relations', *American Economic Review*, vol. 76, pp. 235–9.

Lindbeck, A. and Snower, D. J. (1987) 'Transmission Mechanisms from the Product to the Labor Market', Seminar Paper no 403, Institute for International Economic Studies, University of Stockholm, Sweden.

Lindbeck, A. and Snower, D. J. (1988) *The Insider–Outsider Theory of Employment and Unemployment* (Cambridge, Massachusetts: MIT Press).

Lindbeck, A. and Snower, D. J. (1989) 'Demand- and Supply-Side Policies and Unemployment: Policy Implications of the Insider–Outsider Approach', Seminar Paper no 439, Institute for International Economic Studies, University of Stockholm, Sweden.

Malinvaud, E. (1984) 'Wages and Unemployment', *Economic Journal*, vol. 92, pp. 1–12.

Snessens, H. and Drèze, J. (1986) 'A Discussion of Belgian Unemployment, Combining Traditional Concepts and Disequilibrium Econometrics', *Economica*, vol. 53, pp. 90–119.

5 Two Tools for Analysing Unemployment[1]

Olivier Jean Blanchard

MASSACHUSETTS INSTITUTE OF TECHNOLOGY
and NATIONAL BUREAU OF ECONOMIC RESEARCH

1 INTRODUCTION

Labour markets in developed economies are characterised by large flows of workers, continual job creation and job destruction. This is true of the USA where, on average, 7 per cent of the labour force goes in or out of employment each month. It is also true of Western Europe. Even during the depressed 1980s, the monthly movement in and out of unemployment has been equal on average to 4 per cent of the labour force in the UK, 2.5 per cent in France and 2 per cent in Germany.[2]

Peter Diamond and I have embarked on a research programme designed to understand the macroeconomic implications of this fact. In the process of thinking about the functioning of markets with large flows, we have come to the conclusion that, in identifying the source of movements in unemployment, the joint use of two simple tools is extremely useful. The tools are the oldest of the trade – the Beveridge curve and the Phillips curve. Each contains important information; but it is in combination that they are most useful.[3] This is the theme I want to develop here. I shall do this first by sketching a conceptual framework in which one can interpret both curves, and then by applying the tools to US, UK and German unemployment over the past twenty years.

2 THE SKETCH OF AN ECONOMY WITH LARGE FLOWS

Let me sketch a simple model of an economy with large flows, in which one can interpret movements in the Beveridge and Phillips curves.[4]

Think of an economy in which changes in relative demand, in

102

comparative advantage and in technology lead to a permanent state of flux, with continual job creation and job destruction. If all jobs were in the same place and required the same skills, the reallocation of workers would take place without the coexistence of vacancies and unemployment. But they are not. Workers need to learn new skills, to relocate, to find the right match. Thus, the matching process takes time, leading to the coexistence of jobs looking for workers – vacancies – and workers looking or at least available for jobs – unemployment. The right image here is not – at least for the major industrialised countries – one of an ineffective matching process, but instead of a very effective one: while some workers and some jobs have a hard time finding a match, the flow of hires is large compared to the stocks of vacancies and unemployed workers.

How should one think of wage setting in such an economy? While wage scales, collective bargaining and other legal and institutional restrictions on bilateral bargaining surely play an important role, I want to abstract from those factors and focus on the implications of bilateral bargaining. Thus, think of wages being determined by bilateral bargaining, with the surplus from a match being divided in some proportion between the firm and the worker. Those assumptions imply that wages will move with productivity and with unemployment benefits. And, more importantly here, those assumptions imply that wages will move with market conditions, the crucial variable being the ratio of vacancies to unemployment. Why is this? This ratio can also be interpreted as the ratio of the average duration of a vacancy to the average duration of unemployment.[5] As the ratio increases, turning down a match to wait for the next one becomes more costly for firms, less costly for workers; the workers are therefore in a stronger bargaining position and thus are able to extract a higher wage.

Having sketched the general workings of the economy, we can now turn to the curves.

3 THE TWO CURVES: FINGER EXERCISES

Were the intensity of reallocation, the effectiveness of matching, the level of demand and so on to remain constant, the economy would be in a steady state: the flow of workers through the labour market would be high but approximately constant, unemployment would coexist with vacancies, and the wage would reflect the ratio of unemployment to vacancies. All those things change, however, leading to movements in wages, vacancies and unemployment, and thus to movements in the Beveridge and the Phillips spaces.

The time has come to bite one bullet: clearly, the approach that I have just sketched characterises the relation between the real wage and unemployment, not between inflation – or its rate of change – and unemployment as depicted in the Phillips curve. We – I mean the profession – know more or less how to go from one specification to the other, by assuming for example that wages in new matches are set in nominal terms for the expected duration of a match, and then by having firms mark up prices over wages adjusted for productivity.[6] I have started exploring those issues in this context but shall ignore them here, as it would take me too far from what I want to focus on. I shall do the analysis in terms of real wages, but then look at the empirical Phillips curves with a measure of the change in inflation – which I shall define later – rather than real wages on the vertical axis.

It is traditional to think of movements in unemployment and vacancies as coming primarily from changes in *aggregate activity*. At certain times, aggregate demand increases, leading to faster job creation and slower job destruction. At other times, aggregate demand contracts, leading to slower job creation and faster job destruction. An expansion thus leads to an increase in new vacancies and a decrease in the flow of workers into unemployment. As time passes, unemployment decreases, vacancies increase, and both lead to an increase in the wage. The reverse happens in a recession. Figures 5.1 and 5.2 show the Beveridge and Phillips curves traced by a simple sine wave in aggregate demand in the formal model underlying our argument, roughly calibrated to fit basic US numbers. The Beveridge curve is not a curve but rather looks like a banana, with counter-clockwise movements of unemployment and vacancies. The thickness of the banana depends on the length of the cycle: the longer the economy takes to go from peak to trough, the thinner the banana. The Phillips curve is also not quite a curve, but rather a counter-clockwise loop. Both these counter-clockwise movements were indeed noted by early practitioners of those curves.

While changes in aggregate activity may be the prime movers of unemployment and vacancies, macroeconomic events of the past fifteen years have made it clear that many other factors are also at work. The graphs of empirical Phillips and Beveridge curves below will also make this abundantly clear. Many factors may shift one and/or the other curve. The first class of factors I want to think about

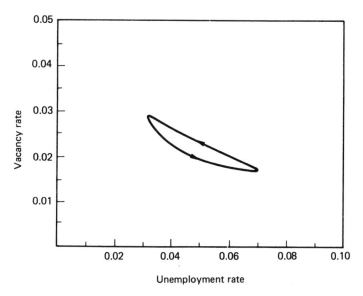

Figure 5.1   The Beveridge curve

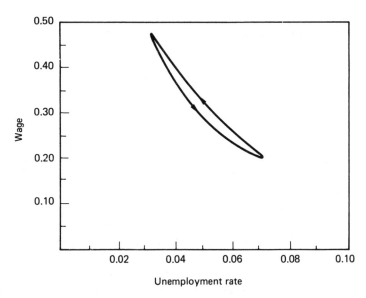

Figure 5.2   The Phillips curve

can be called *reallocation* factors. By this I mean changes in either reallocation intensity or in the effectiveness of the matching process. That such changes could explain a good part of the movement in unemployment even in the USA was argued by Lilien (1982) and has been the subject of much debate since. The role of both reallocation intensity and effectiveness is also at the centre of discussions of European unemployment. The case for such shifts is, *prima facie*, a strong one. Davis and Haltiwanger (1989) have recently shown by looking at changes in employment at the plant level in the USA that cyclical variations in the flows of job creation and job destruction are small in comparison with average flows. Even during the 1982 demand recession, job creation remained high, of the order of 4 per cent per quarter. Thus, small relative changes in the intensity of reallocation may have substantial effects on unemployment.

How do these reallocation factors affect the curves? Suppose that a faster pace of technological change, or of international specialisation lead to an increase in reallocation intensity, thus to both higher flows of job creation and higher flows of job destruction. In sharp contrast to cyclical movements, both unemployment and vacancies increase, reflecting the higher flows of laid-off workers and of newly created jobs. Or suppose instead that the matching process becomes less effective – for example, because the average distance, either purely geographical or in terms of skills, between job creation and destruction is larger. In that case, an unchanged flow of workers is associated with longer duration of both vacancies and unemployment, thus higher levels of unemployment and vacancies. In both cases, increased unemployment is unlikely to lead to a wage decrease, as it is associated with increased vacancies, and a roughly unchanged ratio of unemployment to vacancies.

Figures 5.3 and 5.4 show the shifts in the Beveridge and Phillips curves which result from increased intensity or decreased matching effectiveness in the formal model. In that simple model, both types of changes have the same dynamic effects on unemployment, vacancies and wages. The basic point is that *both* curves shift. At a given level of aggregate activity, both unemployment and vacancies increase, and at any given level of unemployment, the wage will be higher because vacancies are higher, in sharp contrast to cyclical movements.

There is another class of factors which may affect unemployment, those factors which lead firms or workers to extract – or to try to extract – a larger part of the product of their match. I shall call them

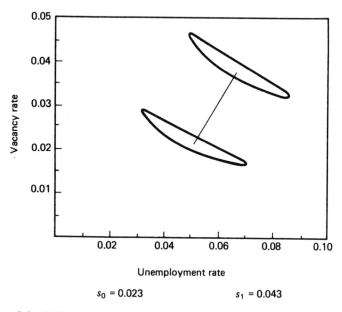

Figure 5.3 Shifts in the Beveridge curve due to reallocation factors

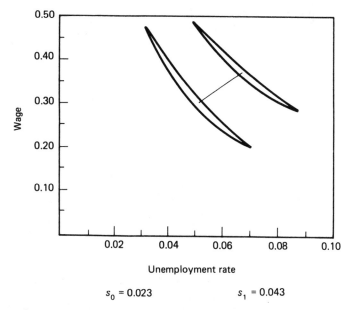

Figure 5.4 Shifts in the Phillips curve due to reallocation factors

bargaining factors. In our formal model, the simplest such factor is an increase in the share of the surplus from a match going to the worker. Such a change increases the wage given unemployment and thus shifts the Phillips curve. But, to a first approximation, it does not shift the Beveridge curve. The 'first approximation' caveat is needed: the change in the wage may affect the intensity of search, the supply of new jobs over time, and so on. There are many other factors, which are likely to shift the Phillips curve and do not affect the Beveridge curve very much. The list is a familiar one from the work on the potential causes of high unemployment. Any changes in market conditions for their products which lead firms to increase their mark-up over wage costs, because of increased monopoly power for example, will also lead to more inflation given unemployment and vacancies, without obvious implications for the Beveridge curve. So will misperceptions of productivity, of the available surplus, something likely to happen after a slowdown in productivity growth for example. In all those cases, the 'first approximation' caveat is again obviously needed: a slowdown in productivity growth may be associated with more – less? – required reallocation. Figures 5.5 and 5.6 show the effects of an increase in the share of the surplus on wages and unemployment. The figures are thoroughly unexciting, but make the basic point: only the Phillips curve shifts.

This suggests a simple empirical strategy. Look at the Beveridge and Phillips curves. Look at whether the economy is moving along those curves, or whether the curves are shifting instead. If they are shifting, look at whether both or only one are shifting. This points to the nature of the shock.[7]

4 A SIMPLE APPLICATION: THE USA

Figures 5.7 and 5.8 give the Beveridge and Phillips curves for 1960–88 for the USA. A word about the data. The USA has no vacancy series, and thus I use for vacancies the Conference Board Help Wanted Index, as adjusted by Abraham (1987); it is my impression, based in part on how useful the series turns out to be in empirical work, that the series is in fact a better proxy for vacancies than many of the vacancy series published for other countries. In the Phillips curve (Figure 5.8) the variable on the vertical axis is $\pi_t - 0.8\pi_{t-1}$, where π is inflation measured using the GNP deflator.[8] I have chosen the number 0.8 as it is roughly the estimated first order serial correlation

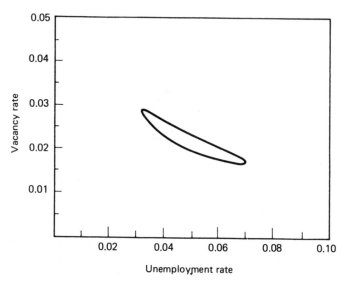

Figure 5.5   Shifts in the Beveridge curve due to bargaining factors

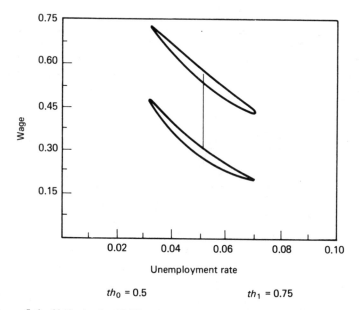

$th_0 = 0.5$ $th_1 = 0.75$

Figure 5.6   Shifts in the Phillips curve due to bargaining factors

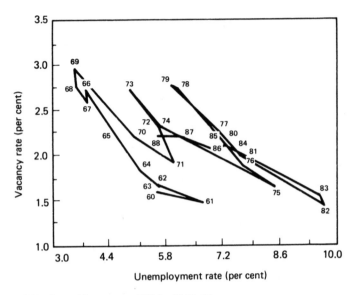

Figure 5.7　Beveridge curve, USA, 1960–88

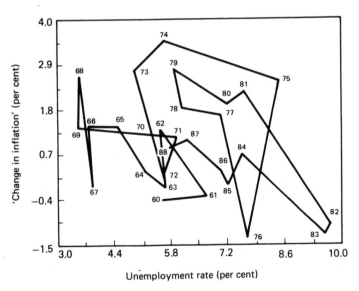

Figure 5.8　Phillips curve, USA, 1960–88

coefficient of inflation during this period. I shall call the variable on the vertical axis 'change in inflation' for short. But keep in mind that the name is not quite right.

The picture given by the Beveridge curve (Figure 5.7) is fairly clear. One can see large swings along a downward sloping locus, as one would expect from movements in aggregate activity. But there is also evidence of shifts to the right, from 1970 to 1982, and nearly all the way back to the left since 1982. The picture given by the Phillips curve is not as clean. 1974 and 1975 stand out, no doubt because of the increase in the price of materials and energy. But one can also see the inverse relation between inflation and unemployment. Again there is evidence of a shift to the right until the early 1980s, and of a shift to the left since then. Thus the fact that both curves shift together over the period points to shifts in reallocation effectiveness or intensity as the main reason for the increase and more recently the decrease in the non-inflationary rate of unemployment.

Let me give a slightly more formal assessment. The right way of using the information on vacancies, unemployment and inflation would be to assume that the joint process for those three variables results from the dynamic effects of three types of shocks, namely cyclical, reallocation and bargaining shocks, and then to use econometrics to identify the shocks and their dynamic effects. This is the approach which Diamond and I have followed in an earlier paper to decompose movements in the Beveridge curve (1989a). I shall use here a dirtier, but simpler and more visual one. If we ignore the thickness of the Beveridge and Phillips loops in response to changes in aggregate activity and assume that shocks to aggregate activity lead to movements along downward-sloping loci in both the Beveridge and Phillips spaces, we can identify these loci and then measure and compare the shifts in both curves. If the shifts are similar, this points to reallocation factors. If they are not, this points to bargaining factors.

The approach suffers from one problem: how does one know the slopes of the loci traced by movements in aggregate activity? Let me avoid that difficulty by estimating the slopes and the shifts in two different, extreme, ways. The truth is probably somewhere in the middle.[9]

In the first, I estimate the slopes of both curves and the shifts by regressing the logarithm of the unemployment rate on inflation, and the logarithm of the unemployment rate on the vacancy rate; I then compare the two series of residuals. This assumes implicitly that the shifts lead to movements in unemployment, with no effect on either

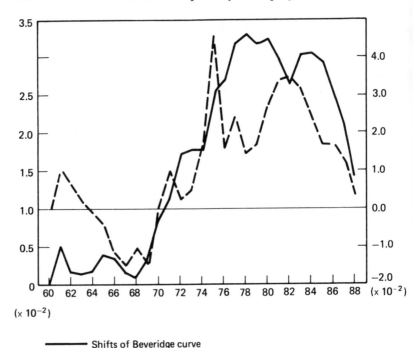

Shifts of Beveridge curve

Shifts of Phillips curve

Figure 5.9   Beveridge and Phillips curve shifts: USA 1960–88 first estimate

inflation or vacancies. Using annual data for 1960 to 1988, the two regressions give:

$$\log u = 0.04 - 7.18 \,(\pi - 0.8\pi(-1)) + \varepsilon_{pc} \quad R^2 = 0.11 \; DW = 0.38$$
$$(-1.9)$$

$$\log u = 2.4 - 0.85 \log v + \varepsilon_{bc} \qquad\qquad R^2 = 0.44 \; DW = 0.14$$
$$(-4.6)$$

where u and v are the unemployment and vacancy rates, and π is inflation using the GNP deflator. The two series of residuals, the estimated shifts, are plotted in Figure 5.9. They clearly move very much together, both on the way up and, since 1982, on the way down. Their correlation is equal to 0.82. At face value, this is a strong evidence for reallocation shifts.

There is however one obvious potential problem with this set of regressions: to the extent that the relation between unemployment

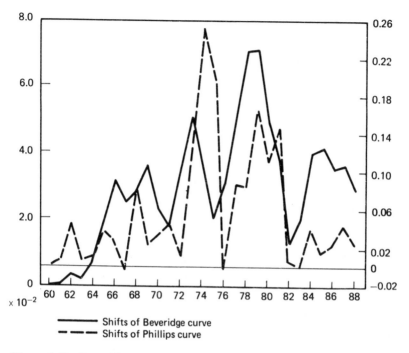

Figure 5.10 Beveridge and Phillips curve shifts, USA, 1960–88, second estimates

and either vacancies or inflation is weak – and indeed it is not very strong, as the R^2s indicate – the residuals will closely track unemployment, which is the left-hand-side variable in both equations. Thus, by construction, they will be highly correlated. This suggests trying the opposite strategy, that of running the regressions the other way, with unemployment as the right hand side variable. Those regressions give:

$$(\pi - \pi(-1)) = 0.04 - 0.016 \log u + \eta_{pc} \quad R^2 = 0.11 \ DW = 1.5$$
$$(-1.9)$$

$$\log v = 1.65 - 0.51 \log u + \eta_{bc} \quad\quad R^2 = 0.44 \ DW = 0.38$$
$$(-4.6)$$

These regressions assume that shifts affect inflation and vacancies, but not unemployment. The shifts are those movements in inflation and vacancies which cannot be explained by movements in unemployment. Figure 5.10 gives the time series for the residuals (each multiplied by minus the inverse of the coefficient on unemployment, so that they have the dimension of shifts in terms of unemployment and are comparable to those in Figure 5.9). As they are uncorrelated by construction with unemployment, they do not look like those in Figure 5.9. They are still however highly correlated: their correlation coefficient is equal to 0.53. Thus, even in this case, reallocation factors seem to be the main culprit behind the increase in the non-inflationary rate of unemployment.

5   A LOOK AT WESTERN EUROPE

The big news on unemployment over the past fifteen years has come not from the USA but from Western Europe. Can we use the same approach there? I shall concentrate on two countries, Germany and the UK, over the period 1970 to 1988.[10] During that period, the German unemployment rate increased from 1 per cent to 9 per cent and in 1989 stood at 8 per cent; the UK unemployment rate increased from 2 per cent to 12 per cent, decreased sharply over the last three years and in 1989 was under 7 per cent.

Figures 5.11 to 5.14 give Phillips and Beveridge curves for both countries. Following the same approach as above, the measure of inflation on the vertical axis, for both Germany and the UK, is $\pi_t - 0.7\pi_{t-1}$; the number 0.7 is roughly equal to the first order serial correlation coefficient of inflation over that period in both countries. The vacancy rate is constructed using registered vacancies series as published by the OECD. How reliable this measure of vacancies is depends on the relation of registered to total vacancies, and there is evidence of shifts in that relation over the sample period. Hence, when carrying out the estimation below, I also use for Germany a series which incorporates a crude adjustment for changes in coverage of registered vacancies.

The German Phillips curve shows clear evidence of steady shifts to the right throughout the period. This captures the well-known fact that high unemployment is now associated with constant rather than sharply declining inflation. Since 1983, the movement appears to be along a new, steep, downward-sloping locus, with no shift back to the left. The Beveridge curve shows a nearly steady movement along a downward-sloping locus until 1983, and a movement back since 1983. Using only the eye, it is impossible to decide whether this movement is a movement along the curve due to a long decrease in aggregate

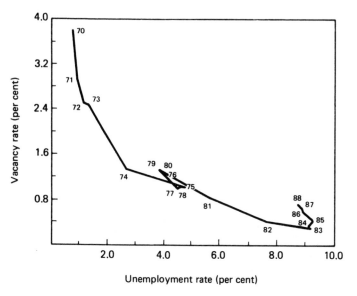

Figure 5.11 Beveridge curve, Germany, 1970–88

Figure 5.12 Phillips curve, Germany, 1970–88

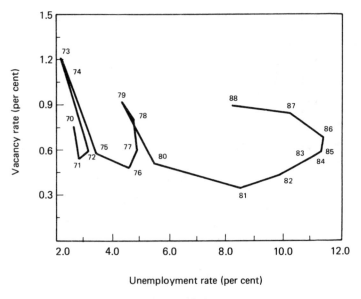

Figure 5.13 Beveridge curve, UK, 1970–88

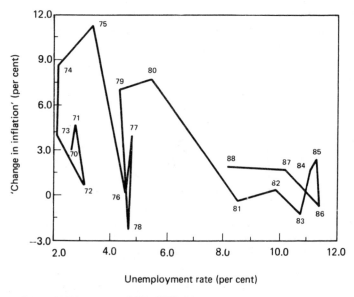

Figure 5.14 Phillips curve, UK, 1970–88

activity, or as a combination of such a movement and a series of shifts of the curve to the right.

The UK Phillips curve also shows clear evidence of steady shifts to the right. Interestingly, and in contrast to Germany, the decrease in unemployment since 1986 appears associated, at least in part, with shifts back of the curve rather than with movements along a new curve. The Beveridge curve also gives a rather different picture from that of Germany, showing clear shifts to the right since 1975. Recent decreases in unemployment appear, just as in the case for the Phillips curve, to be associated with shifts to the left of the curve.

The first visual impression is thus of shifts in the German Phillips curve which may not be associated with similar shifts in the Beveridge curve, pointing to the importance of what I have called bargaining factors in German unemployment. For the UK however, Phillips and Beveridge curves appear to have shifted in tandem, pointing to the importance of reallocation factors. To support this impression, let me again use crude econometrics in a way parallel to that used for the USA.

I estimate the slopes of the curves for both countries by using pre-1970 evidence, more precisely data from the period 1961–71. This is evidence from a long time ago, but things have not been the same since then.[11] For each country and each curve, I estimate the relation in two ways, by using unemployment either on the left or the right of the regression. As estimating simple Phillips and Beveridge curves is hardly new, and space is tight, I shall not report them. The specification is the same as for the USA. In particular, I use a logarithmic specification for the Beveridge curve; while one wants to adopt a specification which implies that the unemployment and vacancy rates are always positive, thus ruling out a linear specification, there are other possible forms one could consider. Because vacancy rates are so low during the period, the exact specification may make a difference to the results; this is another important caveat.

Figures 5.15 and 5.16 plot estimated shifts in the German Beveridge and Phillips curves. Figure 5.15 gives shifts obtained using the curves estimated with unemployment as the dependent variable; this is the figure which is more likely to show highly correlated shifts in the curves. Figure 5.16 gives shifts obtained taking unemployment as the independent variable. Both figures also give alternative Beveridge curve shifts obtained using the alternative measure of vacancies adjusted for changes in coverage which I could construct only up to

118   *Macroeconomic Aspects of Unemployment*

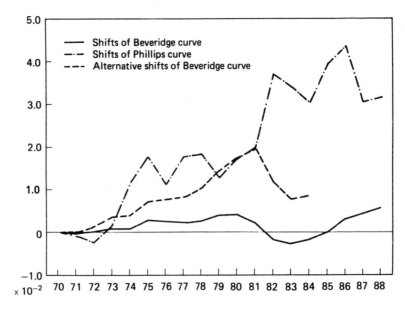

Figure 5.15 Beveridge and Phillips curve shifts, Germany, 1970–88, first estimates

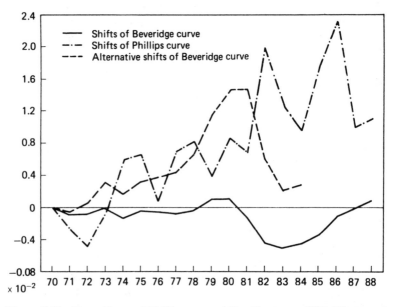

Figure 5.16 Beveridge and Phillips curve shifts, Germany, 1970–88, second estimates

1984. Both figures show the same general picture; the shifts in the Phillips curves are *not* reflected in shifts in the Beveridge curve. When the OECD measure of vacancies is used, there are no significant shifts in the Beveridge curve; put another way, the Beveridge curves estimated using pre-1970 or post-1970 data are nearly identical. When the alternative measure is used, the Beveridge curve shifts up until 1982, but then shifts back after 1982.

Figures 5.17 and 5.18 plot estimated shifts in the Beveridge and Phillips curves for the UK. The figures are defined in the same way. When the Phillips curve is estimated using inflation on the left hand side for the period 1961–71, the coefficient of unemployment is very small; this in turn leads to estimated large and variable shifts in the Phillips curve in Figure 5.18. That figure is presented for completeness, but should not be given much weight. Focusing on Figure 5.17, econometrics confirm the visual impression. Shifts in the Phillips and the Beveridge curves are highly correlated. Except for the period around 1975, the two curves have shifted in the same way over the period; in recent years both have shifted down.

A tentative conclusion is thus that different factors lie behind the common increase in unemployment in Germany and the UK. Bargaining factors appear to dominate in Germany, reallocation factors appear to dominate in the UK. If confirmed, this is an important conclusion. But it leads in turn to another set of questions, one which has been the subject of the debate on hysteresis in European unemployment. What are these mysterious reallocation or bargaining factors which have led to such an increase in unemployment? Is it not in fact more likely that the increase in unemployment, which was in large part triggered by contractions in aggregate demand, has itself led to shifts in the curves, that these shifts are not exogenous, but are themselves the result of prolonged unemployment? In the last section, I touch briefly on these issues, and show how the two curves can shed light on this set of questions as well.

6 SHARPENING THE TOOLS: SHIFTS IN THE CURVES AND PERSISTENCE

How can sustained high unemployment lead to shifts in one or the other curve? The debate on persistence in European unemployment has isolated two such channels, both based on differences between the long-term unemployed and other workers. I shall argue that one implies shifts in the Phillips curve, but not in the Beveridge curve,

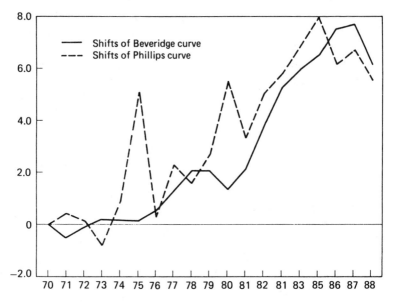

Figure 5.17   Beveridge and Phillips curve shifts, UK, 1970–88, first estimates

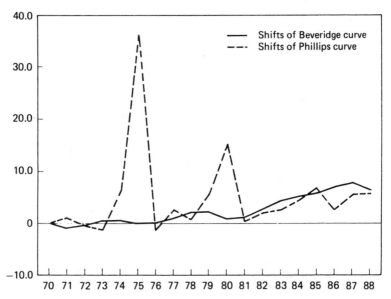

Figure 5.18   Beveridge and Phillips curve shifts, UK, 1970–88, second estimates

while the other implies shifts in both curves. Thus, given our evidence, one appears more relevant for Germany, the other more relevant for the UK.[12]

The first channel has been articulated by Layard and Nickell (1987). They argue that the long-term unemployed eventually give up on searching for jobs, either because they become discouraged, or because they get used to unemployment, or because the stigma of long-term unemployment disappears when there are many long-term unemployed. If we think of the long-term unemployed as simply dropping out, this suggests shifts in both the Beveridge and the Phillips curves. In both cases, the relevant pool of workers is the pool of workers searching for work, not the total pool of unemployed. This channel of persistence is thus consistent with the observed movements in UK unemployment, vacancies and inflation.

The other has been articulated by Blanchard and Summers (1986) and relies on the exclusion of the long-term unemployed from wage bargaining. While it was told initially in the context of collective bargaining, it may arise as well in a market with bilateral bargaining.[13] Suppose that firms, if they have the choice between workers, always hire the most recently laid-off worker. This may reflect the belief of firms that skills may deteriorate – ever so slightly – with unemployment. In this case, a worker who is just laid off knows that his chances of finding a job are higher than for a typical worker in the pool of unemployed. A large increase in unemployment may have, as a result, little effect on wage bargaining. Put another way, the wage will depend on vacancies much more than on unemployment. In terms of our now familiar curves, the Phillips curve will shift. But if workers with different unemployment duration are nearly perfect substitutes, the Beveridge curve will not shift. This channel of persistence is thus more consistent with the movements in the German unemployment, vacancies and inflation.

7 CONCLUSION

The pace of this paper has been fast, and the reader will surely want to see the dots on the i's. But the basic argument is a simple one. Thinking about labour markets as markets with large flows gives a simple way of thinking about the Beveridge and the Phillips curves, and to interpret their movements. Using this strategy, I have concluded that:

1. movements in the non-inflationary rate of unemployment in the USA appear to originate in changes in the reallocation process;
2. movements in the non-inflationary rate of unemployment in the UK appear to be due to changes in the reallocation process, changes due in turn to prolonged high unemployment;
3. by contrast, persistence of high unemployment in Germany appear to come from bargaining factors.

These are first pass conclusions. There is obviously much more information including information about the flows themselves, which must be brought to bear on those issues. But they give a flavour of what can be learned from the joint examination of the Beveridge and Phillips curves.

APPENDIX   A SKETCH OF A MODEL

What follows is a sketch of the model developed in Blanchard and Diamond (1989a, b). The economy is composed of identical workers and identical jobs. Workers can be in one of three states: employed, unemployed or out of the labour force. Let E be the number of employed workers, U the number of unemployed, and N the number of workers not in the labour force. The labour force, $L = E + U$, is given.

Symmetrically, jobs are in one of three states: they can be either filled, unfilled with a vacancy posted ('vacancies' for short), or unfilled with no vacancy posted ('idle capacity'). Each job requires one worker. Let K be the total number of jobs, F the number of filled jobs, V the number of vacancies, and I the number of unfilled jobs with no vacancy posted – that is, idle capacity. Thus, $K = F + V + I$. Obviously F and E are identically equal. K is given.

Job-Creation and Destruction

Each of the K jobs in the economy produces, if filled, a gross revenue of either 1 or 0. Profitability for each job follows a Markov process in continuous time. A productive job becomes unproductive with flow probability π_0. An unproductive job becomes productive with flow probability π_1. At any point in time, some jobs become productive, some jobs become unproductive. This is the mechanism used to capture the large gross flows of job creation and job destruction that exist in the economy.

It is conceptually useful to introduce two other parameters, c and s, defined in terms of π_0 and π_1. For given and constant π_0 and π_1, the proportion of potential jobs which are productive is given by $\pi_1/(\pi_0 + \pi_1)$; we may think of this proportion, which I shall call c (for cycle) as measuring the degree of aggregate activity (or more precisely potential aggregate activity, as the proportion of jobs productive and filled will always be less than c). The instantaneous flow of jobs changing from productive to unproductive (which equals the reverse flow), is equal to $\pi_0\pi_1/(\pi_0 + \pi_1)$ times K; we can think of this ratio, which we shall denote s (for shift), as an index of the intensity of reallocation in the economy.

Matching

The process of matching workers and jobs is captured by a matching function, giving hires, h, as a function of unemployment and vacancies:

$$h = \alpha\, m(U,V) \tag{1}$$

where α is a scale parameter, and m_U, $m_V \geq 0$, $m(0,V)=m(U,0)=0$. The parameter α captures the effectiveness of the matching process, which depends in turn on the dispersion in geographical and skill distributions of jobs and workers, as well as on search intensity.

The Equations of Motion

Assume for simplicity that the only sources of flows out of employment are due to jobs becoming unproductive. Introducing quits would be straightforward. It follows from the assumptions that the behaviour of the labour market is given by a system of two differential equations, which are:

$$dE/dt = \alpha m(U,V)\ -\pi_0 E$$

$$dV/dt = -\alpha m(U,V)+\pi_1 I - \pi_0 V$$

When a job becomes unproductive, the worker is laid off. Thus, the flow from employment to unemployment from this source is equal to $\pi_0 E$. The flow from unemployment to employment is equal to new hires.

For a job to produce 1, it must not only be productive but also be matched with a worker. To do so, a vacancy must be posted and a worker must be recruited. New vacancies come from jobs which were previously unproductive becoming productive; this flow is equal to $\pi_1 I$. Vacancies decrease for two reasons: some are filled by new hires, a flow from V to F; some of the jobs for which vacancies were posted become unproductive, a flow from V to I.

Using the identities above and replacing π_0 and π_1 by c and s gives a system of two equations in unemployment and vacancies:

$$\left. \begin{aligned} dU/dt &= -\alpha m(U,V)+(d+(s/c))(L-U) \\[2mm] dV/dt &= -\alpha m(U,V)+d(L-U) - \\ &\quad (s/(1-c))\,(K-V-L+U) - (s/c)V \end{aligned} \right\} \tag{2}$$

Wage Determination

Wages are determined by Nash bargaining within each match, so that the surplus from the match is shared in some proportion by the firm and the worker.

Flows of benefits to unemployed workers and vacancies are equal to zero. The flow of net output from a match is denoted by y. The joint gain from beginning the employment relationship is $(W_e - W_u + W_f - W_v)$. W_e and W_u are the expected present discounted value of wages when one is currently employed and the expected present discounted value of wages when one is currently unemployed respectively. W_f and W_v are the present expected discounted values of profit from the ownership of a job when the job is currently filled and vacant respectively. This surplus is divided in constant proportion between the firm and the worker:

$$D \equiv W_e - W_u = z(W_f - W_v) \tag{3}$$

Wages are continuously renegotiated to satisfy this equation continuously. Thus all employed workers are earning the same wage. In what follows, I limit myself to the derivation of the steady state wage. While only an approximation, it is a good one, even out of steady state (the simulations presented in the text are based on the general solution, which is given in Blanchard and Diamond, 1989b). To derive the wage, I use the standard arbitrage equation approach, as follows.

In steady state, the discount rate times the present discounted value is equal to the flow of benefits. Thus, the Ws follow:

$$rW_e = w \qquad\qquad\quad + \pi_0(W_u - W_e)$$
$$rW_u = (\alpha m/U)(W_e - W_u)$$
$$rW_f = y - w \qquad\quad + \pi_0(W_i - W_f)$$
$$rW_v = (\alpha m/V)(W_f - W_v) + \pi_0(W_i - W_v)$$
$$rW_i = \qquad\qquad\qquad \pi_1(W_v - W_i)$$

When employed, a worker receives the wage w but the employment relationship ends with flow probability π_0. When unemployed, a worker is receiving no benefit flow and has the flow probability $\alpha m/U$ of finding a job. Similar interpretations apply to the other Ws. Solving those equations for the wage, using equation (3) gives:

$$w/y = (r + \pi_0 + \alpha m/U)z/((r + \pi_0)(1 + z) + z(\alpha m/U) + \alpha m/V)$$

If, as is the case empirically, $\alpha m/U$ and $\alpha m/V$ are large compared with r and π_0, w is approximately equal to:

$$w \cong y(zV/(zV + U)) = zy/(z + (U/V)) \tag{4}$$

so that to a good approximation, the wage depends on the marginal product, y, the share of the surplus, z, and the vacancy unemployment ratio.

Dynamics

The dynamics of vacancies, unemployment and wages follow from equations 1, 2 and 4. Movements in aggregate activity are captured by a sine wave in the parameter, c. Their implications are given in Figures 5.1 and 5.2. Reallocation changes correspond to changes in either s, the intensity of reallocation, or in α the effectiveness of the matching process. Their implications are given in Figures 5.3 and 5.4. Bargaining changes correspond to changes in z, the parameter giving the division of the surplus. Their implications are shown in Figures 5.5 and 5.6.

Notes

1. An earlier version of this paper was presented at the Congrès de la Société Canadienne des Sciences Economiques, May 1989. As will be clear, this paper has grown out of joint work with Peter Diamond, although he bears no responsibility for the contents. I thank Hugh Courtney and Juan Jimeno for research assistance; Katherine Abraham for leading me to data on German vacancies; and Ken Arrow, Pierre Fortin, Robert Solow and Larry Summers for comments.
2. The US numbers are from the monthly *Current Population Survey*, as adjusted by Abowd and Zellner (1985). Corresponding numbers for movements in and out of employment do not exist for Western Europe. What is available are movements in or out of unemployment registers. The numbers are taken from Burda and Wyplosz (1989).
3. I wish we were the first to make this point but we are not. Solow (1964) may have been the first to use both curves to analyse whether a further decrease in unemployment would be inflationary. More recently Layard and Nickell (1987) have used this approach to analyse the sources of European unemployment.
4. For those who trust equations more than words, the appendix, which is based on Blanchard and Diamond (1989a, b) sketches a formal model which underlies the discussion in the text.
5. Let V be vacancies, U unemployment and m the flow of matches. Then U/V is equal to $(U/m)/(V/m)$. U/m is the average duration of unemployment, V/m is the average duration of a vacancy.
6. In the context of our model, this approach leads to inflation unemployment dynamics not unlike those in Calvo (1983).
7. Were there not a long tradition of looking at the joint behaviour of wages, unemployment and vacancies through the Phillips and Beveridge curves, one would probably not want to look at data in this way. The logic of the model just sketched suggests, for example, the use of the ratio of unemployment to vacancies rather than the unemployment rate as the variable on the horizontal axis in the Phillips curve. The tradition, however, is well established and I shall follow it here.
8. Truth in advertising compels me to make an admission here. Instead of estimating the 'price–price Phillips curve', an alternative strategy would

be to estimate the wage equation by itself – that is, the relation between nominal wages, prices, unemployment and vacancies, and productivity. In Blanchard and Diamond (1989b), we have made a first empirical pass at estimating such an equation for the USA, with results which are much less clear cut than those presented here. Reasons why this may be are discussed in that paper, but the discrepancy is worrisome.

9. It may not be. If shifts are correlated during the sample period with movements along the curves, the bias will go the same way under both approaches.

10. The December 1988 OECD *Economic Outlook* gives Beveridge curves for 16 OECD countries for the period 1970–88, which make fascinating reading. Germany and the UK appear broadly representative of those Western European countries which have suffered high unemployment.

11. More precisely, there are good reasons, empirical and theoretical, to think that since 1970 shifts in the curves have been correlated with movements along those curves. This would lead to an obvious bias if I were to use the whole sample to estimate slopes. I return to this issue later.

12. We have not yet extended our formal model to allow for these effects. What follows is based on a combination of work in progress, educated guesses, and bluff.

13. See Blanchard and Diamond (1989c) for a formal model.

References

Abowd, J. and Zellner, A. (1985) 'Estimating Gross Labor-Force Flows', *Journal of Business and Economic Statistics*, vol. 3, no 3, pp. 254–83.

Abraham, K. (1987) 'Help Wanted Advertising, Job Vacancies and Unemployment', *Brookings Papers on Economic Activity*, 1, pp. 207–48.

Blanchard, O. and Diamond, P. (1989a) 'The Beveridge Curve', *Brookings Papers on Economic Activity*, 1, pp. 1–74.

Blanchard, O. and Diamond, P. (1989b) 'The Aggregate Matching Function', in Diamond, P. (ed.) (forthcoming) *Growth Productivity and Unemployment* (Cambridge, Massachusetts: MIT Press).

Blanchard, O. and Diamond, P. (1989c) 'Long Term Unemployment and Wage Determination', unpublished paper, MIT, Cambridge, Massachusetts.

Blanchard, O. and Summers, L. (1986) 'Hysteresis and the European Unemployment Problem', *National Bureau of Economic Research Macroeconomics Annual*, vol. 1, pp. 15–78.

Burda, M. and Wyplosz, C. (1989) 'Inflows, Outflows, Bursts and Heterogeneity', unpublished paper, INSEAD.

Calvo, G. (1983) 'Staggered Prices in a Utility-Maximizing Model', *Journal of Monetary Economics*, vol. 12, no 3, pp. 383–98.

Davis, S. and Haltiwanger, J. (1989) 'Gross Job Creation, Gross Job Destruction, and Intrasectoral Labor Reallocation', unpublished paper, University of Chicago, Illinois, USA.

Layard, R. and Nickell, S. (1987) 'The Labour Market', in Dornbusch, R. and Layard, R. (eds) *The Performance of the British Economy* (Oxford: Oxford University Press) pp. 131–79.

Lilien, D. (1982) 'Sectoral Shifts and Cyclical Unemployment', *Journal of Political Economy*, vol. 90, pp. 777–93.

Solow, R. (1964) 'The Nature and Sources of Unemployment in the United States', *Wicksell Lectures* (Stockholm: Almqvist & Wicksell).

6 The Potential Duration of Unemployment Benefits and the Duration of Unemployment[1]

Lawrence F. Katz
HARVARD UNIVERSITY and NBER

and

Bruce D. Meyer
NORTHWESTERN UNIVERSITY and NBER

1 INTRODUCTION

Western European countries with relatively generous unemployment insurance (UI) systems (such as Belgium, France, Germany, the Netherlands, and the UK) have suffered much larger and more persistent increases in unemployment in the 1980s than has the USA. These differences in West European and US unemployment experience are largely explained by the substantially longer duration of unemployment spells in Europe. Furthermore, much microeconomic evidence indicates that there is a positive relation between the level of UI benefits received and the duration of the unemployment spells of UI recipients.[2] These observations have generated much interest among both academics (for example, Minford, 1985) and the press (for example *The Economist*, 14–20 May 1988, p. 69) in the hypothesis that work disincentives arising from generous unemployment insurance (UI) systems have played an important role in high and persistent European unemployment in the 1980s.

In comparing the UI system in the USA with those in Western Europe, the major differences appear to be in the potential duration of benefits and eligibility requirements for benefits rather than in the

128

level of weekly benefits available to qualified workers. In particular, UI and other assistance lasts for more than twice as long in most European countries than in the USA. The potential duration of benefits varies dramatically across countries. The typical qualified worker is eligible for 6 months of benefits in the USA as compared with over a year of benefits in France, Germany, and Sweden (Burtless, 1987). For some individuals benefits can last indefinitely (although typically at a reduced rate in the form of means-tested assistance after the first year) in Belgium, Ireland and the UK. UI benefits of long duration combined with limited monitoring of efforts to find a job may make an economy more susceptible to increases in long-term unemployment in the face of adverse shocks. In fact, Jackman *et al.* (1989, ch. 4) find that the strong positive relationship between the generosity of the unemployment system and the level of unemployment among OECD countries in the 1980s is driven more by differences in the duration of benefits than by differences in the replacement ratio.

While much microeconomic research has shown that higher levels of benefits are associated with longer durations of unemployment, there is much less empirical research on the impact of the potential duration of benefits on the duration of unemployment.[3] Since the length of available benefits varies substantially among UI systems, an understanding of how potential benefit duration affects the distribution of spells of unemployment is important for determining whether UI differences help explain differences between countries in unemployment.

In this paper, we present new empirical evidence on the impact of the level and potential duration of benefits on the duration of unemployment in the USA. We look at two types of empirical evidence. The first part of our empirical work analyses the unemployment spells of a large sample of household heads. These data allow us to compare spell distributions for UI recipients and non-recipients and to look at differences in the time pattern of exits from unemployment by recalls and by new job acceptances. Sharp increases in both the recall and new-job-finding rates are apparent at durations when benefits are likely to lapse for UI recipients. The absence of such increases in the escape rate from unemployment for non-recipients provides strong evidence of an impact of the potential duration of UI benefits on firm recall policies and workers' willingness to start new jobs.

The second part of our empirical work examines the impact of the level and length of UI benefits on the escape rate from unemployment for a large sample of UI recipients. This continuous wage and benefit history (CWBH) data set, extracted by Moffitt (1985), has the advantage of providing detailed administrative records on the UI system parameters facing individuals. Since the data set covers spells in twelve American states during the period, 1978–83 a fair amount of both cross-section and time-series variation in UI parameters is available. This variation allows us to estimate directly the impact on the escape rate from unemployment of differences in the level and length of benefits and test the predictions of alternative models. We find substantial effects of both the level and length of benefits on spell duration.

The remainder of the paper is organised as follows. Section 2 reviews the predictions of search models of the effects of UI system parameters on the escape rate from unemployment. Section 3 presents our comparison of the unemployment spells of UI recipients and non-recipients. Section 4 applies econometric duration models to administrative data on the spells of UI recipients. Section 5 uses our estimates to simulate the impact of changes in the level and maximum duration of benefits on the mean duration of unemployment, the fraction of workers exhausting benefits, and expected expenditures on UI benefits. Section 6 provides some concluding remarks.

2   THEORETICAL BACKGROUND

In this section, we analyse the likely impact of the level and potential duration of unemployment benefits on the duration of unemployment and the time pattern of the escape rate from unemployment. We discuss the predictions of a standard job search model and of job search models that incorporate the layoff–rehire process.

2.1   Standard Job-Search Model with no Recalls

Mortensen (1977) utilises a dynamic search model with no recall possibility, variable search intensity, a stationary known-wage-offer distribution, and a constant arrival rate of job offers (for a given search intensity) to analyse the effects of UI on the escape rate from unemployment. Mortensen incorporates two key features of the UI system in the USA into the model: benefits are assumed to be paid only for a specified duration rather than in every period of a spell of unemployment and new entrants or workers who quit jobs are not qualified for benefits.

As the remaining number of weeks of benefits available to a qualified unemployed worker decreases, the value of remaining unemployed decreases. This drop causes the reservation wage to fall and search intensity to increase as an individual gets closer to the date when benefits lapse. These changes in behaviour imply that the escape rate from unemployment rises until the date of benefit exhaustion. After benefits are exhausted and given the assumption that the environment is stationary, the escape rate is constant. The time pattern of the exit rate for an unemployed worker initially qualified for UI benefits with potential duration of P_0 periods is illustrated by the solid line in Figure 6.1.[4] If individuals can locate jobs and arrange not to begin work until their benefits run out, one might observe a discrete increase in the escape rate near the point of benefit exhaustion followed by a discrete drop after exhaustion.

Mortensen's model suggests that changes in the level and length of benefits have two opposing influences on the escape rate from unemployment. Increases in either of the benefit parameters have the standard disincentive effect of raising the value of being unemployed, but these increases also raise the value of being employed by increasing the utility associated with being laid off in the future. The second effect, known as the 'entitlement' effect, raises the escape rate from unemployment for workers who currently do not qualify for benefits and for qualified workers close to benefit exhaustion.

The effect of an increase in the potential duration of benefits from P_0 to P_1 is illustrated in Figure 6.1. The standard disincentive effect reduces the escape rate from unemployment for a newly laid-off worker, but the entitlement effect leads to a higher escape rate as the exhaustion point is approached and passed. The impact of an increase in the benefit level from b_0 to b_1 is illustrated in Figure 6.2.

The model suggests the following stylised, reduced-form specification for the escape rate from unemployment, λ:

$$\lambda = \lambda \,(\overset{+}{P}, \overset{-}{P-t}, \overset{+}{b}, b \times (P-t), X) \qquad \text{for } P-t \geq 0$$

where t is the duration of the spell, P is potential duration of benefits, $P-t$ is time until benefit is exhausted, b is the level of benefits, and X is a vector of individual and labour market variables affecting the arrival rate of job offers, search intensity, and choice of reservation wage. As indicated by the positive and negative signs in the

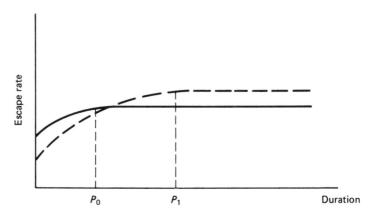

Figure 6.1 The relation of the escape rate and potential benefit duration

specification, the escape rate from unemployment increases as time until exhaustion declines; and higher benefits reduce the escape rate when time until exhaustion is high and increase the escape rate at around exhaustion. Since the entitlement effect is likely to be small, the average duration of unemployment is likely to rise with increases in both the level and potential duration of benefits.

2.2 Recall Prospects, UI Benefits and Unemployment Spell Duration

The standard job search model is not entirely appropriate for analysing the unemployment spells of workers who have been laid off with some possibility of recall. The interpretation of empirical evidence on the duration of insured unemployment spells in the USA requires consideration of the role played by recalls since the majority of insured unemployment spells appear to end in recall (Katz, 1986; Katz and Meyer, 1988). The prospect of recall affects the probability of leaving unemployment directly through the rate of recalls and indirectly by affecting worker search behaviour. Katz (1986) extends a standard model of job search to include an exogenous probability of recall.[5] He shows that under reasonable conditions better recall prospects reduce the new-job-finding rate by raising the reservation wage and reducing the likelihood of search.

The statistical model of unemployment spell durations generated by the job search models extended to allow for recalls is a competing-risks model in which unemployment spells can end either

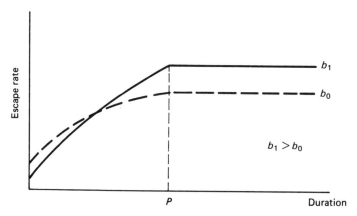

Figure 6.2   The relation of the escape rate and the level of benefits

through recall or the finding of an acceptable new job. The predictions of standard job search models for the way that variables affect the escape rate from unemployment really refer to the new job finding rate and these predictions need not hold for the overall escape rate from unemployment, which is the sum of the recall and new-job-finding rates.

Mortensen (1987) analyses the effects of limited duration UI benefits in a joint wealth-maximising model of job separations that allows for temporary layoffs. Layoffs occur in response to reductions in match-specific (that is, firm specific) productivity. The reservation wage decreases over the course of an unemployment spell as a worker approaches benefit exhaustion. This induces an increasing new-job-finding rate and an increasing recall rate as well. Mortensen shows that for realistic parameter values most of the decline in the reservation wage should occur in the last week or two before exhaustion. The discrete change in the flow value of being unemployed when benefits are exhausted yields the prediction that many firms may recall laid-off workers around the benefit-exhaustion point and that the new-job-finding rate should increase around exhaustion.

3 UI, RECALLS, AND UNEMPLOYMENT SPELLS: EVIDENCE FROM THE PSID

In this section, we compare the distributions of unemployment spell durations of UI recipients and non-recipients in the USA. We analyse employer-initiated unemployment spells in the period 1980–1 for a national sample of household heads derived from Waves 14 and 15 of the Panel Study of Income Dynamics (PSID).[6] The interviews from these two waves of the PSID provide detailed information on each household head's last unemployment spell at least partially contained in the calendar year preceding the interview date.[7] For the last unemployment spell in the calendar year prior to the interview, respondents provide retrospective information on the spell duration. We can also determine whether UI benefits were received during the spell, and whether completed spells ended through recall or the taking of a new job.

The basic sample contains 1115 layoff and plant-closure unemployment spells for household heads between the ages of 20 and 65.[8] This data set has two major advantages. First, it contains a large sample of spells for both UI recipients and non-recipients, and contains information on complete unemployment spells rather than just compensated unemployment. UI benefits were received during some part of the spell for 63 per cent of the observations (703 spells). Second, our data set allows us to separate the escape rate from unemployment into its component parts: the new-job-finding rate and the recall rate.

The PSID data set also has some disadvantages. First, information is only available on whether UI is received at some time during a spell of unemployment. One cannot accurately identify the level or potential duration of the benefits available. Second, response biases for retrospective information on individual unemployment spells can be severe (Mathiowetz and Duncan, 1988).

Basic descriptive statistics for the entire sample, UI recipients, and UI non-recipients are presented in Table 6.1.[9] The importance of recall for job losers in the USA is highlighted by the finding that 52 per cent of the spells ended in recall. The recall rate was 64 per cent for manufacturing workers, 59 per cent for construction workers, 43 per cent for transportation workers, 35 per cent for service workers, and 29 per cent for trade workers.

There are sharp differences in the characteristics of UI recipients and non-recipients. UI recipients have much higher wages than non-recipients. Substantially larger fractions of the UI recipients are white, married, male, and manufacturing workers. The recall rate is also substantially higher for UI recipients. These differences in the characteristics of the two groups help to explain the longer mean spell duration for non-recipients (Katz, 1986).

Table 6.1 Unemployment spells initiated by plant closures, layoffs and firings for UI non-recipients and recipients: descriptive statistics for PSID unemployment spell sample

Variable	Description	Means (standard deviations in brackets)		
		UI non-recipients (UI = 0)	UI recipients (UI = 1)	Total
Duration	unemployment spell duration in weeks	18.64	15.60	16.72
Recall	= 1 if spell ended in recall	0.48	0.55	0.52
New job	= 1 if spell ended in taking a new job	0.28	0.28	0.28
Censored	= 1 if spell is censored at interview date	0.24	0.18	0.20
UI	= 1 if received UI during some part of spell	0.00	1.00	0.63
Unemployment rate	= county unemployment rate	7.09	8.12	7.74
PC	= 1 if spell initiated by plant closure	0.12	0.07	0.09
Wage	Average hourly earnings in calendar year prior to interview (US dollars)	5.69	7.95	7.12
Age	age in years	32.44 (10.48)	33.90 (13.59)	33.34 (10.70)
Non-white	= 1 if non-white	0.61	0.42	0.49
Female	= 1 if female	0.19	0.14	0.16
Married	= 1 if married	0.52	0.71	0.64
Education	years of schooling	11.31 (2.36)	11.42 (2.14)	11.38 (2.22)
Mining	= 1 if in mining or agriculture	0.04	0.03	0.03
Construct	= 1 if construction	0.21	0.17	0.18
Durables	= 1 if durable goods manufacturing	0.16	0.36	0.29
Non-durables	= 1 if non-durable goods manufacturing	0.09	0.15	0.13
Transport	= 1 if transportation or utilities	0.10	0.07	0.08
Trade	= 1 if wholesale or retail trade	0.16	0.08	0.11
Service	= 1 if services	0.24	0.14	0.18
White collar	= 1 if managerial, professional, clerical or sales worker	0.38	0.22	0.28
Sample size		412	703	1115

Sample Hazard Functions for UI Recipients and Non-recipients

The pattern of unemployment spell durations for UI recipients and non-recipients from the PSID sample is illustrated in Figures 6.3 and 6.4. The figures plot the empirical hazards for the two samples with

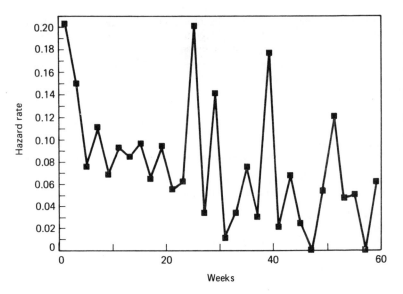

Figure 6.3   Total hazard: UI sample, PSID (two-week intervals)

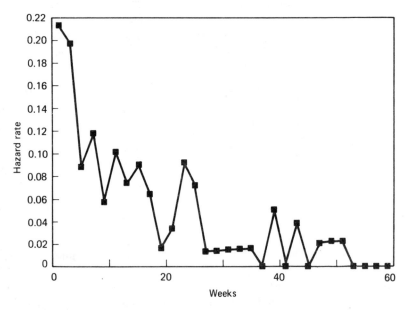

Figure 6.4   Total hazard: non-UI sample, PSID (two-week intervals)

the weekly duration data grouped into two-week intervals for ease of presentation. The overall empirical hazard for a given two-week period is the fraction of spells ongoing at the start of the period which end during the two-week interval. The recall and new job empirical hazards, plotted for the two samples in Figures 6.5 and 6.6, are analogously defined as the fraction of spells ongoing at the start of a period which end during the period through recall and through the finding of a new job respectively.

The figures reveal substantial differences in the pattern of the escape rate from unemployment for UI recipients and non-recipients. The total hazard rates are initially downward-sloping for both groups. The total hazard increases substantially in the 25- to 40-week interval for UI recipients. There are large spikes in the escape rate from unemployment at 26 weeks and at 39 weeks for UI recipients. Spikes of similar magnitude at 26 and 39 weeks are not apparent for UI non-recipients. While the exact placing of the spikes may be an artifact of the tendency for individuals to report long unemployment rates as lasting exactly half a year, three-quarters, or one year, the much greater importance of these spikes for UI recipients strongly suggests that they may be related to the limited duration of UI benefits. Most UI recipients during this period were eligible for either 26 or 39 weeks of benefits in a benefit year. The escape rate from unemployment appears to increase substantially around the time when many UI recipients would be exhausting benefits.

The total rates presented in Figures 6.3 and 6.4 mask sharp differences in the new-job-finding and recall rates illustrated in Figures 6.5 and 6.6. The recall rate drops sharply with spell duration for both UI recipients and non-recipients. Most recalls occur within 8 weeks of the start date of a spell. The new-job-finding rate differs substantially for UI recipients an non-recipients. The new-job-finding rate starts out quite a bit lower and is much more upward-sloping for UI recipients. The lower initial new-job-finding rate for UI recipients may be an artifact of the one week waiting period before UI eligibility in most American states. Individuals expecting short spells may also not bother to apply for benefits. On the other hand, these factors could not plausibly account for the differences in the new-job-finding rate patterns for UI recipients and non-recipients after the first few weeks. The low initial new-job-finding rate and apparent positive duration dependence in the new-job-finding rate for UI recipients provides support for the prediction that UI depresses new-job-finding when the time before benefit is exhausted is long and that the escape

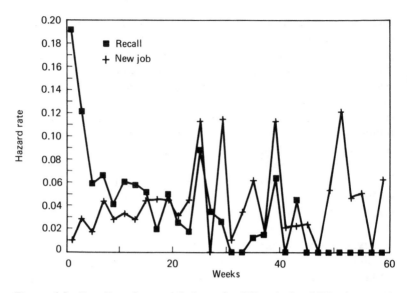

Figure 6.5 Recall and new job hazards: UI sample, PSID (two-week intervals)

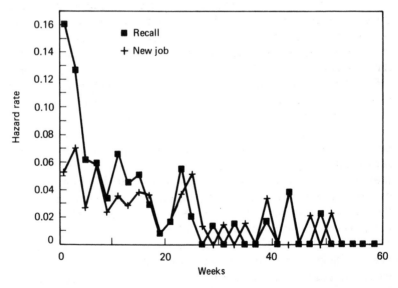

Figure 6.6 Recall and new job hazards: non-UI sample, PSID (two-week intervals)

rate rises with time until benefits are exhausted. The jumps in the recall and new-job-finding rates for UI recipients at likely exhaustion points (26 and 39 weeks) are strong evidence for the prediction that firms take into account the duration of UI benefits in designing recall policies and that workers become much more likely to take new jobs as their benefits run out. The absence of such patterns for non-recipients in the PSID sample strongly suggests that these patterns represent behavioural responses by firms and workers to the incentives created by a UI system with limited benefit duration.

4 HAZARD MODEL ESTIMATES USING THE MOFFITT DATA SET

This section reports hazard model estimates of the effect of the level and length of UI benefits on unemployment durations. We use Continuous Wage and Benefit History (CWBH) UI administrative records on the compensated unemployment spells of a sample of 3365 males from twelve American states during the period 1978–83.[10] The sample is drawn from a data set previously analysed by Moffitt (1985).[11] CWBH data provide accurate information for each individual on the level of UI benefits and their potential duration. Potential duration varies over time since benefits are frequently extended. The number of weeks of benefit receipt is also known exactly.[12] This avoids many of the measurement error problems common in other data sources.

The data set provides enough variation in UI system parameters within and across states and over time to get accurate estimates of the impact of the level and length of UI benefits and the time until benefit is exhausted. The sources of variation in benefit levels in our data are non-linearities in the benefit schedules (different minima and maxima across states), legislative changes during the sample period, and the erosion of real benefit levels due to inflation between legislation changes. Benefit maxima differ substantially across states. For example, the maximum benefit in Missouri is below the average benefit in Pennsylvania in our data set.

There are several sources of variation in the potential duration of benefits in the data. First, there is variability across states in the length of regular benefits provided. During the sample period, Louisiana typically provided 28 weeks. Pennsylvania provided 30 weeks, while most other states provided 26 weeks of benefits. Second, benefits were extended during periods of high unemployment under several federal programmes. The Extended Benefits programme extended benefits 50 per cent beyond state durations, up to a maximum of 39 weeks, whenever the insured unemployment rate was above a trigger level. Two other programmes provided supplemental benefits. At the beginning of the sample period, the Federal Supplemental Benefits programme provided up to a total of 65 weeks of benefits. Beginning in the fall of 1982 the Federal Supplementary Compensation programme provided up to 62 weeks of benefits. Finally, within a state of a point in time the length of benefits may depend on an individual's work history.

A disadvantage of the CWBH data is that it only covers compensated unemployment so that one cannot use it to make inferences about what happens to individuals after benefits are exhausted. Nor does the data set permit one to identify whether spells end through recall or the finding of a new job. Thus one can analyse only the overall unemployment escape rate. Spells that end with the exhaustion of benefits are treated as right-censored since we only know that the spell is at least as long as its length at exhaustion. Spells that are ongoing when the data collection ends are also treated as right-censored.

The duration of unemployment spells is analysed using hazard model techniques. We use a proportional hazards model estimator that allows for time-varying explanatory variables and which estimates non-parametrically the change in the hazard over time. This semi-parametric approach is analysed in detail in Meyer (1986). The estimates are the parameters of a continuous time hazard model and thus retain a clear interpretation. Non-parametrically estimating the change in the hazard over time eliminates the need to impose a potentially restrictive functional form that has little theoretical justification.

Formally, we parameterise the overall hazard rate of exit from unemployment for individual i at time t, $\lambda_i(t)$, using the proportional hazards form. Let T_i be the length of individual i's unemployment spell. Then the hazard at spell length t is

$$\lambda_i(t) = \lim_{h \to 0^+} \frac{\text{prob}\,[t + h > T_i \geq t \mid T_i \geq t]}{h} \tag{1}$$

$$= \lambda_0(t) \exp \{z_i(t)'\beta\}$$

where

$\lambda_0(t)$ is the baseline hazard at time t, which is unknown,
$z_i(t)$ is a vector of time-dependent explanatory variables
for individual i, and
β is a vector of parameters which is unknown.

Our approach estimates β and the baseline hazard parameters $\gamma(t)$ using maximum likelihood techniques, where

$$\gamma(t) = \ln \{\int_{t}^{t+1} \lambda_0(u)du\} \tag{2}$$

The effects of unemployment insurance are measured using functions of the benefit level and the length of benefits. The level of benefits and pre-UI earnings after state and federal taxes are used in the specifications below. We measure the effect of an individual's remaining potential duration of unemployment benefits on the hazard rate using the variables UI 1 to UI 41–54 which form a spline in the time until benefit exhaustion. The coefficient on UI 2–5 is the additional effect on the hazard of having moved 1 week closer to benefit exhaustion when exhaution is 2–5 weeks away. The coefficient on UI 1 is the additional effect on the hazard of moving from 2 weeks to 1 week from exhaustion. Thus, the effect of moving from 6 weeks away to 1 week is four times the UI 2–5 coefficient plus the UI 1 coefficient. The other UI spline coefficients have analogous interpretations.

Formally, let τ be the number of weeks until benefits lapse. τ decreases by one each week, unless benefits are extended thus increasing τ. Then

UI 1   = 1 if $\tau = 1$, and
         0 otherwise

UI 2–5 = min $(6-\tau, 4)$ if $\tau \leq 5$, and
         0 otherwise

UI 6–10 = min $(11-\tau, 5)$ if $\tau \leq 10$, and
          0 otherwise

and similarly for the remaining spline variables.

In some of the later specifications the potential duration of benefits is directly included as an explanatory variable along with the time until benefit exhaustion spline.[13] In addition, interaction terms suggested by the theoretical models reviewed in Section 2 and previous empirical work are included. These variables interact the level of benefits with age, the unemployment rate, and the time until benefit exhaustion. Since benefits are extended in the course of many spells, a variable is included which equals 1 in week *t* if at any time during a spell it was expected that benefits would lapse in week *t*. The unemployment rate variable used in the specifications is the monthly state unemployment rate, which is interpolated to give a weekly series. State dummy variables (fixed effects) are included in the specifications to account for unobserved differences across states that may be correlated with both the generosity of the state UI system and the character of unemployment in the state. The other included variables are age, race, education, marital status and the number of dependents.

Discussion of the Estimates

The coefficient estimates from the specifications are reported in Table 6.2. In all the specifications tried, the UI benefit level has a strong negative effect on the hazard rate. Specification (1) indicates that a 10 per cent increase in the benefit level is associated with a 5.3 per cent decrease in the hazard.[14] A strong effect of the number of weeks until benefits lapse is seen from the exhaustion spline coefficient estimates in Specification (1). The hazard increases 94 per cent when one moves from 6 weeks to 2 weeks before benefits expire. In the last week the hazard increases an additional 78 per cent. Cumulatively, the hazard more than triples as one moves from 6 weeks to 1 week before exhaustion. When it is more than 6 weeks until exhaustion, the time pattern of the hazard is not precisely estimated.

Most states limit the total dollar amount of benefits paid to an individual during a benefit year. The limit typically depends on an individual's base period earnings. If this limit on total payments is binding, an individual may receive a smaller payment in his or her last week of eligibility. Some individuals may not bother to pick up this smaller final payment. The possibility that these smaller final payments could spuriously generate the rise in the hazard just before exhaustion was examined using an additional CWBH sample. The sample includes 38 472 individuals from eight states during 1979–84.

Table 6.2 Semi-parametric hazard model estimates of unemployment duration;[a] Moffitt Data Set ($n=3365$)

Variable	Mean (Standard deviation in brackets)	Coefficient Specification (1)	(2)
UI benefit level (1977 dollars)	104.23 (27.91)	−0.0053 (0.0014)	−0.0040 (0.0015)
Pre-UI weekly earnings after taxes (1977 dollars)	169.51 (66.52)	0.0026 (0.0005)	0.0025 (0.0005)
State unemployment rate	8.70 (2.08)	0.0006 (0.0002)	0.0006 (0.0002)
Age 17–24	0.16	0.234 (0.086)	0.688 (0.201)
Age 25–34	0.34	0.117 (0.076)	0.118 (0.076)
Age 35–44	0.24	0.112 (0.079)	0.109 (0.079)
Age 45–54	0.14	0.034 (0.083)	0.032 (0.083)
Exhaustion spline:			
UI 1		0.577 (0.249)	0.551 (0.250)
UI 2–5		0.166 (0.062)	0.036 (0.099)
UI 6–10		0.005 (0.032)	−0.011 (0.037)
UI 11–25		−0.006 (0.007)	−0.031 (0.015)
UI 26–40		0.006 (0.007)	−0.019 (0.019)
UI 41–54		0.021 (0.138)	
Benefits previously expected to lapse		1.537 (0.188)	1.578 (0.189)
Potential duration of benefits			−0.0247 (0.0153)
Interaction of benefit level and age 17–24			−0.0048 (0.0019)
Interaction of benefit level and ≤ 3 weeks until exhaustion			−0.0039 (0.0027)
Log likelihood value		−8905.1	−8900.6

[a] Variables for education, race, marital status, number of dependents, and 11 state dummy variables are also included. The UI benefit level and pre-UI weekly earnings variables are in 1977 dollars. The numbers in brackets are asymptotic standard errors.

The eight states include seven of the twelve in our subset of the CWBH data set previously analysed by Moffitt. We compared the hazard rate in the week before regular benefits lapsed when the benefit payment was its full amount and when it was reduced because of the limit on total dollar benefits. Those who received Extended Benefits or Federal Supplemental Compensation benefits were excluded. The hazard was 21 per cent higher (0.257 compared to 0.212) when the last payment was less than the full weekly amount. While these comparisons are somewhat crude since we did not control for individual attributes, they do support the hypothesis that a lower benefit amount may cause people not to claim their last week of benefits. Because only a slim majority of the final payments are less than the full amount, this effect could cause only a 12 per cent increase in the overall hazard in the week before benefits lapse. Thus, only a small part of the rise in the hazard just before benefit exhaustion could be explained by this fact.

The estimates reported in Table 6.2 also indicate that the probability of a spell ending is very high in a week in which benefits were scheduled to lapse at some point earlier in a spell. One interpretation of this result is that some firms plan the timing of recalls and some workers arrange the start of a new job to coincide with the end of eligibility for benefits, but do not alter these plans in the face of an extension of benefits. Alternatively, this result could reflect that some people eligible for extended benefits do not claim them. The estimated effects of UI on spell length are nearly identical if this variable is omitted since only a small fraction of spells have unexpected benefit extensions and the coefficient affects the hazard in only one week.

The estimated effect of the benefit level on the length of unemployment spells is at the high end of the distribution of recent estimates. A consensus of the previous estimates of the effect of a 10 percentage point increase in the replacement ratio might be a $\frac{1}{2}$- to 1-week increase in the length of spells.[15] Here the estimate is around $1\frac{1}{2}$ weeks. Larger estimated effects are a plausible result of better data on spell length and the level and length of benefits than in many previous studies.

Specification (2) in Table 6.2 includes several additional variables. The potential duration of benefits is included as in the original paper by Moffitt (1985). This variable is time-varying and often increases from 26 to 39 in the course of a spell as benefits are extended. The entitlement effect captured by Mortensen's (1977) job search model leads to the prediction that the coefficient of potential benefit duration should be positive when the time until exhaustion is also included as a covariate. In fact, the coefficient estimate is negative and substantial in magnitude, although it is not quite significant at conventional levels. A negative coefficient is consistent with the income effects from more generous benefits emphasised by Moffitt and Nicholson (1982). The coefficient estimate implies that a 13-week extension of benefits is associated with a 27 per cent decline in the hazard.

Two benefit level interaction variables are also included in Specification (2). Benefits are interacted with the dummy variable 'Age 17–24'. This variable has a large and significant negative coefficient, indicating that the response of younger people to the benefit level is much more elastic. An interaction between the level of benefits and time until benefit exhaustion of less than or equal to 3 weeks is also added. This coefficient tends to support the hypothesis of Mortensen (1977) that higher benefits will have less of an effect near exhaustion (and may even raise the hazard), but the positive coefficient is not quite significant.

We also note that if Specification (2) is estimated without state fixed effects, the benefit level coefficient almost doubles in absolute value to 0.0073 (standard error 0.0011), while the estimated time until benefit exhaustion and potential benefit duration effects are not greatly altered. The exclusion of fixed effects also causes the state unemployment rate to change sign while retaining statistical significant. It appears that higher unemployment states also tend to have longer spells, but when the unemployment rate rises within a given state the average length of spell drops.

5 SIMULATING THE IMPACT OF CHANGES IN THE LENGTH AND LEVEL OF UI BENEFITS

In this section, we simulate the effect of changes in the level and length of UI benefits on the duration of unemployment spells, the exhaustion rate, and the amount of benefits paid. The simulations are somewhat speculative since they use information on only the unemployment spell durations of UI recipients and so do not illuminate how changes in UI parameters may affect wages, the incidence of layoff unemployment, or the unemployment experience of non-UI recipients through possible displacement effects.

Our simulations use the actual sample distribution of the time-invariant covariates from our subsample of the Moffitt data. The parameter estimates used in the simulations are those in Table 6.2. The simulations assume that the state unemployment rate is constant during each spell and equal to the start-of-spell value for each individual in the sample. It is assumed that everyone is eligible for 39 weeks of benefits (the standard potential duration in a period in which extended benefits are triggered).

The most speculative part of the procedure is making an assumption concerning behaviour after benefits are exhausted. Since the data set covers only compensated unemployment, one cannot use it for inferences concerning post-exhaustion escape rates. We assume that after exhaustion the baseline hazard is equal to the average baseline hazard in our sample and the benefit level is zero. We set the exhaustion spline in the post-exhaustion period equal to 15 weeks before exhaustion. The rationale for this treatment of the exhaustion spline is to avoid the high escape rate from temporary layoffs in the early part of spells and the exhaustion spike found close to the exhaustion point.

5.1   Simulation Methodology

The key quantity used in the simulations is the predicted survivor function for each individual in week t, conditional on the individual's covariates $z_i(\tau)$ up until t. The predicted survivor function in week t is the predicted probability of a spell lasting at least until t and it is defined by the equation

$$
\begin{aligned}
\hat{S}_i(t) &\equiv S_i(t|\hat{\gamma}(\tau), z_i(\tau)'\beta; \tau = 0, \ldots, t-1) \qquad (3)\\
&= \exp\left\{ -\int_0^t \hat{\lambda}_i(u)du \right\}\\
&= \exp\left\{ -\sum_{\tau=0}^{t-1} \exp\left[\hat{\gamma}(\tau) + z_i(\tau)'\beta\right] \right\}
\end{aligned}
$$

where a hat above an expression denotes an estimated quantity. The aggregate survivor function for the sample is then defined by:

$$
\bar{S}(t) \equiv \frac{1}{N} \cdot \sum_{i=1}^{N} \hat{S}_i(t)
$$

where N is the sample size. Given the aggregate survivor function, the predicted mean weeks of unemployment is calculated using the rolling sum $M(t)$, which is the predicted weeks of unemployment accumulated by week t.

$$\text{Weeks accumulated by } t \equiv M(t) \equiv \sum_{\tau=1}^{t} \bar{S}(\tau) \tag{5}$$

In all the simulations $M(104)$, the number of weeks accumulated by the end of two years, was calculated. Since the sum converged rapidly the simulation results would not be very different if we had truncated the sum at 1 or 3 years instead. Thus, predicted mean weeks of unemployment is defined by $M(104)$.

Predicted mean weeks compensated is defined by $M(d)$, where d is the potential duration of benefits. Predicted benefits paid per spell, $B(d)$ is defined by:

$$B(d) \equiv \frac{1}{N} \cdot \sum_{i=1}^{N} \sum_{\tau=1}^{d} \hat{S}_i(\tau) \cdot b_i \tag{6}$$

where b_i is the UI benefit for individual i. Finally, the predicted percentage exhausting UI benefits equals $\bar{S}(d)$.

5.2 Simulation Results

Simulations which use Specification (1) are reported in Table 6.3, and simulations using Specification (2) are reported in Table 6.4. The base case scenario predicted values differ appreciably for the two simulations, but the effects of policy changes are very similar. The base case difference occurs because the simulations assume that potential duration does not change during the unemployment spells, while in the actual Moffitt data the potential duration of benefits rises in the course of many spells as benefits are extended. This effect is captured through the baseline hazard estimates in Specification (1) rather than directly in the potential duration of benefits coefficient as in Specification (2). In both sets of simulations the potential duration of benefits is assumed to be constant over time, but in Specification (1) the baseline hazard estimates implicitly incorporate increases in the potential duration of benefits from extended benefits triggers turning on during the course of a spell.

Table 6.3   Simulations of the impact of UI parameter changes on unemployment outcomes using Specification (1) from Table 6.2 (The numbers in brackets are percentage changes from the base case)

Scenario	Predicted mean weeks of unemployment	Predicted mean weeks compensated	Predicted benefits paid per spell $	Predicted percentage exhausting
Base case (39 weeks)	18.4	16.6	1796	12.9
Benefit level reduced 10%	16.9 (−8.2)	15.5 (−6.6)	1503 (−16.3)	10.4 (−19.4)
Benefit level reduced 20%	15.4 (−16.3)	14.4 (−13.3)	1236 (−31.2)	8.2 (−36.4)
Benefit level reduced 30%	14.1 (−23.4)	13.3 (−19.9)	996 (−44.5)	6.3 (−51.2)
Potential benefit duration reduced to 35 weeks	17.6 (−4.3)	15.7 (−5.4)	1690 (−5.9)	14.6 (+13.2)
Potential benefit duration reduced to 26 weeks	16.2 (−12.0)	13.6 (−18.0)	1461 (−18.7)	20.7 (+60.5)

Table 6.4   Simulations of the impact of UI parameter changes on unemployment outcomes using Specification (2) from Table 6.2 (The numbers in brackets are percentage changes from the base case)

Scenario	Predicted mean weeks of unemployment	Predicted mean weeks compensated	Predicted benefits paid per spell $	Predicted percentage exhausting
Base case (39 weeks)	14.7	13.5	1455	9.0
Benefit level reduced 10%	13.5 (−8.2)	12.5 (−7.4)	1215 (−16.5)	7.2 (−20.0)
Benefit level reduced 20%	12.4 (−15.6)	11.6 (−14.1)	999 (−31.3)	5.7 (−36.7)
Benefit level reduced 30%	11.3 (−23.1)	10.8 (−20.0)	807 (−44.5)	4.4 (−51.1)
Potential benefit duration reduced to 35 weeks	13.9 (−5.4)	12.8 (−5.2)	1376 (−5.4)	9.8 (+8.9)
Potential benefit duration reduced to 26 weeks	12.6 (−14.3)	11.4 (−15.6)	1222 (−16.0)	13.4 (+48.9)

We simulated the impact of changes in UI parameters on the predicted mean completed spell of unemployment and on the mean weeks of compensated unemployment. Tables 6.3 and 6.4 report the following policy experiments: 10, 20 and 30 per cent reductions in the level of benefits, and changes in the potential duration of benefits from 39 to either 35 or 26 weeks. A change in maximum potential benefit duration from 26 to 39 weeks is exactly the natural policy experiment that occurs when extended benefits are triggered in the USA.

Changes in the level of benefits and changes in the potential length of benefits have substantial effects on the mean duration of unemployment of UI recipients. The two sets of simulations provide fairly similar estimates of the impact of policy changes. An increase in the potential duration of benefits from 26 to 39 weeks is predicted to raise the mean unemployment spell duration by 2.1 weeks in both simulations. This is a surprisingly large effect given that most spells are completed well before the 26 weeks of regular benefits run out. An increase in potential benefit duration will mechanically increase the mean compensated spell duration even if benefits have no incentive effect since previously uncompensated unemployment will be classified as compensated unemployment. The predicted effect of an extension of benefits from 26 weeks to 39 weeks if there are no incentive effects from extending benefits (using Specification (2)) is a 0.9 week increase in mean compensated spell duration. Thus most of the impact of extended benefits on compensated unemployment arises through the negative effects of UI on the escape rate from unemployment.

We conclude from an examination of a variety of simulated changes in potential benefit durations that a 1-week extension of benefits increases the mean duration of an unemployment spell by approximately 0.16 to 0.20 weeks. One caveat in interpreting these estimates is that some of the variation in the potential length of benefits arises from the extension of benefits in times of poor macroeconomic conditions. If the time-varying state unemployment rate variable included in our specifications does not fully capture labour market conditions, then our estimates of the impact of increases in potential benefit duration may partly reflect potential benefit durations being high when job availability is low.

Our estimates of the impact of potential benefit duration on the average unemployment spell duration of UI recipients are a little larger than most of those in the literature. Our estimates are slightly larger than Moffitt's (1985) estimate of 0.15 weeks from a model that does not include state dummy variables. Moffitt and Nicholson (1982) find using a static labour supply estimation framework that a one week extension raises the average unemployment duration by 0.10 week. Moffitt and Nicholson's sample consists of 'long-term' unemployed workers who had exhausted their benefits; such individuals may plausibly be less sensitive to benefits than a more representative group of UI recipients such as in our data set. In a study of Canadian UI recipients, Ham and Rea (1987) find that a 1-week increase in the duration of benefits increases the mean duration to the start of a new job by 0.26–0.33 weeks in a competing risks framework.[16]

The hypothetical UI parameter changes examined in the simulations have substantial effects on the amount of benefits paid per spell. A reduction in the level of benefits by 10 per cent has an impact on the UI budget similar to a reduction in the potential duration of benefits from 39 to 26 weeks. The simulations indicate that increases in potential benefit duration have much larger adverse incentive effects on unemployment than do changes in the level of benefits that have the same effect on the UI budget. The simulations in Table 6.4 show that the budget cut from the base case accomplished through a 10 per cent reduction in benefits reduces mean unemployment by 1.2 weeks, while a similar budget cut made through eliminating extended benefits generates almost twice as large a reduction in mean unemployment.

These findings suggest that a government with a fixed UI budget faces a sharp trade-off between incentives and insurance in the design of the level and time sequence of UI payments. A balanced budget combination of a reduction in the level with an increase in the maximum duration of benefits has strong adverse incentive effects although it does provide greater protection for those who are unlucky in their attempts to gain re-employment.

5.3   The Impact of Extended Benefits on the Income of the Unemployed

Broadly, our results suggest that the behavioural effects of UI are extremely important. The estimated incentive effects of extended benefits are large enough to allow the possibility that a benefit extension could actually reduce the total money income of UI recipients. If the benefit extension did not affect unemployment duration or re-employment earnings, then increasing the weeks of unemployment in which benefits are received would raise the income of the unemployed. On the other hand, if a higher duration of benefits increases unemployment duration and does not affect re-employment wages, the extension of benefits may reduce the income (although probably not the welfare) of UI recipients if re-employment wages are higher than UI benefits.

The following simple calculations are instructive concerning the incentive effects of increases in benefit duration. We make the strong assumption that re-employment weekly wages are unaffected by the availability of extended benefits. Under this assumption, the change in a UI recipient's money income arising from the extension of benefits is given by the formula:

$$\Delta \text{ Income } = \{\Delta \text{ (Weeks of compensated unemployment)}$$
$$\times \text{ (Weekly UI benefit)}\} - \{\Delta \text{ (Total weeks}$$
$$\text{of unemployment)} \times \text{ (Re-employment}$$
$$\text{weekly wage)}\}$$

In Table 6.5 we present the predicted impact on the income of a UI recipient (with pre-UI weekly earnings equal to our sample average of $170) of an increase in potential benefit duration from 26 to 39 weeks. We use the simulations discussed above based on specifications (1) and (2) from Table 6.2. We consider three cases for each specification. The first case assumes there are no behavioural effects of extended benefits. The second case assumes that extended benefits increase unemployment by the amounts shown in our simulation results (in Tables 6.3 and 6.4) and that re-employment wages are 90 per cent of pre-UI weekly wages. The final case assumes these same behavioural effects on the duration of unemployment, but assumes that re-employment wages are only 60 per cent of pre-UI weekly wages. Katz and Meyer (1988) find that the typical UI recipient who gains re-employment within a year of layoff has (initial) re-employment weekly earnings that are approximately 10 per cent less than pre-UI weekly earnings. On the other hand, those who were not recalled, and exhausted benefits, averaged 50 per cent losses in weekly earnings.

The calculations presented in Table 6.5 suggest that extending benefits may reduce the total money income of UI recipients. If one assumes that re-employment earnings are 90 per cent of previous

Table 6.5 The effect of an increase in potential benefit duration from 26 to 39 weeks on the income of a typical UI recipient[a] (1977 US$)

Scenario	Change in unemployment income	Change in wage income	Net change in income
Specification (1) from Table 6.2			
No behavioural effects of UI	179	0	179
Behavioural effects:			
Re-employment weekly wage equals 90% of pre-UI weekly earnings	336	−337	−1
Re-employment weekly wage equals 60% of pre-UI weekly earnings	336	−225	111
Specification (2) from Table 6.2			
No behavioural effects of UI	98	0	98
Behavioural effects:			
Re-employment weekly wage equals 90% of pre-UI weekly earnings	223	−321	−98
Re-employment weekly wage equals 60% of pre-UI weekly earnings	223	−214	9

[a] These calculations assume a pre-UI weekly wage of $170. All figures are in 1977 dollars. The change in income of a UI recipient arising from the extension of benefits is given by the formula:

$$\Delta \text{Income} = \{\Delta(\text{Weeks of compensated unemployment}) \times (\text{Weekly UI benefit})\} - \{\Delta(\text{Total Weeks of unemployment}) \times (\text{Re-employment weekly wage})\}.$$

earnings, then both specifications yield the prediction that the income of the typical UI recipient falls in response to an increase in potential benefit duration from 26 to 39 weeks. If workers whose behaviour is most strongly affected by extended benefits have low re-employment wages, then it is likely that extended benefits raise the money income of UI recipients. Of course, these simple calculations ignore the increases in leisure accruing to UI recipients from greater unemployment and do not take into account the possibility that extended benefits may allow workers to make better job matches raising future earnings from employment.

6 CONCLUSIONS

The evidence presented in this paper indicates that the potential duration of UI benefits has a strong impact on the duration of the unemployment spells of UI recipients in the USA. Our examination of data from the PSID indicates that the distributions of unemployment spell durations of UI recipients and non-recipients are appreciably different. Substantial increases in both the recall rate and new-job-finding rate are apparent for UI recipients around the time when benefits are likely to lapse. Large increases in the escape rate from unemployment in the several weeks before exhaustion are also apparent for a large sample of UI recipients for which administrative data allows us to date accurately the end of the spell and the point at which benefits are exhausted. It seems safe to conclude that potential benefit duration has significant behavioural effects on the recall policies of firms and the new-job-finding strategies of workers. Overall, our results imply that a 1-week increase in potential benefit duration increases the average duration of the unemployment spells of UI recipients by about 0.16 to 0.20 weeks. Furthermore, our estimates indicate that policies that extend benefits have much greater adverse incentive effects on the duration of unemployment than policies with the same predicted impact on the government budget which raise the level of benefits.

Two caveats about our results should be kept in mind. First, while lower unemployment benefits might decrease the length of UI recipients' spells of unemployment, the spells of non-UI recipients might rise because of congestion/displacement effects. If aggregate employment is determined by the level of demand, and the matching of particular workers to jobs is not important, shorter unemployment spells for one group would imply longer spells on average for others. This effect would imply that our estimates of the microeconomic effects of UI on unemployment may be an overestimate of the macroeconomic effects. Second, we have concentrated on transitions from unemployment into employment, and we have ignored the impact of UI on the incidence of layoffs and on labour force participation decisions. A more encompassing analysis of the effects of UI might yield different conclusions about the aggregate effects of changes in the level and length of UI benefits.

Notes

1. This paper represents a shortened version of our study 'The Impact of the Potential Duration of Unemployment Benefits on the Duration of Unemployment', *Journal of Public Economics* (1990) vol. 41, pp. 45–72, with the kind permission of Physical Sciences and Engineering Division, Elsevier Science Publishers. We thank Robert Moffitt for providing data and answering numerous questions. We are grateful to Gary Burtless, Dale Mortensen, Nick Stern, Lawrence Summers, and an anonymous referee for helpful comments. Financial support from the following sources is also gratefully acknowledged: National Science Foundation Grants SES 88-09200 (Katz) and SES 88-21721 (Meyer); an NBER Olin Fellowship in Economics (Katz); and the Industrial Relations Section at Princeton University (Meyer). The data used in this paper will be made available upon request.
2. See, for example, Classen (1977) and Solon (1985) for estimates of the impact of benefit levels on unemployment duration in the USA, and Narendranathan *et al.* (1985) for estimates for the UK. Atkinson *et al.* (1984) present evidence that casts some doubt on the robustness of findings concerning the impact of benefit levels on the re-employment probability in the UK.
3. Moffitt and Nicholson (1982), Moffitt (1985), and Ham and Rea (1987) are among the few sophisticated econometric studies of the impact of potential benefit duration on the duration of unemployment.
4. Figure 6.1 is drawn assuming the marginal utility of leisure is independent of income.
5. Burdett and Mortensen (1978) and Pissarides (1982) also analyse job-search models that incorporate the possibility of recalls.
6. A description of the Panel Study of Income Dynamics (PSID) can be found in Survey Research Center (1987).
7. The questions concerning individual unemployment spells were asked only of household heads who were labour force participants at the time of the interview.
8. A household head's last spell from the calendar year prior to the interview date made it into the sample if (1) the spell ended in recall to

the pre-separation employer; (2) the spell ended in the taking of a new job and the head was separated from his or her last job by a plant closing, layoff, or firing; (3) the spell is censored at the interview date and the head is categorised as on temporary layoff; or (4) the spell is censored at the interview date and the head is categorised as unemployed having been separated from last job by plant closing, layoff or firing. Observations satisfying the above criteria were deleted if they had missing information on spell duration, spell start date, UI receipt, or pre-separation occupation and industry.

9. The extremely high proportion of non-whites in the sample results from the oversampling of low income households in the PSID. The empirical findings are qualitatively similar to those presented in this section when observations from only the 'random' portion of the PSID are used.

10. The twelve states are Georgia, Idaho, Louisiana, Missouri, New Mexico, New York, North Carolina, Pennsylvania, South Carolina, Vermont, Washington, and Wisconsin.

11. The original Moffitt (1985) data set contains 4628 observations. 1227 observations are excluded because of missing data on age, schooling, dependents or marital status. 36 observations are excluded because the recorded spell is longer than the reported potential duration of benefits.

12. The spells in the Moffitt data are periods of benefit receipt. Spells that are interrupted by short periods when benefits are not received are concatenated. This modified spell of benefit receipt may do a better job of grouping together periods of similar behaviour.

13. It is possible to allow the hazard rate to depend on time (t), time until exhaustion $(P_t - t)$ and potential benefit duration (P_t) because P_t is a time-varying covariate in this sample. P_t changes over the course of many of the spells as extended or supplemental benefits begin or expire.

14. When UI benefits and previous earnings are entered in logarithms the effect of benefits is somewhat higher (Meyer, 1988).

15. See Burtless (1986) for a survey of estimates based on US data.

16. Since some of the spells in their sample end in recall, it is difficult to translate this finding into an estimate of the effect on the mean duration of unemployment.

References

Atkinson, A. B., Gomulka, J., Micklewright, J., and Rau, N. (1984) 'Unemployment Benefit, Duration, and Incentives in Britain', *Journal of Public Economics*, vol. 23, pp. 3–26.

Burdett, K. and Mortensen, D. (1978) 'Labor Supply Under Uncertainty', *Research in Labor Economics*, vol. 2, pp. 109–57.

Burtless, G. (1986) 'Unemployment Insurance and Labor Supply: A Survey', unpublished mimeo, The Brookings Institution, Washington DC, USA.

Burtless, G. (1987) 'Jobless Pay and High European Unemployment', in Lawrence, R. and Schultze, G. (eds) *Barriers to European Growth* (Washington, DC: The Brookings Institution).

Classen, K. (1977) 'The Effect of Unemployment Insurance on the Duration of Unemployment and Subsequent Earnings', *Industrial and Labor Relations Review*, vol. 30, pp. 438–44.

Economist, The, 14–20 May 1988.

Ham, J. C. and Rea, S. A. Jr (1987) 'Unemployment Insurance and Male Unemployment Duration in Canada', *Journal of Labor Economics*, vol. 5, pp. 325–53.

Jackman, R., Layard, R., Nickell, S., and Wadwhani, S. (1989) *Unemployment*, unpublished manuscript, London School of Economics, London.

Katz, L. F. (1986) 'Layoffs, Recall and the Duration of Unemployment', *NBER Working Paper*, no 1825.

Katz, L. F. and Meyer, B. D. (1988) 'Unemployment Insurance, Recall Expectations, and Unemployment Outcomes', *NBER Working Paper*, no 2594.

Mathiowetz, N. A. and Duncan, G. J. (1988) 'Out of Work, Out of Mind: Response Errors in Retrospective Reports of Unemployment', *Journal of Business and Economic Statistics*, vol. 6, pp. 221–9.

Meyer, B. D. (1986) 'Semiparametric Estimation of Hazard Models', unpublished mimeo, MIT, Cambridge, Massachusetts.

Meyer, B. D. (1988) 'Unemployment Insurance and Unemployment Spells', *NBER Working Paper*, no 2546.

Minford, P. (1985) *Unemployment: Cause and Cure* (Oxford: Basil Blackwell).

Moffitt, R. (1985) 'Unemployment Insurance and the Distribution of Unemployment Spells', *Journal of Econometrics*, vol. 28, pp. 85–101.

Moffitt, R. and Nicholson, W. (1982) 'The Effect of Unemployment Insurance on Unemployment: The Case of Federal Supplemental Benefits', *Review of Economics and Statistics*, vol. 64, pp. 1–11.

Mortensen, D. T. (1977) 'Unemployment Insurance and Job Search Outcomes', *Industrial and Labor Relations Review*, vol. 30, pp. 595–612.

Mortensen, D. T. (1987) 'A Structural Model of UI Benefit Effects on the Incidence and Duration of Unemployment', unpublished mimeo, Northwestern University, Evanston, Illinois.

Narendranathan, W., Nickell, S. and Stern, J. (1985) 'Unemployment Benefits Revisited', *Economic Journal*, vol. 95, pp. 307–29.

Pissarides, C. A. (1982) 'Job Search and the Duration of Layoff Unemployment', *Quarterly Journal of Economics*, vol. 97, pp. 595–612.

Solon, G. (1985) 'Work Incentive Effects of Taxing Unemployment Benefits', *Econometrica*, vol. 53, pp. 295–306.

Survey Research Center (1987) *User Guide to the Panel Study of Income Dynamics* (Ann Arbor, Michigan: University of Michigan).

Part II

Economics of Integration

7 The European Monetary System Ten Years On: The System's Architecture, Problems and Perspectives

Rainer S. Masera[1]

ISTITUTO MOBILIARE ITALIANO, ROME

1 INTRODUCTION

Operational experience with the European Monetary System (EMS), coupled with theoretical analysis (see, in particular, Obstfeld, 1988 and Wyplosz, 1986), have convinced me that a system of fixed exchange rates that can be adjusted discretely, and which therefore offers substantial opportunities for speculative profits, will be difficult to maintain under conditions of complete capital mobility, even with unlimited very short-term reciprocal lines of credit in place. We are faced with a difficult road ahead, but the *leit-motiv* of this paper is 'keep going and you won't stop'.

In the ten years since the inception of the EMS numerous assessments have been made of its performance with analyses highlighting the strong and weak points, especially Giavazzi (1989) and CER (1988). The subject has already been addressed by Masera (1987), so this paper focuses on the problems that will have to be tackled in the near future if the EMS is to develop into an integrated financial and monetary area. On the one hand, this presupposes complete substitutability of financial assets denominated in European currencies and held in member countries and, on the other, increasingly stable exchange rates, leading, in the end, to fixity (Kenen, 1976).

The urgency of these problems is enhanced by the more intense competition between financial systems associated with the creation of an integrated market, especially in view of the probability that this will involve the European financial industry in a phase of Schumpeterian

159

'creative destruction', not only as a result of the quantum increase in the size of markets but also because it will be necessary to cut costs in a period marked by rapid technological innovation and financial deregulation, coupled with a revision of supervisory operating procedures.

There are three main problems requiring immediate and simultaneous attention if an orderly process of financial and monetary unification is to be possible in Europe. In addition to the integration of monetary and exchange rate policies, it will be necessary to address the issues of harmonising financial and prudential regulations and making the taxation of financial incomes more uniform. Both these factors contribute to the establishment of an integrated market and their importance is enhanced by complete freedom of capital movements.

This paper touches only briefly on the harmonisation of financial regulations and taxation – issues treated in detail elsewhere by Masera (1989a and 1989b) and concentrates on the integration of monetary and foreign exchange policies. The problems are analysed primarily with reference to Italy, in order to bring out clearly the steps that will have to be taken if the Italian economy is to develop in line with the rest of Europe.

2 THE HARMONISATION OF FINANCIAL REGULATIONS

We are currently faced with two very different approaches to financial regulation in Europe: the British approach, in which a key role is played by markets, whose development determines the structure of the system of intermediaries and their importance; and, at the other extreme, the approach exemplified by Germany, in which banks play a primary role and have close links with industry.

The freedom to supply financial services, which will become effective on 1 January 1993, implies the right of every licensed bank to engage in a series of predetermined activities in every Community country in conformity with the rules and under the supervision of its home country. This application of the *principle of mutual recognition* – which amounts to a 'Copernican revolution' compared with the previous doctrine of *total harmonisation* – will lead to competition between the various regulatory frameworks and financial systems, with a gradual convergence to the model that best meets the needs of the market (Steinherr and Gilbert, 1989; Banca d'Italia, 1989a; IMI-EC Affairs Section, 1989).

There is thus the problem of suitably applying minimal harmonisation and mutual recognition: the harmonisation implemented in accordance with Community directives and supranational law will be followed by further harmonisation in response to competition and the need for each credit system to compete on equal terms with those of the other Community countries.

The creation of a core of standard regulations is intended to perform the task of avoiding excessive deregulation and limiting the danger of instability and distorted competition; while minimal harmonisation of the operational methods of prudential supervision is intended to prevent the less regulated systems from enjoying an unjustified competitive advantage, which would provoke a downward levelling of regulations to the least strict standards. *Ex ante* it is by no means easy to identify the equilibrium point of all these different requirements, especially in view of the substantial disparities between the national systems discussed above. In particular, the relationship between institutions and the market appears to be strongly influenced by the *global rules* that govern each system, bearing in mind that the development of financial markets as separate entities is a feature of those economies in which the importance of the banking system is less, in terms of its links with other financial sectors and industry.

The growing interpenetration of the financial and banking markets implies that both should be set within a regulatory framework that will guarantee stability while avoiding rigidity. Otherwise, the effect would be to put a straitjacket on competition between operators in different sectors in the area where it is liveliest, that is along the demarcation line between them. Such flexibility in the rules governing operators' behaviour can only be achieved by providing for close and pragmatic coordination between the authorities responsible for developing and carrying out supervisory controls.

The efforts to bring about regulatory convergence, notably in connection with entry requirements, activity-related capital adequacy and pricing, together with those to link the various financial supervisory bodies, both within each country and internationally, are among the most far-reaching problems on the road to an integrated monetary area and require clear decisions. Their solution cannot be left simply to competition between regulatory systems – a point stressed also by Sarcinelli (1988) – but will have to be consciously tackled in the light of the indications that economic theory can provide.

Recent analytical studies of regulatory problems reveal the complexity of the factors that interact in the various levels of the decision-making process. Simplified models focusing variously on stability and transparency or on stability and efficiency as the basis for control appear inadequate. What is required is the identification of the cases in which market mechanisms are inadequate and need to be supplemented by regulation.

The asymmetric information approach and reputation theory provide instruments for an innovatory analysis of the problem of regulation in the financial field. In particular, traditional approaches emphasise the static aspects of allocative efficiency and the microeconomic aspects of stability. Today, the 'objective divisions' between banking activities, the securities business and insurance no longer exist. In the new conditions of truly global markets (BIS, 1986), innovation, the reduction in the technological cost of operations and the resulting economies of scale and scope make dynamic efficiency of paramount importance. On the other hand, the fact that individual operators and informed investors are expected to identify suitable institutions, instruments and operations that nonetheless involve a known element of risk requires that unsound financial institutions and operators be subject to the discipline of the market. Only when this condition holds are savers and final borrowers spurred into making the necessary autonomous assessment of risk and financial operators encouraged to invest in developing their reputations, transparency, capital strength and profitability.

In short, if the primary reason for exercising control is the gap between private and social benefits, competition between regulatory authorities will not be the most effective means of maximising social welfare. The problem of establishing a European supervisory authority that would operate pragmatically and, if necessary, in opposition to national authorities should be tackled at the same time as a central monetary institution is created.

3   THE HARMONISATION OF TAX REGULATIONS

The need for greater tax harmonisation is evident, since disparities in this field would not only be incompatible with a future single currency but are already an obstacle to the creation of an internal market in which there is complete freedom of capital movements (Commission of the European Communities, 1988; European Council, 1988). If they were allowed to remain, the differences in the taxation of the income from financial assets in the various member countries (Banca d'Italia, 1989b; Studi Finanziari, 1989) would encourage artificial arbitrage operations. Today's disparities in the taxation of interest, dividends and capital gains would give rise in an integrated capital market to serious distortions both in the location of intermediaries and the size of national markets and in the structure of net yields. Such distortions, moreover, would have undesired effects on exchange rates and lead to calls for the reintroduction of capital controls, thereby moving us away from the objective of monetary unification and the creation of the single market.

Failure to achieve sufficient fiscal uniformity would result in a tendency to bring the taxation of 'unearned' income into line with the least onerous system, with very low or zero rates of taxation and a consequent increase in the burden borne by 'earned' income. Moreover, the need for greater harmonisation is not restricted to the relevant legislation, since whenever the tax on investment income is not withheld at source or is withheld 'on account' – so that full payment is left to the investor's 'fiscal conscience' – there is a very significant difference in many European countries between theory and practice, as described in the Lebègue report (Conseil National du Credit, 1988) on the organisation and prospects of the securities market in France.

Since the *assessment* of investment income also involves considerable difficulties and care needs to be taken to prevent the progressiveness of personal income taxes from discouraging financial saving, a universal system of 'in settlement' withholding tax levied at source might be the easiest and fastest way of ensuring basic fiscal neutrality. As things stand today, such a withholding tax could be levied at a rate of around 20 per cent.

There also appears to be a need for the structures and rates of personal income taxes to be made more uniform, by moving in the direction already taken by the major industrial countries towards a smaller number of tax brackets and thereby establishing *de facto* a system midway between a fully progressive system and a flat-rate system.

4   THE HARMONISATION OF MONETARY AND EXCHANGE-RATE POLICIES

Last, but definitely not least, there are the problems associated with the need for closer coordination of monetary policies and further convergence of economic fundamentals and exchange rates. Failure to move in the direction of enhanced exchange-rate stability would severely hinder the orderly competition between member-countries' financial assets and the efficient allocation of saving. Financial assets denominated in different currencies would no longer be perfect substitutable, which is the indispensable precondition for complete integration.

Autonomous control by each member-country of its money supply and exchange rate is not compatible, in principle, with the aim of creating a unified European financial market, especially since reaping the benefits of financial integration will ultimately depend on the ability to ensure unchanging exchange rates after a period of enhanced stability and, in the end, a single currency.

The analysis of monetary and exchange rate policy problems can be divided conceptually into two parts: the analysis of the *technical problems* regarding the mechanisms for creating money and determining exchange rates, and the analysis of the *'institutional'* problems regarding the identification of the authorities that should regulate these mechanisms. There are analogies with the functions performed in each country by central banks, but there are also significant differences and complications. It needs to be recognised, in fact, that we are dealing with the conditions analysed by coordination theory (Hamada, 1976; Canzoneri and Gray, 1985); even if the cooperative solution is the best overall, there is always the risk that a country will seek to modify the most efficient systemic solution to try to improve its own position (Basevi, 1986).

4.1   Technical Systemic Problems

As long as there are differences between the policies pursued by EMS countries and the international situation continues to exert a destabilising influence on the system, the liberalisation of capital movements risks being accompanied by large speculative flows in expectation of realignments of the central rates. On the other hand, the incomplete convergence of the fundamental economic variables means that we cannot yet do without such changes (Baffi, 1989).

Complete monetary unification thus cannot be achieved without a change in the mechanisms of the EMS. The solution I would propose in this connection is two-pronged:

- all the participating countries should undertake to keep the variations in their bilateral central rates within a predetermined range, say 3–4 per cent, in each year; and
- every country, including the United Kingdom, Spain and Italy should immediately adopt 3.0–3.5 per cent bilateral fluctuation margins.[2]

Realignments involving changes in central rates that cause a 'break' in market quotations provide speculators with a one-way bet. By contrast, if the new and the old fluctuation bands, equal to twice the instantaneous margin, as shown in Masera (1987, Appendix 2), overlap, market quotations are not subject to discrete changes when a realignment is agreed, on the assumption that the exchange rate shifts, in the case of a revaluation, from the upper part of the old band to the lower part of the new one.

The determination of a fluctuation band that will satisfy the foregoing condition thus depends both on the variation in central rates required over time to maintain balance-of-payments equilibrium and on the frequency with which it is desirable, on average, to carry out realignments.[3] As regards the latter aspect, there appear to be two conflicting requirements: on the one hand, realignments cannot be put off for so long that they become obviously inevitable; on the other, the system cannot be transformed into a *crawling peg* with small but frequent adjustments, despite this having been proposed in some quarters. Such a course would annul the fundamental disciplinary effect and credibility of the system, which are consistent with the objective of gradually achieving monetary unification. In the present circumstances, an average frequency of between 12 and 18 months would appear to reconcile these requirements.

As regards changes in central rates, the current inflation differentials – especially with regard to domestic costs in the EMS countries – and the prospective changes in real factors requiring further variations in equilibrium exchange rates would allow member countries to undertake to keep the variations in their bilateral central rates below 3–4 per cent per year. The adoption of this constraint should nonetheless be accompanied, as discussed below, by an undertaking to modify the main mechanisms governing the development of costs that are not consistent with the objective of monetary stability.

Adequate fluctuation of both exchange and interest rates around a more stable central value, coupled with recourse to intervention on the forward foreign exchange market and a commitment to respect an upper limit on central rate variations, would make it possible to counter destabilising movements of speculative capital and to progress towards the goal of monetary unification. This would be achieved without having to accept the hypothesis of Europe advancing at two different speeds in the process of monetary integration, an approach that could be dangerous and which could impose difficult choices on some countries, especially Italy.

Subsequently, both the constraints – presumptive in the case of central rates and operational in that of the fluctuation band – should be gradually tightened, in conformity with the goal of monetary and financial unification. Notably, the maximum permitted variation in central rates should be reduced to zero over a period of five years or so.

It should be noted here that the exchange rate policies pursued so far within the EMS, implying an upward drift of the real exchange rate of some currencies and the depreciation of others – the strong currencies – cannot serve as a model for the phase of monetary integration that we are now entering. The pendulum of central rate variations has swung too far in the direction of infrequent intervention and created a situation that is, on balance, undesirable. In particular, not changing the lira/DM central rate for more than two years has caused current account distortions.[4] Moreover, as the gap between price levels widens, the market becomes subjectively more convinced of the probability of a realignment. The differential between real interest rates thus tends to overestimate the difference between yields expressed in a common currency, as shown by Masera and Bini Smaghi (Masera, 1987). In other words, in order to counter the impact on capital movements it is necessary – with reference to the foregoing bilateral example – to keep interest rates in Italy above, and those in Germany below, the domestic equilibrium level. Thus the distortions in the current account are supplemented by others of a financial nature, which are particularly onerous in Italy's case in view of the large public debt.

4.2   Some Remarks Concerning Italy

More than any other country, Italy will need to back the double commitment to reduce fluctuation margins and limit changes in

Table 7.1 Indices of productivity and money wages and salaries in industry (excluding construction) and the public sector in Italy (1970=100)

	Productivity in industry (excluding construction)[1]	Productivity in the public sector[2]	Per capita money wages and salaries in industry	Per capita money wages and salaries in the public sector
1970	100.0	100.0	100.0	100.0
1971	100.0	103.0	112.3	115.0
1972	107.6	103.9	125.1	126.2
1973	116.6	102.4	148.4	141.4
1974	122.5	101.3	185.8	164.0
1975	113.6	95.6	229.9	183.8
1976	125.9	97.2	284.4	216.2
1977	129.6	95.4	335.0	265.5
1978	135.3	95.3	385.3	318.0
1979	144.3	99.4	463.2	388.1
1980	150.9	100.2	544.9	492.7
1981	153.8	99.1	660.7	635.1
1982	156.4	97.5	776.8	728.9
1983	162.8	91.7	909.9	845.4
1984	176.8	92.9	1044.3	939.5
1985	184.1	94.5	1164.1	1025.7
1986	189.5	97.4	1247.2	1106.7
1987	198.4	100.9	1352.7	1236.8
1988	206.0	n.a.	1459.7	1358.6

Notes: n.a.: not available.
  1 Value added at constant prices per employee.
  2 Estimates for the period 1970–8 by Formez: physical indicators for the activities of Justice, Education, Museums, Hospitals, State Telephone, Post Office, State Railways, etc. Figures for 1979–87 based on physical indicators for the activities of the Post Office and the State Railways.

Sources: ISTAT, Contabilità nazionale (national accounts) and Annuario Statistico (statistical yearbook).

central rates with measures correcting the domestic factors that generate upward pressure on costs and prices, notably wages and the budget deficit. In particular, it will be necessary to guarantee a close link between increases in money wages and improvements in productivity, especially in the public sector. As the public sector is not affected by international competition and is influenced by a policy favouring employment, it has not improved its efficiency or productivity to the same extent as the private sector, especially industry excluding construction (see Table 7.1), which was clearly stimulated by the combined effect of Italy's unaccommodating exchange-rate policy and fierce international competition. By contrast, the divergence of nominal costs and real productivity in the public sector has exacerbated the difficulty of controlling the public finances,

Economics of Integration

Table 7.2 Labour costs, productivity and prices in Italy (Average annual percentage changes)

	Agriculture	Industry	Services	Total
1970–1980				
Labour costs[1]	22.66	18.77	17.46	18.45
Productivity[2]	3.40	3.59	1.32	2.76
Prices[3]	14.64	14.18	15.87	15.06
Consumer prices[4]				14.15
1980–1988				
Labour costs[1]	11.45	13.06	12.39	12.77
Productivity[2]	3.30	3.33	−0.06	1.50
Prices[3]	6.95	9.99	12.32	11.23
Consumer prices[4]				10.61

Notes: 1 Per employee
2 Value added per worker at constant prices
3 Deflator of value added
4 Consumer price index for blue and white collar households
Source: ISTAT, Contabilità nazionale (national accounts); revised series from 1970

already aggravated by the burden imposed by the public debt. For this reason, the distinction made here is between industry and general government, rather than the more usual one between industry, agriculture and services. In reality, while the improvement in agricultural productivity has kept pace with that of industry, productivity in private services has risen no faster than that of public services. As Fiaccavento (1989) has shown in a recent paper, from which the figures for Table 7.2 were taken, the new national accounts series indicate that the productivity of services actually decreased at an average annual rate of 0.06 per cent between 1980 and 1988, while rates of increase of 3.33 per cent and 3.30 per cent were recorded in industry and agriculture respectively.

In the future, the creation of a single market, and hence the opening of private services to international competition, is likely to produce similar effects to those generated in industry and agriculture, as shown by Dell'Aringa (1989). Another reason for focusing on the public sector here is that, in contrast to other EC countries, the mechanisms for determining public sector wages and salaries are less rigorous than in the private sector, with a tenuous link between earnings and productivity that risks causing Italy to be left behind in the monetary integration of Europe.

The difficulty of measuring productivity in the public sector is, of course, well known. While it is reasonable to assume that the prices of goods freely exchanged in the market reflect the value that consumers attach to them, provided that market conditions are not too far from perfect competition, the valuation of public services is more complicated. In the national accounts they are valued on the basis of costs incurred in their production, so that if labour productivity is measured in the conventional way as the ratio of total value added to the number of employees, any increase will not differ significantly from that in real per capita earnings.

It is therefore necessary to have recourse to 'physical' measures of output, which are often not available or only partially significant unless used very carefully. The data for carrying out such calculations are limited and in any case tend to contain a large subjective component, apart from the fact that they are usually available after considerable delay. For these reasons, the analyses in question are restricted to specialist publications and fail to influence economic policy decisions. In this paper estimates of public sector productivity calculated by Formez (1987) have been used, updated on the basis of physical indicators for the Post Office and the State Railways (see note 2 to Table 7.1)

Notwithstanding these measurement difficulties, the figures available lead to an unambiguous conclusion: some of the public sector's lower rate of productivity improvement compared with industry can be justified on the grounds that the nature of the services prevents more efficient production techniques from being adopted in many sectors (in education, for example, there is obviously a limit beyond which labour intensity cannot be reduced); most of the gap, however, has to be attributed to the greater 'inefficiency' with which public resources are managed, since internal controls are rarely an effective substitute for the stimulus of competition or able to overcome the greater inertia in adopting the optimal combination of the factors of production in the sectors where this is technically possible.

The rate of increase in public sector wages in the 1970s and 1980s has nonetheless not differed significantly from that of industry (see Table 7.1), leading to what Baumol calls an 'unbalanced pattern of growth'. It is worth noting, moreover, that the overall increase in public sector wages during the period in which the EMS has been in operation have actually exceeded that of industry, covering the gap accumulated during the mid-1970s, thereby confirming the view put forward in this paper that exchange rate constraint does not impose

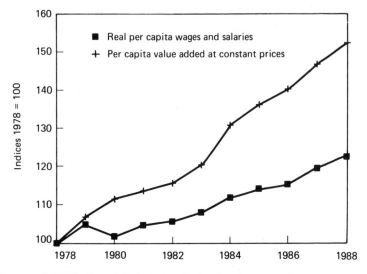

Source: ISTAT, Contabilità nazionale (national accounts)

Figure 7.1   Real wages and salaries and productivity in industry (excluding construction) in Italy

discipline on the public sector in the same way that it does on the private sector, which is exposed to international competition.

Focusing on the ten years of the EMS, the data reveal two rein-forcing scissor-like divergences: on the one hand, earnings in the public sector have grown faster than in industry and on the other, the virtual stagnation of productivity in the public sector has been ac-companied by a significant improvement in that of industry. Between 1978 and 1987 the index of productivity in industry excluding con-struction rose by 46.7 per cent, while that of the public sector rose by less than 6 per cent. By contrast, the indices of real per capita wages and salaries, that is the compensation of employees, in the two sectors rose by 19 per cent and 32 per cent respectively, as shown in Figures 7.1 and 7.2. These developments are summarised in the inverse ratio of the growth in real earnings to productivity in the two sectors.

These results for Italy have been compared with the corresponding figures for Germany. The choice of these two countries is designed to provide a clear example of the differences that still exist between the economies participating in the European Exchange Rate Mechanism. Moreover, if the objective is to achieve monetary and exchange rate

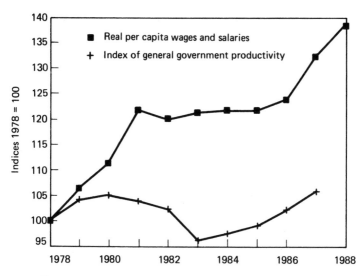

Sources: ISTAT, Contabilità nazionale (national accounts) and Annuario statistico (statistical yearbook)

Figure 7.2 Real wages and salaries and productivity in the public sector in Italy

integration with Germany, this country has to be considered as providing the base line. The comparison with Germany accentuates the opening of the 'scissors'. On the one hand, the increase in public-sector earnings in Germany was 13 per cent less than that recorded in industry (as shown in Figures 7.4 and 7.5, pp. 173, 174); on the other, even though statistics on public-sector productivity in Germany are not available, it appears clear from an analysis of the services supplied that productivity increased more than in Italy.[5] This conclusion is supported by the results of a recent survey by Nomisma (1988) of the productivity of public services in selected countries. Between 1970 and 1986 the index of railway productivity rose by 36.5 per cent in Germany and by only 0.4 per cent in Italy; as for the postal service, in the period 1975–86 productivity rose by 9.4 per cent in Germany and fell by 9.6 per cent in Italy.

The divergence is also due, however, to the ratio of the index of productivity in industry (excluding construction) to that of real earnings, having been higher in Italy than in Germany ever since the inception of the EMS, as is indicated by Figure 7.6 (p. 174). Between 1978 and 1987 the productivity gains in Italian industry (excluding

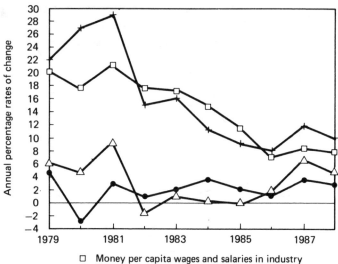

Source: ISTAT, Contabilità nazionale (national accounts)

Figure 7.3   Real and money wages and salaries in industry (excluding construction) and the public sector in Italy

construction) exceeded the rise in real earnings by 23 per cent, while the figure for Germany was less than 1.0 per cent. The burden of protecting the competitiveness of the Italian economy has thus been borne exclusively by the industrial sector, which has had to compensate for the negative performance of the public sector. Despite the increases in real earnings in Italian industry having been smaller than those in productivity, there was nonetheless a significant divergence between real and money wages as shown in Figure 7.3. Obviously, if it were no longer possible to modify the exchange rate, this divergence would inevitably cause a loss of competitiveness.

The international comparison highlights the need for Italy to adopt a policy for public sector incomes that links increases in money wages more tightly to productivity, a principle that has been extensively ignored in recent years. As already mentioned, while market mechanisms and the exchange rate constraint, coupled with international competition, are sufficient to ensure this linkage in the sectors producing tradable goods and services, in the public sector it can only be

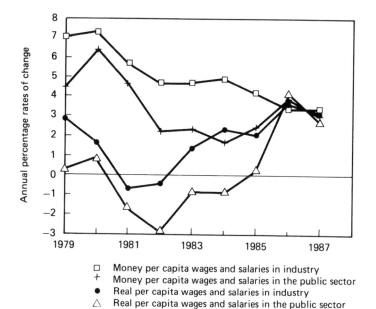

Source: OECD, National Accounts

Figure 7.4   Real and money wages and salaries in industry (excluding construction) and the public sector in Germany

achieved as a result of explicit political action. In my opinion, it would be the first and the most important demonstration of control over the growth in the current expenditure of the public sector as a whole. It would create the conditions for achieving a degree of monetary stability that would permit the pursuit of objectives for employment and competitiveness, without the external restraint returning to suffocate economic growth and the burden of the public debt provoking financial instability.

Even in the private sector of the Italian economy, especially industry, a major problem is that of divorcing wage demands from inflation expectations and strengthening the link between increases in money wages and productivity. This is essential if the competitiveness of industry and market services is not to be undermined by the implementation of the plan to achieve increasing exchange rate stability *vis-à-vis* countries, such as Germany, that have made a close relationship between money wage dynamics and productivity the linchpin of their industrial relations. Figure 7.7 clearly shows, in fact,

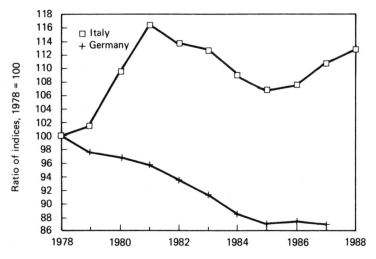

Sources: ISTAT, Contabilità nazionale, (national accounts); OECD, National Accounts

Figure 7.5   Ratio of the indices of wages and salaries in industry (excluding construction) and the public sector in Italy and Germany

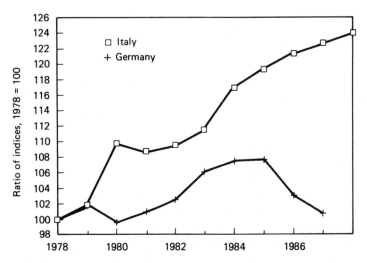

Sources: ISTAT, Contabilità nazionale, (national accounts); OECD, National Accounts

Figure 7.6   Ratio of the indices of productivity and real wages and salaries in industry (excluding construction) in Italy and Germany

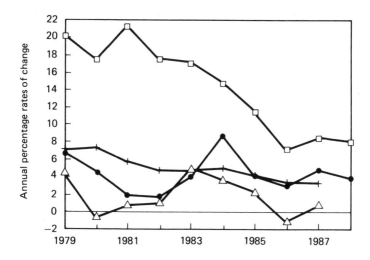

□   Money per capita wages and salaries in industry in Italy
    +   Money per capita wages and salaries in industry in Germany
    ●   Productivity in industry in Italy
    △   Productivity in industry in Germany

Sources: ISTAT, Contabilità nazionale, (national accounts); OECD, National
        Accounts

Figure 7.7   Money wages and salaries and productivity in industry (excluding construction) in Italy and Germany

---

that the gap between the rates of increase in money wages and
productivity in Italian industry is still significantly larger than that
recorded in German industry, despite its having narrowed considerably since the inception of the EMS.

In the light of the foregoing considerations, there appear to be
good grounds for concluding that there will have to be a substantial
change in the mechanisms of wage formation in Italy. It will only be
possible to break out of the vicious circle of inflation fuelled by
increases in costs and expectations of inflation, if wage demands are
made consistent with the hypothesis of zero inflation and earnings are
therefore effectively linked to productivity. The scope for greater
efficiency in the private and public services sectors is considerable, so
that plenty of room exists for increases in real earnings, provided
these are made dependent on the actual achievement of 'real' results.
The reform of the mechanisms of wage formation, which would
contribute significantly to curbing the growth of current government

expenditure, could be accompanied by monetary reform. Italy could precede its European partners (see Section 4.3 below) and anchor the 'new lira' to the ECU. This would permit the public debt to be converted into 'new lire', with a large saving in interest payments.[6]

Models based on the approach developed by Barro and Gordon (1983) indicate that the credibility of the government is the crucial factor in the determination of prices and wages in the private sector. Even more than the commitment to a stable exchange rate and hence to control over the money supply, it is the action of the government in fixing public sector wages and salaries that determines businessmen's expectations. Taken together, the two measures proposed here would, therefore, go a long way towards curbing inflationary expectations. The sectoral adjustment measures already formulated by the government in the Amato plan would produce synergetically complementary effects and complete the strategy for the restoration of public finances to a sound footing.

The reduction in public expenditure, both on current account and for interest payments, would have a beneficial effect on the budget deficit and hence on inflation, creating a virtuous circle in which decreases in the deficit in *nominal* terms would be both the condition and the consequence of decreases in *real* terms. Anchoring the 'new lira' to the ECU would set a seal on the elimination of the gap separating Italy from its partners as regards rates of increase in real and nominal wages and prices. The monetary reform would also defuse expectations of inflation and confirm the switch to the new regime. This virtuous circle would be further strengthened by a mechanism described elsewhere (Masera, 1986). Briefly, a reduction in the rate of inflation brings an immediate reduction in the debt burden since, in the short term, changes in the cost of servicing the public debt in real terms are directly related in a proportional manner to the rate of inflation.

4.3 Institutional Problems[7]

Another problem closely related to that of enhancing the overall disciplinary effect of the exchange rate constraint is that of strengthening monetary cooperation, with the adoption of 'rules of the game' consistent with the goal of unification.

One possible coordination formula involves an 'asymmetrical' solution: the country whose currency is the linchpin of the system ensures that the growth of its monetary aggregates is consistent with domestic price stability. It is up to the other countries in the system to manage their exchange rates *vis-à-vis* the dominant currency through appropriate changes in interest rates. This formula has the advantage – which is not to be undervalued – of providing the whole system with a nominal anchor that benefits from the discipline and monetary 'reputation' of the leader country. However, in the context of a common economic policy framework based on cooperation and designed to promote the growth of the European economy as a whole, this solution appears unacceptable to the other EMS countries, and the leader country itself might be unwilling to accept the constraint inherent in pursuing a passive exchange-rate policy within the area with the resulting reduced freedom in the use of anti-inflationary instruments.

Another formula – one I personally prefer – is based on the coordinated management by the central banks of the Community of the growth rates of both the domestic component of the monetary base and domestic credit. In the aggregate, this would imply a joint decision on the total creation of a monetary base in the area. The following steps would have to be taken to achieve these objectives without weakening the fundamental commitment to monetary stability:

- the present powers of the Committee of Governors of the EC central banks would be enlarged to permit the joint *ex ante* fixing of monetary targets and the coordinated management and control of financial and credit aggregates. In order to strengthen the control of intramarginal exchange rate fluctuations, the impulses generated by the foreign component of the monetary base would have to be promptly reflected in changes in interest rate differentials. More generally, liquidity and credit creation would have to be carefully controlled and coordinated in the context of overall portfolio equilibrium;
- the Committee of Governors would develop a common policy *vis-à-vis* third currencies leading to concerted intervention at the European level; and, most importantly,
- all the European currencies making up the ECU would have to participate in the exchange rate mechanism on an equal footing.

If these steps were accompanied by guarantees regarding the exercise of unaccommodating control over individual countries' monetary and exchange rate policies, the Committee could initially act as a European

Monetary 'Board' and subsequently turn into a European Monetary 'Fund' with member countries as the shareholders and with an organisational structure that would permit it, not only to govern the credit mechanisms needed to ensure balance of payments adjustment, but also to manage on its own account the related exchange and interest rate risks.

This approach requires the 'Fund' to have a legal entity and to be administratively and operationally autonomous, so as to constitute the nucleus of a European central bank, which would enjoy institutional guarantees analogous to those of the central banks, with total independence in ensuring monetary stability. It is also necessary to stress the importance of the continuous monitoring of monetary and exchange rate policy in conjunction with the central banks of the member-states.

At this point, it would be only a short step to create a federal central bank with full 'constitutional' guarantees of its independence, in line with the recent suggestion of the President of the Bundesbank. It is worth recalling in this connection that the US Federal Reserve System was conceived in the context of the gold standard as a 'system' of twelve federal banks that were coordinated but enjoyed a considerable degree of autonomy in their 'domestic' credit markets.

Within this framework it would also be desirable, as discussed by Dini (1989) to cast the ECU in a central role, both as an international reserve asset and as a European currency in parallel with national currencies. In my opinion this would require not only the removal of the restrictions on the acceptability of official ECUs, but also the creation of a link between the official and the private ECU markets allowing central banks to transform their official ECU assets into private ECU balances and *vice versa*. This can be done through an institution, such as the Bank for International Settlements (BIS) that would act both as a clearing house for private ECUs and as the recognised holder of official ECUs.

The Committee of Governors, and subsequently the European Monetary Board, would be responsible for supervising ECU creation, subjecting it to controls analogous, especially as regards reserve requirements (preferably denominated in high-powered ECUs), to those in force for national currencies and taking account of the growth in the latter. This organisation would also be responsible for the centralised management of a part of Europe's foreign currency reserves as well as the actual creation of official ECUs and the operation of the short-term credit support mechanisms serving to discourage and counter speculative attacks on participating currencies.

The development of the ECU would encourage the necessary harmonisation of the taxation of financial assets in the Community. In the situation described above the ECU, if necessary redefined, could in the end become the European currency. The separate national currencies would be gradually anchored to the ECU and become identified with *the* European currency. The ECU liabilities of the Board would constitute Europe's monetary base. Account would naturally have to be taken of the gradual increase in the ECUs in circulation and of their distribution within the Community in order to ensure the control of total monetary assets and credit flows.

The assumption that the Board will have to become a 'sovereign' body raises the question whether it should also be made responsible for monetary supervision at the supranational level, the importance of which in an integrated market for capital and financial services has been already emphasised. In my view, these functions should be performed by a different organisation which, while working in close contact with the Board, would be autonomous. Such a body should provide the necessary, and appropriately dialectic, link between the Board and the various national supervisory authorities.

5 CONCLUSIONS

This paper has focused on three problems that will have to be tackled in the short-term to enable the financial integration of Europe to proceed in an orderly manner: national regulatory systems, the taxation of financial assets and enhanced exchange rate stability in a context of closely coordinated monetary policies. Though there are, of course, other problems, this paper has attempted to identify the nature of these three issues and to indicate possible ways of resolving them.

Today's general move towards greater exchange rate cohesion and monetary stability, set within the framework of a system that is rigorous, but nonetheless able to forestall and counter destabilising currency speculation, means that domestic costs will have to be stable, if integration is to provide the foundation for economic growth and a gradual reduction in unemployment. If European financial integration is to make progress, there will have to be a greater convergence of economic fundamentals. In Italy's case, the challenge of 1992 is inextricably related, on the one hand, to the rehabilitation of its public finances, and on the other, to changes in the mechanisms for determining money wages that will make Italian earnings rise at a 'European' rate and link increases to 'real' improvements in productivity and efficiency. Market mechanisms and exchange rate constraint will force the private sector to move in the desired direction, and the intensification of competition in services, as a result of the single market, will sharpen the spur. In the public sector, by contrast, appropriate action by the political authorities will be necessary.

Notes

1. I am grateful to I. Cipolletta, S. Del Punta, G. Faustini, F. Guelpa and N. Sartor for their comments on an earlier draft of this paper.
2. At present the instantaneous margin is equal to 2.25 per cent for every currency except the lira (6 per cent) and the pound and the peseta, which formally have infinite margins.
3. Denoting the maximum bilateral realignment by $\bar{\Delta}e_{ij}$, the frequency of realignments in annual terms by f, and the fluctuation band common to every country by b, the considerations set out in the text enable the desired width of the band to be expressed in terms of the following inequality: $b \geqslant \bar{\Delta}e_{ij}/f$. If the band were narrower, a realignment would probably cause a discrete 'jump' in market quotations. In practice, it would be preferable for the band to equal rather than exceed the second term, since, provided it remains credible, the narrower the band, the greater its stabilising effect on expectations.
4. The last realignment in the EMS took place on 12 January 1987. From the end of 1987 to the time of writing (April 1989) the lira/DM rate of exchange remained virtually unchanged at around 735 lire = 1 DM.
5. It is interesting that the applications made both in Germany, to the federal institutions, and to international organisations for estimates of the development of public sector productivity indicate that such statistics are not available.
6. With the current (April 1989) levels of interest rates, there would be a reduction of nearly three points in the rate paid on the public debt as a result of its conversion into ECUs. Every one point reduction implies a corresponding decrease in a full year of nearly 10 000 billion current lire in the borrowing requirement.
7. Written prior to the release of the Delors Committee Report (*Report on Economic and Monetary Union in the European Community*), the recommendations advanced here dovetail remarkably well with the contents of that more detailed and comprehensive treatment. Readers familiar with that report will note the substantial agreement here, down to the choice of institutional vehicles and the phasing-in of changes, with the first

and second stages towards monetary union as laid out in the report. At a more general level, both documents cover the difficult central policy and political choices required for meaningful union: (a) concerted macroeconomic management, (b) transfer of sovereignty in monetary and exchange rate policies, (c) amendment of the Treaty of Rome in order to establish the essential European central banking apparatus, (d) the approach to a central currency, and eventual replacement of national currencies through fully fixed exchange rates. Last, it is worth noting that the Delors Committee also rejected the 'asymmetrical' formula for achieving the coordination of monetary policy.

References

Baffi, P. (1989) 'Due momenti del negoziato sullo SME: la banda larga e l'adesione del Regno Unito', Proceedings of the Conference on '*The European Monetary System Ten Years after its Inception: Results and Prospects*', organised by the Ministry of Foreign Affairs and IMI, Rome, December.

Banca d'Italia (1989a) 'Intermediazione finanziaria non bancaria e gruppi bancari plurifunzionali: le esigenze di regolamentazione prudenziale', *Temi di discussione*, no 113.

Banca d'Italia (1989b) 'La tassazione delle rendite finanziarie nella CEE alla luce della liberalizzazione valutaria', *Temi di discussione*, no 114.

Barro, R. J. and Gordon, D. (1983) 'Rules, Discretion and Reputation in a Model of Monetary Policy', *Journal of Monetary Policy*, July.

Basevi, G. (1986) 'Il sistema dei cambi', in Padoa-Schioppa, T. (ed.) *Il sistema dei cambi oggi* (Bologna: Il Mulino).

BIS (1986) *Recent Innovations in International Banking*, April.

Canzoneri, M. and Gray, J. (1985) 'Monetary Policy Games and the Consequences of Non-Cooperative Behaviour', *International Economic Review*, no 3.

CER (1988) *Lo SME dieci anni dopo*, Rome, December.

Commission of the European Communities (1988) 'Mésures fiscales à adopter par la Communautée en liaison avec la libéralisation des mouvements de capitaux', Commission Communication to the Council.

Conseil National du Crédit (1988) *La fiscalité de l'épargne dans le cadre du marché intérieur européen*; the Lebègue report, June.

Dell'Aringa, C. (1989) 'Produttività e retribuzioni: esperienze di relazioni industriali', *Rassegna di statistiche del lavoro*, no 1.

Dini, L. (1989) 'A Single Currency for Europe: Economic Policy and Financial Choices', Conference paper given at the conference on *A Single Currency for Europe*, Confindustria Rome, February.

European Council (1988) 'Conclusions of the Presidency', meeting held in Hanover on 27 and 28 June.

Fiaccavento, C. (1989) 'L'economia italiana tra ciclo e trend', paper given at a seminar held at IMI on 16 March.

Formez (1987) *La produttività nella Pubblica Amministrazione*, Edizioni Il Sole 24 Ore, Milan.

Giavazzi, F. (1989) 'The Exchange-Rate Question in Europe', *Discussion Paper Series*, no 298, CEPR, January.

Hamada, K. (1976) 'A Strategic Analysis of Monetary Interdependence', *Journal of Political Economy*, no 4.

IMI – EC Affairs section (1989) 'Il mercato unico degli enti creditizi', February.

Kenen, P. (1976) 'Capital Mobility and Financial Integration: a Survey', *Princeton Studies in International Finance*, no 39.

Masera, R. S. (1986) 'The Balancing of Public Finance in Italy: Four Arguments', *Rivista di Politica Economica*, no 20.

Masera, R. S. (1987) *L'unificazione monetaria e lo SME – l'esperienza dei primi otto anni*, (Bologna: Il Mulino).

Masera, R. S. (1989a) 'Monetary and Financial Markets in Europe: Regulation and Market Forces', *Review of Economic Conditions in Italy*, Banco di Roma, no 1.

Masera, R. S. (1989b) *Finanza, moneta e risparmio: la prospettiva del'92*, (Rome: Luiss University).

Nomisma (1988) *Produttività e competitività*, Bologna, December.

Obstfeld, M. (1988) 'Competitiveness, Realignments and Speculation: the Role of Financial Markets' in Giavazzi, F., Micossi, S. and Miller, M. (eds) (1988) *The European Monetary System*, (Cambridge, UK: Cambridge University Press).

Sarcinelli, M. (1988) 'L'integrazione finanziaria europea e la sfida politica del 1992: è l'approccio di mercato sufficiente?', *Moneta e Credito*, December.

Steinherr, A. and Gilbert, P. (1989) 'The Impact of Financial Market Integration on the European Banking Industry', Research Report, no 1, Centre for European Policy Studies, January.

Studi Finanziari (1989) 'Il trattamento fiscale dei proventi delle attività finanziarie', February.

Wyplosz, C. (1986) 'Capital Controls and Balance of Payments', *Journal of International Money and Finance*, June.

8 European Integration and Regional Development Policy in Portugal

Manuel C. L. Porto
UNIVERSITY OF COIMBRA, PORTUGAL

1 INTRODUCTION

Regional policy has assumed a far greater importance since Portugal joined the European Community (EC). On the one hand, the opening up of the economy can accentuate existing imbalances, while on the other, integration into the community has provided Portugal with an opportunity to redress various imbalances and improve economic performance within a relatively short time-span.

After describing the imbalances that exist in Portugal in the EC context in Section 2, the institutional framework for promoting regional policy is explored in Section 3; Section 4 shows how funds have been applied and finally, Sections 5 and 6 evaluate the experience of Portugal to date and attempt to draw some conclusions.

2 REGIONAL IMBALANCES IN PORTUGAL[1]

In contrast to most Western European economies, economic activity in Portugal has been concentrated around the coastal zones rather than the hinterland, as shown in Table 8.1. For example, two-thirds of the population live in one-quarter of the country's land area, between the coastal districts of Braga in the north and Setúbal in the south. This same area accounts for over 80 per cent of the contribution to Gross Domestic Product (GDP) made by industry and the service sector.

Within this area, the concentration of activity in the two districts of Lisbon and Oporto is even more marked. Together they account for

183

Table 8.1   Regional GDP per inhabitant 1959–85
(Index, average for Portugal = 100)

Regions	1959	1970	1980	1985
North	85	80	85	86
Coast	91	86	91	91
Interior	60	53	56	55
Centre	75	69	81	79
Coast	85	79	94	87
Interior	62	55	59	63
Lisbon	153	158	131	133
Coast	169	174	138	141
Interior	92	79	90	83
Alentejo	94	75	85	81
Algarve	69	64	92	86
Portugal	100	100	100	100
Coefficient of variation	0.3847	0.4669	0.2859	0.2975

Note: See note 2 and Figure 8.2 for composition of regions.
Source: Instituto Nacional de Estatistica (INE).

only 6 per cent of the country's land area, but 40 per cent of the population and around half the country's industrial and service contribution to GDP. If economic success is measured in terms of GDP per head of population, then only the coastal districts of Lisbon and Setubal exceed the national average, while the interior North and Centre Regions are little above half the national average, as shown in Table 8.1.

These imbalances, implying a serious squandering of national potential, are even more serious in the Community context and the integration process – with the free movement of goods, services and factors of production – may be expected to accentuate this polarisation. Table 8.2 compares GDP per inhabitant in the twelve EC countries in 1985. It will be seen that Portugal had the lowest average figure while several countries enjoyed more than twice the Portuguese level of GDP per inhabitant. Moreover, if inter-regional comparisons are made, per capita GDP in a region such as Hamburg in Germany was eight times that of a poor region in Portugal, and that of the Ile-de-France in France, six times as high.

Table 8.2 GDP per inhabitant in EC countries, 1985
(Index numbers, EC average = 100)

	Average	*Regional*	
		Maximum	*Minimum*
Portugal	50	n.a.	n.a.
Greece	56	60	43
Ireland	69	n.a.	n.a.
Spain	77	98	47
Italy	91	136	54
UK	102	149	82
Holland	105	116	79
Belgium	109	137	83
France	121	170	85
Germany	113	200	81
Denmark	125	147	107
Luxembourg	127		
EC	100		

Note: n.a. not available

Source: EC Commission, *The Regions of the Enlarged Community: Third Periodic Report on the Social and Economic Situation and Development of the Regions of the Community*, 1987, Appendix, p. 27.

However, prior to joining the Community, Portugal had already opened up her trade with the ten existing EC countries. Thus, on joining the Community, over 55 per cent of her exports and 35 per cent of her imports were already with EC member countries. As regards the mobility of the factors of production, by 1985 over half (52 per cent) of all inward foreign investment originated in the Community compared to 42 per cent in 1979. Similarly, the majority of Portuguese emigrant workers moved to Community countries.

This open situation contrasted vividly with the closed situation that existed between Spain and Portugal, despite the common border. In 1985, Spain accounted for only 4 per cent of Portugal's exports and 7 per cent of her imports; less than 4 per cent of foreign investment originated in Spain; only 0.1 per cent of Portugal's legal emigrants settled in Spain between 1960 and 1975, compared with the 58 per cent moving to EC countries during the same period. This was a paradoxical situation, arising to a great extent from Spain's exclusion from the steps which, since the war, had opened up the Portuguese economy – the OEEC, EFTA, GATT and EC trade agreements (see Macedo, Corado and Porto, 1988).

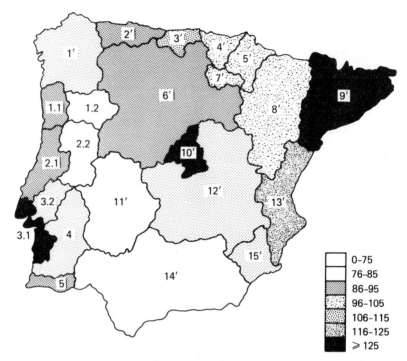

Index, Average value for country = 100
(with separate calculations for each of
the countries); Portugal 1985, Spain, 1986/7.
See note 3 for key to Spain's regions

Figure 8.1   GDP per inhabitant in Spain and Portugal

However, since Portugal joined the EC, this trend has been reversed. By 1988, 11 per cent of Portuguese exports were destined for
Spain and imports from Spain accounted for 13.5 per cent of Portugal's total import bill. Similarly, Spain accounted for 22 per cent of
foreign investment in Portugal in 1987.

The closer links between the two countries will have important
economic consequences, though these will probably differ sharply
from region to region. Given their geographical proximity it can be
expected that the richer Spanish regions will have strong polarisation
effects on the poorer regions of Portugal (Gaspar, 1987). The regional variation in GDP per inhabitant for Portugal and Spain is
shown in Figure 8.1. It will be seen that the least-developed areas of
both countries, with the exception of Madrid, are located in the

central regions. So the breaking down of barriers with Spain and the improved land transport network, could open up new opportunities for the less-favoured interior regions, reducing the present inequalities and leading to a more efficient use of both countries' resources.

3 INSTITUTIONAL MEANS OF PROMOTING REGIONAL DEVELOPMENT IN PORTUGAL

The problems of Portugal's spatial imbalances were first analysed some twenty years ago. The two first Development Plans, for 1952–8 and 1959–64, made no mention of these problems, and although the Intermediate Development Plan of 1965–7 refers to spatial inequalities, there was no suggestion of preparing a regional development strategy.

The Third Development Plan, covering 1968–73, can therefore be considered a milestone, as it devoted a whole chapter to regional development policy. It identified four planning regions for mainland Portugal and laid down certain basic parameters for economic and social development, together with the means of achieving them. At the same time, the first regional institutions to promote socio-economic development were set up – the Regional Consultative Planning Commissions, since 1979 renamed Regional Coordinating Commissions (CCRs).

These Commissions have played a vital role in developing the country's regional policy. They are now responsible for local authority technical support, physical planning and environmental issues as well as socio-economic planning. In 1986 they were integrated in the Ministry of Planning and Territorial Administration and have been made responsible for preparing investment projects for submission to the EC structural funds. The CCR regions are shown in Figure 8.2.

4 REGIONAL DEPLOYMENT OF COMMUNITY STRUCTURAL FUNDS

The benefits of European integration extend far beyond the receipt of structural funds, even though they amount to some 13 per cent of total investment. The opening-up of commerce and the freer

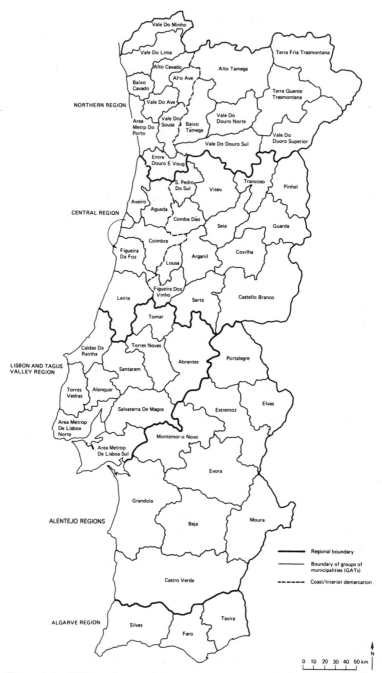

Figure 8.2   CCR regions and municipalities of Portugal

movement of the factors of production have made an important contribution to the results achieved by the Portuguese economy. In the three years since integration, real growth in Portuguese investment was 9.4, 19.5 and 16.5 per cent respectively in 1986, 1987 and 1988, compared with a fall of 1.3 per cent in 1985. During the same period, GDP increased by 4.5, 4.8 and 4.1 per cent annually, compared with 3.5 per cent in 1985, while unemployment fell from 9 per cent in the last quarter of 1985 to 5.6 per cent in the last quarter of 1988.

The real impact of structural funds, namely those of the European Regional Development Fund (ERDF), needs to be assessed from the point of view of the stimulation of a country's economic capacity. The ERDF is intended to encourage greater regional equality, but the logic of a regional development policy can only be justified in the medium term in terms of increased general welfare, while avoiding external diseconomies of large agglomerations and increasing the efficiency of the use of resources at a regional level. In order to maximise external economies and eliminate market imperfections, which obstruct competition, it follows that intervention should take place at the points of divergence. To achieve these goals the various Community intervention mechanisms should be coordinated so as to reinforce each other, as stressed in the recent reform of the Community structural funds, carried out under EEC Regulations 2052/88 and 4253/88, setting out new procedures 'in relation to the purposes of the Funds for structural ends, the efficiency and coordination of their application, the intervention of the European Investment Bank (EIB) and other existing financial instruments'.

An important aspect of regional policy should be to encourage integrated development programmes using local resources. Examples of successful industrial projects in rural areas in EC countries are cited by Quevit (1986), Becatini (1987), Barquero (1988) and the CCRC (1989). An important factor contributing to the success of these schemes has been the rapid progress made in communication techniques, which have helped to overcome the problems of geographical separation.

Within the EC context, the case of Portugal is a good example of how the national interest should be linked to that of EC regional development, showing the benefits of avoiding external diseconomies of concentration and taking advantage of the competitive conditions that exist in most of the regions of Portugal. In the coastal urban conurbations, principally Lisbon, the degree of concentration frustrates these competitive conditions, while increasing costly external diseconomies of various factors, such as transport congestion, land costs and housing bottlenecks. The concentration of power and bureaucracy at the centre encourages the continuation there of inefficiencies within the state administration and the state supported corporations and creates difficulties for those seeking to run businesses in other regions, which would otherwise enjoy a comparative competitive advantage. Despite this, there are many instances, often in rural areas, where small and medium-sized businesses, which have proved competitive in relation to other European enterprises, have been successfully created, showing the role that regional development can have. This phenomenon has occurred mainly in the North and Centre regions, which by the end of the 1970s accounted for 60 per cent of Portuguese industrial exports.

Portugal's geographical location is such that any improvement in the country's land transport system, both road and rail, which connects the developed coastal areas to other EC member-countries, also helps the less-developed interior, because the improved network provides the interior with access to the rest of Europe. This is illustrated in Figure 8.3. Together with the opening-up of the frontier between Spain and Portugal, this should stimulate development along the common border. These zones enjoy some of the major factors of competitive advantage which account for the current, and doubtless future, patterns of Portugal's international trade (see Courakis and Roque, 1987).

The allocation of all structural funds to Portugal, not just those of the ERDF, needs to be analysed in the light of the above criteria. Even where funds, such as the European Agricultural Guidance and Guarantee Fund (EAGGF) or the European Social Fund (ESF), were not set up primarily to promote greater regional balance, the creation of external economies and the removal of market imperfections in the spatial context should be taken into account. And coordination between the funds is also required, as stressed above. This applies as well to financial support given by the European Investment Bank (EIB).

4.1   The Institutional Framework for the Allocation of EC Funds

In order to prepare regional projects for Community funding, an institutional framework was set up under the national coordination of the Minister of Planning and Territorial Administration, by a resolution of the Council of Ministers in January 1986. A subsequent resolution established the guidelines and methods for applying these

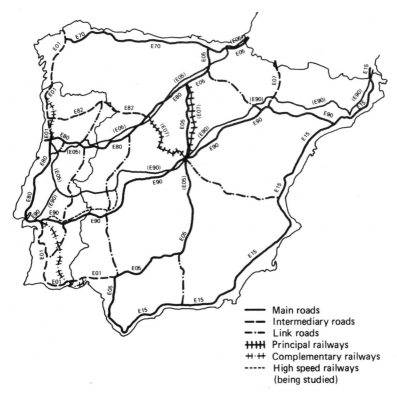

Figure 8.3 Major international road and rail links

funds.[4] The criteria stressed the need to take account of the relationship between national and regional priorities and how to use the intervention instruments for programmes, projects, studies and integrated development operations (Pires, 1987). Particular mention was made of the need to take into account the Regional Development Programme (Programa de Desenvolvimento Regional, PDR), the Broad Planning Guidelines (Grandes Opções do Plano, GOP) and the annual State budgets. The interacting objectives of economic growth and spatial harmonisation were to be pursued simultaneously, to create competitive conditions within an integrated European Community.

A number of different procedures for selecting suitable projects for ERDF financing were laid down. For ERDF investment in public infrastructure a basic distinction was drawn between projects handled by the central administration and public corporations and those handled by local authorities. The former are presented in the first instance to the Study and Planning offices of the respective ministries, whereas the latter go to the appropriate Coordinating Commission, but require municipal backing through the Regional Council.[5] Finally, the General Directorate for Regional Development prepares and presents all projects for the approval of the Portuguese government.

As regards the financing of manufacturing and service sector projects, the Sistema de Estimulos de Base Regional (SEBR), the incentive system then in force (in 1986) to obtain finance in Portugal, was not accepted by those responsible for regional policy within the EC and so no projects in those sectors received ERDF funding during the first two years. For 1988, a new system – the Programa Nacional de Interesse Comunitário de Incentivo à Actividade Productiva, (PNICIAP) (National Programme of Community Interest for Incentives to Production) – was set up and approved.[6] This system incorporated three incentive investment schemes: the Sistema de Incentivos de base Regional (SIBR) (Regional Base Incentive System);[7] the Sistema de Incentivos Financeiros ao Investimento no Turismo, SIFIT) (System of Financial Incentives for Investment in Tourism)[8] and the Sistema de Incentivos ao Potencial Endógeno (SIPE) (System of Incentives for Indigenous Potential). In addition, there are the EAGGF – Guidance and ESF funds, administered by the Ministry of Agriculture, Fisheries and Food and the Ministry of Social Security respectively, which, like the ERDF, come under the final coordination of the Minister of Planning and Territorial Administration. Lastly, use of EIB funds was carried out under a flexible system, in some cases allowing direct links with the Bank.

Three years is too short a period for any significant regional restructuring to have been achieved, so a future reassessment of the extent to which Community funds may have achieved that objective will be required. Nevertheless, some tentative preliminary conclusions on the effects of Community funding by type of fund can be drawn in the light of the stated criteria. These are discussed below.

4.2 Use of the ERDF

Indicative quotas are agreed annually for each member-country. As a result of the new limits set out in January 1986,[9] when the two new countries joined the EC, Portugal was allocated between 10.66 and

Table 8.3 Allocation of ERDF funds to Portugal
(value in billion Portuguese escudos)

	1986		1987		1988		Total	
	Value	*Per cent of total*	*Value*	*Per cent of total*	*Value*	*Per cent of total*	*Value*	*Per cent of total*
Central administration	19.7	34	17.1	28	23.2	34	59.9	32
State corporations, etc.	16.4	29	18.9	31	11.3	16	46.7	25
Local authorities (mainland)	14.1	24	15.1	25	18.5	27	47.7	26
Production ventures	–	–	–	–	9.8	14	9.8	5
Autonomous region of Azores & Madeira	7.4	13	9.2	15	6.2	9	22.8	12
Total	57.6	100	60.3	100	69.0	100	186.8	100

Source: Direcção Geral do Desenvolvimento Regional, (DGDR) (General Directorate for Regional Development)

14.20 per cent of total ERDF funds. And a high level of disbursement to Portugal was achieved, reaching 12 and 11 per cent of total funds in 1986 and 1987 respectively. Within the country quotas were established by type of user as follows:

- Central administration — 30–35 per cent
- State corporations, etc. — 15–17.5 per cent
- Local authorities: mainland — 15–17.5 per cent
- Production projects — 22–27 per cent
- Autonomous regions of Azores and Madeira — 8–13 per cent
  Total — 90–110 per cent

As already mentioned, because the Community refused to accept the SEBR system, no funds could be allocated to production projects in 1986 and 1987. The resulting distribution of funds by class of user is shown in Table 8.3. It will be seen that in general the state corporations and local authorities absorbed the quotas not used by the production sector, whereas the central administration and autonomous regions remained within their quota allocation.

Table 8.4   Deployment of ERDF funds by country (million ECU)

Country	Industry/ service sector		Infra- structure		Studies		Pro- grammes & Article 15		Total	
	1986	1987	1986	1987	1986	1987	1986	1987	1986	1987
Belgium	3	1	12	7	0.01	–	3	14	19	23
Denmark	1	5	7	4	0.02	0.1	3	3	11	13
France	19	3	210	133	0.14	5.0	30	135	259	276
Germany	54	63	29	51	0.14	–	–	–	83	114
Greece	2	2	290	192	–	–	18	108	310	302
Holland	–	–	23	15	0.04	–	5	5	28	20
Ireland	22	25	103	69	–	0.1	1	67	125	161
Italy	186	121	627	789	0.35	0.1	–	31	813	941
Luxembourg	–	–	–	2	–	–	1	1	1	3
Portugal	–	–	381	360	–	0.2	–	29	381	389
Spain	11	–	630	633	–	–	–	27	641	660
UK	84	44	372	451	1.43	1.0	56	132	513	628
Total	382	264	2685	2708	3.30	6.4	117	554	3184	3530

Source: J. Palma Andrés, CCRC, 1989.

The resulting concentration of investment in infrastructure was strongly marked in Portugal, although in all other EC countries except Germany, more funds were allocated to infrastructure than to the industrial and service sectors, as can be seen from Table 8.4.

4.2.1   Basic Public Infrastructure

Some assessment of the degree of success in meeting the twin objectives of a more even regional balance and a better use of national resources through a more equitable geographical distribution of funds, may be obtained by examining the allocation by region, and the breakdown into coastal and interior areas as shown in Table 8.5. Because of the existing inequalities, not only is the absolute amount important, but also the allocation per head, which takes account of the population living there.

It would appear that although funds in 1986 and 1987 made some contribution to reducing the regional imbalances, with low per capita values for the Lisbon and Tagus Valley region, in 1988 this most favoured region obtained over 40 per cent of all ERDF funds, resulting in a per capita value above the national average. Consider-

Table 8.5 ERDF expenditure on public infrastructure by region
(value in thousand Portuguese escudos)

	1986		1987		1988		Total	
	Per cent	Per head	Per cent	Per head	Per cent	Per head	Per cent	Per head
North	26	3.7	47	6.6	28	4.0	34	14.3
Coast	12	2.1	42	7.0	23	3.9	26	13.0
Interior	14	11.8	5	4.5	5	4.4	8	20.7
Centre	34	9.9	17	5.0	14	4.2	22	19.1
Coast	20	11.4	12	6.8	5	3.1	12	21.3
Interior	14	8.4	5	3.0	9	5.4	9	16.8
Lisbon and Tagus Valley	8	1.2	13	2.0	43	6.5	22	9.7
Alentejo	26	23.3	13	12.1	7	6.4	15	41.8
Algarve	5	7.6	10	15.1	8	12.6	8	35.3
Mainland Portugal	100	5.2	100	5.3	100	5.4	100	15.9

Sources: DGDR and INE.

ing the interior as distinct from the coastal zones of the North and Centre, only in 1986 were the per capita values above the national average, since when no contribution was made to promoting a better regional equilibrium.

It is also interesting to see whether it makes any significant difference which authority is responsible for administering funds. The results of this analysis are shown in Tables 8.6 and 8.7. The funds for national infrastructure investment administered by the state and state corporations (or similar corporations) are more than twice as large as those administered by local authorities. However, as the effects of such investments usually extend beyond the regions or subregions in which they were made, their benefits cannot be evaluated only at the regional level. For example, the thermal energy programme in Sines, Alentejo, which accounted for more than 90 per cent of the investment made by the state and state corporations in this region in 1986 and 1987, contributed significantly to the entire nation's energy infrastructure. Similarly, the investment in roads in the interior North Region in 1986, the coastal Centre Region in 1986 and 1987,

Table 8.6　ERDF expenditure on national infrastructure 1986–8 (value in thousand Portuguese escudos)

	1986		1987		1988		Total	
	Per cent	Per head	Per cent	Per head	Per cent	Per head	Per cent	Per head
North	27	2.7	54	5.3	26	2.4	36	10.4
Coast	11	1.3	50	6.0	24	2.7	28	10.0
Interior	16	9.8	3	2.0	2	0.8	7	12.6
Centre	38	7.9	14	2.9	8	1.6	20	12.4
Coast	26	10.4	11	4.4	4	1.4	14	16.2
Interior	12	5.3	3	1.2	4	1.7	7	8.2
Lisbon and Tagus Valley	3	0.3	8	0.8	52	5.1	20	6.2
Alentejo	28	18.2	14	9.3	4	2.5	16	30.0
Algarve	4	4.6	11	11.3	10	9.7	8	25.6
Mainland Total	100	3.7	100	3.7	100	3.5	100	10.9

Source:　DGDR and INE.

and Alentejo in 1988 improved the national road network, not only within and between these regions, but also with Spain and other EC countries. For this reason, an examination of local authority invest-ment might be a better guide to the extent to which spatial equilib-rium between the regions was achieved.

In order to achieve a minimal national balance, ERDF's National Regulation, article 6, lays down that municipal investment funds should be allocated in proportion to the Region's participation in the Financial Equilibrium Fund (FEF). This ensured that investment took account of population and other relevant economic and social factors.[10] It is usual for the Regional Councils to apply different criteria when submitting projects for approval. Not surprisingly, the results have also been influenced by the initiative and competence developed by some local authorities in preparing, presenting and lobbying for the acceptance of their projects, as well as the inherent technical merits of the proposal.

Table 8.7 shows local authority investment by region from 1986 to 1988. It will be seen that over these three years, three regions – the

Table 8.7 ERDF and FEF expenditure on local authority infrastructure 1986–8 (value in thousand Portuguese escudos)

	1986 ERDF		FEF	1987 ERDF		FEF	1988 ERDF		FEF	Total ERDF		FEF
	Per cent	Per head	Per cent	Per cent	Per head	Per cent	Per cent	Per head	Per cent	Per cent	Per head	Per cent
North												
Coast	25	1.0	33	30	1.3	33	32	1.6	34	29	3.9	33
Interior	17	0.8	22	20	1.0	22	21	1.3	22	19	3.1	22
	9	2.0	11	10	2.6	11	11	3.5	11	10	8.1	11
Centre												
Coast	25	2.0	23	24	2.1	23	25	2.7	23	25	6.8	23
Interior	6	1.0	13	14	2.4	13	8	1.7	13	10	5.1	13
	19	3.1	10	10	1.8	10	17	3.6	10	15	8.5	10
Lisbon and Tagus Valley	22	0.9	26	27	1.2	27	26	1.4	27	25	3.5	27
Alentejo	20	5.1	11	10	2.7	11	12	4.0	11	14	11.8	11
Algarve	7	3.0	6	8	3.8	6	5	2.9	5	7	9.7	6
Mainland Portugal	100	1.4	100	100	1.6	100	100	1.9	100	100	4.9	100

Source: DGDR and INE.

Table 8.8   The VALOREN and STAR programmes
(value in thousand Portuguese escudos)

| Regions | VALOREN | | | | STAR | |
| | Public | | Private | | | |
	Per cent	Per head	Per cent	Per head	Per cent	Per head
North	45	0.5	25	0.1	52	0.9
Centre	32	0.5	53	0.2	18	0.6
Lisbon and Tagus Valley	12	0.1	18	0.0	22	0.4
Alentejo	4	0.4	4	0.1	1	0.1
Algarve	7	0.7	0	0.0	7	1.3
Mainland Portugal	100	0.4	100	0.1	100	0.6

Source: DGDR and INE.

Centre, Alentejo and Algarve – obtained the highest levels of investment per head of population, usually exceeding the FEF percentage. As regards the distribution between coastal and interior areas, in all three years the interior of the North and of the Centre had per capita values above the national average and nearly always above the corresponding coastal value. Overall, the Centre interior received a percentage considerably higher than the FEF percentage while the North interior received a little below it.

4.2.2   Sector Programmes – VALOREN and STAR

Two projects, VALOREN, which encourage the use of indigenous resources in expanding energy, and STAR, a major telecommunications development programme, provide interesting case studies. Investment in these two programmes by region is shown in Table 8.8. The most interesting feature of both programmes is the concentration of investment in the two regions of the North and Centre – over 75 per cent for VALOREN and nearly 70 per cent for STAR. Data for the breakdown between coastal and interior areas were not available, but probably given the nature of the VALOREN project, a higher proportion was invested in the interior.[11]

4.2.3 Production Ventures

As already mentioned, ERDF funds began to be used in 1988 for production ventures, with the first two tranches in April and August. Regional allocation was to some extent based on legal criteria, which encouraged job creation or a reduction in regional disequilibrium. But the results also reflected the prevailing structural conditions and local initiative. Investment under this head is shown in Table 8.9. SIBR funds were distributed fairly evenly among the three regions of the North, Centre and Lisbon and Tagus Valley, which implies a much higher level of expenditure per head of population in the Centre Region.[12] The Algarve, it will be noted, benefited least.

SIFIT, on the other hand, achieved a high degree of equality in terms of investment per head of population, with the exception of the Algarve, which received no funds from the first tranche, but 23 per cent of the second tranche. Again, no breakdown was available between the coastal and interior areas, but because of legal priorities, the interior probably received the higher proportion of funds.

4.3 Use of EAGGF – Guidance

These funds apply to horizontal Community programmes covered by EEC Regulation 797/85 and 355/77 as well as vertical community programmes specific to Portugal, such as the cut-back of wine-growing under Regulation 2239/86 or the Special Programme for the Development of Portuguese Agriculture (PEDAP) under Regulation 3828/85, which also covers fishing, aquiculture and fishing fleets. Table 8.10 shows the distribution of multisector agricultural aid finance, together with the gross added value for agriculture by each Coordinating Commission area for comparison. Only Alentejo received a much higher percentage of funds than GDP contribution – 23 per cent of total EAGGF–Guidance funds compared with its 17 per cent contribution to agricultural GDP, while the Centre received less than its contribution – 20 per cent of funds compared with 27 per cent contribution to agricultural GDP. Of course, actual agricultural production may vary considerably from potential capacity in the regions, so some differences in the percentages should be expected. But it seems that these differences were also due to structural factors such as size of property and management capacity (Cunha, 1986)

The three most important agricultural sectoral programmes went to finance the definitive abandonment of wine growing, olive production and the forestry action programme. The regional deployment

Table 8.9 ERDF funds: SIBR and SIFIT programmes 1988 (value in thousand Portuguese escudos)

| | SIBR 1988 | | | | | | SIFIT 1988 | | | | | |
| | April tranche | | August tranche | | Total | | April tranche | | August tranche | | Total | |
Regions	Per cent	Per head	Per cent	Per head	Per cent	Per head	Per cent	Per head	Per cent	Per head	Per cent	Per head
North	29	1.0	30	1.0	30	2.0	44	0.3	29	0.2	36	0.4
Centre	41	2.8	20	1.4	31	4.2	22	0.3	14	0.2	18	0.4
Lisbon and Tagus Valley	22	0.8	45	1.6	34	2.3	22	0.1	29	0.2	26	0.3
Alentejo	7	1.4	3	0.6	5	2.0	12	0.4	5	0.2	9	0.6
Algarve	1	0.4	2	0.6	1	1.0	–	–	23	1.5	12	1.5
Mainland Portugal	100	1.2	100	1.2	100	2.5	100	0.2	100	0.2	100	0.4

Source: DGDR and INE.

Table 8.10   EAGGF – Guidance: multisector agriculture

Region[1]	Total[2] Per cent	Gross added valued to agriculture (Per cent of total)
North	26	25
Douro to Minho	17	17
Trás-os-Montes	9	8
Centre	20	27
Beira coast	13	16
Beira interior	7	11
Lisbon and Tagus Valley	26	25
Alentejo	23	17
Algarve	5	6
Mainland Portugal	100	100

Notes: 1. EAGGF data relate to agricultural regions, which differ somewhat from the areas of the Coordinating Commission nor do they correspond precisely to the coast–interior divisions in Figure 8.2.
 2. Includes Reg. (EC) 797/85; Reg. (EC) 355/77; Reg. (EC) 3828/85 with funds of 23.78, 11.11 and 11.39 billion Portuguese escudos respectively. EAGGF – Guidance funds allocated totalled nearly 60 billion Portuguese escudos.

Source: DGDR and IFADAP.

of funds together with their sectoral contribution is shown in Table 8.11. Clearly, wide regional differences are to be expected for specific sectors reflecting the varying agricultural potential of the different regions, but again such differences appear to have been accentuated by institutional factors. It is worth noting that Ribatejo and the West accounted for 82 per cent of all finance under the wine growing cut-back scheme, and while it is by far the biggest wine producing area it contributes less than 50 per cent of total income from wine. As for olive production, the two regions of Ribatejo and the West and Alentejo accounted for about 80 per cent of programme finance, although Alentejo might have been expected to obtain more than the 44 per cent allocated as it contributes 52 per cent of production. In

Table 8.11   EAGGF – Guidance: wine- and olive-production and forestry

Region[1]	Vineyard cut-back[2]		Olive production[3]		Forestry Action Programme (PAF)	
	fund aid	gross added value	fund aid	gross added value	fund aid	gross added value
			(Per cent of total)			
North	5	38	12	17	44	15
Douro to Minho	2	21	–	2	n.a.	n.a.
Trás-os-Montes	3	17	12	15	n.a.	n.a.
Centre	7	16	8	15	33	34
Beira coast	3	11	2	3	n.a.	n.a.
Beira interior	4	5	6	12	n.a.	n.a.
Ribatejo and West	82	43	36	10	7	19
Alentejo	3	2	44	52	8	30
Algarve	3	–	–	5	8	2
Mainland Portugal	100	100	100	100	100	100

Notes: 1. See Note 1 to Table 8.10.
2. Reg. (EC) 2239/86 – total funds of approximately 0.7 billion Portuguese escudos.
3. Reg. (EC) 3828/85 – total funds of approximately 0.8 billion Portuguese escudos.
4. Funds of approximately 7.23 billion Portuguese escudos to districts as defined in Table 8.1 and Figure 8.1.

Source: IFADAP and INE 1985.

the case of the forestry action programme, the main beneficiaries were the North Region (44 per cent) and the Centre region (33 per cent), with the North receiving much more than its contribution to national production (15 per cent). Ribatejo and the West and Alentejo made little use of this programme although they contributed nearly half of the total income generated by the sector.

Lastly, it seems that the allocation of money from the EAGGF–Guidance to the fishing industry depended not only on physical conditions (harbours and ports), but also on other factors, particularly the business acumen within different regions (see Table 8.12). Obviously, investment was concentrated along the coast. Funds for

Table 8.12   EAGGF – Guidance: fishing and fisheries

Region[1]	Fishing industry[2]	Construction and modernisation of fishing fleet etc.[3]
		(Per cent of total)
North	25	10
Douro to Minho	24	10
Trás-os-Montes	2	–
Centre	15	50
Beira coast	13	50
Beira interior	2	–
Ribatejo and West	42	25
Alentejo	–	1
Algarve	17	14
Mainland Portugal	100	100

Notes: 1. See Note 1 to Table 8.10.
2. Reg. (EC) 355/77 – total funds of approximately 1.4 billion Portuguese escudos.
3. Reg. (EC) 4028/86 – total funds of approximately 4.36 billion Portuguese escudos.

Source: IFADAP.

the fishing industry were largely allocated to the Ribatejo and West region, which accounted for over 40 per cent of all funds, while the remainder was divided fairly evenly between the other regions. But half the funds for modernising the fishing fleet went to the Centre Region, largely because of the initiative of firms located near the ports of Aveiro and, to a lesser degree, Figueira da Foz.

4.4   Use of ESF Finance

These funds can have an important influence on the efficient use of resources in the labour market, through professional training and management and the eradication of market imperfections, especially through the dissemination of better information on employment opportunities. In a country where a large percentage of the population is still engaged in the primary sector – over one-fifth of the

Table 8.13 ESF: Regional distribution (value in thousand Portuguese escudos)

Region	1986		1987		1988		Total[1]	
	Per cent	Per head	Per cent	Per head	Per cent	Per head	Per cent	Per head
North	12	2.9	35	6.3	15	3.6	19	12.7
Coast	10	2.8	32	6.6	14	3.7	17	13.1
Interior	2	3.5	3	4.1	1	2.8	2	10.4
Centre	31	10.1	37	8.9	14	4.4	27	23.4
Coast	29	14.3	33	12.0	11	5.0	23	31.3
Interior	2	2.4	4	3.0	3	3.2	4	8.6
Lisbon and Tagus Valley	55	12.0	25	3.9	69	14.2	52	30.2
Alentejo	1	1.0	1	1.6	1	1.3	1	3.9
Algarve	1	2.1	2	2.5	1	2.2	1	6.7
Mainland Portugal	100	7.8	100	5.7	100	7.4	100	20.8

Note: 1. Total funds of approximately 144 billion Portuguese escudos.

Source: Secretary of State for Employment and INE.

labour force in 1985 – the redeployment of labour to the secondary and tertiary sectors is particularly important.

The breakdown of funds between regions is shown in Table 8.13. Yet again, the more developed Lisbon and Tagus Valley Region received the major share of funds, obtaining 55 per cent in 1986 and nearly 70 per cent in 1988. Even in per capita terms, the region was strongly favoured; in 1988, for example, it received three times more per capita than any other region and ten times more than the much less developed region of Alentejo. This makes it clear that the ESF aggravated the imbalance in Portugal and failed to help those areas which would most have benefited from special treatment.

This distribution of funds to the better-off region of the country is probably the result of the decision-making centre being concentrated in Lisbon and most of the firms proposing projects which qualify for Social Fund support also being located there. The results indicate that the spatial distribution to date has failed to redress labour imbalances through the redeployment of labour and the provision of training, both essential to improving competitiveness.

4.5 EIB Finance

The last source of funds available for the promotion of integrated development is the European Investment Bank (EIB). EIB funds had been available to Portugal since 1976, although the amounts were small compared with those available from 1986. The distribution of area specific EIB funds by region is given in Table 8.14. Alentejo, it will be noted, obtained the largest share of area-specific funds, both prior to accession (30 per cent) and subsequently (about 50 per cent), despite the absence of an allocation in 1986. Because the region is so sparsely populated this resulted in per capita figures many times higher than those for the other regions. However, many of the projects funded were of national importance, with benefits accruing far beyond this region.

There were sizeable differences in the distribution of funds pre- and post-accession to the other regions. Prior to accession, the Centre obtained a larger share of funds than the North or Lisbon and Tagus Valley, which was accentuated in the per capita figures. After entry into the EC, the North increased its share, coming second after Alentejo in total over the three years 1986–8, with a share of over 40 per cent of total funds in 1988.

As regards the distribution between coast and interior, it will be seen that none of the area specific funds went to the North after entry to the EC, although a World Bank programme did to some extent compensate for this. In the Centre region the interior maintained a similar share of the country's funds before and after 1986 and between 1986 and 1988 obtained over twice as much per capita as had been allocated to the coastal area, although this was still below the national average.

5 GENERAL ASSESSMENT OF THE PORTUGUESE CASE

While the use of funds should have been aimed at improving the country's economic structure, particularly through regional development, there were nevertheless other economic considerations, not least the need to obtain as much finance as possible from the various funds. In fact, Portugal has succeeded in absorbing considerable

Table 8.14 EIB: regional distribution¹ (value in thousand Portuguese escudos)

Region	Pre-accession Total		Pre-accession 1986		Post-accession 1987		Post-accession 1988		Total¹	
	Per cent	*Per head*	*Per cent*	*Per head*	*Per cent*	*Per head*	*Per cent*	*Per head*	*Per cent*	*Per head*
North	21	2.3	35	0.6	8	0.7	42	6.4	29	7.7
Interior	9	5.9	–	–	–	–	–	–	–	–
Coast	12	1.6	35	0.7	8	0.9	42	7.6	29	9.2
Centre	31	7.0	54	1.9	3	0.6	11	3.6	11	6.1
Interior	10	4.6	14	1.0	3	1.2	9	6.2	7	8.4
Coast	21	9.2	40	2.8	–	–	2	1.1	4	3.9
Lisbon and Tagus Valley	13	1.5	11	0.2	–	–	9	1.4	5	1.6
Alentejo	30	21.5	–	–	81	52.4	36	36.1	51	88.5
Algarve	5	6.2	–	–	8	8.9	2	3.3	4	12.2
Mainland Portugal	100	4.1	100	0.7	100	3.7	100	5.7	100	10.1

Note: 1. Throughout this period area specific funds totalled 127.2 billion Portuguese escudos out of a total of approximately 204.1 billion Portuguese escudos; the corresponding figures before accession were 39.5 billion out of 52.6 billion and after accession 87.7 billion out of 151.5 billion.

Source: EIB.

funds since joining the EC, despite the need to adapt to new mechanisms and inevitable institutional delays. As already mentioned, an institutional delay was also responsible for the concentration of investment in public infrastructure programmes during the first two years of operation.

Clearly funds should have been used to develop the potential of the less favoured areas – notably in the interior – where the breaking down of the frontier with Spain and improvements to the road transportation network are improving the competitive environment, instead of channelling funds to areas such as Lisbon, where too heavy a concentration of investment has brought harmful external diseconomies. In this respect, the analysis has yielded some interesting results. On the one hand, it has shown the successes and failures of different funds to meet the objective of improving equilibrium, on the other it has highlighted a number of structural obstacles which frustrate the achievement of this objective.

As regards the regional use of ERDF funds to finance public sector infrastructure projects, the data show that after the promotion of some improvement in equilibrium in 1986 and 1987, the most favoured region of Lisbon and the Tagus Valley in 1988 received over 40 per cent of the total funds.

Bearing in mind the economic underdevelopment of the interior and the opportunity offered by integration, the interior should have been more specifically targeted. The results show that only in 1986 were the per capita values of expenditure on public infrastructure for the interior regions above the national average. However, the values for the interior regions were comparatively high for infrastructure investment by local authorities. And the distribution of EIB funds markedly favoured the interior zone of the Centre Region but not the interior zone of the North Region, which received no such funds after accession.

As to the use made of other funds, it would appear that the prevailing structural conditions in Portugal, together with the legal criteria for selection, affected the distribution of funds. This occurred in the case of the SIBR and the private element of the VALOREN, where very low values were recorded in Algarve and Alentejo compared to high values in the North and Centre Regions, and in the second tranche of the SIBR in the Lisbon and Tagus Valley Region. The Centre also did particularly well out of the EAGGF programme for the modernisation of the fishing fleet. In all cases, the success in the North and Centre Region already mentioned was to a great extent due to the nature of the market structure, comprising dynamic small and medium-sized businesses. In the case of the VALOREN project, the physical characteristics of the regions also contributed to the project's success.

On the other hand, the low level of take-up of EAGGF–Guidance finance in the North – with the exception of the forestry sector, and the Centre – as compared with Ribatejo and West and Alentejo, may in large part be attributed to social and institutional factors. These latter two regions undoubtedly benefited from their stronger management structure and the number of larger-sized properties.

Finally, it is important to recognise that institutional factors (the centralisation of the power of decision), and the level of expertise in preparing, following-up and executing projects help to explain the increasing concentration of ESF funds in the Lisbon area. This without doubt caused distortions, detrimental to the other regions, whose local economies could, and should, have benefited far more from these funds.

6   CONCLUSIONS

The conclusions which can be drawn from the Portuguese case may also be relevant to an assessment of Community regional policy in general.

It is clear that there must be no trade-off between the goal of increased regional equilibrium and that of higher growth rates for countries generally. In Portugal underperformance has in part been the result of external diseconomies in the main centres of economic activity, notably Lisbon, and the inefficient use of national resources, particularly in the less-developed regions. In order to meet the challenge of the single European market, regional development should be an essential target for the Portuguese authorities.

The analysis has also highlighted some areas of failure in the regional allocation of funds to meet the national and European objectives laid down. This is equally true of public and private sector funding. In many cases, the inefficient distribution of funds was the consequence of the very structural conditions which the funds themselves were designed to amend. In certain instances, the allocation of funds achieved the very opposite of what was intended, so that funds were channelled – for structural reasons – to programmes or projects which contributed to the creation of yet greater imbalances and inefficiencies within the Portuguese economy.

It can, therefore, be concluded that the authorities must not have a merely passive role (or in some cases an actively harmful role) but must intervene positively to ensure that funds are allocated in such a way as to achieve the most efficient use of all resources, avoiding external diseconomies, creating external economies and clearing the markets.

Notes

1. Throughout this paper, unless otherwise stated, Portugal refers to mainland Portugal and excludes the autonomous regions of the Azores and Madeira.
2. Portugal's regions and districts have been grouped as follows:

   North   Coast includes Viana do Castelo, Braga, Porto
               Interior   includes Vila Real, Bragança
   Centre   Coast includes Aveiro, Coimbra, Leiria
               Interior   includes Viseu, Guarda, Castelo Branco
   Lisbon   Coast includes Lisbon, Setúbal
               Interior   includes Santarém
   Alentejo includes the districts of Portalegre, Evora, Beja
   Algarve includes the district of Faro.

   This grouping differs from the Comissoẽs de Coordenação Regionais (CCR's) areas, corresponding to the Unidades Territoriais para Fins Estatisticos (NUTs) as at present defined – see Figure 8.2.

3. Key to Spain's regions:
   1' Galicia; 2' Asturias; 3' Cantabria; 4' Basque region; 5' Navarre; 6' Castile-Leon; 7' Rioja; 8' Aragon; 9' Catalonia; 10' Madrid; 11' Estremadura; 12' Castile-La-Mancha; 13' Valencia; 14' Andalusia; 15' Murcia.
4. Resolution 44/86 of 5 June approved the 'Regulation of Application' to the National Territory of the ERDF. The regions of Azores and Madeira operate different procedures.
5. The Regional Council within the ambit of each Coordinating Commission is made up of the mayors elected by each group of municipalities (see Figure 8.2) and representatives from the metropolitan areas of Porto and Lisbon.
6. Presented to the Commission of the EC by the Portuguese Government on 10 June 1987 under cover of article 10 of the ERDF regulation, and accepted by the ERDF Committee the following November. PNICIAP also became responsible for the financing of Agentes de Dinamização Economica (Economic Dynamising Agents).
7. Created by Decree 15-A/88. Decree 483/B88 in December amalgamated SIBR with SINPEDIP.
8. Set up by Decree 420/87 and regulated by Order 976/87, both in December.

9. EC quotas for different countries are laid down in Article 4 No 3 of the 1984 Regulation, with new limits established on 1 January 1986, when Spain and Portugal joined the EC.
10. Article 10 of the Local Finance Law (Law 1/87) (the FEF) includes an equal distribution (10 per cent) plus funds calculated on number of inhabitants; area; direct taxation per capita; municipal road network; number of dwellings; number of parishes and level of socio-economic development. This tends to allocate funds in favour of the less developed zones.
11. Figures available for the Centre Region confirm this. Of the 80 per cent allocated to the interior, 34 per cent was used in the very deprived Pinhal subregion.
12. The Centre's success was related to its positive social and economic characteristics, and the dynamic business community in which small and medium-sized businesses play a big part.

References

Barquero, A. V. (1988) *Desarrollo Local. Una Estrategia de Creacion de Empleo* (Madrid: Ediciones Piramide).

Becatini, G. (ed.) (1987) *Mercato e Forze Locali: Il Distretto Industriale* (Bologna: Il Mulino).

Comisão de Coordenação da Regiao Centro (CCRC) (1989) 'Industrializacao em Meios Rurais e Competitividade Internacional', 1989 International Seminar, Coimbra.

Courakis, A. and Roque, F. (1987) 'On the Informational Content of Technology Variables in Explaining Trade Patterns', paper presented at the Conference on Trade Patterns and Policies in Southern Europe, ISE, Lisbon.

Cunha, A. (1986) 'The Impact of the Common Agricultural Policy on the Agricultural Development of the Portuguese Regions', (unpublished) M.Ph. thesis, University of Reading, UK.

Gaspar, J. (1987) *Ocupação e Organização do Espaço. Retrospectiva e Tendências em Portugal. Ós proximós 20 anos* (Lisbon: Calouste Gulbenkian Foundation) vol. 1.

Macedo, J. B., Corado, C. and Porto, M. (1988) *The Timing and Sequency of Trade Liberalisation Policies: Portugal 1948–86* Working Paper 114 (Lisbon: Faculdad de Economia, Universidad Nova de Lisboa, and Washington DC: World Bank).

Pires, L. M. (1987) *Guia para os Utilizadores Portugueses*, Fundo Europeu de Desenvolvimento Regional (FEDER) (Lisbon: Banco de Fomento Nacional 2nd ed.)

Quevit, M. (1986) *Le Pari de l'Industrialisation Rurale* (Lausanne: Editions Regionales Européennes)

Part III
Econometrics

9 The Interplay of Theory and Data in the Study of International Trade

Edward E. Leamer[1]
UCLA, CALIFORNIA

1 INTRODUCTION

This is a survey of the empirical studies of the determinants of the commodity structure of international trade.[2] In the context of this review, two deeper questions are addressed:

1. What role does empirical work actually play in the development of our discipline?
2. What role should empirical work play in the development of our discipline?

The subject of economics is and probably always will be highly theoretical in the sense that much of what economists believe comes from the manipulation of thought experiments rather than from observation of real phenomena. Pause a moment to reflect on your first introduction to the simple model of supply and demand. Did you come to believe in this model because of compelling empirical evidence, or did you spend most of your time learning how to manipulate it? If the former, exactly what empirical support was offered for the model?

Usually introductions to economics make very little reference to real phenomena. Students are sometimes asked to imagine their responses to a higher price. If asked to wear a purchaser's hat, most imagine that they would purchase less, though some think otherwise. If asked to wear a supplier's hat, most imagine that they would probably sell more, though again some think otherwise. The notions of a demand response and a supply response are thus connected to reality, at least so we imagine. But this kind of introspective 'empirical' work forms a very inadequate basis for the market model. In

213

addition, an individual's response to a change in price would have to be unique and therefore describable in terms of a mathematical function. That requires some extra imagination. But an even greater degree of imagination is required to form the belief that the intersection of the aggregated demand and aggregated supply curves has special meaning. This price–quantity couple is said to select the price at which 'most' trades take place and to identify the total number of trades. Does this remarkable hypothesis have an empirical basis or is it just a case of imagination out of control? How did you come to believe in this model? In most introductory economics courses the emphasis is on manipulation – shifting one curve while holding constant the other. If there were genuine interest in the empirical validity of the model surely some effort would be made to identify real settings in which the model works well and other settings in which it is not especially apt.

Indoctrination through manipulation is a feature of most graduate programmes in economics. Most of the time is spent learning how to manipulate complicated mathematical models. Hardly any is spent studying the factual basis of these models, or any facts at all. Indeed, many of the models presented to students are so abstract that they seem unlikely ever to have any relation to real world phenomena.

International economics is no exception.[3] Most time is spent manipulating ever more complicated models. New models and those who have the mathematical skills to manipulate them receive most of the adulation. Indeed, it is difficult even to come up with a single name of an international economist whose fame depends on a finding, not a model.[4]

The teaching of international economics usually proceeds through four different models, each of which is extensively manipulated to derive many interesting conclusions. These models are:

(i)   the Ricardian model with a single labour input and with technological differences between countries;
(ii) the Ricardo–Viner model with a single mobile factor, labour, and a set of specific factors which are immobile across industries;
(iii) the Heckscher–Ohlin (H–O) model with at least two factors and at least two commodities;
(iv) a variety of models with increasing returns to scale and market power at the level of the firm.

These models serve as vehicles for discussing the sources of international comparative advantage. These sources are (a) differences in technology, (b) differences in factor supples, (c) economies of scale (d) differences in tastes, and (e) barriers to trade.

The first question that we address is: what role does empirical work actually play in the development of international economics? More specifically: how have empirical findings influenced professional opinions regarding the sources of comparative advantage? Two empirical findings seem to have had a major impact. The first was Leontief's (1953) discovery that US imports were more capital-intensive than US exports. This was widely regarded as a great blow against the H–O model, which was met by a variety of theoretical responses that either amplified or altered the H–O model. The second major empirical finding was the extensive amount of 'intra-industry' trade catalogued by Grubel and Lloyd (1975). The extent of intra-industry trade is also regarded as a blow against the H–O model and is at least partly responsible for the large theoretical literature on models with increasing returns to scale and product differentiation. Other than these two results, beliefs about the sources of international comparative advantage have not been greatly affected by any observations.

That seems a bit disappointing, which leads to the second question: what role should empirical work play in the development of our discipline? This is a more difficult question. It is one thing to grumble that the discipline is too theoretical. It is another thing to understand why this is so and what might alter the situation. Economic models would predict roughly equal net values of the marginal piece of theory and the marginal piece of empirical work. This equilibrium could be altered by a tax on theory or a subsidy for empirical work. It is possible that tastes could be changed. An academic group that relies on its own internal judgements to evaluate its output rather than on an external market may have tastes that are amenable to manipulation. But I think the best solution is innovative effort to improve the quality of the empirical work that is done. What we need is better, more consequential empirical work that will replace the marginal theory.

How can empirical work be improved? My ideas on this are summarised in the following series of questions:

1. Does the empirical work have a solid base in economic theory?

2. Are the hypotheses phrased in a way that puts intellectual capital
   at risk?
   (a) Is there an alternative hypothesis?
   (b) Is the null hypothesis sensible?
      (i) Is the null hypothesis sharp?
      (ii) Is the counterfactual vague and/or absurd?

It may seem obvious that empirical work should have a solid base
in economic theory, but in fact it is usually extraordinarily difficult to
translate a theoretical model into an empirical application. There are
many examples of work in international economics in which the
translation of the theory into an empirical exercise was casual and
'intuitive', and which were later discovered to have been fatally
flawed.

It may also seem obvious that influential empirical work requires
interesting and refutable hypotheses. But in fact a lot of time is
wasted testing hypotheses that are surely false, a fact that is revealed
whenever the data sets are large enough. The sharp hypotheses that
are represented by each of the four models listed above, or each of
the five sources, are not sensibly tested. These models are only tools,
each of which is appropriate in some circumstances and inappropriate
in others. Empirical studies should therefore not attempt to test the
validity of the theories. Instead, empirical work should identify the
circumstances under which each of the tools is most appropriate, or
should measure the 'amount' of trade that is due to each of the
sources. Neither of these tasks has been accomplished or often even
attempted. It is not clear how to define precise counterfactuals that
might lie behind the question regarding the relative importance of the
various sources of comparative advantage for the case of technological differences and increasing returns to scale. It is difficult to phrase
a counterfactual that is neither vague nor absurd.

2 WHY IS NOT EMPIRICAL WORK MORE INFLUENTIAL?

The methodological parable of hypothesis formulation, testing and
reformulation does not offer much insight into the directions that are
taken by the main intellectual currents of economics. This is no doubt
partly the result of the difficulties of drawing convincing inferences
from non-experimental data. But part of the problem is caused by the
way that empirical work is conducted. A basic shortcoming of much

empirical work is that the answers to the following questions are a resounding 'No':

1. Does the empirical work have a solid base in economic theory?
2. Are the hypotheses phrased in a way that puts intellectual capital at risk?

Many studies in international economics have floundered because they were inadequately linked to any fully articulated theory. One example is the Leontief paradox, which according to Leamer (1980) is no paradox at all if the Heckscher–Ohlin–Vanek (H–O–V) model is used as a guide. Another example is a cross-commodity multiple regression study which, again using the H–O–V theory, cannot produce the empirical regularities that most authors presume (Leamer and Bowen, 1981).

Cross-industry comparisons are based implicitly on the suspicious assumption that all industries are identical after controlling for a casually selected set of variables. Distinct 'competing' models are often combined empirically merely by the inclusion in a linear regression of one variable for each of the separate models. A proper foundation for this kind of regression would be a composite theory that described the simultaneous effect of all the influences. When there are only distinct models capturing different features of reality, it may make sense to report simple correlations rather than partial correlations offered by multiple regression analysis.

Even when the theory is clear, empirical studies can have limited impact because they put too little intellectual capital at risk. Part of the reason that there is little at risk is that the next two questions generally also have the same answer 'No':

2(a) Is there an alternative hypothesis?
2(b) Is the null hypothesis sensible?

The usefulness of a clearly stated alternative hypothesis seems clear but many studies take a single model as given and concentrate on finding estimates of its parameters. Even my own work, Leamer (1984), lacks a sensible and testable alternative hypothesis to the Heckscher–Ohlin model and in its absence this empirical study only measures the accuracy of the model and does not test it against a clear alternative. Nevertheless, this work can be influential if the Heckscher–Ohlin model is shown to be surprisingly accurate and if the data suggest surprising conclusions regarding the factor supplies that critically determine the direction of trade. But it would have been much better to have been able to describe precisely how economies of scale might affect the regressions.

The lack of an alternative is an important shortcoming. But a more important problem is that the hypotheses we study are usually not very 'sensible'. The reason they are not sensible is that the answers to the following pair of questions are both 'Yes':

2b (i) Is the null hypothesis sharp?
2b(ii) Is the counterfactual vague and/or absurd?

Possibly one of the greatest shortcomings of empirical work in economics is the excessive focus on sharp hypotheses that are clearly false and rejectable if the data are informative enough. Here are some false hypotheses: purchasing power parity, factor price equalisation, the 'efficiency' of markets (zero transactions costs), the 'law of demand' (for example, symmetry of a system of demand functions). The hypotheses that theorists derive are guides; they are not intended to be exact descriptions of reality. What is desperately needed, instead of wasting time 'testing' hypotheses that are clearly false, is some clear thinking about how the sharp hypotheses provided by theorists can be translated into interesting and verifiable approximate hypotheses.

Another problem is that many hypotheses make reference to vague counterfactuals. For example, it is not clear what is the counterfactual implicit in most studies of 'the effect of market concentration on trade performance'. There is a need to be more specific, partly to improve communication and partly because the relationship between concentration and trade performance may depend on the sources of variation of concentration.

2.1 Sharp Hypotheses: Are They Worth Testing?

It is my contention that most interesting refutable hypotheses will take one of two forms: 'There is no reason to alter your opinions about the way the economic system operates', or 'A (popular) theory is a good guide for decision making'. In order to test the first kind of hypothesis it is necessary to be as clear as possible in defining what it is that economists think. Then empirical work should attempt to identify 'news'; that is, evidence that is intellectually upsetting. In order to test the second hypothesis it is necessary to be explicit about the use to which a model is put. Then empirical work should attempt to demonstrate that the theory leads to significant errors of decision making.

For example, the theory of purchasing power parity (PPP) is false. A little bit of travelling is all it takes to make clear that commodity arbitrage across space is not instantaneous. Thus there is no point in testing the sharp version of PPP, notwithstanding dozens of papers that claim to do so. Nonetheless, the theory does raise interesting hypothesis-testing questions such as: does arbitrage work more slowly than most economists imagine? does arbitrage work so slowly that PPP is not a useful guide for policy making and prediction? These two questions amount to the question: 'Is PPP approximately correct?' The first question defines the adequacy of an approximation in terms of conformity to the current state of mind of economists; the second question defines the adequacy of an approximation in the context of a decision problem. In order to phrase these questions precisely it is necessary to determine what it is that economists think and what it is that they do with their models.

A defect of most 'tests' of economic hypotheses is that no consideration is given to defining the sense in which the hypothesis is approximately correct. This is not merely an oversight, since it is far from easy in most circumstances to select a suitable measure of the accuracy of an approximation. Furthermore, there are no conventions that can be relied upon for testing approximate hypotheses analogous to the (sad) convention of testing sharp hypotheses at a fixed level of significance. Most researchers test the sharp hypotheses at fixed levels of significance. If the sharp hypothesis is really a surrogate for an approximate hypothesis, then the significance level for testing the sharp hypothesis ought to be a decreasing level of sample size. Otherwise, as the sample size grows, the approximate hypothesis will surely be rejected, whether it is true or not.

These comments apply specifically to studies of comparative advantage: there are no sharp hypotheses that are worth studying. The best that empirical work can do is to influence how economists think about the sources of comparative advantage, and possibly to influence their attitudes toward the efficacy of trade policy. But most of the empirical work has not focused on this goal. Possibly that is why it has not been all that consequential.

2.2 Factor Price Equalisation

The factor price equalisation theorem is a good example since economists have not made the mistake of 'testing' it. The theorem
identifies conditions under which the international exchange of commodities brings about the complete equalisation internationally of
wages and the returns to all other factors of production. Among the
assumptions are constant returns to scale of production, free internal
mobility of factors, and equal numbers of tradable goods and factors.
No one takes these assumptions to be perfect descriptions of reality.
Nor does anyone think that factor prices are exactly equalised by
international trade. Nonetheless, the theorem is given a great deal of
attention.

The question being addressed by the factor price equalisation
theorem is: what is the effect of international trade on the returns to
factors? The proof is not especially difficult or elegant, but it is
efficient and correct. The theorem is mathematically fragile and is a
good way of listing the reasons why factor prices may not be equalised by trade. The theorem is surprising since complete equalisation
would not have been expected. The conclusion is obviously important since it suggests that trade barriers may have major effects on
factor prices. All these things are true, but not, I believe, the real
reason why the theorem attracts attention. The most important
reason is that the factor price equalisation theorem is used as a
rhetorical device to support the broader argument that trade in goods
tends to equalise the returns to factors and in particular to lower the
return to relatively scarce factors and to raise the return to relatively
abundant factors. The force of the argument relies heavily, but
implicitly, on the sturdiness of the theorem: if the assumptions are
'approximately' correct then factor prices will be 'approximately'
equalised by trade.

It should come as no surprise that there are no empirical tests of
this rhetorical device. There are studies of the extent to which
measurement errors contribute to the impression that factor prices
are greatly different. And there are studies of the effect of trade
liberalisation on factor prices. But it would be pointless to test the
literal interpretation of the factor price equalisation theorem since
the theorem may be rejected at the outset without recourse to any
data.

Many other theorems which are also only rhetorical devices have
been subjected to empirical testing. These theorems will surely be

rejected if the data sets are rich enough. Purchasing power parity is a good example.

2.3 Counterfactuals

'The problems which can afflict counterfactuals are two: vagueness and absurdity.' 'Vagueness is solved by explicitness.' But 'the less vague the theory, the more likely is a counterfactual using the theory to encounter absurdity.' McCloskey (1987), 'Counterfactuals', *The New Palgrave*.

The thought experiments implicit in manipulating some explanatory variables like tax rates are sufficiently clear. But the changes that might be required to manipulate other explanatory variables like the number of firms in an industry may be vague and/or absurd. Of the four basic variables that are hypothesised to determine trade, the most clear counterfactuals refer to changes in the level of artificial barriers. Changes in the levels of resource supplies like the population or the capital stock are not as clear. Just how do we imagine that the level of the population might be altered? The exact meaning of counterfactuals referring to economies of scale, technological differences and taste differences are almost a complete mystery.

Vagueness and absurdity of econometric counterfactuals can often be alleviated by hypothesising a second equation which expresses the explanatory variable of interest in terms of some other variable or variables that are more clearly manipulable. An explicit consideration of the components of variability of the explanatory variable in the primary equation may give rise to the realisation that its effect depends on how it is varied.

Here is an example of a model that may seem initially to admit a clear counterfactual, but which on further reflection is not so clear. The model is made genuinely clear by adding a couple of equations that characterise more completely the nature of the counterfactual that is under consideration. Suppose that a randomly selected group of students is 'encouraged' to study more, and subsequently they do study more than a control group and also get higher grades. Based on observations of this group, the following regression is estimated:

$$Test_i = \alpha + \beta Study_i + \delta Enc_i$$

where *Enc* is a zero-one variable indicating whether the subject was encouraged to study, *Test* is the test score, and *Study* is the hours of studying. This data set yields a particular positive estimate of β. Is this evidence that 'studying' improves grades? It is important to make clear the kind of intervention that is implicit in this statement.

Two points need to be understood. First, β, the effect of studying on the test score, probably depends on the form of encouragement. For example, studying that is 'encouraged' by monetary payments can be expected to have a greater effect on test scores than studying at gun point. Second, the only kinds of interventions that are logically possible manipulate the level and character of encouragement and not studying directly. Thus, research that claims to demonstrate that 'studying' improves grades cannot unambiguously be used as evidence that students should be encouraged to study harder, unless the form of the encouragement conforms closely with the experiment. It is convenient to refer to 'the effect of studying' on test scores only if reasonably diverse kinds of encouragement that led to the same amount of studying all had the same effect on test scores.

This discussion can be made more precise by referring to a model of the form:

$$Test_i = \alpha + \beta_i Study_i + \delta_1 Carrot_i + \delta_2 Stick_i$$

$$Study_i = \theta_0 + \theta_1 Carrot_i + \theta_2 Stick_i$$

$$\beta_i = \gamma_0 + \gamma_1 Carrot_i + \gamma_2 Stick_i$$

where 'encouragement' is either a 'carrot' or a 'stick', and where the effect of studying on test scores depends on the form of the encouragement. In the context of this model it is easily seen that the effect of studying on test scores depends on whether the encouragement is a carrot or a stick. One could sensibly refer to 'the' effect of studying only if $\gamma_1 = \gamma_2 = 0$. Incidentally, if only one form of encouragement is used, this model implies a separate coefficient of studying for those who are encouraged and those who are not. This would be one way of studying the sensitivity of the studying effect to the form of the encouragement.

An example closer to the concerns of this paper is the hypothesis that market structure affects trade performance. Economists interested in the forces that determine export performance have estimated regressions with some measure of trade of the industry as the dependent variable and a set of industry characteristics including the number of firms in the industry as explanatory variables:

$$Trade = \beta(Number\ of\ firms) + \gamma\ x$$

where x stands for a rather large collection of other variables that describe an industry.

What question does β answer? What is the nature of the change in the industry that is imagined when all other characteristics are held constant and the number of firms is varied? This seems to me to be a very unclear counterfactual. Are firms to be sprinkled from heaven onto the industries? To paraphrase J. S. Mill: two industries which were alike in everything except the number of firms would have the same number of firms as well.[5]

What this model needs is a second equation expressing the number of firms in an industry as a function of some variables which can more clearly be manipulated, at least hypothetically. For example:

$$Number\ of\ firms = \theta\ Anti + \delta\ Scale$$

where *Anti* might be the level of anti-trust activity directed at the industry and *Scale* might be a technical measure of the returns to scale. Incidentally, this is not meant to suggest necessarily that the level of anti-trust activity is a suitable exogenous variable, only that altering the level of anti-trust activity is a clear counterfactual; altering the number of firms is not. Furthermore, the coefficient β on the number of firms in the trade equation is likely to depend on the reasons why the number of firms varies by industry. Thus the model possibly needs to express β in terms of the variables that determine the number of firms, as was done above for the studying/test score system.

3   EMPIRICAL STUDIES OF THE RICARDIAN MODEL OF COMPARATIVE ADVANTAGE

A simple model of comparative advantage was offered by Ricardo in 1817. This familiar model includes two countries (England and Portugal), two goods (cloth and wine), a single input (labour), and constant ratios of output to input. The purpose of this model seems to lie primarily in the area of political philosophy, not economic science. Ricardo brilliantly makes the argument that both countries benefit from trade, even if one has an absolute productive advantage in both goods. Thus the imposition of trade barriers makes one and possibly both worse off. But it is difficult to detect anything genuinely empirical about this model. What are its testable propositions? Here are three:

1. *International trade is beneficial.* This proposition has been subjected to a great deal of theoretical scrutiny. Theorists have pointed out that some individuals may be made worse off if the ownership of productive factors is unequal and if factors are sector-specific. Theorists have proposed many other models with features such as economies of scale, non-competitive market structures, etc., in which the proposition may not be true. But, to my knowledge, there has never been an attempt to test the very basic premise of economics that individuals and/or economies possess enough knowledge and skill to ensure that 'voluntary' trades can occur only if both parties 'expect' to be made better off. Furthermore, I cannot imagine how this proposition might be tested. Surely this is a Lakatosian 'hard core' proposition that is protected from falsification by the undefinable word 'voluntary'.

2. *The observed terms of trade are bounded between the comparative labour-cost ratios of the two countries.* This proposition is too closely associated with the very simple one-factor, two-goods, two-country model to be worthy of empirical scrutiny. And multi-dimensional generalisations of the Ricardian constant cost model, such as the one-factor, many-good, many-country model, are complex enough to make the link between the theory and the empirical work very difficult. It should thus not come as a surprise that (to my knowledge) there have been no studies of the relationships between relative prices of different commodities and relative labour costs. For that matter, if one were to do a serious study of the technological determinants of commodity prices, one would surely include more than just the labour input.

3. *A country exports the commodity in which it has a comparative labour-cost advantage and imports the commodity in which it has a comparative disadvantage.* Again this proposition is too closely associated with the very simple model to be worthy of empirical scrutiny. But loose versions of this proposition were the first to be studied empirically. Before discussing these studies, we need to

increase the dimensions of the Ricardian model, and also allow for imperfect substitutability between foreign and domestic goods.

Haberler (1933) and Viner (1937) generalise the simple Ricardian model to the case of two countries and many goods, producing the familiar 'chain of comparative advantage'. This chain is formed by ordering commodities by their relative comparative labour productivities in the two countries. Multiplying the inverse of these productivity ratios by the relative wage ratios in the two countries produces an ordered set of relative prices. One country produces the first subset of commodities with price ratios less than one, and the other country produces the second set of commodities with price ratios exceeding one. The borderline between these two sets of commodities depends on demand conditions, but the ordering does not.

The sharp implications of this theory concerning the extent of specialisation can quickly be rejected by any data set. At even finely defined commodity categories, complete specialisation is not the rule. Clearly the model needs amendment. The tradition, sometimes only implicit, is to treat goods produced by different countries as imperfect substitutes. This may be a casual way to deal with aggregation problems caused by the fact that only commodity aggregates are observed.

The following is a Ricardian model of price formation coupled with the assumption that goods produced by different countries are imperfect substitutes. Given that there is only labour input, we can use the labour productivity in industry k in a country i and the prevailing wage to solve for the price of the commodity. Let

Q_{ik} = output of industry k in country i

L_{ik} = labour used in industry k in country i

q_{ik} = labour productivity = Q_{ik}/L_{ik}

If labour is uniform in quality, mobile across industries, and the only input, then we can define

w_i = the wage rate in country i

and solve for the product price

$$p_{ik} = \text{wage}_i/(\text{output per man})_{ik} = w_i/q_{ik}$$

Further, assume that the relative demand for the commodity offered by countries i and i' satisfies the relationship:

$$X_{ik}/X_{i'k} = f_k(p_{i'k}/p_{ik}) = f_k[(q_{ik}/q_{i'k})/(w_i/w_{i'})]$$

where X_{ik} = exports of commodity k by country i.

In words this last result asserts that export success depends on relative labour productivity. However, this is not enough to justify the cross-commodity comparisons that are now to be discussed because of the commodity subscript on the demand function f_k. It is also necessary to eliminate this commodity subscript by assuming that the elasticity of substitution between goods produced at different locations is the same for all goods $f_k = f$. This seems pretty doubtful.

The earliest study of the commodity composition of international trade by MacDougall (1951) implicitly uses this framework and explains the export performance of the USA relative to the UK in terms of the relative labour productivity. Using 1937 data MacDougall finds the export ratio $X_{ik}/X_{i'k} > 1$ whenever the US productivity advantage $q_{ik}/q_{i'k} > 2$ and notes that wage rates in the US were approximately twice wages in the UK. This seems supportive of the Ricardian model, but MacDougall notes that even in industries in which the UK has a strong comparative advantage, the UK share of the US market is small. He suggests that trade barriers may be the reason and finds that US tariffs did offset the UK's comparative-cost advantage in many products.

Balassa (1963) extends the work of MacDougall and offers 'An Empirical Demonstration of the Classical Comparative Cost Theory'. Two of his results based on 1950 data for 28 manufacturing industries are:

$$X_k = -53.3 + 0.721 \, P_k \qquad\qquad R^2 = 0.64$$

$$X_k = -181.2 + 0.691 \, P_k + 0.14 \, W_k \qquad R^2 = 0.81$$
$$ (0.167) \quad\;\; (0.102)$$

where X_k = the export ratio $X_{ik}/X_{i'k}$, P_k = the productivity ratio $q_{ik}/q_{i'k}$, and W_k is the wage ratio: $(\text{US wage})_k/(\text{UK wage})_k$. Balassa's first result seems to support the comparative cost model in the sense that US export performance tends to be relatively good in industries in which it has a relatively large labour productivity. The second result is something of a mystery. Why should high wages lead to export success? This is very suggestive of a multi-factor model including human capital as one of the inputs.[6]

What can we learn from this? What answers can we offer to our two basic questions: does the empirical work have a solid basis in an acceptable economic theory? and are the empirical hypotheses phrased in a way that puts intellectual capital at risk? My answers are: 'Not really' and 'I don't think so'. The Ricardian model is not sensibly interpreted literally when it is studied empirically, and the non-literal translations of the model seem to have a lot of loose ends. And what we can learn from the Ricardian regressions seems to me very limited. Is it a surprise that the USA did relatively well compared with the UK in industries in which its labour productivity is relatively high? What is the alternative model? And why do these labour productivities differ? I do not find appealing the notion that there are technological differences between the UK and the USA that confer comparative advantage on one or the other. Maybe it is only an aggregation phenomenon.

4 EMPIRICAL STUDIES OF THE HECKSCHER–OHLIN MODEL

Economists generally regard the H–O model as superior to the Ricardian model for the intellectual reason that it offers a 'deeper' and more 'appealing' explanation of trade which does not have to resort to the 'gimmick' of technological differences. England trades cloth for wine with Portugal not because the technological knowledge of cloth production is unavailable in Portugal or because grape growing and wine production are a genetic mystery to the British, but rather because the Portuguese are relatively well supplied with land in a grape growing climate and relatively poorly supplied with capital.

An elegant version of the H–O general equilibrium model is based on the assumptions of:

(a) identical homothetic tastes;
(b) constant returns to scale and identical technologies;
(c) perfect competition in the goods and factor markets;
(d) costless international exchange of commodities;
(e) internationally immobile factors of production that can move

costlessly among industries within a country;
(f) equal numbers of goods and factors;
(g) sufficient similarities in factor endowments that countries are all in the same 'cone of diversification'.

These assumptions imply that all countries have the same factor prices (factor price equalisation) and identical input-output ratios. These assumptions also imply that the vector of net exports is a linear function of the vector of factor supplies.

The production side of the even general equilibrium model can be summarised by the system of equations:

$$Q = A^{-1} V \tag{1}$$

$$w = A'^{-1} p \tag{2}$$

$$A = A(w, t) \tag{3}$$

where Q is the vector of outputs, V is the vector of factor supplies, A is the input–output matrix with elements equal to the amount of a factor used to produce a unit of a good, p is the vector of commodity prices, and w is the vector of factor returns. Equation (1), which translates factor supplies V into outputs Q, is the inverted form of the factor market equilibrium conditions equating the supply of factors V to the demand for factors AQ. Equation (2), which translates product prices into factor prices, is the inverted form of the zero profit conditions equating product prices p to production costs $A'w$. Equation (3) expresses the dependence of input intensities on factor prices w and on the state of technology t, $A(w, t)$ being the cost minimising choice of input intensities at time t. The assumption of constant returns to scale implies that A depends on the factor returns w but not on the scale of output Q.

The consumption side of the model is neutralised by the assumption of identical homothetic tastes. Then, in the absence of barriers to trade, all individuals face the same commodity prices, and they consume in the same proportions:

$$C = sC_w = sA^{-1} V_w \tag{4}$$

where C is the consumption vector, C_w is the world consumption vector, V_w is the vector of world resource supplies, and s is the consumption share. Thus trade is

$$T = Q - C = A^{-1} V - sA^{-1} V_w = A^{-1} (V - sV_w). \qquad (5)$$

The consumption share s will depend on the level of output and also on the size of the trade balance, $B = \pi'T$, where π is the vector of external prices which in the absence of trade barriers would equal the internal prices p. Premultiplying (5) by the vector of prices π and then rearranging produces the consumption share:

$$s = (\pi' A^{-1} V - B)/ \pi' A^{-1} V_w = (GNP - B)/GNP \qquad (6)$$

This is often called the Heckscher–Ohlin–Vanek model referring to Vanek's (1968) use of the assumption of homothetic tastes. Using this H–O–V model, trade is a linear function of the endowments. The more basic Heckscher–Ohlin proposition is that trade arises because of the unequal distribution of resources across countries. A pure H–O model thus implies that if the ratios of resources were the same in all countries then there would be no trade. Several of the assumptions listed above can be altered without affecting this basic H–O proposition. These assumptions only introduce non-linearities in the relationship between trade and factor supplies.

One assumption that cries out for change is that of equal numbers of commodities and factors. An alternative is that the number of commodities exceeds the number of factors. Then factor price equalisation need not occur, and if countries are sufficiently different in their relative factor supplies, they will have different factor prices and they will produce different subsets of commodities which use intensively their relatively cheap factors.

4.1 Factor Content Studies of the Heckscher–Ohlin Model

The first and by far the most influential study of the H–O model was done by Leontief (1953), who found that US imports in 1947 were more capital intensive relative to labour than US exports. This empirical 'paradox' sparked a search of great breadth and intensity for a theory that could explain it. Among the explanations were labour skills, trade barriers, natural resource abundance, capital-biased consumption, and technological differences.

It turns out that the Leontief finding is compatible with the USA being capital abundant (Leamer, 1980). This is a good illustration of the need for a clear conceptual framework when empirical work is being carried out since in its absence substantial mistakes can be made. One suspicious step in Leontief's calculation is the separate computation of the factor content of exports and imports, whereas the H–O–V theory relates to net exports. The H–O–V theory implies that the factor content of trade satisfies the relationship $F \equiv AT = V - sV_w$, where the consumption share is $s = (\mathrm{GNP} - B)/\mathrm{GNP}_w$. From this set of equations we can separate the capital and labour content of trade:

$$F_K = X_K - M_K = K - sK_w, \quad F_L = X_L - M_L = L - sL_w$$

where X and M refer to exports and imports respectively. Leamer (1980) shows that the Leontief finding, that exports are less capital intensive than imports, $X_K/X_L < M_K/M_L$, is compatible with capital abundance, $K/L > K_w/L_w$. Using $X_K = M_K + K - sK_w$, and $X_L = M_L + L - sL_w$, it is possible to write

$$X_K/X_L - M_K/M_L \propto \frac{K_w/L_w}{M_K/M_L}\left[\frac{K}{K_w} - s\right] - \left[\frac{L}{L_w} - s\right]$$

where the proportion symbol indicates that a positive number multiplies this expression to create an equality. From this expression it is easy to see that if capital is more abundant than labour and if the consumption share separates the abundance ratios, $K/K_w > s > L/L_w$, then exports must be more capital intensive than imports, $X_K/X_L > M_K/M_L$. (Under these conditions, both parts of the expression are positive.) But if the consumption share is small enough so that $K/K_w > L/L_w > s$ and if imports are capital intensive, $(K_w/L_w)/(M_K/M_L) < 1$, then the last term can be sufficiently negative for imports to be more capital intensive than exports even though the country is relatively capital abundant. This cannot happen if there are only two factors, but a three-factor example is given by Leamer (1980) and corrected by Heravi (1986).

A correct way to use the H–O–V theory to infer the relative abundance of factors from the factor content of trade refers to the factor content adjusted for the trade imbalance, $F^A = AT - V_w B/\mathrm{GNP}_w$. Using (5) and (6), this adjusted factor content is

$$F^A = AT - V_w B/\mathrm{GNP}_w = V - (\mathrm{GNP}_i/\mathrm{GNP}_w)V_w$$

Multiplying each side by $(V_{wk})/(\mathrm{GNP}_i/\mathrm{GNP}_w)$ produces:

$$Z_{ik} \equiv (R^A_{ik}/V_{wk})/(\mathrm{GNP}_i/\mathrm{GNP}_w) = (V_{ik}/V_{wk})/(\mathrm{GNP}_i/\mathrm{GNP}_w) - 1 \qquad (7)$$

Table 9.1   Ratio of adjusted net trade in factor to national endowment, 1967
(per cent)

	USA	UK	Japan
Capital	0.08	−12.86	−5.47
Labour	−0.25	0.63	0.10
Professional/technical	0.23	1.77	0.44
Manager	−0.11	2.04	0.48
Clerical	−0.19	1.37	0.33
Sales	−1.10	1.30	−0.05
Service	−0.68	1.32	−0.03
Agriculture	1.54	−18.57	−1.54
Production	−0.34	1.11	1.18
Land			
Arable	19.45	−313.42	−341.42
Forest	−23.82	−2573.99	−268.58
Pasture	−1.63	−91.89	−1998.58

Source: Bowen, Leamer and Sveikauskus (1987).

The ratio of the resource share (V_{ik}/V_{wk}) to the GNP share ($\text{GNP}_i/\text{GNP}_w$) of the right-hand side of this expression is a measure of the abundance of factor i. On the left-hand side of this expression is the exported share of the domestic supply adjusted for the trade imbalance. Thus the theory suggests there are two ways to measure factor abundance: directly by $(V_{ik}/V_{wk})/(\text{GNP}_i/\text{GNP}_w) - 1$, or through the adjusted factor content of trade $(F^A_{ik}/V_{wk})/(\text{GNP}_i/\text{GNP}_w)$.

Measures of the adjusted factor content of trade for the USA, the UK and Japan in 1967 using the US factor intensities are reported in Table 9.1.

The qualitative content of equation (7) has been studied in at least two ways: by examining the signs of the numbers Z_{ik} or their rank ordering. A Leontief type of study compares the numbers Z_{ik} for different factors k, say capital and labour. If $Z_K > Z_L$ where K and L refer to capital and labour, then trade reveals that the country is capital abundant compared with labour. Indeed that is Leamer's (1980) comment on Leontief: if the calculation is done correctly then the USA is revealed to be relatively capital abundant. This is also true for the 1967 data reported in Table 9.1 since the US capital number of 0.08 per cent exceeds the overall labour number of −0.25 per cent. According to the data in Table 9.1, the USA was most abundant in arable land and most scarce in forest land. It is also possible to make comparisons across countries. The UK was more scarce in capital than Japan which was more scarce than the USA. The UK was most abundant in labour overall. Japan was scarcest in arable land. A test of the H–O theory compares these numbers with direct measures of factor abundance. Tests of this form are what Bowen, Leamer and Sveikauskus (1987) call rank tests since they compare the rank order of factor abundance measured directly and through the factor content of trade.

It is also possible to perform 'sign' tests that compare the signs of the left and right of (7). This was first done by Brecher and Choudhri (1982), who mention that a feature of Leontief's data is that the net export of labour services is positive, even after adjusting for the trade imbalance. Using the right-hand side of (7), this implies that the US per capita Gross National Product (GNP) is less than world per capita GNP, which is impossible to square with the facts. Another way to describe sign tests is that they compare the resource abundance of one factor with an average of all the other factors, since the GNP ratio is an earnings weighted average of all the factor abundance ratios. By examining the signs in Table 9.1 we infer that the USA was abundant in capital, professional workers and arable land and scarce in unskilled labour. Both the UK and Japan were scarce in capital and land and abundant in labour. Sign tests would compare these signs with the corresponding signs of direct measures of the factor abundance (7).

Bowen, Leamer and Sveikauskus (1987) in a study of 1967 data for 27 countries and twelve factors found about 35 per cent violations of the signs implied by (7) and about 50 per cent violations of the ranks. This seems disappointing, but what was to be expected? In the absence of a clearly stated alternative theory, it seems impossible to determine just how many violations are enough to cast substantial doubt on the theory. Here we are troubled by one of our four basic questions: 'What can we hope to learn about the behaviour of real economies from this empirical work?'

4.2 Cross-commodity Comparisons

The Heckscher–Ohlin model has often been studied empirically with cross-commodity comparisons implicitly based on the assumption that the export performance 'should' depend on the characteristics of the industry. Simple correlations were rather common early in the literature, but these gave way to multiple correlations in the 1970s. For example, Keesing (1966) reports some simple correlations of

Table 9.2   Simple correlations of labour share and export performance, 1966 (US exports)/(group of 14 countries exports)

Skill groups	46 industries	35 industries[1]
Scientists and engineers	0.49	0.72
Technicians and draughtsmen	0.37	0.55
Other professionals	0.41	0.58
Managers	0.16	0.06
Machinists	0.22	0.37
Other skilled manual workers	0.11	0.21
Clerical and sales	0.35	0.44
Unskilled and semi-skilled	–0.45	–0.64

Note: 1. Excluding natural resource industries.

Source: Keesing (1966).

---

export performance (US Exports)/(Group of Fourteen Countries Exports) with skill intensities that are reported in Table 9.2. These results are suggestive of human capital abundance in the USA because the largest positive correlations occur at the highest skill levels and because the unskilled labour share is negatively correlated with export performance.

A typical multiple regression is that of Baldwin (1971) (reported incompletely):

$$X_k = -1.37 \, (K/L)_k + \sum_f \beta_f \, p_{fk} - 421s_k + 343u_k \qquad R^2 = 0.44$$

where

X_k = US (adjusted) net exports of commodity k in 1962
$(K/L)_k$ = capital/labour ratio in industry k
p_{fk} = percentage of labour force in skill group f
s_k = an index of scale economies
u_k = an index of the rate of unionisation.

One conclusion from this regression might be that the negative sign on the capital-intensity variable is suggestive of the Leontief paradox that the USA does not export goods that are capital-intensive.

These simple correlations and multiple regressions raise a number of questions:

• How should the export performance variable be scaled? Keesing scales by the exports of a comparison group of fourteen countries. Baldwin uses the unscaled data, which seems a bit uncomfortable since all his explanatory variables are scaled.

- Is it more appropriate to use simple correlations or multiple regressions?
- How should the 'importance' of a resource be inferred? By the size of the simple correlation? By the t-statistic in the multiple regressions?
- Is it legitimate to exclude the natural resource industries?
- Is it legitimate to include measures like the indices of scale and unionisation?

These questions can only be answered with reference to a clear theoretical framework.

It has been argued in several papers (Leamer and Bowen, 1981, Leamer, 1984 and Leamer, 1988) that cross-industry regressions generally have an unclear theoretical foundation. In deciding the kind of equation to estimate, the first important question is how to scale the dependent variable in a way that makes cross-industry comparisons sensible. Just using output or trade does not seem very sensible because some commodity groups form a large share of output and consumption whereas others form a small share. If no attempt is made to control for scale, any explanatory variable that is correlated with the size of the commodity group will pick up the scale effect. To put this another way, without some way to correct for the relative size of different commodity groups, the estimates will be highly sensitive to the level of aggregation. The scale effect has traditionally been controlled by dividing the dependent variable by some measure of market size. The ideal candidate would seem to be total world output. What seems to lie behind this normalisation is the intuitive notion that a country's share of world output can be expected to depend on the input mix of the commodity. Thus countries that are abundant in capital 'ought' to have larger shares of capital intensive industries than of labour intensive industries. But what seems intuitively clear is not always true. To explore this formally, let us focus on the production side of the Heckscher–Ohlin model with equal numbers of factors and goods and with sufficient similarity of endowment supplies for all countries to have the same factor prices and use the same input mixes.

The model (1)–(6) can serve as a theoretical foundation for a study of the determinants of the structure of production and trade. Equation (1) identifies a set of relationships between outputs, factor intensities and factor supplies. If data are collected for a single country only, then the endowment vector V is necessarily constant and (1) explains the level of production of each commodity as a function of the factor intensities A. This equation suggests that the 'correct' variables to include in the equation are elements of the inverse of A, not elements of A. Usually, however, the dependent variable is not selected to be the level of output, which can vary enormously if data are in monetary units and oddly if data are in other units. It is traditional to normalise by a variable that represents the 'size' of the commodity in world markets. A natural divisor is the level of the world's ouput of the commodity. By Cramer's rule, the share of the country output of commodity one is

$$Q_1/Q_{1w} = \det\,(V, A_2, A_3, ..., A_N)/\,\det(V_w, A_2, A_3, ..., A_N)$$

where A_j refers to a column of the matrix A, Q_{1w} is the world output of commodity one and V_w is the world's vector of factor endowments. Leamer (1988) makes the point that this formula indicates that the share of world output of commodity one does not depend on A_1, the input mix in industry one! This model thus suggests that it is entirely inappropriate to regress output shares on characteristics of industries.

Many cross-industry regression studies in the literature have not used world shares as the dependent variable. Typically, the dependent variable is the trade-dependence ratio equal to the level of net exports as a share of domestic consumption. Exactly the same comment applies if the model (1)–(6) is used. Using Cramer's rule we can solve for the trade dependence ratio for the first commodity as:

$$T_1/C_1 = \det\,(V - sV_w, A_2, A_3, ..., A_n)/\,\det(sV_w, A_2, A_3, ..., A_n)$$

The same result thus applies: the trade dependence ratio in industry one is altogether unrelated to the characteristics of that industry.

Another comment on cross-commodity regressions is offered by Leamer and Bowen (1981). It has been a tradition to regress trade on factor intensities and to assume that the signs of the coefficients reveal the relative abundance of factors. For example, a country that is relatively well-endowed with capital is expected to have a positive coefficient on the capital variable when trade is regressed on a set of factor intensities. But as Leamer and Bowen (1981) observe, there is no assurance that this is true. The regression vector formed when the unscaled trade data T are regressed on the input intensities A is $(AA')^{-1} AT = (AA')^{-1} (V - sV_w)$, which has the same sign as $(V - sV_w)$ only under special circumstances.

The 'intuition' about the correlation of trade and factor intensities may refer to the simple correlation, not the multiple correlation. The simple correlation between trade and the capital input, for example, is:

$$\text{Corr}\ (T, A_K) = (T'\ A_K - 1'T1'A_K/p)\ /\ \sqrt{(T'T - (1'T)^2/p)}$$
$$\sqrt{(A_K'A_K - (1'A_K)^2/p)}$$
$$= (K - sK_w)\ /\ p\ \sqrt{\text{Var}\ (T)}\ \sqrt{\text{Var}(A_K)}$$

where p is the number of commodities and where I have used $T'A_K = K - sK_w$ and the trade balance restriction $1'T = 0$. Thus, if trade is balanced, $B = 0$, the sign of the simple correlation is the same as the sign of the excess factor supply $K - sK_w$. For example, a country that is well endowed in capital will have trade positively correlated with capital intensity. By this type of reasoning, the simple correlations in Table 9.2 suggest that the USA was relatively abundant in all the skilled labour categories and relatively scarce in unskilled labour.

More than just the sign, it is natural to suspect that the simple correlation between trade and factor intensity is highest for the factor that is most 'important', scientists and engineers in Table 9.2, for example. In theory, the absolute size of the correlation depends on the degree of 'peculiarity' of this resource supply $K/K_w - s$ and also on the term $K_w/\ \sqrt{\text{Var}(A_K)} = 1/(\text{Var}(A_K/K_w))^{1/2}$. The number A_{Kj}/K_w is the inverse of the amount of the output of commodity j that would be produced in the world if j used only capital. Thus the term $\text{Var}(A_K/K_w)$ compares in a scale-free way the variability of resource use across industries. In that sense, the correlation is high if the supply of the resource is unusual and if the intensities are highly variable across industries.

4.3 Studies of the Heckscher–Ohlin Model Based on Cross-Country Comparisons

Cross-country comparisons are another way to study the validity of the Heckscher–Ohlin theorem. Studies of this type hold the commodity fixed and use the country as the experimental unit. Normally the tool of analysis is multiple regression with some measure of trade performance as the dependent variable and various characteristics of countries as the explanatory variable. Chenery (1960), Chenery and Taylor (1968) and Chenery and Syrquin (1975) were some of the earliest studies of this type, although these studies did not deal with details of the structure of trade but rather with more aggregate features of the economy like the ratio of gross imports to GNP. Leamer (1974) was one of the first to study commodity composition questions, contrasting the performance of three groups of variables as predictors of imports disaggregated by commodity; these groups are resistance (tariffs and distance), stage of development (GNP and population) and resource supplies (capital, labour, education and R&D). Leamer finds that the development group is generally most important in helping to predict import patterns. Some typical results from Leamer (1984) are reported in Table 9.3. These are beta-values from regressions of four commodity aggregates on 11 resource supplies. The data refer to trade and resource supplies of 60 countries in 1975. Based on these beta-values, comparative advantage in cereals is associated with an abundance of highly skilled labour, land of type 3 and oil. Comparative advantage in the three manufactures is associated with the supply of moderately skilled workers and capital, and is negatively related to the supply of land.

The theory underlying much of this work is casual at best. This contrasts with Leamer (1984) which takes equation (5) of the H–O–V model, $T = A^{-1} (V - sV_w)$, as the clearly stated foundation for calculating regressions of net exports on factor supplies. One function of such an estimation exercise is implicitly to infer the value of A^{-1} and to study how this changes over time. The question that is implicitly addressed is: 'What resource supplies determine comparative advantage?'

4.4 Studies of the Heckscher–Ohlin Model Using Two-Dimensional Data

Since Leamer and Bowen (1981), Leamer has often observed that the Heckscher–Ohlin model links three separately observable phenomena: trade, resource supplies and technological input coefficients. A full test of the theory accordingly must begin with separate measures of each of these three concepts and must explore the extent to which the observed data violate the Heckscher–Ohlin restrictions.

Hufbauer (1970) is a notable early study that employs measure-

Table 9.3   Beta-values of net export regressions

	Cereals	Labour Intensive Manufactures	Capital Intensive Manufactures	Machinery
Capital	−0.17	0.08	0.78	0.49
Labour 1	0.74	−1.13	−1.80	−0.39
Labour 2	−0.55	0.93	0.85	0.18
Labour 3	−0.15	0.08	0.37	0.02
Land 1	0.09	−0.04	−0.03	−0.01
Land 2	0.03	−0.02	−0.01	0.00
Land 3	0.26	−0.04	−0.15	−0.06
Land 4	0.05	−0.15	−0.10	−0.11
Coal	0.03	−0.14	−0.09	−0.02
Minerals	0.00	−0.03	−0.03	−0.01
Oil	0.72	−0.24	−0.60	−0.21

Note: Labour is disaggregated by skill; land by climate.

Source: Leamer (1984).

ments of all three concepts. Some typical results are reported in Table 9.4. The countries in this list are ordered according to their capital per man, with Canada being the most abundant in capital and Pakistan the least abundant. The capital per man in exports is compared with the capital per man in imports in the next two columns. It should be noted that the US data display the 'Leontief paradox' that imports are more capital intensive than exports. This is not true for the other countries at the top of the list. Hufbauer reports that the capital per man (first column) has a correlation of 0.625 with the capital per man in exports (second column) and a correlation of −0.353 with capital per man in imports (third column). This is regarded as confirming the Heckscher–Ohlin model: capital abundant countries tend to have capital intensive exports and labour intensive imports.

There are four comments that can be made about this study:

1. The study uses measures of all three concepts: factor supplies, trade and technological input intensities. As already mentioned, a

Table 9.4   Capital per man

	Abundance	Exports	Imports
Canada	8 850	17 529	11 051
USA	7 950	11 441	13 139
Norway	6 100	16 693	10 476
Sweden	5 400	12 873	11 373
Netherlands	4 750	11 768	11 706
Korea	850	8 004	14 900
India	500	7 339	12 019
Pakistan	500	5 725	12 371

Source: Hufbauer (1970).

full test of the Heckscher–Ohlin model must surely make reference to all of these.

2. Hufbauer's analysis does not refer explicitly to any model. It separates imports from exports, which landed Leontief in trouble.
3. It is curious that the capital per man in exports varies greatly across countries in contrast to the capital per man in imports. I would not have expected this result based on my understanding of the Heckscher–Ohlin model. What might account for it? Perhaps the uneven model helps understand this. In the Heckscher–Ohlin model with many goods and two inputs, countries concentrate production on just two of the goods and import all the rest. The two produced goods have similar capital intensities. In words, countries have a diversified import structure but a concentrated export structure. Another possible explanation is trade barriers which might plausibly force product diversification for imports but not exports.
4. Competing models and/or factors that might explain trade are 'tested' by comparing the size of the correlations that they produce. The list of theories is noticeably inclusive: factor proportions, human skills, scale economies, stage of production, technological gap, product cycle and preference similarity.

Bowen, Leamer and Sveikauskus (1987) also use measurements of all three concepts but link their work to a carefully formulated model, namely the H–O–V model as captured by equation (7) which determines the adjusted factor content of trade as a function of resource supplies. Recognising the impossibility of testing a theory without an alternative, these authors generalise the H–O–V model to allow for:

(a) non-homothetic tastes characterised by linear Engel curves;
(b) technological differences among countries that affect all technological coefficients proportionately;
(c) various kinds of measurement errors.

In the words of Bowen, Leamer and Sveikauskus (1987, p. 805):

> The data suggest errors in measurement in both trade and national factor supplies, and favor the hypothesis of neutral technological differences across countries. However, the form of the technological differences favored by the data involves a number of implausible estimates, including some in which factors yield strictly negative outputs. Thus . . . The Heckscher–Ohlin model does poorly, but we do not have anything that does better.

4.5 Comment on the Studies of the Ricardian Model

One of the basic questions that is posed in the introduction is: What is the theoretical basis for this empirical work? The studies of the Ricardian model that regress measures of relative export performance on measures of relative labour productivities are only loosely connected with the Ricardian model. We can also ask if the Ricardian regressions make sense from the standpoint of the H–O model. Clearly, the answer is 'no' if the even H–O model is used since it implies that labour productivities are the same in all countries. Cross-commodity empirical studies suggested by the H–O model thus usually proceed as if this were so and use the input intensities from one country as explanatory variables rather than ratios of intensities from different countries. The H–O regressions take the form $X_{ik}/X_{i'k} = f(q_{ik})$ where X_{ik} equal exports of commodity i by country k and q_{ik} is the corresponding labour productivity measured in one of the countries. This contrasts with the Ricardian equation which uses the *relative* labour productivities: $X_{ik}/X_{i'k} = f(q_{ik}/q_{i'k})$.

In a search to give the Ricardian regression some meaning from the standpoint of this version of the H–O model, it seems natural to consider aggregation over goods or over factors. Aggregation is something that must always be considered since real data on commodities and factors necessarily refer to aggregates. In particular, differences in labour productivities may be a consequence of aggregation even though at the level of the commodity labour productivities are equal. The labour productivity within a commodity aggregate is equal to $\sum p_k Q_k / \sum L_k = \sum (p_k Q_k / L_k) L_k / \sum L_k$ which is the weighted average of labour productivities with weights equal to the labour used in sector k. This aggregate labour productivity will thus be relatively high in countries with labour allocations concentrating on those industries within the aggregate with relatively high labour productivities. If the summation in this expression extends over all commodities, then the labour productivity is GNP per man which is an increasing function of the relative supplies of the non-labour factors. Those countries with relatively high GNP per man will therefore have relatively large allocation of labour to the industries with relatively high productivities. This can make the measured productivities for commodity aggregates different in the two countries even though they are identical at the level of individual commodities. Aggregates composed of commodities with uniform values of output per man will of course have the same level of aggregate output per man in both countries since the weights do not matter. But aggregates composed of commodities with variable labour productivities will tend to have high measured labour productivities in the capital abundant country because it allocates relatively large shares of its work force to the components with relatively high labour productivities.

This discussion of aggregation does not give a very sensible foundation to the Ricardian regressions since the proposition that the USA has a comparative advantage in those commodities with relatively high labour productivities amounts to the odd claim that the USA has a comparative advantage in the commodity aggregates composed of variable labour productivities.

As argued by Deardorff (1984), the uneven H–O model can give greater content to the Ricardian regressions because factor prices are not necessarily equalised and labour productivities may differ across countries. The supply price of commodity k in country i depends on the factor return vector and the input vector by the zero profit condition (2): $p_{ik} = \sum_f w_{if} A_{ifk}$. The relative supply price of two different countries is thus $p_{ik} / p_{i'k} = \sum_f w_{if} A_{ifk} / \sum_f w_{i'f} A_{i'fk}$ which depends on factor intensity differences and also factor return differences. This cannot be exactly expressed simply in terms of relative labour productivities even if there are only two factors, since other factors matter, but differences in labour productivities do account for part of the differences in relative prices.[7]

5   EMPIRICAL STUDIES OF INTRA-INDUSTRY TRADE

The puzzling phenomenon of intra-industry trade has sparked a large theoretical literature dealing with differentiated goods produced with increasing returns to scale. Accompanying these theoretical pieces are a number of empirical studies of the determinants of intra-industry trade. In this area of research there is special difficulty in forming interesting empirical questions because the linkage of the theory and the data analyses of necessity is often casual. Here are some of the problems:

1. It is often difficult to find any variable that closely measures the hypothetical construct stipulated by the theory. For example, Loertscher and Wolter (1980), measure 'the potential for large scale production' by value added per establishment. But it is not clear what this has to do with the fixed costs and differentiated products that are the bases for models of intra-industry trade. An industry that accounts for much of GNP may be supplied by many very large establishments each producing at the efficient scale, and nonetheless have industry output that exhibits constant returns to scale. A better variable might be value added per establishment relative to some measure of the total market of the good.
2. The theory consists of a set of separate models, each intended to capture one feature. There is ordinarily little attempt made theoretically to combine these models into one composite. They are combined empirically merely by inclusion of separate variables representing each model in a single linear regression equation. But in the absence of a clear combined theory, it may make more sense to look at simple correlations, rather than partial correlations, since there is no assurance that the other influences are properly controlled merely by throwing them into a regression.
3. Studies that combine data from many industries are especially suspect, since the theoretical underpinnings of these studies are often weak. Economists would distrust estimates of price elasticity of demand based on observations of price and quantity collected from many industries. Some of this distrust should carry over to all cross-industry studies.

4. Null and alternative hypotheses are not often stated and are usually quite difficult to form. As argued above, these hypotheses should refer either to economists' states of mind or to the uses for which the model is intended. For reasons (1) and (2) (measurement difficulties and the absence of a combined theory), we really cannot claim to have much genuine knowledge of even the signs of the coefficients. And the uses of these models seem pretty distant and unclear.
5. The counterfactuals that are implicit in the estimated regressions are often unclear. What exactly, for example, is meant by a change in value added per establishment?
6. It is sometimes difficult to determine whether a projected empirical regularity is due to the existence of economies of scale or more importantly to the assumption about the nature of tastes.

With all these difficulties, it is not surprising that the impact that these empirical findings might have on our understanding of the role of economies of scale is limited to a simple measurement of the amount of intra-industry trade for various commodity groups and countries. These measurements do cast doubt on the H–O model which does not seem capable of offering a very satisfying explanation of intra-industry trade.

An example of the kind of empirical work that has accompanied models of intra-industry trade is a study by Loertscher and Wolter (1980) who report:

Drawing on the literature quoted above the following hypotheses *seem warranted*: (my italics)
Intra-industry trade among countries is intense if:
– the average of their levels of development is high.
– the difference in their levels of development is relatively small.
– the average of their market sizes is large.
– the difference in their sizes is small.
– barriers to trade are low.
Intra-industry trade in an industry is intense if:
– the potential for product differentiation is high and market entry in narrow product lines is impeded by significant barriers.
– transaction costs are low.
– the definition of an industry is comprehensive.

I have added the italics in this quotation to emphasise the casual link between the theory and the empirical work. The regression that

Table 9.5   Country- and industry-specific determinants of intra-industry
trade, OECD countries; cross-section 1972/73

	Estimate	*F-value*
Country-specific variables		
Development stage differential	−0.106	47.95
Average development stage	$(0.259)(10^{-1})$	1.68
Market size differential	$(−0.146)(10^{-5})$	82.71
Average market size	$(0.296)(10^{-5})$	108.17
Distance	$(−0.485)(10^{-4})$	44.52
Customs unions dummy	0.382	64.89
Language group dummy	0.171	6.43
Border trade dummy	0.268	20.41
Cultural group dummy	$(−0.423)(10^{-2})$	0.01
Industry-specific variables		
Product differentiation	$(0.733)(10^{-3})$	0.45
Scale economies	$(−0.311)(10^{-1})$	91.23
Transactions costs	$(−0.225)(10^{-3})$	3.71
Level of aggregation	$(0.137)(10^{-1})$	3.05
Product group	0.112	5.56

Adjusted $R^2 = 0.070$, degrees of freedom = 6975.

Source: Loertscher and Wolter (1980).

Loertscher and Wolter compute explains a measure of intra-industry trade indexed by importer, exporter and commodity in terms of a set of variables selected to represent the various hypothetical determinants of intra-industry trade. One of their results is reported in Table 9.5.

From my perspective it is difficult to know what to make of a regression of this type. Most of the coefficients are statistically highly significant, as might be expected with so large a sample size. The precision with which these coefficients are estimated is misleading, however, since the fit as measured by the R^2 is very low. One thing the low R^2 means is that the signs of the estimated coefficients are not resistant to measurement-error adjustments. In fact, it is likely that any sign pattern of estimated coefficients would be possible if a little measurement error were assumed in a few of the variables. For the technical reasons, consult Klepper and Leamer (1984). Actually, the authors' reaction (p. 287) to the 'wrong' sign on the scale economies variable is indeed mismeasurement.

But the real difficulties of interpreting a regression of this type come from the tenuous link between the theory and the regression.

Models do suggest that intra-industry trade is positively associated with scale economies. But no composite model has been presented which suggests that, controlling for all these other variables, the scale effect is positive. Without a theory to tell what other things to control, it is difficult to interpret a partial correlation which controls for a haphazardly selected group of other variables. Then it may make sense to look at the simple correlation.

Helpman's (1987) study of the effect of size dispersion on the amount of trade and the amount of intra-industry trade is noteworthy in its attempt to link more closely the theory and the empirical study. Neglecting Helpman's correction for trade imbalances, his size similarity index of a 'group I' of countries is defined to be a negative function of the variance of GNP shares:[8]

$$SIM = 1 - \sum (s_j)^2 = 1 - (1/n) - \text{Var}(s_j)$$

where s_j is the GNP share of country i in total GNP of 'group I'. Total intra-group trade is

$$V_I = \sum_{i \neq j} X_{ij}$$

where X_{ij} is the value of exports from i to j. Helpman's model implies that the total trade increases with similarity:

$$V_I/\text{GNP}_I = (\text{GNP}_I/\text{GNP}_w) \times SIM$$

Helpman finds that for a group of fourteen of the most industrialised countries both GNP similarity and trade intensity have increased more or less constantly from 1956 to 1981, giving the appearance that the model is supported.

One of the basic questions now arises: 'What is the theoretical basis for this empirical work?' To express it differently: what is being tested? Economies of scale appear to be central but, in fact, the result just described comes from the consumption side of the model and makes no serious reference to the production side. In particular, suppose that we make the 'Armington' assumption that products are distinguished by location of production and further assume that tastes are identical and homothetic and that trade is balanced. Then purchases by country i of country j's product are equal to $s_i \text{GDP}_j = s_i s_j / \text{GDP}_w$, where s_i is country i's GDP share. Summing this over all importers and exporters produces the result:

$$V_t = \sum_{i \neq j} s_i\, s_j / \text{GDP}_w = (1 - \sum_i s_i^2)/\text{GDP}_w$$

which is just the model that Helpman studies. If this model fits poorly, it is due to a failure of the proposition that all individuals consume the same share of total output of US wine, French wine, German automobiles, etc. It need not have anything to do with the method of production or the nature of competition. The same result can be obtained by appending a different model of consumption onto the basic H–O model of production.

Helpman also reports that his theory 'suggests' that: 'The share of intra-industry trade in bilateral trade flows should be larger for countries with similar incomes per capita. . . . In order to examine the consistency of this hypothesis with the data', Helpman calculates bilateral intra-industry trade as:

$$S_{ij} = 2 \sum_k \min(X_{ijk}, X_{jik})/\sum_i (X_{ijk} + X_{jik})$$

where k indexes commodities. For each of twelve different years this measure of intra-industry trade is explained in terms of three variables:

$$X_1 = \log|(\text{GDP}_i/POP_i) - (\text{GDP}_j/POP_j)|$$

$$X_2 = \min(\log(\text{GDP}_i), \log(\text{GDP}_j))$$

$$X_3 = \max(\log(\text{GDP}_i), \log(\text{GDP}_j))$$

The results for the extreme years were as shown in Table 9.6.

From these regressions we may conclude that intra-industry trade is more intense between countries that are similar either in terms of per capita gross domestic product (GDP) or in terms of GDP itself, though this is more difficult to detect in the latter period. The conclusion regarding the effect of similarity in the levels of GDP refers to the fact that the coefficient on the minimum GDP is positive and the coefficient on the maximum GDP is negative and approximately the same absolute size. It also appears that the coefficient on the minimum GDP is the larger in absolute value, suggesting that country size as well as similarity contributes to intra-industry trade. A second regression reported by Helpman separates GDP size from GDP similarity and confirms that both seem to contribute positively to intra-industry trade.

Table 9.6   Regressions for intra-industry trade

	X_1	X_2	X_3	R^2
1970:	−0.044	0.055	−0.014	0.266
	(−3.141)	(4.153)	(−1.105)	
1981:	−0.006	0.027	−0.020	0.039
	(−0.370)	(1.686)	(−1.283)	

Note: t-values in parentheses; n = 14 × 13/2 = 91.

Source: Helpman (1987).

This work has unearthed several interesting empirical regularities but there remains a great deal that could be done on the role of economies of scale in international relationships. For example, among the unanswered questions are:

How much of total trade is due to economies of scale?
How much of the gains from trade are due to economies of scale?
What role do tastes have in determining the result?
Why does the regression fit so poorly?
Which industries are best described by models of imperfect competition?

And so on.

6   EMPIRICAL STUDIES OF THE EFFECT OF DEMAND

Trade, of course, is the difference between production and consumption. Most of the theoretical literature in international economics concentrates on the production side and often uses assumptions that neutralise demand as a determinant of the composition of trade. An early and notable exception is Linder (1961), who argues that differences in taste are a deterrent to trade because of the costs of tailoring a product to fit local conditions. This is usually interpreted to mean that the intensity of bilateral trade decreases with differences in per capita income. The H–O model, on the other hand, 'suggests' the reverse association because countries with substantially different per capita incomes are 'likely' to have different resource endowments, offer different baskets of goods for trade and therefore become trading partners.

Table 9.7 Gravity equations: 1970 trade

Country	$DIFF_Y$	DIST	$DIFF_L$	ASSOC	BORDER	R^2	λ
West Germany	0.01	−4.65	−0.29	−0.22	0.56	0.55	0.001
	(0.01)	(5.00)	(0.06)	(0.55)	(1.45)		
Japan	−2.18	−11.52	−1.40			0.13	0.3
	(0.08)	(2.70)	(0.12)				
USA	3.20	−8.22	−2.40		0.28	0.27	0.1
	(1.15)	(3.33)	(0.31)		(0.40)		

Notes: t-statistics in parentheses
$DIFF_Y$ = Absolute difference in income per capita
$DIFF$ = Great circle difference between economic centers
$DIFF_L$ = Absolute difference in land per capita
ASSOC   = Common membership in free trade associations
BORDER = Common border
λ   = Box–Cox parameter
Source: Hoftyzer (1984).

Most of the theoretical work deals with the commodity composition of trade, not the partner composition. The Linder hypothesis has traditionally been interpreted in terms of its implications for partner composition by including a measure of similarity of per capita GNPs in 'gravity equations' that explain bilateral trade. The Linder hypothesis as it relates to the commodity composition has been studied recently by Hunter and Markusen (1988) who estimate a system of demand equations and study its implications for total trade. An interesting example of the gravity model is reported by Hoftyzer (1984) who presents a model that explains the bilateral trade of each of eleven importers using data for fifty-eight exporters. His results for three of the importers are reported in Table 9.7.

The Linder hypothesis is interpreted to mean that the dissimilarity of countries as measured by the difference in per capita incomes will lower the intensity of trade. In other words the coefficient on $DIFF_Y$ should be negative. Hoftyzer (1984) finds otherwise in the sense that for a few countries the estimated coefficient is negative, but for most it is positive. This contrasts with some more positive results by other authors, which Hoftyzer argues are due to their failure to control for border effects and membership in free trade associations and their failure to consider other functional forms which he does through the Box–Cox analysis. However, this finding is in conflict with Helpman's (1987) time series finding that the rapid growth of trade over the past three decades was associated with a convergence of per capita incomes.

To return to the two basic questions: 'Does this work have a solid base in economic theory?' No, not really. 'Are the hypotheses phrased in a way that puts intellectual capital at risk?' I think so. Even though the theoretical foundation is murky, the finding of Hoftyzer (1984) seems to unsettle the Linder viewpoint. According to Hoftyzer (1984) trade may seem intense between similar countries, but that can be explained first by the fact that they are neighbours and/or members of free trade associations and second, that whatever relationship exists, it is not log-linear. This is a memorable result that affects my understanding of the role of demand as a determinant of trade patterns.

The questions remain. What exactly is being studied here? What is the counterfactual? Is the question as simple as determining the sign of the difference variable after accounting for a list of randomly selected other variables? That is an interesting question, but it seems a very limited one. Maybe the deeper issues have to do with the gains from trade and the effects of trade policy on welfare. Are the gains from trade less if the trade is Linder trade as opposed to Heckscher–Ohlin trade?

7 CONCLUSION

From the standpoint of an econometrician and a data analyst, it is a disappointing observation that data do not play a more obvious and more substantial role in determining the course of professional opinion in international economics. This disappointment has produced here what may seem like a very critical review. But I make these criticisms constructively. I want us to do better; I want myself to do better. I think we can. I think we need to devote much more energy to the interface between theory and data analysis. We need to form interesting and decidable hypotheses. We should not waste so much time testing obviously false theoretical propositions that were never intended as more than approximations. These are not the only reasons why international economics is not especially empirical, but attention to these concerns should have the desirable effect of increasing the role of data.

Notes

1. The author gratefully acknowledges the support from NSF grant SES-8708399 and the comments and assistance of Graeme Woodbridge.
2. General reviews of the empirical work in international economics have been offered by Deardorff (1984) and Stern (1975). Of necessity this paper overlaps with these excellent reviews.
3. It is not an exception even though the level of mathematical sophistication is not as high as in some other fields.
4. In surveys of graduate students at five of the best economics departments, Klamer and Colander (1990) find that the following economists are listed as 'most respected': J. M. Keynes, Kenneth Arrow, Paul Samuelson, Karl Marx and Adam Smith.
5. 'Two nations which agreed in everything except their commercial policy would agree also in that', J. S. Mill (1872) *A System of Logic*, 8th edn, (London: Longmans; reprinted in 1956). Quoted in McCloskey, (1987).
6. Bhagwati (1964) makes the comment that a critical step in the logic above is the linkage between relative product prices and relative labour productivities, but he finds no significant relation exists.
7. Deardorff's (1984) (loose) argument is based on the observation that countries with relatively high labour costs will use more capital-intensive techniques and have higher labour productivities. He notes that the responsiveness of labour productivities in the two-factor model satisfies, $d\log(Q/L)/d\log(w/r) = \sigma\,\theta$ where σ is the elasticity of substitution between capital and labour, and θ is the capital share. Thus if the elasticity of substitution were the same in all industries, differences in factor prices would cause the greatest differences in labour productivities in industries with the greatest share of capital. The looseness in the argument is that statement 'Now suppose that the more capital abundant country has a comparative advantage in more capital intensive goods, as the Heckscher–Ohlin model predicts . . .' I am not sure that the H–O model does make this prediction.
8. Helpman calls this a 'dispersion' index though it is a measure of how similar are the sizes of different countries.

References

Balassa, B. (1963) 'An Empirical Demonstration of Classical Comparative Cost Theory', *Review of Economics and Statistics*, vol. 45, August.

Baldwin, R. E., (1971) 'Determinants of the Commodity Structure of US Trade', *American Economic Review*, vol. 61, no 1, pp. 126–46.

Bhagwati, J. (1964) 'The Pure Theory of International Trade: A Survey', *Economic Journal*, vol. 74, March, pp. 1–84.

Bowen, H. P., Leamer, E. E. and Sveikauskus, L. (1987) 'Multicountry, Multifactor Tests of the Factor Abundance Theory', *American Economic Review*, vol. 77, no 5, December.

Brecher, R. A. and Choudhri, E. U. (1982) 'The Leontief Paradox, Continued', *Journal of Political Economy*, vol. 90, no 4, pp. 820–3.

Chenery, H. B. (1960) 'Patterns of Industrial Growth', *American Economic Review*, vol. 50, no 1, pp. 624–54.

Chenery, H. B. and Syrquin, M. (1975) *Patterns of Development, 1950–1970*, (Oxford: Oxford University Press).

Chenery, H. B. and Taylor, L. (1968) 'Development Patterns: Among Countries and Over Time', *Review of Economics and Statistics*, November, vol. 50, no 4, pp. 391–416.

Deardorff, A. V. (1984) 'Testing Trade Theories and Predicting Trade Flows' in Jones, R. W. & Kenen, P. B. (eds) *Handbook of International Economics*, vol. 1 (Amsterdam: North-Holland).

Grubel, H. G. and Lloyd, P. J. (1975) *'Intra Industry Trade'*, (London: Macmillan).

Haberler, G. (1933) *The Theory of International Trade*, translated by Stonier, A. and Benham, F. 1936 (London: W. Hodge).

Helpman, E. (1987) 'Imperfect Competition and International Trade: Evidence from Fourteen Industrialised Countries', *Journal of the Japanese and International Economies*, vol. 1, June.

Heravi, I. (1986) 'The Leontief Paradox, Reconsidered: Correction', *Journal of Political Economy*, vol. 94, no 5, p. 1120.

Hoftyzer, J. (1984) 'A Further Analysis of the Linder Trade Thesis', *Quarterly Review of Economics and Business*, vol. 24, no 2, pp. 57–90.

Hufbauer, G. C. (1970) 'The Impact of National Characteristics and Technology on the Commodity Composition of Trade in Manufactured Goods', in Vernon, R. (ed.) *The Technology Factor in International Trade*, (New York: Columbia University Press) pp. 145–231.

Hunter, L. C. and Markusen, J. R. (1988) 'Per Capita Income As a Determinant of Trade', in Feenstra, R. C. (ed.) *Empirical Methods for International Trade'* (Cambridge, Mass.: MIT Press).

Keesing, D. B. (1966) 'Labour Skills and Comparative Advantage', *American Economic Review*, vol. 56, no 2, pp. 249–58.

Klamer, A. and Colander, D. (1990) *The Making of an Economist* (Boulder: Westview Press).

Klepper, S. and Leamer, E. E. (1984) 'Consistent Sets of Estimates for Regression with All Variables Measured with Error', *Econometrica*, vol. 52, pp. 163–83.

Leamer, E. E. (1974) 'The Commodity Composition of International Trade in Manufactures: An Empirical Analysis', *Oxford Economic Papers*, vol. 26, no 3, pp. 350–74.

Leamer, E. E. (1980) 'The Leontief Paradox Reconsidered', *Journal of Political Economy*, vol. 88, pp. 495–503.

Leamer, E. E. (1984) *Sources of Comparative Advantage, Theory and Evidence* (Cambridge, Massachussetts: MIT Press).

Leamer, E. E. (1988) 'Cross-Section Estimation of the Effects of Trade Barriers' in Feenstra, R. C. (ed.) *Empirical Methods for International Trade* (Cambridge, Massachussetts: MIT Press).

Leamer, E. E. and Bowen, H. P. (1981) 'Cross-Section Tests of the Heckscher–Ohlin Theorem: Comment', *American Economic Review*, vol. 71, pp. 1040–3.

Leontief, W. W. (1953) 'Domestic Production and Foreign Trade: The

American Capital Position Re-examined', *Proceedings of the American Philosophical Society*, September, pp. 332–49.

Linder, S. B. (1961) *An Essay on Trade and Transformation* (New York: John Wiley).

Loertscher, R. and Wolter, F. (1980) 'Determinants of Intra-Industry Trade: Among Countries and Across Countries', *Weltwirtschaftliches Archiv*, vol. 116, pp. 280–93.

MacDougall, G. D. A. (1951) 'British and American Exports: A Study Suggested by the Theory of Comparative Costs, Part I', *Economic Journal*, vol. 61, December.

McCloskey, D. N. (1987) 'Counterfactuals' in Eatwell, J., Millgate, M. and Newman, P. (eds) *The New Palgrave* (London: Macmillan).

Stern, R. M. (1975) 'Testing Trade Theories' in Kenens, P. B. (ed.) *International Trade and Finance: Frontiers for Research* (New York: Cambridge University Press), pp. 3–49.

Vanek, J. (1963) *The Natural Resource Content of United States Foreign Trade, 1870–1955* (Cambridge, Massachussetts: MIT Press).

Vanek, J. (1968) 'The Factor Proportions Theory: The N-Factor Case', *Kyklos*, vol. 21, no 4, pp. 749–56.

Viner, J. (1937) *Studies in the Theory of International Trade* (New York: Harper).

10 Price Elasticities from Survey Data: Extensions and Indonesian Results

Angus Deaton[1]
PRINCETON UNIVERSITY

1 INTRODUCTION

For many questions of public policy, it is important to know how consumers change their expenditures on goods in response to changes in prices. For developing countries, there are typically rather few time series data from which price elasticities can be inferred. By contrast, cross-sectional household expenditure surveys are available for many LDCs. In Deaton (1986, 1987) I developed a methodology for using such household survey data to detect spatial variation in prices, and to estimate price elasticities by comparing spatial price variation to spatial demand patterns. In the first paper, I showed how to estimate the own-price elasticity for a single good by comparing its demand to its price. In the second paper, the methodology was extended to cover systems of demand functions, so that cross-price elasticities could be estimated, and substitution patterns studied.

Both papers, although giving satisfactory results for data from the Ivory Coast, contain a number of unresolved problems. Perhaps the most serious of these is the use of double-logarithmic demand equations. Not only are such demand functions inconsistent with basic theory, but more importantly, they cannot be used to model households that do not purchase all goods. As a result, many sample points have to be deleted prior to estimation. Even if the selection did not introduce bias, the estimated demand functions are thereby conditioned on positive consumption. However, for most policy purposes, it is the *unconditional* demands that are of interest. The revenue effects of a tax change depend on how total demand is altered, and not on whether changes take place at the extensive or intensive margins.

In the published version of the first paper, Deaton (1988), the logarithmic formulation was abandoned, but the analysis was confined to the single commodity case, and thus to measurement of own-price responses. The current paper provides a unified statement of the methodology for the system case without using double logarithmic forms, and is intended to supercede previous treatments. Section 2 of the paper summarises the model, and describes the estimation procedure. A brief Monte Carlo experiment illustrates how the procedure works in practice, as well as the consequences of following alternative estimation strategies of the kind that have appeared in the literature. Section 3 presents an application of the new version of the model to data from the 1981 SUSENAS Indonesian household survey. Results are given for a moderately large demand system of eleven commodities. Another application of the same techniques can be found in Laraki's (1988) analysis of food subsidies and demand patterns in Morocco. The Appendix derives standard errors for the estimators presented in Section 2. A SAS computer program that implements these procedures is available from the author or from the Welfare and Human Resources Division of the World Bank in Washington, DC.

2   MODEL FORMULATION AND ESTIMATION

The framework for the analysis is a model of consumer behaviour in which households choose how much of a commodity to buy, and in what quality or grade. Commodities are considered as collections of heterogeneous goods within which consumers can choose more or less expensive items, so that the unit value of a commodity, the price paid per physical unit, is a matter of choice. Both quantity and quality choice are functions of household income, household characteristics, and price. Prices of any one good will typically affect the quantities and qualities chosen of all goods.

To estimate such a model, data are required on household expenditures on a range of goods, as well as on physical quantities purchased. Weight may well be the most natural measure of physical quantity, but it is by no means the only one. For example, it might be convenient to consider a commodity 'flour and flour products' that contained purchases of both flour and bread. In such a case, it would not be sensible to add kilos of bread to kilos of flour, but rather to convert bread to its flour equivalent before adding. Calories may also be a convenient common unit in which to aggregate. While all household budget surveys collect data on household expenditures, not all ask questions about physical quantities. The methods of this paper cannot be applied to survey data without such information.

The second major data requirement, and one that is satisfied by virtually all household surveys, is that households be geographically 'clustered' within the sample. Survey organisations nearly always adopt such a design because it minimises transport costs, and allows a group of households to be interviewed at the same time. For current purposes, clustering is important because it means that households within each cluster can be assumed to face the same prices for market goods. Note that the validity of the 'same price' assumption requires not only the geographical proximity of the households, but also that they be interviewed at approximately the same time.

The model with which I shall work is as follows. For household i in cluster c, there are two equations for good G:

$$w_{Gic} = \alpha_G^0 + \beta_G^0 \ln x_{ic} + \gamma_G^0 \cdot z_{ic} + \sum_{H=1}^{N} \theta_{GH} \ln p_{Hc}$$

$$+ (f_{Gc} + u_{Gic}^0) \tag{1}$$

$$\ln v_{Gic} = \alpha_G^1 + \beta_G^1 \ln x_{ic} + \gamma_G^1 \cdot z_{ic} + \sum_{H=1}^{N} \psi_{GH} \ln p_{Hc} + u_{Gic}^1 \tag{2}$$

In equation (1), w_{Gic} is the budget share of good G in household i's budget, defined as expenditure on the good divided by total expenditure on all goods and services, x_{ic}. This share is assumed to be a linear function of the logarithm of total expenditure, of the logarithms of the prices of all of the N goods, and of a vector of household characteristics z_{ic}. The remaining terms are f_{Gc}, a cluster fixed effect for good G, and an idiosyncratic residual u_{Gic}^0. The second equation relates to the unit value of good G, v_G, defined as the expenditure on the good divided by the quantity bought. The logarithm of the unit value is a function of the same variables that appear in the share equation, with the exception of the cluster fixed effect. The basic idea is that the logarithm of unit value is the logarithm of quality plus the logarithm of price. In consequence, if there were no quality effects, unit values would move proportionally with price. However, prices, income, and characteristics all affect the choice of quality and so all appear in the unit value equation. Although it is difficult to rule out the possibility of cluster fixed effects in the unit value equation, the model depends on their exclusion; since prices are not measured, the identification of the model requires a direct link between prices and unit values, a link that would be broken by the presence of fixed effects.

One non-standard feature of the equations (1) and (2) is that the prices for the goods, $\ln p_{Gc}$, are not observed, so that it is not possible to estimate the equations directly. Note that prices are assumed to be the same for all households in cluster c, so that there is no i suffix on these variables. The budget share in equation (1) is observed for all households, but the unit value for good G in equation (2) is observed only for those households that record at least one purchase in the market for that commodity. Households with zero budget shares do not generate a corresponding unit value, just as in the labour supply literature, individuals who do not work do not have recorded wage rates. However, in the current case there will also be households with a positive budget share but for whom there is no recorded unit value. This occurs if households consume own-produced goods whose value has to be imputed. Different surveys will generally have different imputation rules, and it will only rarely be the case that the prices used for imputation can be treated as genuine observations on unit values. For each cluster c, I shall denote by n_c the number of households in the cluster, and by n_{cG}^+ the number of households that have observations on both the budget share and the unit value of good G.

Equation (1) looks very much like the 'Almost Ideal' demand system of Deaton and Muellbauer (1980) in which budget shares are a linear function of the logarithms of real expenditure and prices. However, there are a number of reasons why the model here is different. First, equation (1) and (2) should not be regarded as a direct representation of preferences, but simply as the regression functions of budget shares and unit values conditional on the included right-hand side variables. Zero expenditures are included, so that the conditional expectation is taken over purchasers and non-purchasers alike. There is no guarantee that there exist preferences that generate a regression function like (1). Instead of following the traditional methodology of postulating a linear structural model and then dealing with the zero censoring separately and subsequently, I am directly postulating that the conditional expectations, or regression functions take the form (1) and (2). Such a procedure has several advantages. As argued in the introduction, it is this regression function that is of interest for policy, and estimation of the underlying structural model is not required. Estimation is simplified because I am dealing with a linear model and not with a Tobit or its multivariate generalisation. Further, it is the regression function which is identified from the data, and it is far from clear whether it is possible to disentangle the effects of the censoring from the underlying functional form without essentially arbitrary and untestable identifying assumptions. Of course, there still remains unresolved the question of whether (1) is a plausible functional form for the budget shares, given that the zero observations are included.

The second reason why (1) and (2) differ from a model like the almost ideal demand system is that we are no longer within the framework of a standard demand model where quantities are a function of prices and the budget. Here, consumers choose both quantity and quality, so that expenditure is the product not only of quantity and price, but of quantity, quality, and price. As a consequence, the analysis must take account of price and income elasticities of quality, and the existence of these effects also complicates the relationship between the parameters and the elasticities that we are ultimately interested in measuring.

The parameters β_G^0 in (1) and β_G^1 in (2) determine the total expenditure elasticities of quantity and quality. Since $\beta_G^1 = \partial \ln v_G / \partial \ln x$, and since unit value is price multiplied by quality, the parameter is simply the expenditure elasticity of quality. If (1) is differentiated with respect to $\ln x$, and ε_G is the (quantity) demand elasticity, we have:

$$\partial \ln w_G / \partial \ln x = \beta_G^0 / w_G = \varepsilon_G + \beta_G^1 - 1 \qquad (3)$$

since the logarithm of the share is the sum of the logarithms of quantity and quality less the logarithm of expenditure. Rearranging,

$$\varepsilon_G = (1 - \beta_G^1) + (\beta_G^0 / w_G) \qquad (4)$$

Turning to the price elasticities, ψ_{GH} is the matrix of own and cross-price elasticities of the unit values; if price were to have no effect on quality, Ψ would be the identity matrix. In general, the elasticities of quality with respect to price are $\psi_{GH} - \delta_{GH}$, for Kronecker delta δ_{GH}. If ε_{GH} is the standard matrix of own and cross-price elasticities of quantities, then, differentiating (1) with respect to $\ln p_H$, we have

$$\partial \ln w_G / \partial \ln p_H = \varepsilon_{GH} + \psi_{GH} = \theta_{GH} / w_G \qquad (5)$$

so that:

$$\varepsilon_{GH} = -\psi_{GH} + \theta_{GH}/w_G \tag{6}$$

It is the estimation of the quantities ε_{GH} and ε_G to which I give the most attention in what follows, although note that, for some purposes, interest might focus on the income and price elasticities of quantity and quality together, i.e. on $\varepsilon_G + \beta_G^1$ and $\varepsilon_{GH} + \psi_{GH} - \delta_{GH}$, quantities that are easily calculated if required. Note that the elasticity formulae typically contain both parameters and data, and will therefore vary across the sample. I shall typically ignore this variation and evaluate formulae at the sample means of the data.

Given that prices are not observed, all of the parameters cannot be estimated without further prior information. The basic result that yields identification is a formula that links the effects of prices on quality choice to conventional price and total expenditure elasticities. Given a separability assumption about the basic goods that comprise each heterogeneous commodity, it is shown in Deaton (1988) that:

$$\psi_{GH} = \delta_{GH} + \beta_G^1 \, \varepsilon_{GH}/\varepsilon_G \tag{7}$$

According to (7), the price of good H only affects the quality of good G to the extent that there is a cross-price quantity elasticity ε_{GH}. Given such an elasticity, the effect works through the change in the total quantity of good G: β_G^1/ε_G is the elasticity of quality of G with respect to total expenditure on G.

Assuming that (7) holds at the sample means, (4) and (6) can be used to substitute for ε_{GH} and ε_G in (7), we obtain a relationship linking the underlying parameters:

$$\psi_{GH} = \delta_{GH} + \frac{\beta_G^1 \, (\theta_{GH}/w_G - \psi_{GH})}{(1 - \beta_G^1) + \beta_G^0/w_G} \tag{8}$$

It is convenient to define the vector ξ by

$$\xi_G = \beta_G^1/[(1 - \beta_G^1)w_G + \beta_G^0] \tag{9}$$

so that, in matrix notation, (8) becomes

$$\Psi = I + D(\xi)\Theta - D(\xi)D(w)\Psi \tag{10}$$

where I is the $(N \times N)$ identity matrix and $D(x)$ denotes a diagonal matrix with the vector x on its diagonal.

I am now in a position to discuss the method of estimation. There are both important analogies and important differences between the methods used here and the methods of estimation routinely used for panel data. In panel data, we typically have a short time series on a large cross-section of individuals. Error structures are specified that allow either fixed or random effects for each individual, and estimates are sought that will be consistent as the number of individuals in the cross-section increases with the number of time series observations held constant. In the current application, the role of the individuals is taken by the clusters or villages in the survey, and the repeat, time series observations, are replaced by the individual households within each cluster. In sample surveys, the cluster size does not vary very much across surveys, sample sizes, or countries, and is usually between six and fifteen households. In consequence, as in the case of panel data, I require estimators that are consistent as the number of clusters increases, holding cluster size constant. As far as error specification is concerned, equation (1) assumes that there is a fixed effect in the demand equation. This allows each household in each cluster to share an idiosyncratic cluster effect that could represent shared preferences (villages are often homogeneous with respect to race, tribe, religion, or occupation), or weather, or distance, or many other factors. Such a specification allows for arbitrary patterns of spatial correlations in consumption patterns; the spatial autocorrelation models estimated by Case (1988), and shown by her to be important, are special cases of the model estimated here.

It is very important that the fixed effects be permitted to be correlated with the included exogenous variables, particularly income, and it is this feature that rules out the use of a 'random' effect for each cluster, and the associated error components model. For the unit value equation (2), the addition of a fixed effect would destroy identification because the unit values would no longer give any useful information about the prices. However both random errors u^0 and u^1 in (1) and (2) are allowed to have cluster components; in particular, there is no supposition that measurement error cancels out over the households in each cluster. When there are only a few sample households in the village, the average measurement error for the cluster will typically have lower variance than the measurement error for each household, but that does not mean that it can be ignored. I note finally that while in most panel data sets there are the same number of time series observations on each individual, it is typically not the case here that there are the same number of sample households per cluster; even when intended by design, non-response always introduces some variation. This variation introduces some additional complexity into the algebra but raises no issues of principle.

The estimation takes place in two stages. At the first, equations (1) and (2) are estimated equation by equation by ordinary least squares (OLS) with cluster means subtracted from all data. The subtraction of cluster means removes, not only the fixed effects in (1), but also the cluster invariant prices in both equations. The resulting 'within' estimates of β_G^0, γ_G^0, β_G^1, and γ_G^1, are consistent in spite of the lack of information on prices and fixed effects. Denote these parameter estimates as $\tilde{\beta}_G^0$, $\tilde{\gamma}_G^0$, $\tilde{\beta}_G^1$, and $\tilde{\gamma}_G^1$. Although I shall not be dealing here with a 'complete set' of demand equations, in which the budget shares of the goods add to unity, these parameter estimates respect the adding-up conditions in the sense that, for a complete system the vectors of parameter estimates $\tilde{\beta}^0$ and $\tilde{\gamma}^0$ add to zero. This result is a consequence of the fact that for a system of OLS estimators $B = (X'X)^{-1}(X'Y)$, where Y is the matrix of observations on the budget shares, $Y\iota = X\gamma$ implies $B\iota = \gamma$, for vector of units ι. In this case the budget shares add to unity, so that γ is zero except for the element corresponding to the constant term in X. All this only works if zero observations on consumption are *included*. Otherwise, the sample of included households is different for each commodity, we no longer have a simple multivariate regression set, and the result does not apply.

Note that, from (4) and (9), the estimates of the total expenditure elasticities of quantity and quality, as well as the parameters ξ are functions only of these first stage parameters. Denote the residuals from the two sets of regressions as ε_{Gic}^0 and ε_{Gic}^1. These can be used to give consistent estimates of the variances and covariances of the residuals in (1) and (2) as follows:

$$\tilde{\sigma}_{GH}^{0\,0} = (n - C - k)^{-1} \sum_c \sum_i e_{Gic}^0 e_{Hic}^0 \tag{11a}$$

$$\tilde{\sigma}_{GG}^{1\,1} = (n_G^+ - C - k)^{-1} \sum_c \sum_i (e_{Gic}^1)^2 \tag{11b}$$

$$\tilde{\sigma}_{GG}^{1\,0} = (n_G^+ - C - k)^{-1} \sum_c \sum_i e_{Gic}^0 e_{Gic}^1 \tag{11c}$$

where n_G^+ is the sum of n_{cG}^+ over clusters and n is the total number of households. In (11b) and (11c) the summation is taken over all households that record unit values, while in (11a), it runs over all households. Note that equations (11b) and (11c) estimate only variances and covariances within goods, and that the covariances of the residuals *between* goods are assumed to be zero both within the unit value equation and between the two equations.

In principle there is no difficulty in estimating the full matrices of inter-good covariances, and the appropriate formulae are the obvious extensions to (11b) and (11c). The formulae given below also apply to the more general case. However, in many applications there are relatively few households recording market purchases, and the estimation of off-diagonal elements for σ_{GH}^{10} and σ_{GH}^{11} could only be based on households that record purchases for *both* goods. Even then, each element of the estimated matrix would be formed from a different number of residuals, a fact that would have to be allowed for in calculating standard errors. The important covariances here are those between the budget shares and unit values for the same good. Expenditures and quantities are inevitably measured with error, so that when unit values are calculated by dividing one by the other, there will generally be a correlation between the residuals in the budget share and unit value equations.

All the first stage estimators will be consistent as the sample size tends to infinity, even if the number of clusters increases at the same rate as the total sample size, as it would in the practically relevant case where cluster size is held constant. Of course the consistency comes at a price, that the parameters (including the variances) are the same for all clusters, so that the within-cluster information can be pooled over a large number of clusters.

The second stage of estimation begins by using the first stage estimates to calculate the parts of mean cluster shares and unit values that are not accounted for by the first stage variables. Define $\bar{y}_{G.c}^{0}$ and $\bar{y}_{G.c}^{1}$ by

$$\bar{y}_{G.c}^{0} = w_{G.c} - \beta_{G}^{0}\ln x_{.c} - \bar{\gamma}_{G}^{0} \cdot z_{.c} = w_{G.c} - x_{.c} \cdot \bar{\pi}_{G}^{0} \tag{12a}$$

$$\bar{y}_{G.c}^{1} = \ln v_{G.c} - \beta_{G}^{1}\ln x_{.c} - \bar{\gamma}_{G}^{1} \cdot z_{.c} = \ln v_{G.c} - x_{.c} \cdot \bar{\pi}_{G}^{1} \tag{12b}$$

where, in a slight abuse of notation, $x_{.c}$ is the vector of explanatory variables at the first stage, and π_{G}^{0} and π_{G}^{1} are the parameters for the two equations. Define the matrix Q as the variance – covariance matrix across clusters of the theoretical magnitudes $y_{G.c}^{0}$, defined as above but using the true parameters β^{0} and γ^{0}. S is the corresponding matrix for $y_{G.c}^{1}$, and R the covariance matrix, that is:

$$q_{GH} = \text{cov}(y^0_{G.c}, y^0_{H.c}), \ s_{GH} = \text{cov}(y^1_{G.c}, y^1_{H.c}),$$
$$r_{GH} = \text{cov}(y^0_{G.c}, y^1_{H.c}) \tag{13}$$

It is also convenient to have a matrix notation for the matrices of residual variances and covariances. Denote the population counterparts corresponding to (11a), (11b) and (11c) by Σ, Ω, and Γ respectively. As defined above, and as implemented in the computer code, the last two of these are diagonal matrices, but nothing in the theory prevents a more general interpretation.

From the population version of (12), and taking probability limits over all clusters:

$$S = \Psi M \Psi' + \Omega N_+^{-1} \tag{14}$$

$$R = \Psi M \Theta' + \Gamma N^{-1} \tag{15}$$

where M is the variance–covariance matrix of the unobservable price vector, $N_+^1 = \text{plim} C^{-1} \sum_c D(n_c^+)^{-1}$, with $D(n_c^+)$ a diagonal matrix formed from the elements of n_{cG}^+ and N^{-1} is the corresponding matrix for the n_cs. Equating sample moments to their population counterparts, calculate the matrix $\tilde{B}$ according to:

$$\tilde{B} = (\tilde{S} - \tilde{\Omega} T_+^{-1})^{-1} (\tilde{R} - \tilde{\Gamma} T_A^{-1}) \tag{16}$$

where a superimposed '~' (tilde) denotes an estimate and the diagonal matrices T_A and T_+ are the sample counterparts of N and N_+, and are given by:

$$T_A^{-1} = C^{-1} \sum_c [D(n_c)]^{-1}, \ T_+^{-1} = C^{-1} \sum_c [D(n_c^+)]^{-1} \tag{17}$$

and C is the total number of clusters in the sample. As the sample size goes to infinity with cluster sizes remaining fixed, $\tilde{B}$ will tend to its population counterpart, that is:

$$\text{plim } \tilde{B} = B = (\Psi')^{-1}\Theta' \tag{18}$$

It is not required that the cluster size become large; by pooling across clusters at the first stage, the first stage parameters are consistent as the number of clusters increases. Similarly, the estimation of price effects rests entirely on the between cluster variation, and the estimate of B will tend to its true value as the number of clusters grows large.

Estimates of B do not allow direct recovery of Ψ and Θ. However, equation (10) together with (18) allows Θ to be calculated from

$$\Theta = B'\{I - D(\xi)B' + D(\xi)D(w)\}^{-1} \tag{19}$$

The matrix of price elasticities E, from (6), is $\{D(w)\}^{-1}\Theta - \Psi$, so that, substituting:

$$E = [D(w)^{-1} B' - I][I - D(\xi)B' + D(\xi)D(w)]^{-1} \tag{20}$$

Estimates of Θ and E are calculated from (19) and (20) by replacing theoretical magnitudes with estimates from the first and second stages and by using the sample mean budget shares for the w-vector.

The Appendix derives variances and covariances for the parameters and for the elasticities, as well as test statistics for Slutsky symmetry. The remainder of this section reports a very limited Monte Carlo experiment with a 'stripped-down' version of the model. The model I have investigated is one in which there are neither cross-price nor quality effects; the focus is rather on the effects of the measurement error, particularly in the unit value equation. The true model is formed from the following versions of (1) and (2):

$$w_{ic} = \alpha^0 + \beta^0 \ln x_{ic} + \theta \ln p_c + f_c + u_{ic}^0 \tag{21}$$

$$\ln v_{ic} = \ln p_c + u_{ic}^1 \tag{22}$$

There is only one good, and the absence of quality effects means that the unit value is simply a noisy measure of price. The parameter α^0 is set to zero, β^0 to 0.02, and θ, which is the parameter on which I shall focus, to 0.046; this value, together with the other assumptions to be made, generates a price elasticity of -0.67 at the mean of the budget share. Total expenditure x and the unobservable p are each generated by independent drawings from lognormal distributions, $\ln x$ with mean 4.6 and standard deviation 0.5, and $\ln p$ with mean zero and standard deviation 0.1. These values were drawn afresh at each experiment rather than held fixed in repeated samples; this appears to be the appropriate way to model repeated sample surveys from the same underlying population. I made no attempt to induce any cluster structure into the $\ln x$s; all observations are independent drawings.

The fixed effects f_c are generated as $0.01\ (\ln x_c{-}4.6){+}0.0159\varepsilon$, where 4.6 is the mean of $\ln x$, $\ln x_c$ is the cluster mean of $\ln x_{ic}$, and ε is drawn from $N(0, 1)$. This procedure is chosen so as to generate a correlation of 0.3 between the fixed effects and $\ln x$. Finally, the two error terms u^0 and u^1 are independently drawn from normal distributions, each with mean zero, and standard deviations of 0.0005 and 0.1 respectively. The independence of u^0 and u^1 corresponds to the case where errors of measurement in expenditures and prices are independent, so that there will be a *negative* correlation between measured quantity and measured unit value. While there is a good deal of arbitrariness in the choice of these parameters, they generate data that bear at least superficial resemblance to the results reported below.

The experiments were carried out as follows. Given a cluster size n_c, assumed to be the same for all clusters, and a number of clusters C, 500 'sample surveys' were generated according to the rules above, and the estimate of θ calculated using equation (16). No use was made of the absence of quality effects in the price equation, so that the unit values were regressed on $\ln x$ at the first stage as described in the text above. Based on the previous literature, two additional estimators were calculated. The first, referred to as the 'between-cluster' estimator, has a first stage that is identical to that for the 'correct' estimator, but at the second stage the corrections for the estimated measurement errors are omitted. Referring to equation (16), the estimate would be $\tilde{S}^{-1}\tilde{R}$. The basic idea is to ignore the within-cluster information, relying on the averaging within clusters to reduce the measurement error in prices, see Strauss (1982) for a similar argument in the context of farm-household behaviour in Sierra Leone. The second, the 'logarithmic' estimator follows the standard procedure of double logarithmic regression – see, for example, Timmer and Alderman (1979) and Timmer (1981). In the experiments, $\ln q$ was calculated as $\ln w{+}\ln x{-}\ln p$, and then the individual household data were used to regress $\ln q$ on a constant, $\ln x$ and $\ln v$. To compare the estimated elasticity with the parameter θ, it was multiplied by the sample mean budget share and added to 1. A simple errors-in-variables analysis shows that, provided the true elasticity is greater than -1, as it is here, this estimator will be biased downward by the spurious negative correlation between $\ln q$ and $\ln v$.

The results are shown in graphic form in Figures 10.1, 10.2, and 10.3. In Figure 10.1, there are 100 clusters, each of size 2. (In the empirical results below, the situation is much better than this, and

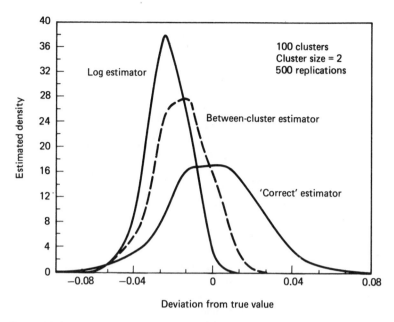

Figure 10.1   Three estimators: smoothed densities

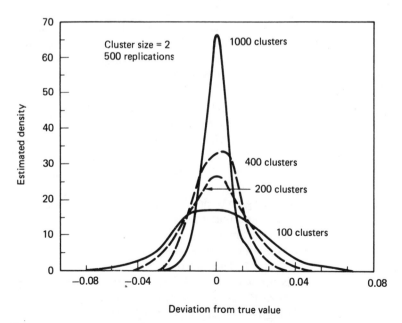

Figure 10.2   Effects of numbers of clusters

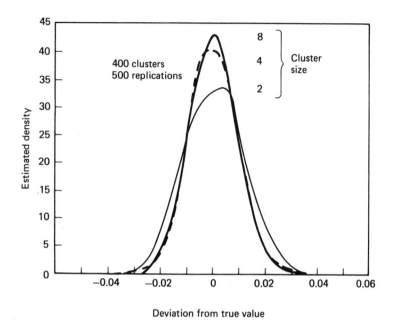

Figure 10.3   Effects of cluster size

there are typically more than 2000 clusters with 4–6 households in each.) The estimated densities are shown for each of the three estimators. They are calculated from the underlying 500 estimates by using a kernel density estimator with a Gaussian kernel and a band width of $1.06.m^{-0.2}.\min\{sd, iqr/1.34\}$, where sd and iqr are the standard deviation and inter-quartile range of the estimates, and $m=500$ is the number of replications, see Silverman (1986, pp. 45–7). Unlike the other two estimators, the 'correct' estimator is correctly centred, but has noticeably greater spread. The between estimator is biased downward; averaging over clusters does not eliminate the measurement error in the unit values, so that the variance of 'prices' is overstated, thus producing an understatement when it is divided into the covariance of prices and budget shares. The expected downward bias in the logarithmic estimator is also apparent; in this case the elasticity would be estimated as close to –1 instead of its true value (at the sample mean) of –0.67. The variance of the log estimator is the least because it uses the whole sample, not just the between-cluster data. That of the 'correct' estimator is relatively wide because of the necessity of estimating the within-cluster error variances. The sampling variability of these variances causes a loss of precision but is required to correct the bias and inconsistency in the other two estimators. Not shown here is the bias of the total expenditure elasticity from the log estimator; by ignoring the fixed effects, the estimated expenditure elasticity is contaminated by the correlation between $\ln x$ and f, not to mention the measurement error in $\ln v$.

Figures 10.2 and 10.3 show the effects of increasing, first, the number of clusters, and second, the number of households in each cluster. Figure 10.2 shows the expected narrowing of the distribution as the number of clusters increases from 100 to 1000 with the cluster size at its worst possible value of 2. As theory would suggest, the standard deviations of the four densities are proportional to $C^{-0.5}$, and even with these relatively unfavourable sample sizes, the asymptotic standard errors derived in the Appendix are an excellent approximation to the empirical standard deviations. For the four cases shown, with cluster size 2 and with 100, 200, 400 and 1000 clusters, the actual standard deviations with the theoretical asymptotic standard errors in brackets are, respectively, 0.0210 (0.0220), 0.0149 (0.0151), 0.0105 (0.0107), and 0.0067 (0.0067). Figure 10.3 shows that larger cluster sizes are better than smaller ones, but the effect is not very marked. Again, this is what is predicted by the theory. Even with infinite numbers of households in each cluster, the estimates would not converge; information about prices comes only from the cross-section of clusters. Again the asymptotic standard errors are a good guide to the actual results; for cluster sizes 4 and 8, the actual standard deviations, followed by the theoretical standard errors in brackets, are 0.0092 (0.0093) and 0.0086 (0.0088). Unless there is something special about these simulations (and they are the only ones that I have tried), the theory in the Appendix would seem to provide useful formulae for standard errors, especially given that, in practice, sample sizes are likely to be much larger than those in the simulation.

3   RESULTS FROM RURAL JAVA

The model described in Section 2 was used to estimate a demand system of eleven foods using data from the 1981 SUSENAS household survey of Indonesia. Since spatial price variation is likely to be more marked in rural areas, and since survey clusters are more widely spaced in the countryside, I report results only for rural households. In order to keep a sample that is relatively homogeneous, I further restrict

Table 10.1   Commodities, sample sizes, and budget shares, Java, 1981

	Households in clusters where some purchases	Households recording purchases	Clusters where some purchase	Budget share (averaged over households in column 1)
		(Numbers)		Per cent
Rice	12 914	9 245	2 804	24.53
Wheat	5 228	1 703	1 061	0.52
Maize	3 926	1 593	815	5.77
Cassava	6 441	2 539	1 343	1.39
Roots	5 716	2 021	1 185	0.60
Vegetables	14 419	14 115	3 181	5.57
Legumes	13 939	12 055	3 070	3.66
Fruit	10 114	4 652	2 124	1.88
Meat	4 928	1 526	1 001	2.07
Fresh fish	9 262	5 046	1 925	2.95
Dried fish	13 327	10 665	2 871	2.83

Source: SUSENAS, *Household Survey of Indonesia*, 1987.

attention to Java. Even so, the potential maximum sample is 14 487 households. Table 10.1 lists the eleven foods, together with their average budget shares, and the numbers of households providing information about each. Although households that record no expenditure are included in the analysis, whole clusters with zero expenditures are excluded because there is no way of estimating a price for them. There are 3202 sample clusters in rural Java in all, and the third column of Table 10.1 shows how many clusters record at least one household making a purchase for each of the goods. The first and second columns show how many households are in these clusters, and how many make purchases. Overall, there are just under five households per cluster. Even selecting out clusters where no household makes a purchase, the number of purchasers per cluster varies from 4.4 for vegetables to around 1.5 for meat. Expenditure on rice accounts for nearly a quarter of the budget while the other foods account for another quarter between them.

Table 10.2 presents some of the results from the first stage estimation. At this stage, cluster means are removed from all variables, and shares and logarithms of unit values regressed on the logarithm of household per capita expenditure, the logarithm of total house-

Table 10.2 First stage estimates of quantity and quality effects

	β^0	$t(\beta^0)$	β^1	$t(\beta^1)$	ε	$t(\varepsilon)$
Rice	−0.1179	−56.7	0.0290	9.0	0.490	57.6
Wheat	0.0035	6.6	0.0993	1.1	1.567	23.4
Maize	−0.0526	−19.1	−0.0003	−0.0	0.088	3.3
Cassava	−0.0118	−14.9	0.0168	0.7	0.139	3.5
Roots	−0.0008	−1.7	0.1653	2.8	0.709	13.9
Vegetables	−0.0206	−33.7	−0.0402	−1.8	0.670	25.2
Legumes	−0.0039	−5.9	0.0422	4.6	0.850	42.3
Fruit	0.0086	12.4	0.0725	2.7	1.385	40.0
Meat	0.0287	18.2	0.0885	1.9	2.296	43.4
Fresh fish	0.0090	8.8	0.2232	8.5	1.082	35.0
Dried fish	−0.0105	−17.6	0.0639	5.7	0.566	25.5

Notes: β^0 is the coefficient of the budget share, and β^1 the coefficient of the unit value on the logarithm of household expenditure per capita.
β^1 is the total expenditure elasticity for quality.
ε is the calculated total expenditure elasticity of quantity.

---

hold size, a set of demographic variables (the numbers of household members in each of thirteen age and sex categories as a ratio of household size), and nine educational dummies. The first four columns show, together with their t-values, the coefficients β^0 and β^1, which estimate the effects of the logarithm of total expenditure on the shares and the unit values. The last two columns show the total expenditure elasticities of quantity calculated according to equation (4).

The quality elasticities β^1 relate to unit values, defined as expenditure per kilo, where the latter is calculated by adding weights across all goods in the group. Such a procedure makes sense for most of the goods, but is less than satisfactory for such categories as fresh fish, vegetables, or fruit, where I am (literally for fruit) adding apples and oranges. A more sophisticated calorie-based treatment would be an obvious next step. However, note that even if kilos of 'fruit' are of little interest on their own account, total weight is likely to be well correlated with more satisfactory indicators of volume if the composition within the category is more or less constant across the sample. In any case, and with the exception of roots and fresh fish, the estimates in Table 10.2 show very little response of unit value to total expenditure. For two goods, maize and vegetables, there are insignificant negative effects, while for the others, the elasticities are less than 10 per cent. Even when the quality elasticity is relatively large, as in fresh fish, the effect is hardly dramatic. An estimated expenditure

Table 10.3 First stage variances, covariances, and cluster sizes

	σ^{00}	σ^{11}	σ^{10}	t_A	t_+
Rice	0.004915	0.00671	0.00072	3.85	2.31
Wheat	0.000138	0.50110	0.00122	4.28	1.28
Maize	0.002678	0.05991	0.00172	4.11	1.40
Cassava	0.000349	0.06175	0.00066	4.09	1.41
Roots	0.000100	0.30061	0.00023	4.14	1.33
Vegetables	0.000467	0.58771	−0.00180	3.74	3.59
Legumes	0.000530	0.08454	0.00041	3.76	2.99
Fruit	0.000450	0.21981	0.00119	4.08	1.59
Meat	0.001369	0.15164	0.00153	4.20	1.24
Fresh fish	0.000865	0.23510	0.00212	4.08	1.76
Dried fish	0.000413	0.10134	0.00082	3.92	2.68

Notes: σ^{00}, σ^{11}, and σ^{10} are the residual variances of the share equation, the unit value equation, and the covariance between them, respectively. t_A and t_+ are the elements of the matrices T_A and T_+, and are appropriately defined 'averages' of numbers of households per cluster, in total, and reporting purchases of the good.

elasticity of fish *expenditure* of 1.31 is decomposed into an estimated quantity elasticity of fish of 1.08, with the difference of 0.22 representing the upgrading of quality at higher incomes. The quantity elasticities are ordered much as would be expected, with cassava and rice near the bottom, and meat, fresh fish, and wheat near the top.

Table 10.3 reports the estimates of variances and covariances from the first stage estimates. The first column gives the diagonal of the matrix $\tilde{\Sigma}$, the residual variances from the share equation; the square roots of these numbers can be compared with the average budget shares from Table 10.1 to give some idea of fit. The second column is the diagonal of Ω, while the third column, which is the most interesting, presents the covariances between the residuals in the two equations. The estimates of σ^{10} are important because they are informative about the importance of measurement error and because their magnitude affects the size of the corrections that are made to what otherwise would be an OLS regression of cluster average shares on cluster average prices, see equation (16) above. A natural starting point for discussion is the supposition that the errors of measurement in reported expenditures are orthogonal to the errors of measurement in reported quantities. If so, the error in the unit value will have a positive covariance with the error in the share, and that is what occurs in Table 10.3 in all cases except for vegetables. The last may

Table 10.4   Cross-cluster variances and covariances and corrections

	Cov(w, ln$p$)	Var(ln$p$)	Ratio (1)	Ratio (2)	e_1	e_2
Rice	0.00203	0.0158	0.1284	0.1429	−0.48	−0.42
Wheat	0.00113	0.9545	0.0012	0.0015	−0.77	−0.71
Maize	0.00223	0.1499	0.0149	0.0169	−0.74	−0.71
Cassava	0.00117	0.1663	0.0071	0.0082	−0.49	−0.41
Roots	−0.00038	0.6486	−0.0006	−0.0010	−1.10	−1.17
Vegetables	−0.00184	0.5862	−0.0031	−0.0032	−1.06	−1.06
Legumes	−0.00032	0.1203	−0.0027	−0.0047	−1.07	−1.13
Fruit	0.00033	0.2424	0.0014	0.0004	−0.93	−0.98
Meat	−0.00010	0.2281	−0.0004	−0.0044	−1.02	−1.21
Fresh fish	0.00165	0.3311	0.0050	0.0057	−0.83	−0.81
Dried fish	0.00345	0.1404	0.0246	0.0316	−0.13	0.12

Notes: The covariances and variances are evaluated across cluster means.
Ratio (1) is the ratio of the covariance to the variance.
Ratio (2) is the ratio of the covariance less σ^{10}/t_A to the variance less σ^{11}/t_+.
e_1 and e_2 are the own-price elasticities calculated ignoring all cross-price and quality effects using ratio (1) and ratio (2) respectively.

---

reflect a different reporting bias, or just the general inappropriateness of adding together the weights of different vegetables. The scale of σ^{10} will be determined by the budget share of the good, so that, once again, it is useful to deflate the estimates by the average budget share. Particularly noticeable is the very small figure for the most important commodity, rice, where σ^{10}/w is 0.0029, suggesting that measurement errors on expenditures have a standard error of only about 5 per cent. For the other commodities, similar computations give much larger figures.

From an econometric point of view, the importance of allowing for measurement error is determined by the size of the corrections to S and R made by subtracting ΩT_A^{-1} and ΓT_+^{-1}. Table 10.4 is one way of assessing the extent to which measurement error affects the estimates. The first and second columns show the cross-cluster variance of mean unit value and its covariance with the budget share, where both quantities have been purged of the effects of the first stage variables. The ratio of covariance to variance, ratio (1), is the OLS regression coefficient in the regression of mean budget share on mean unit value. If there were no quality effects, no cross-price effects, and no measurement error, this ratio, divided by the budget share, would be one plus the own-price elasticity, e_1 in the table. As has already been seen, the quality effects are small in any case, and as will be seen, allowing for cross-price effects has only a minor effect on the own-price elasticities, so the simple estimates here are more useful than might appear. If the calculation is complicated only to the extent of allowing for measurement error, still ignoring cross-price and quality effects, the covariance is corrected by substracting σ^{10}/t from Table 10.3, the variance by subtracting σ^{11}/t_+, and the ratio and the elasticity recalculated. Hence ratio (2) and e_2 in the table.

Given the general uncertainty about price elasticities, the last two columns are remarkably close. Only for dried fish, and to a lesser extent for meat, does the correction make an appreciable difference. For some commodities, for example rice, the estimated size of the measurement error is small relative to the substantive variances and covariances so that ratio (1) and ratio (2) are similar. This finding replicates earlier work on the demand for rice in Indonesia by Case (1988). For other goods, allowing for measurement error makes a large proportional difference to the ratio of covariance to variance, but since the ratio itself is small, the estimated elasticity remains close to minus one. In either case, similar results would have been obtained by simply ignoring the measurement error, provided, of course, that the regression is one of average cluster demand on average cluster price. However, it is important to note that this result provides no support for a regression, at the household level, of log quantity on log price. Such a regression is restricted to households that make positive purchases and the results on the restricted sample are likely to be (and in this case are) very different. Even simple regressions of budget shares on ln$x$ have very different coefficients depending on whether or not zeros are excluded, particularly for those commodities where there are a large number of households not purchasing. Further, by working at the household level, rather than with cluster means, there is no averaging to reduce the effects of measurement error relative to the effects of genuine price variation.

The matrix of own and cross-price elasticities is presented in Table 10.5. All the estimated own-price elasticities are negative, as they should be. Note however that the 'default' own-price elasticity is not zero but minus one, a value that is attained when B and β^1 are zero, see equation (20). The own-price elasticities are also close to the preliminary estimates in Table 10.4; allowing for cross-price effects is not very important for measuring own-price elasticities, at least in these data. For four commodities – vegetables, legumes, fruit, and meat – the price elasticity is not significantly different from this default value, a phenomenon that may reflect problems with defining quantities. For all goods except meat, and for all goods with price

273

Table 10.5 Own- and cross-price elasticities, Java, 1981

	1 Rice	2 Wheat	3 Maize	4 Cassava	5 Roots	6 Vegetables	7 Legumes	8 Fruit	9 Meat	10 Fresh fish	11 Dried fish
1 Rice	-0.424 (5.1)	-0.005 (0.3)	-0.032 (0.9)	0.088 (3.1)	0.025 (1.8)	-0.057 (3.2)	0.065 (2.0)	0.130 (2.9)	-0.064 (1.6)	0.053 (2.1)	1.213 (6.3)
2 Wheat	0.461 (1.6)	-0.692 (13.8)	0.011 (0.1)	-0.000 (0.0)	-0.188 (3.8)	0.284 (4.6)	-0.127 (1.1)	-0.211 (1.3)	-0.226 (1.6)	0.089 (1.0)	-0.128 (1.1)
3 Maize	1.245 (4.9)	0.090 (2.1)	-0.822 (7.5)	-0.256 (3.0)	-0.100 (2.4)	0.602 (9.5)	0.006 (0.1)	-0.247 (1.8)	0.167 (1.4)	-0.444 (5.6)	-0.111 (1.1)
4 Cassava	0.151 (0.5)	0.078 (1.4)	0.186 (1.4)	-0.325 (2.8)	-0.003 (0.1)	0.121 (1.7)	0.013 (0.1)	-0.461 (2.5)	0.184 (1.1)	0.054 (0.5)	-0.671 (5.0)
5 Roots	0.795 (3.9)	0.125 (3.6)	0.150 (1.9)	0.084 (1.2)	-0.953 (22.0)	0.080 (1.8)	-0.122 (1.5)	-0.072 (0.6)	0.080 (0.8)	0.181 (2.9)	-0.253 (3.1)
6 Vegetables	-0.047 (0.4)	-0.057 (3.1)	-0.100 (2.3)	0.101 (2.7)	0.030 (1.6)	-1.113 (28.5)	-0.081 (1.9)	-0.064 (1.1)	-0.064 (1.2)	0.050 (1.5)	-0.173 (4.0)
7 Legumes	0.108 (0.8)	-0.038 (1.6)	-0.200 (3.5)	-0.050 (1.0)	0.034 (1.4)	-0.118 (3.8)	-0.954 (0.8)	-0.097 (1.3)	0.202 (3.0)	-0.084 (1.9)	-0.134 (2.4)
8 Fruit	0.354 (2.1)	-0.013 (0.4)	-0.003 (0.0)	0.171 (2.9)	-0.068 (2.3)	0.056 (1.5)	-0.088 (1.3)	-0.953 (0.5)	-0.092 (1.1)	0.071 (1.4)	-0.070 (1.0)
9 Meat	-0.190 (0.8)	-0.075 (1.7)	-0.060 (0.6)	-0.173 (2.0)	-0.158 (3.6)	0.176 (3.2)	0.030 (0.3)	-0.376 (2.7)	-1.091 (0.7)	-0.036 (0.5)	0.196 (1.9)
10 Fresh fish	0.399 (2.0)	0.028 (0.8)	0.244 (3.0)	-0.017 (0.2)	-0.099 (2.8)	0.316 (7.0)	0.026 (0.3)	-0.009 (0.1)	0.047 (0.5)	-0.762 (3.8)	0.259 (3.2)
11 Dried fish	0.391 (2.0)	0.029 (0.8)	0.151 (1.9)	0.057 (0.8)	-0.057 (1.7)	0.379 (8.4)	-0.023 (0.3)	-0.105 (1.0)	-0.057 (0.6)	0.667 (10.4)	-0.239 (9.4)

Notes: The column is the good whose price is changing, and the row is the good affected. Hence, a 1 per cent increase in the price of vegetables is estimated to increase the consumption of wheat by 0.284 per cent. The figures below the elasticities are (absolute) asymptotic t-values.

elasticities significantly different from minus one, the price elasticities
are estimated to lie between minus one and zero. There are no goods
with very large estimated own-price elasticities, and there is some
tendency for the goods that have the lowest total expenditure elasticities (dried fish, cassava, rice) to have absolutely low price elasticities, something that might be expected for goods that are
genuinely 'necessary'.

The important rice price elasticity is estimated to be -0.42, which
can be compared with the figures of -0.55 or -0.62 (depending on
detailed assumptions) estimated from a subsample of 5218 households in Java from the same survey by van de Walle (1988). Van de
Walle used a log–log specification and the difference in the estimates
is in the direction that the theory would predict. However, the
divergence is not very large; the vast majority of households consume
rice, and van de Walle argues that the rice price may be relatively
well measured. Timmer and Alderman (1979) and Timmer (1981)
also report price elasticities for rice and cassava from the 1976 survey.
Again they use a double logarithmic formulation but apply the
model, not to the micro data, but to cell means of income classes by
province, sector, and time period. They estimate different elasticities
for different income groups, and find figures that are numerically very
much larger than those reported here. Most income groups have rice
price elasticities below -1, and the average is -1.1, while for fresh
cassava, the average price elasticity is -0.8, as opposed to -0.33 in
Table 10.5. Timmer and Alderman also report a cross-price elasticity
of cassava with respect to the rice price of 0.77 (0.15 here) but fail to
find a significant cross-price effect from cassava to rice (0.09 here).
There are many possible reasons for these discrepancies, but again
the double logarithmic quantity on unit value specification must be a
prime suspect. I also find it implausible that such basic staples should
display such high price elasticities, if only because there are few
obvious substitutes. However, the opposite position has also been
argued: that poor, near-subsistence consumers will substitute between minimum cost calorie-based diets as relative prices change.

There are a considerable number of estimates of cross-price elasticities that are significantly different from zero. It is not difficult to
invent 'explanations' to account for almost any observed pattern of
responses, but it is undoubtedly the case that some of the figures
make a good deal more sense than others. For example, the elasticities are gross elasticities, with income effects included, so that it
would be reasonable to expect many of the numbers in the first

Table 10.6 Deviations from symmetry

	2	3	4	5	6	7	8	9	10	11
1	0.1	**7.4**	**−2.1**	−0.1	1.4	−0.9	−2.1	2.1	0.3	**−4.1**
	0.0	4.6	2.5	0.3	1.9	0.9	1.8	1.9	0.4	4.0
2		0.5	0.1	**0.2**	**−0.5**	−0.1	0.1	−0.0	0.3	0.1
		1.9	1.0	5.1	4.6	0.8	0.3	0.2	0.2	1.2
3			**1.7**	**0.7**	**−3.8**	−0.6	1.6	−0.8	**3.4**	1.1
			3.3	2.8	8.6	1.0	2.0	1.1	6.6	1.8
4				0.1	0.4	−0.2	**1.0**	−0.6	−0.1	**1.1**
				0.7	1.9	0.6	3.6	1.9	0.3	4.1
5					0.1	0.2	−0.1	**−0.3**	**−0.4**	−0.0
					1.1	2.0	0.9	3.3	3.6	0.1
6						0.1	0.5	**0.9**	**0.7**	**2.0**
						0.2	1.6	3.0	3.2	7.4
7							0.2	−0.6	0.4	0.4
							0.7	1.7	1.5	1.3
8								−0.6	−0.2	−0.2
								1.7	0.5	0.6
9									0.1	−0.7
									0.4	1.9
10										**1.1**
										3.6

Note: the upper entry in row i, column j is (100 times) the quantity $w_j e_{ji} - w_i e_{ij} + w_j w_i (e_j - e_i)$, which should be zero under Slutsky symmetry. The lower figures are absolute asymptotic t-values. Deviations with t-values greater than 2 are shown in bold.

column to reflect the large negative income effects generated by increases in the price of rice. Yet most of these estimates are *positive*, and there are substantial proportional increases in the demand for maize, roots, fruit and fish when the price of rice rises. For this to make sense, the other omitted categories must show an overall complementarity with rice. Some other cross-price effects, for example the strong substitutability between fresh and dried fish, look a good deal more satisfactory. Table 10.6 shows the deviations from symmetry evaluated according to equation (39), together with their absolute t-values. Sixteen of the fifty-five cross-terms are significantly different from zero, and the overall Wald statistic for the null of symmetry is 415.8, a number that is well in excess of conventional critical values of a χ^2, even with 55 degrees of freedom. In Deaton (1987), I reported a favourable symmetry test for the Ivory Coast;

however, in that case there were only five goods and fewer than 200 clusters, as distinct from eleven goods and 2000 clusters in the current example. With such large samples, standard hypothesis tests will always tend to reject if no attempt is made to trade off Type I and Type II errors, and a case can be made for using a Bayesian procedure, such as that advocated by Schwartz (1978). This would reject the null only for test statistics greater than 55 times the log of the sample size, or 418.0. While such a procedure is not universally accepted, it is perhaps reasonable to conclude that the evidence is not overwhelmingly against the symmetry hypothesis.

4 CONCLUSIONS

This paper has proposed a method for using large scale household survey data for the estimation of a system of demand equations, making use of spatial variation in price to identify and estimate a matrix of own and cross-price elasticities. Compared with earlier formulations (Deaton, 1987 and 1988), the model presented here contains a more satisfactory specification of the demand functions, as well as a derivation of the rather complex formulae for variances and covariances of the estimates. The admittedly limited Monte Carlo evidence presented in Section 2 does not suggest any practical problems in using the procedure or the formulae for the standard errors. Large scale sample surveys provide the sort of data where asymptotic theory is likely to provide a very good approximation.

Estimates are presented for an eleven-commodity system for Indonesia. To the extent that it is possible to judge, the parameter estimates are plausible. For rice and cassava, the own-price elasticities are a good deal smaller (that is, closer to zero) than some previous estimates, but the direction of the discrepancy is as predicted by the theory developed here. If judged by a large sample posterior odds test, the estimates are consistent with Slutsky symmetry, but the hypothesis would be rejected by a strict classical statistician (as would most sharp hypotheses on a sample of more than 14 000 observations.)

While the model appears to work well in the application, there are a number of unresolved issues that ought to be noted. The model is very close to being exactly identified and so it is difficult to construct the sort of cross-checks that would lend it greater conviction. Plausibility of demand elasticities is not in itself a very powerful test. It would be extremely desirable to have data with direct measures of market prices against which this method could be compared. The model would also be improved by allowing a more general functional form for the Engel curve in equation (1). Given that zero observations are included, there are even less grounds than usual for assuming linearity. An ideal, but technically difficult solution, would be a semi-parametric form in which the Engel effects are dealt with non-parametrically. Although much remains to be done, the results reported here would nevertheless support the cautious use of the procedure in practical applications.

APPENDIX

This appendix describes the procedures for deriving standard errors for the parameters B, as well as the derived quantities Θ, and E. As pointed out by a referee, the estimator in Section 2 works by equating sample with theoretical moments, and so belongs to the generalised methods of moments (GMM) class of estimators. The general theory of this class has been worked out by Hansen (1982), so that one approach to deriving standard errors would be to apply Hansen's formulae. The sequential nature of the procedure can be handled by the results given by Newey (1984). The GMM method can be used to explore efficiency considerations, as well as to check the extent to which it is possible to relax the assumptions of homoskedasticity and normality which are made below. However, the algebra involved is still extraordinarily heavy, and following this route all the way would be a research project in its own right. Given computer software that would handle symbolic matrix differentiation, it would be a useful exercise to re-do the calculations below using the GMM method. Here, I proceed directly under the assumption that the error terms in (1) and (2) are independently and identically distributed normal.

I start with the variance – covariance matrix of the estimate of the matrix B; this is the most straightforward to deal with, and the variances of the elements of E are derived from it. The basic procedure is the 'delta-method', see, for example, Fuller (1987, p. 108). Expand $\bar{B}$ from equation (16) around the true value B, so that

$$(\bar{B} - B) = (S - \Omega T_+^{-1})^{-1} [(\bar{R} - R) - (\bar{\Gamma} - \Gamma)T_A^{-1}$$
$$- (\bar{S} - S)B + (\bar{\Omega} - \Omega)T_+^{-1}B] \tag{A1}$$

The derivations are simplified by adopting the following notation from Deaton (1987). Define the following matrices:

$$H = \begin{bmatrix} Q & R' \\ R & S \end{bmatrix} \qquad \Lambda = \begin{bmatrix} Z & \Gamma' \\ \Gamma & \Omega \end{bmatrix} \tag{A2}$$

together with $J=(0_N|I_N)$ an $N \times 2N$ matrix of ones and zeros, and $P' = (I_N|-B')$. Then (A1) becomes

$$(\check{B} - B) = (A^{-1}J[(\check{H} - H) - (\check{\Lambda} - \Lambda)T^{-1}]P \tag{A3}$$

where $A = (S - \Omega T_+^{-1})$ and T is a $2N \times 2N$ diagonal matrix with T_A on the first N elements of the diagonal and T_+ on the second N elements. Equation (A3) traces the sources of variance in $\check{B}$ back to the estimation uncertainties in $\check{H}$ and in $\check{\Lambda}$. The latter comes entirely from the first stage estimation and can be dealt with straightforwardly using the fact that $\check{\Lambda}$ is a Wishart matrix. It is the estimation error in $\check{H}$ that is complicated because there are two independent sources: (a) the estimation error that comes from the estimation of parameters at the first stage, and (b) the inherent uncertainty that comes from estimating population from sample covariance matrices, an uncertainty that would be present even if the first stage parameters were known. In Deaton (1987), albeit using a different functional form, I incorrectly assumed that source (a) could be asymptotically ignored. The numerical results in that paper are barely affected by the error, but in general, both sources of variance need to be taken into account, even in large samples.

To decompose further the estimation error $(\check{H} - H)$, rewrite (12) in the form

$$\check{Y}^0 = Y^0 - X(\check{\Pi}^0 - \Pi^0) \tag{A4a}$$

$$\check{Y}^1 = Y^1 - X(\check{\Pi}^1 - \Pi^1) \tag{A4b}$$

where Y^0 and Y^1 are the $C \times N$ matrices of cluster means of budget shares and log unit values, each with the grand mean removed, X is the corresponding $C \times K$ matrix of cluster means of first stage explanatory variables, again with the grand mean removed, and Π^0 and Π^1 are $K \times N$ matrices of first stage parameters. By aligning the matrices to define $Y = (Y^0 | Y^1)$, a $C \times 2N$ matrix, and similarly for $\Pi = (\Pi^0 | \Pi^1)$, (A4a) and (A4b) can be combined to give

$$\check{Y} = Y - X(\check{\Pi} - \Pi) \tag{A5}$$

The matrix $\check{H}$ is then simply $C^{-1}\check{Y}'\check{Y}$, and I denote the corresponding estimate with known first-stage parameters as $\hat{H}$, i.e. $\hat{H} = C^{-1}Y'Y$. Write M for the covariance matrix $C^{-1}X'Y$, so that, to the first-order

$$\check{H} = \hat{H} - M'(\check{\Pi} - \Pi) - (\check{\Pi} - \Pi)'M \tag{A6}$$

Substituting in (A3), we have

$$(\check{B} - B) = A^{-1}J[(\hat{H} - H) - M'(\check{\Pi} - \Pi) - (\check{\Pi} - \Pi)'M$$
$$- (\check{\Lambda} - \Lambda)T^{-1}]P \tag{A7}$$

which isolates the three sources of variance in the estimate of B. The first expression in the brackets, $\hat{H} - H$, comes from the second stage between cluster residuals, and has a standard Wishart form. The variability in the estimates of Π and of Λ comes from the first stage within cluster residuals. Since the within estimates are orthogonal to the between estimates, there is no covariance between the first term and the last three. Further, since the Π-parameters are obtained by linear regression at the first stage, their estimates are asymptotically independent of the estimates of the variances and covariances of the residuals, and thus of the estimates of Λ. Note finally that no allowance need be made for the variability of M that comes from the variability of Y, since the effects through (A6) are of the second order. Given this, I have economised on notation by not replacing M in (A7) by its population counterpart.

In 'vec' notation (A7) takes the form:

$$
\begin{aligned}
\text{vec}(\tilde{B} - B) &= (P' \otimes A^{-1} J)[\text{vec } (\tilde{H} - H) - \text{vec } \{M'(\tilde{\Pi} - \Pi)\} \\
&\quad - \text{vec } \{(\tilde{\Pi} - \Pi)'\tilde{M}\} - \text{vec } \{(\tilde{\Lambda} - \Lambda)T^{-1}\}] \\
&= (P' \otimes A^{-1}J)[\text{vec } (\tilde{H} - H) - (I+K)(I \otimes M') \text{ vec } (\tilde{\Pi} - \Pi)] \\
&\quad - (P'T^{-1} \otimes A^{-1}J) \text{ vec } (\tilde{\Lambda} - \Lambda)
\end{aligned} \tag{A8}
$$

where K is the $2N^2 \times 2N^2$ commutation matrix with the property that $K\text{vec}(A) = K\text{vec}(A')$, for arbitrary conformable matrix A, see Magnus and Neudecker (1986). Given that both $\tilde{H}$ and $\tilde{\Lambda}$ are Wishart matrices, we have:

$$
E[\text{vec } (\tilde{H} - H) \text{ vec } (\tilde{H} - H)'] = C^{-1}(H \otimes H)(I+K) \tag{A9}
$$

$$
E[\text{vec } (\tilde{\Lambda} - \Lambda) \text{ vec } (\tilde{\Lambda} - \Lambda)'] = (n - C - k)^{-1} (\Lambda \otimes \Lambda)(I+K) \tag{A10}
$$

while, since Π is estimated at the first stage from the standard multivariate regression model:

$$
E[\text{vec } (\tilde{\Pi} - \Pi) \text{ vec } (\tilde{\Pi} - \Pi)'] = \Lambda \otimes (W'W)^{-1} \tag{A11}
$$

where W is the matrix of explanatory variables for the within-regression at the first stage. Note that the matrices W and X relate to the same variables, but that X consists of deviations of cluster means from the grand mean, while W consists of deviations of individual observations from their cluster means.

Combining equations (A8) through (A11) yields

$$
V[\text{v\~ec}(\tilde{B})] = V_1 + V_2 + V_3 \tag{A12}
$$

$$
V_1 = C^{-1}(P'HP \otimes A^{-1}JHJ'A^{-1}) + C^{-1}(P'HJ'A^{-1} \otimes A^{-1}JHP)K
$$

$$
\begin{aligned}
V_2 &= (n - C - k)^{-1} (P'T^{-1}\Lambda T^{-1}P \otimes A^{-1}J\Lambda J'A^{-1}) \\
&\quad + (n - C - k)^{-1} (P'T^{-1}\Lambda J'A^{-1} \otimes A^{-1} J\Lambda T^{-1}P)K
\end{aligned}
$$

$$
V_3 = (P' \otimes A^{-1}J)(I+K)(\Lambda \otimes M'(W'W)^{-1}M)(I+K)(P \otimes J'A^{-1})
$$

Athough (A12) is the simplest way to write the variance covariance matrix, the expression for V_3 involves a larger than necessary matrix, since the matrix in the centre is $4N^2 \times 4N^2$, which can be large enough to cause storage difficulties. The following equivalent expression uses smaller matrices:

$$
\begin{aligned}
V_3 &= P'\Lambda P \otimes A^{-1} JM'(W'W)^{-1} MJ'A^{-1} \\
&+ P'M'(W'W)^{-1}MP \otimes A^{-1}J\Lambda J'A^{-1} \\
&+ (P'M'(W'W)^{-1} MJ'A^{-1} \otimes A^{-1}J\Lambda P)K \\
&+ (P'\Lambda J'A^{-1} \otimes A^{-1} JM'(W'W)^{-1} MP)K
\end{aligned} \tag{A13}
$$

Note finally that there is some ambiguity in implementing V_3 because (A11) does not reflect the fact that the unit value equations are estimated on a smaller sample than are the share equations. There are several ways of fixing this that give the right answer in large samples. Here I take $W'W$ as the matrix from the share regressions, and scale Ω, the bottom right-hand matrix of Λ, by n/n^+, where n^+ is the average over goods of the numbers of observations entering the unit value equations. Since the first stage parameters are based on a sample that is typically ten times larger than the sample at the second stage, both V_2 and V_3 usually make very small contributions to the total variance.

Although the above formulae give variances and covariances for all the parameters that are estimated, in most applications interest will focus, not on the B-parameters, but on the estimates of elasticities that are derived from them. In principle, it is straightforward to use the delta method to estimate variances and covariances of functions of the elements of B. In practice, the algebra is extremely tedious. An outline is included here for completeness, and to support the computer code. Start with the total expenditure elasticities, ε_G, which depend only on the first stage parameters β_G^0 and β_G^1, see equation (4). Write the total differential of (4) in the form $d\varepsilon = \Phi_1 d\Pi' e = (e' \otimes \Phi_1) K \text{vec} d\Pi$, where e is a (basis) vector of zeros with a one in the position occupied by $\ln x$ in the matrix of first-stage variables, where Π, as before, is the $K \times 2N$ matrix of first-stage parameters, and $\Phi_1 = [I \,|\, -D(w)^{-1}]$ is the $N \times 2N$ Jacobian matrix of partial derivatives. It then follows that

$$
V(\hat{\varepsilon}) = (e' \otimes \Phi_1) K(\Lambda \otimes (W'W)^{-1})K(e \otimes \Phi_1') = \omega \Phi_1 \Lambda \Phi_1' \tag{A14}
$$

where $\omega = e'(W'W)^{-1}e$ is the element in the diagonal of $(W'W)^{-1}$ corresponding to $\ln x$.

Turning next to the price elasticities E, transpose equation (20) and take total differentials to give

$$
dE' = G.dB[D(w)^{-1} + D(\xi)E'] + G[B - D(w)]dD(\xi).E' \tag{A15}
$$

where $G = [I - B\xi + D(\xi)D(w)]^{-1}$. Hence, in vec notation

$$
\begin{aligned}
\text{vec}(dE') &= \{[D(w)^{-1} + ED(\xi)] \otimes G\} \text{vec}dB \\
&+ \{E \otimes G[B - D(w)]\} \text{vec}D(d\xi)
\end{aligned} \tag{A16}
$$

To evaluate the second term on the right-hand side, note that ξ_G given by (9), like ε_G above, is a function only of the first stage parameters β_G^0 and β_G^1. Define the $N \times 2N$ matrix $\Phi_2 = [D(\varrho^0)|D(\varrho^1)]$, where $\varrho_G^0 = \partial \xi_G / \partial \beta_G^0$, and $\varrho_G^1 = \partial \xi_G / \partial \beta_G^1$ evaluated from (9), so that in parallel with the discussion of ε above, we have $d\xi = \Phi_2 d\Pi' e = (e' \otimes \Phi_2) K \text{vec} d\Pi$. The 'diagonalisation' matrix L, an $N^2 \times N$ matrix of ones and zeros, is defined by its property $L\xi = \text{vec} [D(\xi)]$, for any N-vector ξ. It can be used to express $\text{vec} D(d\xi)$ as $Ld\xi = L(e' \otimes \Phi_2) K \text{vec} d\Pi$, so that combining (A8) and (A16):

$$\text{vec}(\bar{E}' - E') = F_1 \text{vec}(\bar{H} - H) + F_2 \text{vec}(\bar{\Lambda} - \Lambda)$$
$$+ F_3 \text{vec}(\bar{\Pi} - \Pi) \tag{A17}$$

$$F_1 = [D(w)^{-1} + ED(\xi)]P' \otimes GA^{-1}J$$

$$F_2 = -[D(w)^{-1} + ED(\xi)]P'T^{-1} \otimes GA^{-1}J$$

$$F_3 = \{E \otimes G[B - D(w)]\}L(e' \otimes \Phi_2)K - F_1(I + K)(I \otimes M')$$

so that, given the asymptotic independence of the estimates of H, Λ, and Π, a formula for the variance–covariance matrix can be derived. Unfortunately, this straightforward procedure leads to large matrices, including, for example, the last commutation matrix above, which has $4N^2K^2$ elements. After some manipulation, it is possible to derive the following expressions which contain matrices no larger then max $(4N^2, 2NK)$:

$$V(\text{vec}\bar{E}') = C^{-1}V_a + (n - k - C)^{-1}V_b + V_{11} + V_{12} + V'_{12}$$
$$+ V_{22} \tag{A18}$$

$$V_a(P, H) = [D(w)^{-1} + ED(\xi)]P'HP[D(w)^{-1} + D(\xi)E']$$
$$\otimes GA^{-1} JHJ' A^{-1} G'$$

$$V_b = V_a(PT^{-1}, \Lambda)$$

$$V_{11} = \omega\{E \otimes G[B - D(w)]\} L\Phi_2\Lambda\Phi'_2L' \{E'$$
$$\otimes [B' - D(w)]G'\}$$

$$V_{12} = -\{E \otimes G[B - D(w)]\} L\{e' (W'W)^{-1} MP [D(w)^{-1}$$
$$+ D(\xi)E'] \otimes \Phi_2\Lambda J' A^{-1} G'\}$$
$$- \{E \otimes G[B - D(w)]\} L\{e' (W'W)^{-1} MJ' A^{-1} G'$$
$$\otimes \Phi_2\Lambda P [D(w)^{-1} + D(\xi)E']\}K$$

$$V_{22} = \{[D(w)^{-1} + ED(\xi)] \otimes G\} V_3 \{[D(w)^{-1}$$
$$+ D(\xi)E'] \otimes G'\}$$

In the consumer-demand literature, there has frequently been an interest in examining the matrix of cross-price effects for evidence of Slutsky symmetry. In the notation used here, symmetry is satisfied at the budget shares w if the following condition holds:

$$\Delta = D(w)E + D(w)\varepsilon w' - E'D(w) - we'D(w) = 0 \tag{A19}$$

In vec notation, this can be written

$$\delta = \text{vec}(\Delta) = (K - I)\,[I \otimes D(w)]\,\text{vec}E'$$
$$+ (K - I)\,[D(w) \otimes w]\,\varepsilon = 0 \tag{A20}$$

An estimate of Δ can be calculated from the estimates of E and ε, and a Wald test constructed given a variance–covariance matrix for Δ. Note that Δ is the difference between a matrix and its transpose, so has a zero diagonal, and an upper right triangle that is minus its lower right triangle. In consequence, only the elements of δ corresponding to the bottom left-hand triangle (below the diagonal) of Δ need be used for inference. Denoting these by δ^*, and the corresponding variance–covariance matrix by $V(\delta^*)$, the Wald test is $\delta^{*'}\,\{V(\delta^*)\}^{-1}\delta^*$. The matrix $V(\delta^*)$ is selected from the elements of $V(\delta)$ obtained from using (A20) above. Note that the variance–covariance matrices for $\text{vec}\bar{E}'$ and for $\bar{\varepsilon}$ have already been obtained, so that the only further requirement is for the covariance $\text{cov}(\text{vec}\bar{E}',\,\bar{\varepsilon}')$. Referring to (A17) gives:

$$C_v = E[\text{vec}(\bar{E}' - E')\,(\bar{\varepsilon} - \varepsilon)'] = F_3[\Lambda \otimes (W'W)^{-1}]K(e \otimes \Phi_1') \tag{A21}$$

which, after substitution from (A17) and rearrangement gives:

$$C_v = \{E \otimes G[B - D(w)]\}L\Phi_2\Lambda\Phi_1'\omega$$
$$- [D(w)^{-1} + ED(\xi)]P'M'\,(W'W)^{-1}\,e \otimes GA^{-1}\,J\Lambda\Phi_1'$$
$$- [D(w)^{-1} + ED(\xi)]P'\Lambda\Phi_1' \otimes GA^{-1}\,JM'(W'W)^{-1}\,e \tag{A22}$$

The variance–covariance matrix of $\bar{\delta}$ is then constructed from the outer product of the estimate of (A20), substituting from (A14) and (A18) for the two variances, and from (A22) and its transpose for the two covariances.

Notes

1. The author would like to thank Dwayne Benjamin who provided outstanding research assistance. The research reported here was carried out for the Welfare and Human Resources Division of the World Bank. The World Bank does not accept responsibility for the views expressed herein, which are those of the author and should not be attributed to the World Bank or to its affiliated organisations. This paper was first published in the

Journal of Econometrics (1990) vol. 44; permission to reprint it here is gratefully acknowledged.

References

Case, A. C. (1988) 'Analyzing Spatial Patterns in Developing Country Data', unpublished Ph.D. thesis, Department of Economics, Princeton University, Princeton, NJ, USA.

Deaton, A. S. (1986) 'Quality, Quantity, and Spatial Variation of Price', unpublished paper, Woodrow Wilson School, Princeton University, Princeton, NJ, USA.

Deaton, A. S. (1987) 'Estimation of Own and Cross-price Elasticities from Survey Data', *Journal of Econometrics*, vol. 36, pp. 7–30.

Deaton, A. S. (1988) 'Quality, Quantity, and Spatial Variation of Price', *American Economic Review*, vol. 78, pp. 418–30.

Deaton, A. S., and Muellbauer, J. (1980) 'An Almost Ideal Demand System', *American Economic Review*, vol. 70, pp. 312–26.

Fuller, W. A. (1987) *Measurement Error Models* (New York: John Wiley).

Hansen, L. P. (1982) 'Large Sample Properties of Generalized Methods of Moments Estimators', *Econometrica*, vol. 50, pp. 1029–54.

Laraki, K. (1988) 'The Nutritional, Welfare, and Budgetary Effects of Price Reform in Developing Countries; Food Subsidies in Morocco', unpublished paper, Welfare and Human Resources Unit, The World Bank, Washington DC, USA.

Magnus, J. R. and Neudecker, H. (1986) 'Symmetry, 0–1 Matrices and Jacobians: A Review', *Econometric Theory*, vol. 2, pp. 157–90.

Newey, W. K. (1984) 'A Method of Moments Interpretation of Sequential Estimators', *Economics Letters*, vol. 14, pp. 201–6.

Schwartz, G. (1978) 'Estimating the Dimension of a Model', *Annals of Statistics*, vol. 6, pp. 461–4.

Silverman, B. (1986) *Density Estimation for Statistics and Data Analysis* (London and New York: Methuen).

Strauss, J. (1982) 'Determinants of Food Consumption in Rural Sierra Leone', *Journal of Development Economics*, vol. 11, pp. 327–53.

Timmer, C. P. (1981) 'Is there "Curvature" in the Slutsky Matrix?', *Review of Economics and Statistics*, vol. 63, pp. 395–402.

Timmer, C. P. and Alderman, H. (1979) 'Estimating Consumption Parameters for Food Policy Analysis', *American Journal of Agricultural Economics*, vol. 61, pp. 982–7.

van de Walle, D. (1988) 'On the Use of the SUSENAS for Modelling Consumer Behavior', *Bulletin of Indonesian Economic Studies*, vol. 24, pp. 107–22.

11 Family Labour Supply Decisions in Rural Peru

Paul J. Gertler[1]

RAND CORPORATION CALIFORNIA

and

John L. Newman[1]

WORLD BANK, WASHINGTON, DC.

1 INTRODUCTION

Raising rural incomes and increasing agricultural production are two of the primary challenges facing policy-makers in developing countries. While increasing agricultural production calls for policies that raise the return to agricultural activities, higher rural incomes could be achieved by raising both agricultural and non-agricultural returns. The resulting impacts on incomes and agricultural production depend heavily upon the family labour supply responses in both agricultural and non-agricultural activities. Because raising the return of one work activity relative to the other can induce a reallocation of labour between activities, both sectors must be considered jointly. For instance, if an increase in agricultural production comes at the expense of work in non-agricultural activities rather than leisure, the net effect on rural incomes may be negligible. If, at the same time, these policies result in a decline in agricultural output, then the cost of this decline needs to be considered in the evaluation of the policies.

Changes in the returns to work may induce a reallocation of labour not only between work activities but also among family members. Understanding the interactions among family members and activities is necessary in deciding how to generate the increases in the returns to work. Some policies, such as investing in infrastructure, are targeted towards communities and families and will influence the returns of all family members. Other policies, such as education, can be targeted to individuals within a household. For example, it may be possible to promote female education or to direct agricultural extension efforts towards the type of activities typically done by women on the farm. If policies are targeted on raising the returns of individuals with strong labour supply responses, these individuals could significantly increase their personal contributions to family income and production. However, the net effect of these policies on *family* income and production depends on the labour supply responses of all family members, not just the targeted group. Estimating the net effect of targeted policies requires that explicit account be taken of interactions in labour supply of different family members.

A second reason for being interested in the family allocation of labour is that families may not internalise the costs of their decisions. For example, if parents respond to higher returns to work by increasing the labour supply of their children, they may reduce educational investments and, consequently, their children's future productivity. In other words, they may not internalise the future private and social returns to investments in education. As another example, if elderly family members work more, their future health status may be adversely affected. To the extent that the family may not pay all the costs of health care, its choice in allocating labour among family members may not internalise the costs of having elderly members work. Policy makers may want to alter the relative returns of different types of individuals in an effort to maximise family incomes and output and to minimise the adverse effects of the externalities. For these reasons, labour supply responses to income-enhancing policies should be examined within the context of family labour supply.

The typical model of family labour supply considers the case where the husband works full-time for a wage and the wife may or may not work (Ashenfelter and Heckman, 1974; Gronau, 1977; Graham and Green, 1984; Hausman and Ruud, 1984; Kooreman and Kapteyn, 1987; Ransom, 1987). In developing countries, family labour supply behaviour can be considerably more complicated. This paper considers the family labour supply of land-owning households in Peru. The complexities in the behaviour of these families generate difficulties for the typical model. There are a large and variable number of family members who may choose to work both on and off the farm. The number of potential workers in our sample ranges from 1 to 14 and over 60 per cent of the households have more than three family members who work. A substantial number of the potential workers either do not work (14 per cent) or work in more than one activity (22 per cent). Self-employment in agriculture and business, where the returns can depend on the hours worked, are the most important activities.

While theoretical models of rural household labour supply (Rosenzweig, 1978; Huffman and Lange, 1989; and Singh, Squire, and Strauss, 1986, recognise the interdependence and endogeneity of farm production and off-farm labour supply, these issues have not yet been adequately addressed in the models' empirical implementations. The empirical models typically have focused either on only one activity (farm or off-farm work) or on tests of the implications of the theoretical model regarding market equilibrium.[2] A second issue in the agricultural labour supply literature is whether production decisions (in this case, labour supply decisions) can be analysed independently of consumption decisions. If workers can take their marginal return functions as given, as would be the case if there is a well functioning rural labour market, then production and consumption decisions would be independent. If there is no labour market to fix the marginal returns, then the production and consumption decisions would be linked.[3]

In this paper, we formulate a general model of family decisions on labour supply and consumption that does *not* assume independence between the decisions. The model allows for a variable number of family members, each of whom may engage in multiple activities, and for the leisure of one family member to affect the labour supply of another. We also allow the marginal return functions to depend on the hours worked in that activity and provide a test for this dependence. We model family decisions as a simultaneous system of equations, where the system consists of a family consumption equation and farm and off-farm labour supply equations for each potential worker in the family. The number of equations in the system for any particular family will depend on the number of potential workers in the family and, hence, will vary across families. We use the model to simulate the effects of increases in consumer and producer prices and the education of prime age males and females on family consumption and labour supply of households in rural Peru.

2 A GENERAL MODEL OF FAMILY LABOUR SUPPLY

In this section we derive a model of family labour supply that allows for a variable number of family members each of whom may engage in multiple activities.[4] We first specify the model and then discuss identification and estimation.

2.1 Specification

Consider a family with N members whose utility function is:

$$U = U(C, L \mid Z) \tag{1}$$

where C is the value of total (aggregate) household consumption, L is a $(N \times 1)$ vector of the leisure of different family members, and Z is a $(ZZ \times 1)$ vector of exogenous taste-shifters. The taste-shifters can include family variables such as the characteristics of the head and family structure and individual variables such as the age and health status of each member. This specification of the family utility function implicitly assumes that families use a two stage decision-making process that first allocates resources among total family consumption and the leisure of each member, and then allocates consumption among members. We focus on the first stage as it determines labour supply behaviour.

The family faces a budget constraint and N time constraints, one for each member. Each family member can engage in a possible $m = 1, \ldots M$ activities. The family's budget constraint is:

$$V + \sum_{m=1}^{M} Q_m(H_m \mid F_m, X_{m1}, \ldots, X_{mN}) = P\,C \tag{2}$$

where V is non-labour income, $Q_m(H_m \mid X_m)$ is the total value to the family of engaging in the mth activity, H_m is a $(N \times 1)$ vector of hours of work in the mth activity for all N potential workers in the family, F_m is a $(K \times 1)$ vector of family-level exogenous variables that influence the returns to the mth activity, and the X_{mi} are $(J \times 1)$ vectors of exogenous variables corresponding to each family member that influence the returns to the mth activity. P is the price of consumption good. If activity m involves working for a wage, then Q_m is the income earned by the family in that activity. If activity m involves production, then Q_m is the value of that production.

The time constraints are:

$$\sum_{m=1}^{M} H_m + L = T \tag{3}$$

where T is a $(N \times 1)$ vector of total time available for the family and $H_m \geq 0$ for all m.

The optimisation problem involves choosing the hours that each member supplies to the various activities and the total value of family consumption so as to maximise utility subject to budget, time and non-negativity constraints. Maximising utility subject to the budget and time constraints yields the following set of first order conditions for H_m and C:

$$H_m \left(\frac{1}{\lambda} \frac{\partial U (C, L \mid Z)}{\partial L} - \frac{\partial Q_m (H_m \mid F_m, X_{m1}, \ldots, X_{mN})}{\partial H_m} \right) = 0$$

$$H_m \geq 0 \qquad \forall \, m \tag{4}$$

$$\frac{1}{\lambda} \frac{\partial U (C, L \mid Z)}{\partial C} = p \tag{5}$$

where, via the time constraint, $L = T - \sum_{m=1}^{M} H_m$. The term λ is the Lagrange multiplier on the budget constraint and in equilibrium is equal to the family's marginal utility of income.

We assume that the marginal values of leisure and the marginal value of consumption can be written as linear functions of their arguments. Thus, the family's marginal value of leisure for all n family members and the marginal value of consumption can be written:

$$\frac{1}{\lambda} \frac{\partial U}{\partial L} = A_{LO} + A_{Lc}C + A_{LL}L + A_{Lz}Z + A_{Lzc}Z \cdot C + \psi_L \tag{6}$$

$$\frac{1}{\lambda} \frac{\partial U}{\partial C} = A_{co} + A_{cc}C + A'_{Lc}L + A_{cz}Z + L'A_{Lzc}Z + \psi_c \tag{7}$$

where A_{LL} is $(N \times N)$, A_{Lz} and A_{Lzc} are $(N \times ZZ)$ with ZZ being the dimension of the vector of taste-shifters, A_{LO}, ψ_L, and A_{Lc} are $(N \times 1)$, A_{co}, A_{cc}, and ψ_c are (1×1), and A_{cz} is $(1 \times ZZ)$.

There exists one marginal value of consumption function for the family and one marginal value of leisure function for each family member. The marginal functions are not independent, for they are obtained by partially differentiating the same family value function. This places a restriction across the marginal value of leisure functions of different family members, namely that A_{LL} is a symmetric matrix. In addition, there are two restrictions across the marginal values of leisure and family consumption. The coefficient on family consumption in the approximation to the marginal values of leisure must be equal to the corresponding coefficient on leisure in the marginal value of consumption. The coefficient on the interaction of the taste-shifters (Z) with family consumption in the marginal values of leisure must be equal to the corresponding coefficients on the interaction of Z with leisure in the marginal value of consumption.

The coefficients in (6) indicate how the family's marginal value of leisure of individual i changes with respect to family consumption, each family member's leisure (including individual i's own leisure), and the taste-shifters.

As with the marginal value of leisure functions, the coefficients in (7) indicate how the family's marginal value of consumption changes with respect its arguments. The error term represents random taste effects. We expect A_{cc} to be negative, which would imply a diminishing marginal value of consumption. In our empirical work, we classify individuals into six age and sex groups and allow each group to have a distinct marginal value function and require the coefficients of the marginal value function to be the same for all individuals within the same group. The *marginal values* can still differ because the taste-shifters include individual characteristics that vary within the group.

With this specification, the family's marginal values of leisure and marginal value of consumption can be rewritten as:

$$\frac{1}{\lambda} \frac{\partial U}{\partial L} = A_{Lo}^g + A_{Lc}^g C + A_{LL}^g L + A_{Lz}^g Z + A_{Lzc}^g Z \cdot C + \psi_L \quad (8)$$

$$\frac{1}{\lambda} \frac{\partial U}{\partial C} = A_{co} + A_{cc} C + A_{Lc}^{g'} L + A_{cz} Z + L' A_{Lzc}^g Z + \psi_c \quad (9)$$

where the g superscripts on the A matrices indicate that within-group equality restrictions are imposed.

We also assume that the marginal return functions can be written as linear functions of their arguments. Thus,

$$\frac{\partial Q_m}{\partial H_m} = B_m + B_{mH} H_m + X_m B_{mx} + B_{mF} F_m + \eta_m, \quad \forall m \quad (10)$$

where B_m is a $(N \times 1)$ vector of coefficients, B_{mH} is a $(N \times N)$ matrix of coefficients, X_m is a $(N \times NJ)$ block diagonal matrix with the X_{mi} $(J \times 1)$ vectors along the diagonal, B_{mx} is a $(NJ \times 1)$ vector of coefficients, and B_{mF} is a $(N \times K)$ vector of coefficients.

There is a separate marginal return function for each individual in each activity. We allow the marginal return functions to depend on the hours worked since in non-wage activities, such as farming and self-employment, marginal productivity may vary with the level of activity. The marginal return functions also depend on a vector of characteristics X_{mi} such as age, experience and education. This vector may include variables that enter Z. The vectors may differ by activity since, for example, variables such as land do not affect the return to market labour, while business assets do not affect the return to agricultural labour. The errors in the marginal return function represent random productivity shocks.

In the case of wage work, the marginal return is the wage, which may not be a function of individual i's hours worked. As with the marginal value functions, the marginal return functions for different family members are obtained from a common family function, in this case a common family production function for Q_m. Specifying a linear marginal return function as in (10) implies that Q_m can be approximated by a quadratic function. As specified, equation (10) embodies an assumption that the marginal return functions are separable across family members and activities. That is, i's *marginal* (but not total) return depends only on i's own hours worked in that activity and does not depend on the hours spent working in that activity by other family members or on the hours working in any other activity. While this assumption facilitates the estimation, it is not necessary. The assumptions on the production technology required to identify the model are discussed in the section on identification.

In our estimation, we restrict the coefficients of the marginal return functions (10) in any particular activity to be the same for all family members within each of the six age and sex groups. The coefficients in the marginal return functions are still allowed to differ across activities and groups. Moreover, the restriction does not imply that all individuals within the same age and sex group have the same marginal returns. Although the coefficients are the same within a group, the individual characteristics can differ. Thus, for an individual i in group g, the marginal return function is:

$$\frac{\partial Q_m}{\partial H_m} = B_m^g + B_{mH}^g H_m + X_m B_{mx}^g + B_{mF}^g F_m + \eta_m, \quad \forall m \quad (11)$$

where again the g superscripts indicate that the within-group restrictions are imposed.

Substituting the above approximations for the marginal return functions and the marginal values of leisure and consumption into the first order conditions yields the family consumption and labour supply functions. Substituting the marginal value of consumption into equation (5) and solving for C yields the family consumption equation:

$$C = -\frac{1}{A_{cc}} \left(A_{cO} + A_{Lc}^{g'} L + A_{cz} Z + L' \cdot A_{Lzc}^g Z + \psi_c - P \right) \quad (12)$$

The labour supply functions for an individual i in group g can be obtained by substituting the time constraints back into the marginal values of leisure, substituting the marginal value of leisure and the marginal return into equation (4) and solving for h_{mi}. The solutions are:

$$h_{mi} = \frac{1}{b_{mi}^g + a_{ii}^g} \left(a_{i0}^g + a_{ic}^g C + a_{iz}^g Z + a_{izc}^g Z \cdot C \right.$$

$$+ a_{ii}^g \sum_{j \neq m}^{M} (T - h_{ij}) + A_{iL}^g L_i - b_{mi}^g - b_{mHi}^g H_{-i}$$

$$\left. - X_m b_{mX}^g - b_{mF}^g F_m + \psi_i - \eta_{mi} \right) \quad \text{if RHS} > 0$$

$$h_{mi} = 0 \quad \text{otherwise} \quad (13)$$

where: L_{-i} is a $[(N-1) \times 1]$ vector obtained by eliminating the ith row from L, H_{-i} is a $[(N-1) \times 1]$ vector obtained by eliminating the ith row from H.

The one equality restriction that can be imposed is that in accordance with the theoretical model; the effect of i's leisure on i's labour supply is restricted to be the same as that of any other member of the same age and sex group. In addition, there are a set of restrictions on coefficients that arise because i's labour supply both on and off the farm is derived by equating each marginal return separately to the same value – the marginal utility of i's leisure. If farm work is activity 1 and off-farm work activity 2, the coefficients of the variables that enter through the marginal value of i's leisure $(C, Z \cdot C, \sum h_{ij}, L_{-i}, Z)$ in the off-farm equation will be $(b_{1i}^g + a_{ii}^g)/(b_{2i}^g + a_{ii}^g)$ times the corresponding coefficients in the off-farm equation. To ensure consistency with our family decision making model, we impose these restrictions in the estimation.

The denominator of each of the coefficients in the labour supply equations is the difference between the effects of an additional hour on the marginal return function and on the family's marginal value of individual i's leisure. If the marginal return function does not depend on the hours spent in that activity (that is: $b_{mi}^g = 0$), then the coefficient on the total leisure from one's own group will be equal to negative one. Thus, one may test whether the marginal return function depends on the hours spent in that activity and whether b_{mi}^g is positive or negative. At the optimum, we expect the return function to be weakly declining with an additional hour spent in that activity (that is, $b_{mi}^g \leq 0$). If the number of alternative activities considered is more than two, one may also test whether the coefficients on the hours worked in each of the other activities are equal, as predicted by the theory.

2.2 Forming a Family

Equations (13) present the labour supply equations for a single individual of a given age and sex group. However, we are interested in the labour supply of *all* potential workers in the family and in the family's consumption level. This requires that we consider the family as the unit of analysis. While the first order condition for family consumption (equation (12)) naturally has the family as the unit of observation, the labour supply equations for farm and off-farm work have the individual as the unit of observation. A family connection is maintained in the latter two equations because the family's level of consumption and the leisure of other family members appear on the right-hand sides. However, it is clearly not sufficient to estimate equations (13) on individual data and claim that what is estimated is a family model. The family variables appearing on the right-hand side are endogenous. In order to aggregate from an individual's to the family's labour supply, one must consider a simultaneous system of equations, where the system consists of a family consumption equation and the farm and off-farm labour supply equations for each potential worker in the family.

The number of equations in the system for any particular family will depend on the number of potential workers in the family and, hence, will vary across families. Families with more than one member in a particular age and sex group still have two labour supply functions for each family member. In our model, the *parameters* of the labour supply functions for the two individuals in the same age and sex group will be the same, but the values of the exogenous variables will differ. If a family does not have a member in a particular age and sex group, then there is no leisure for that group included on the right-hand side of the labour supply functions of other groups. Thus, our estimation problem is to derive consistent estimates of the coefficients for family consumption and for farm and off-farm labour supply for six well-defined age and sex groups. These labour-supply functions form building blocks for constructing a system of equations specific to each family.

In addition to the presence of different family structures, a second important feature of our family model is that the endogenous hours of work are censored, rather than continuous. The censoring arises because an individual may or may not participate in an activity and creates difficulties in the calculation of expected values of the endogenous variables conditional on the characteristics of the family. In a simultaneous system with continuous endogenous variables, there is a single reduced form that is used to calculate the expected values of the endogenous variables. With censored variables, there are multiple reduced forms, depending on which regime each individual in the family is in – working only on the farm, only off the farm, both on and off the farm or not at all. The unconditional expected hours of work must be calculated by multiplying the expected hours of work in the activity conditional on being in a particular regime times the probability of being in that regime. Moreover, with censoring, the calculation of the conditional expected values of the endogenous variables will involve calculating the mean of an error distribution with a non-zero mean. This mean must be solved by numerical integration over the multivariate error distribution.

If consistent estimates of the coefficients in our model can be obtained, then the expected values of the endogenous variables can be calculated as follows. Using the estimated coefficients and the family characteristics, form a family-specific system of equations, with the number of equations in the system depending on the number of potential workers in the family. Solve the non-linear system of equations separately for each family in the sample. The solution yields estimates of expected family consumption, expected hours of working for each family member conditional on being in any particular regime, and the expected probability of that individual being in the regime. From the predicted probability and conditional hours, one may construct the unconditional hours of work. Comparative static results may be obtained by changing one of the exogenous variables and resolving the non-linear system for each family in the sample.

2.3 Estimation and Identification

We now turn to the problem of obtaining consistent estimates of the coefficients of our model. The key estimation problem is the potential corners arising from family members choosing not to participate in a particular activity or not to work at all. This problem would exist even in a model of individual labour supply.

In the vast majority of the families in rural Peru, at least one person in the age and sex group works. In 99 per cent of the households with males aged 20 to 59 there is at least one male of that group working and in 94 per cent of the households with females aged 20 to 59 there is at least one female of that group working. Even among households with females aged 60 and over, 73 per cent of the households have at least one elderly woman working. In rural Peru, the problem with corners arises more from non-participation in a given activity than from potential workers not working at all.

Because the other leisure variables appearing on the right-hand sides of equations (12) and (13) may be considered as approximately continuous, we choose not to estimate the coefficients using full information maximum likelihood. Instead, we take a simpler limited information approach. We estimate the two labour supply functions jointly for each age and sex group, but separately from each other and from our estimation of the family consumption function. We use instruments for family consumption and leisure in the labour supply equations and for leisure in the family consumption equation.[5]

Although the family consumption equation can then be estimated in the second step by OLS, the farm and off-farm labour supply functions comprise a two-equation simultaneous system where both dependent variables are truncated. This cannot be estimated by OLS.

Assuming the error terms follow a bivariate normal distribution, our econometric specification is exactly the simultaneous Tobit problem of Amemiya (1974) and Maddala (1983).[6] We estimate the two labour-supply equations by maximising the likelihood function of the simultaneous Tobit.[7]

In both the full- and limited-information approaches to the estimation of the family system, conditions for identification must be met. Consider first the identification issue in our limited-information approach. Equations (12) and (13) all contain right-hand-side endogenous variables. It is the availability of valid instruments that determines the number of right-hand-side endogenous variables that can be considered. Consumption prices and non-labour income will always be valid instruments. If they are the *only* ones available, then only consumption and total leisure of all family members could be included as arguments of the family value function. In this case, the family consumption equation (12) would contain a single right-hand-side endogenous variable, the total leisure of all family members. This equation would be identified since, given the total leisure, non-labour income should not enter the first order conditions for family consumption but would be correlated with the total leisure of the family. The equation for h_{1i} would contain three right-hand-side endogenous variables, h_{i2}, the total leisure of all other family members, and family consumption. Given family consumption and the leisure of all other family members, non-labour income and consumer prices should not enter the first order conditions determining h_{1i}. Since h_{2i} enters this equation, a further condition for identification is that there exist variables that affect the return to h_{2i} that do not affect the return to h_{1i}. Possible instruments are assets used in only one activity or activity-specific training and experience of the individual. Similar considerations apply for identification of the equation determining h_{2i}.

If one is to include more than one type of leisure, more identifying variables are required. No variable that enters the family's value function would be a candidate for a valid instrument because any such variable should enter all labour supply functions for all types of individuals as well as the first order condition for family consumption. Identification must follow from what is assumed about the nature of the marginal return functions.

The least restrictive assumption about the marginal return functions that will still permit identification of the simultaneous system is that the marginal return functions are separable across activities.

Then, variables that affect the marginal return to activity i but not j could be used to instrument for the hours in activity i that appears as a right-hand-side endogenous variable in the labour supply to activity i. This would permit, for example, individual i's marginal return to working on the farm to depend on the hours of work and experience on the farm of other family members. With separability across activities, variables that affect the marginal return *off* the farm of other family members could serve as instruments for the endogenous hours of work of other family members. Such variables would be correlated with other family members' hours of work on the farm but would be uncorrelated with the errors in the labour-supply equation determining individual i's work on the farm.

To simplify the estimation, we make the stronger assumption that the marginal return functions are separable across activities and family members.[8] This allows the characteristics of other family members to affect the total (but not the marginal) return from individual i's hours of work. In the case where all the work was wage work, separability of the marginal returns across individuals would be automatically satisfied. The marginal return to individual j would be the wage of that individual. Individual j's education and experience would be expected to affect individual j's wage, but not that of individual i. With non-wage work, the assumption that the marginal returns are separable is more restrictive. However, the model has a number of over-identifying restrictions which provides a test of our separability assumption. We can test whether the presence of other family members affects i's labour supply only through the marginal value of leisure or whether there is also an effect coming through the marginal return function.

In summary, we pursue a limited information approach to obtain consistent estimates of the coefficients of the family consumption equation and the farm and off-farm labour supply functions for each of six age and sex groups. Although we do not have to estimate the whole system together to get consistent estimates of the parameters, we emphasise that the comparative static results must be obtained by solving the entire non-linear system.

3   THE DATA

Data used in this study are drawn from the Peruvian Living Standards Survey (PLSS)), conducted between July 1985 and July 1986 as a collaborative effort between the Instituto Nacional de Estadistica (INE) in Peru and The World Bank. A random sample of 5120 households was chosen to reflect the distribution of the population in urban and rural areas and in four natural regions. The households were chosen with an equal probability of being selected in any given month to minimise the impact of seasonal variation. This multipurpose survey collected information on family background and resources available to the households. Thus, it gathered data on health, education and training, migration, housing, fertility, income, expenditures, assets, labour force, and farm and business activities. In rural areas, the household-level information was complemented by a community questionnaire which gathered information on public services, transportation, communication, and prices.[9] From this survey, we selected all households outside the metropolitan Lima area with land holdings greater than 0.01 hectares.

The arguments of the marginal value functions are family consumption and the total leisure of the six age and sex groups. The measure of total family consumption includes imputed returns from consumer durables and a valuation for their own consumption of agricultural crops.[10] So as to reflect June 1985 values it is deflated by a temporal price index specific to one of thirteen regions. The total hours of leisure for an individual is calculated as the total hours in the week minus the hours spent in farm work and the hours spent in off-farm work.[11] Because the number of family members in each group is held constant, the coefficients on the effect of total leisure will truly reflect additional leisure rather than the presence of additional family members. Leisure includes hours spent working at home, taking care of children, and attending school. In subsequent analyses we plan to analyse home production and hours of schooling jointly with market work.

The variables included in the set of taste-shifters are household structure variables and the schooling of the head of the household. We use the actual number of family members in each of the six age and sex groups, but because the presence of young children is potentially endogenous to current labour-supply decisions, we use predicted values of the number of children aged 0 to 9 present in the home. We use as instruments the distance to family planning clinics and to health centres. The distance variables are obtained from the community questionnaire and pertain to the distance from the village to the nearest clinic or hospital. To reduce the number of coefficients to be estimated, we only interacted one taste-shifter variable (the schooling of the head) with family consumption and leisure of the six age and sex groups.

Non-labour income is used as one of the instruments in the first stage. It is measured as the sum of retirement and pension benefits, medical or life insurance, interest on savings accounts or other forms of savings, dividends on bonds and profit shares, rentals for buildings, machinery, and vehicles, and inheritances. The consumer prices that appear as instruments in the first stage and in the family consumption equation are obtained from the community questionnaire and include those of aspirin, cooking oil, noodles, and potatoes. We use the median price within each of thirteen regions that are used by INE of Peru in their presentation of disaggregated data. We do not pretend that these four prices provide us with four identifying variables. They are included separately in lieu of having weights to construct a consumer price index.

The marginal return to work on the farm is assumed to depend on the hours the individual works on the farm, the wage of hired workers in agriculture, the family's farm assets, the log of land holdings, seasonal dummies, agricultural producer prices, and vector of individual characteristics. The personal characteristics are age, education, a dummy variable equal to 1 if married, and the years of experience in agricultural work. The omitted season is that of June, July and August. The family's farm assets are measured as the total value of equipment and the value of livestock. Regional variables include a producer price index and a dummy equal to 1 if there is electricity in the community. The producer price index is calculated from the median price of the sixteen most important agricultural crops in Peru, which account for 80 per cent of the value of all production. With fixed weights, variation in the producer prices arises from price variation over thirteen regions of the country. Ideally, it would be desirable to calculate the index only from the price of cash crops so as to avoid correlation between producer and consumer price indices.

The marginal return to work off the farm is assumed to depend on the hours the individual works off the farm, the family's assets devoted to non-farm family enterprises, the complementary inputs in the area of residence (proxied by the availability of electricity), and a vector of individual characteristics.[12] These characteristics are age, education, a dummy variable equal to 1 if married, and the years of experience in nonagricultural work.

4   RESULTS

As previously discussed, the effect of any given variable on family consumption and labour supply can only be ascertained by solving the non-linear system of equations for the family. For this reason, we present the tables of estimated coefficients from the family consumption and labour supply equations in an Appendix. In this section, we highlight the relations between leisure of the different age and sex groups and between leisure and family consumption that are the novel features of the model. We defer discussion of the full comparative static effects of the explanatory variables to the next section.

The first six columns of Table 11.1 are extracts from Tables 11.A1 to 11.A4 (appearing in the Appendix) the coefficients on the endogenous variables appearing on the right-hand side of the farm labour supply functions of the six age and sex groups. These coefficients provide information on the structural coefficients of our model. The coefficient on leisure of one's own group, $[(a_{ii}^g/(b_{1i}^g + a_{ii}^g)]$, reveals information about b_{1i}^g (how the marginal return function varies with an additional hour of work). For prime-age and elderly males and females, this coefficient is positive, significantly less than one, implying that b_{1i}^g is negative. Thus, for these age and sex groups we would reject the hypothesis that the marginal returns to farm work do not depend on the hours worked. Our results suggest that individuals in these groups are on the declining portion of their marginal return functions in farm work. For young males and females, the coefficient is small and negative. This may be because a_{ii}^g is small, implying that given their children's hours of leisure, the family's marginal value of their children's leisure is not declining with additional leisure, or because b_{1i}^g is large and positive, that is, the children are on the upward sloping portion of their marginal return functions. Without also estimating production functions that would yield estimates of b_{1i}^g, it is impossible to distinguish between these explanations.

The coefficient of the leisure of young males aged 12–19 on farm work of prime-age males and the coefficient of the leisure of the prime-age males on farm work of young males are both negative and significant. Although both coefficients have the same numerator, they have different denominators. Again from equation (13), the coefficient on the total leisure of group j on the farm labour supply of an individual in group g is $(a_{ij}^g/(b_{1i}^g + a_{ii}^g))$. Since the denominator is

Table 11.1 Key variables in the theoretical model

| | Coefficients in farm labour supply | | | | | | Coefficients in family consumption |
| | Aged 12–19 | | Aged 20–59 | | Aged 60 and over | | |
	Males	Females	Males	Females	Males	Females	in family consumption
Leisure males 12–19	-0.03	-0.08	-0.07**	-0.07	-0.14	-0.37*	3.87
Leisure females 12–19	0.03	-0.05	-0.03	-0.08**	0.19	-0.10	2.30
Leisure males 20–59	-0.32*	-0.09	0.54*	0.03	-0.15	0.33	-11.14**
Leisure females 20–59	0.10	-0.11**	-0.02	0.10*	0.10	0.05	7.42*
Leisure males 60 and over	-0.06	0.14	0.05	0.03	0.21	0.05	0.97
Leisure females 60 and over	0.05	-0.07	0.00	0.02	-0.02	0.18**	6.84*
Family consumption/1000	-3.43**	-0.52	-4.24*	-2.05**	-0.40	-0.62	
(Fam cons./1000) * Schooling head	-0.20	-0.59*	-0.31*	-0.41*	-0.48	0.00	
Schooling of head	0.31	1.29*	1.55*	1.05*	0.20	-0.29	52.98*
Leisure males 12–19 * Schooling head							0.02
Leisure females 12–19 * Schooling head							0.27*
Leisure males 20–59 * Schooling head							0.44*
Leisure females 20–59 * Schooling head							-0.10
Leisure males 60 and over * Schooling head							-0.17
Leisure females 60 and over * Schooling head							-0.06
Ratio of $(b^g_{1i} + a^g_{ii})/(b^g_{2i} + a^g_{ii})$	-1.59*	1.17*	1.30*	-0.05	0.64	0.72*	
Sample size	1153	1213	1879	1978	390	409	1950

* significant at 5 per cent level

negative, the estimated negative coefficient suggests that the numerator a_{ij}^g is positive. This means that the leisure of these two groups are complementary. Increases in the leisure of the one group will increase the family's marginal valuation of the other group's leisure. In addition, the coefficient of the leisure of young females aged 12–19 on farm work of prime-age females and the coefficient of the leisure of prime-age females on farm work of young females are both negative and significant. This implies that the leisure of these two groups are complements.

For all but the elderly females, the coefficient on the schooling of the head in the labour supply equation is positive, implying that a_{gz} is negative. This coefficient does not reflect the full effect of the schooling of the head because schooling of the head is interacted with family consumption and leisure in the value function. Thus, the effect of schooling per head can only be obtained through the comparative static exercise.

The coefficients of the leisure, family consumption, schooling of head, predicted children, number of individuals within each age and sex group, and schooling-consumption interaction variables in the off-farm labour supply equation are obtained by multiplying the corresponding coefficients in the farm labour supply equation by a common ratio for each age and sex group. In the simultaneous Tobit estimation we can obtain an estimate of this ratio which, for any group g, is equal to $(b_{1i}^g + a_{ii}^g / (b_{2i}^g + a_{ii}^g)$. Depending on the size and size of b_{1i}^g and b_{2i}^g, this ratio can be either positive or negative. The negative and significant sign on males aged 12–19 means that the leisure, family consumption, and interaction terms will have the opposite signs in the off-farm labour-supply equation.

The restriction that the coefficients of the number of individuals within each age and sex group differ in the two labour supply equations by the same ratio was imposed because our prior was that these variables should only affect the labour supply through the marginal value of leisure and not through the marginal return functions. This restriction can be tested. If the number of family members within a given age and sex group affects the marginal returns, then one would expect to reject the restriction that the coefficients across the two labour supply equations differ by a common ratio. For prime age males and females we could not reject the restriction. For the other groups, we would reject the restriction, but not resoundingly so. In future work, we plan to relax the separability of the marginal return function across family members in the same activity, but the results of our tests suggest to us that we are not committing grave errors by assuming the separability of marginal return functions across family-members.

The elements a_{ic}^g of the matrix A_{Lc}^g, the interaction terms between family consumption and leisure of the different age and sex groups in the value function, appear in both the family consumption and in the labour supply equations. The coefficients on family consumption in the leisure equations appear in the seventh row of Table 11.1. They are all negative which, together with the finding that the denominator is negative, implies that all a_{ic}^g are positive. That is, for all groups, leisure is complementary with family consumption.

The first six rows of the last column of Table 11.1 also provide information on the sign of a_{ic}^g. From equation (12), the coefficient on the total leisure of group g is $(-A_{Lc}^g/A_{cc})$. Table A5 in the Appendix indicates that two of the four consumption prices are negative and significant, one is negative but not precisely estimated, and one is essentially zero and insignificant. This suggests that A_{cc} is negative, implying that the marginal value of family consumption decreases with additional consumption, as expected. For all but the leisure of prime age males, the results from the family consumption equation imply that leisure is complementary with family consumption. This is in agreement with the results from the labour supply equations. For prime age males, the estimates from the family consumption equation imply that the leisure of prime age males is a substitute with family consumption rather than a complement as implied by the labour supply equations. The different implications are due to our inability to place cross-equation restrictions given the data at our disposal. With better information on prices and information on output, we could impose these restrictions. Despite the differences in interpretations of the coefficients, we may still solve for the family consumption and hours of work in the comparative statics that will solve our non-linear system.

The coefficients of the interaction terms of family consumption and schooling of the head in the labour supply coefficients and the corresponding interaction terms of leisure and schooling of the head in the family consumption equation have the same numerator. Where significant in the family consumption and labour supply equations, the results have the same implication for a_{icz}^g, namely that it is positive. The higher the schooling per head, the more additional consumption increases the marginal value of leisure.

Finally, we should note that the logical consistency condition was not imposed in the simultaneous Tobit estimation of the labour supply equations and was always satisfied.

5 COMPARATIVE STATICS

In this section we present the results of different counterfactual simulations. Based on the estimated coefficients and observed values of the explanatory variables, for each family we solve the non-linear system of equations for family consumption and farm and off-farm labour supply of each potential worker. Given observed characteristics and the estimated coefficients of the model, we calculate the probability that the individual will be in one of four regimes – working both on and off the farm, working only on the farm, working only off the farm, and not working – and the predicted hours of work in each activity conditional on being in a particular regime. The unconditional predicted hours are then obtained for each individual by multiplying the conditional predicted hours by the individual's predicted probability of being in that regime. Thus, in calculating the unconditional hours, only data on the observed variables were employed. The sample information that an individual was actually in a particular regime was not used.

For a random sample of 10 per cent of the families, we calculate comparative static results of increases in producer prices, consumer prices, and the education of prime age females and males on family consumption, probabilities of being in any particular regime, and the unconditional hours working on and off the farm. Table 11.2 presents the base case for the comparative statics. It is obtained by solving the system with the actual values of the family. The comparative static results are obtained by changing one of the explanatory variables and re-solving the non-linear system, again for each family in the sample. Given the non-linearity and the multiple reduced forms in our system of equations, it is only by going through the comparative static exercises that one can ascertain the complete effect of a variable on the endogenous variables.

Table 11.3 presents the results from a simulation of a 20 per cent increase in producer prices. *Ceteris paribus*, higher producer prices are associated with higher prime age male labour, higher leisure of all other family members, and 2.5 per cent higher monthly family consumption. Prime age males work 2.2 hours more per week on the farm, with about 60 per cent of that increase coming from a reduction

Table 11.2 Base case

| | Aged 12–19 | | Aged 20–59 | | Aged 60 and over | |
	Males	Females	Males	Females	Males	Females
Predicted probability						
Working on farm	69.6	51.5	64.0	50.1	71.3	65.3
Working off farm	3.7	3.7	6.3	9.8	1.6	1.4
Working in both	7.0	10.5	28.4	29.5	18.4	24.7
Not working	19.7	34.4	0.8	10.6	8.7	8.2
Unconditional hours						
Working on farm	25.3	17.5	43.3	24.7	37.7	44.9
Working off farm	2.4	3.3	11.0	9.5	4.9	9.0
Family Consumption		1361.2				

Table 11.3 Changes due to increase of 20 per cent in producer prices

| | Aged 12–19 | | Aged 20–59 | | Aged 60 and over | |
	Males	Females	Males	Females	Males	Females
Changes in predicted probabilities						
Working on farm	–1.1	–0.7	2.3	–1.6	–0.2	–0.9
Working off farm	0.1	0.0	–1.0	1.3	0.1	0.2
Working in both	–0.4	–0.3	–1.2	–1.3	0.0	–0.2
Not working	1.4	0.9	–0.1	1.6	0.1	1.0
Changes in unconditional hours						
Working on farm	–1.1	–0.5	2.2	–2.0	–0.5	–2.1
Working off farm	–0.1	–0.1	–0.9	0.0	0.0	0.0
Total leisure	1.2	0.6	–1.3	2.0	0.5	2.1
Percentage change in family consumption		2.5				

in their leisure and about 40 per cent from a reduction in the hours they work off the farm. From the predicted probabilities, one observes that the increased work comes mainly from reductions in leisure among men who were already working, rather than inducing men who were not working to start working. Other family members enjoy an increase in leisure. Most of the increased leisure of these groups comes from a reduction in farm work, rather than off-farm

Table 11.4 Changes due to increase of 20 per cent in consumer prices

	Aged 12–19		Aged 20–59		Aged 60 and over	
	Males	Females	Males	Females	Males	Females
Changes in predicted probabilities						
Working on farm	2.9	0.8	–1.2	0.8	0.0	0.4
Working off farm	–0.8	0.1	–0.2	–0.8	–0.1	–0.1
Working in both	–0.7	0.9	1.6	0.7	0.4	0.1
Not working	–1.4	–1.9	–0.2	–0.7	–0.3	–0.4
Changes in unconditional hours						
Working on farm	1.6	0.8	1.4	1.0	0.6	1.0
Working off farm	–0.4	0.3	0.7	0.0	0.1	0.0
Total leisure	–1.2	–1.1	–2.1	–1.0	–0.7	–1.0
Percentage change in family consumption		–28.4				

work. In addition, all other age and sex groups except elderly males have a 1 per cent or higher increase in the probability of not working. The largest reductions in farm work (and, hence, the biggest increases in leisure) occur among young males and prime age and elderly females. Young females, who work less on the farm, have a smaller absolute decrease in their hours worked on the farm.

Table 11.4 presents the results from a simulation of increasing consumer prices by 20 per cent. The higher consumer prices are associated with more hours of work of all family members. Despite the additional labour, monthly family consumption still falls by 28.4 per cent. Prime age males have the largest increase in their hours of work (2.1 hours), with the unconditional hours working on the farm increasing by twice that of hours off the farm. This does not mean that prime age males turn to specialising in farm work. The changes in predicted probabilities indicate that the higher consumption prices are associated with more prime age males engaged in both farm and off-farm work. The largest reduction in non-participation occurs among young males and females. Higher consumption prices are associated with nearly 2 per cent higher labour force participation rates among young females.

Our results suggest that the impact of increases in consumer prices on family consumption could be large. Given that the measures we use for the price variables are far from ideal, the results from the

Table 11.5 Changes due to increase of one year in prime age male
schooling

	Aged 12–19		Aged 20–59		Aged 60 and over	
	Males	*Females*	*Males*	*Females*	*Males*	*Females*
Changes in predicted probabilities						
Working on farm	0.0	–0.1	–2.0	0.0	0.0	0.0
Working off farm	0.0	0.0	0.6	0.0	0.0	0.0
Working in both	0.0	0.1	1.4	0.0	0.0	0.0
Not working	0.1	0.0	0.0	0.0	0.0	0.0
Changes in unconditional hours						
Working on farm	–0.1	0.0	–1.1	0.0	0.0	0.0
Working off farm	0.0	0.0	0.9	0.0	0.0	0.0
Total leisure	0.1	0.0	0.2	0.0	0.0	0.0
Percentage change in family consumption		6.3				

simulation of the increase in consumer prices should be interpreted
with caution. Moreover, the results are obtained from a cross-
sectional analysis and do not necessarily reflect the family's response
to changes in consumer prices over time.

Table 11.5 presents the results from a simulation of increasing the
education of prime age males by one year, from a mean of 4.4 to 5.4
years. This simulation holds constant for the schooling of the head.
Prime age males work more off the farm and less on the farm.
Participation rates in farm-work only fall by 2 per cent while participation in both activities increase by 1.4 per cent and in off-farm work
only increases by 0.6 per cent. While there is no increase in non-
participation rates, the prime age males who are working enjoy
0.2 hours more of leisure a week. Despite this reallocation, we were
unable to detect any effect on family consumption. There was a small
increase in the leisure of young males, in keeping with our finding
that the leisure of these two groups are complements.

Table 11.6 presents the results from a simulation of increasing the
education of prime age females by one year, from a mean of 2.5 to
3.5 years. This increase appears to have an effect on only the
activities of the prime age females. The higher education is associated
with a reallocation of labour of prime age females from farm to

Table 11.6   Changes due to increase of one year in prime age female schooling

	Aged 12–19		Aged 20–59		Aged 60 and over	
	Males	Females	Males	Females	Males	Females
Changes in predicted probabilities						
Working on farm	0.0	0.0	0.0	–1.5	0.0	0.0
Working off farm	0.0	0.0	0.0	0.7	0.0	0.0
Working in both	0.0	0.0	0.0	0.8	0.0	0.0
Not working	0.0	0.0	0.0	0.0	0.0	0.0
Changes in unconditional hours						
Working on farm	0.0	0.0	0.0	–0.5	0.0	0.0
Working off farm	0.0	0.0	0.0	0.5	0.0	0.0
Total leisure	0.0	0.0	0.0	0.0	0.0	0.0
Percentage change in family consumption		0.0				

off-farm work, with no change in their leisure. There is no apparent effect on family consumption and since there are no changes in family consumption or the leisure of prime age females, there are no effects on the labour supply of other family members.

The reallocations of labour from farm to off-farm work with either male or female education areas were to be expected. Higher education must increase the marginal return of off-farm work *relative* to farm work at the margin, otherwise there would not have been a reallocation of labour. However, the almost non-existent effect on family consumption suggests that the inframarginal effects of education on the two marginal return functions may be small. This may be due to the low levels of education prevailing in rural Peru or it may be because of the way we have specified the education variable. In other countries we would not necessarily expect the same results.

6 CONCLUSIONS

Our approach to estimating family consumption and labour supply decisions may be briefly summarised as follows. We consider that the family consumption and labour supply decisions of each family generate a distinct non-linear system. The key to identification of the system lies in the assumptions regarding the separability of marginal return functions across family members and activities. We classify each individual into one of six age and sex groups and restrict the coefficients of the marginal value and marginal return functions to be the same within any group. The system for each family is then constructed from the labour supply and marginal value functions appropriate for the particular composition of the family. We take a limited information approach to the estimation of the coefficients, but calculate comparative static results by solving each family's non-linear system separately.

Our findings suggest that higher producer prices are associated with increased work on the farm by prime age males. Because part of their supply response comes from substituting away from off-farm work and because other family members reduce their work on the farm, the increase in family consumption is lower than if all the additional hours were taken from leisure and there was no reallocation of family labour. This suggests that looking at changes in leisure together with changes in consumption levels provides a better indicator of the effects of such changes on family welfare.

We also find that higher consumption prices are associated with increased labour on the part of all family members, but lower consumption levels. Young males and females, in particular, had higher participation rates where, *ceteris paribus*, consumer prices were higher. Having marginal workers work more is evidently one of the ways that families attempt to maintain income levels. Because the leisure category for these workers includes schooling, their current participation may lead to lower levels of output in the future. While higher education of prime age males and females is associated with more off-farm relative to farm work, holding the schooling of the head constant, the education had little effect on family consumption.

Further progress in developing the general model of family decision making set forth in this paper requires estimating production functions jointly with the first order conditions for labour supply and family consumption. This would have the advantage of ensuring that the family's choices also satisfy the budget constraint. It would also allow one to identify the parameters of the marginal value function separately from the production function parameters. With such estimated coefficients, one could estimate not only changes in consumption, but also obtain estimates of how the family's welfare changes with changes in both consumption and leisure.

The general model developed for farm and off-farm work in Peru is applicable to other analyses of multiple activities and/or interdependent family time allocations. Examples include analyses of the effect of the availability of child care on the mother's work at home and in the market, of the effect of illness of one family member on activities of another, and the effect of infrastructure investment on the family's decision on allocating their children's time among market work, home work, and school attendance.

APPENDIX

Table 11A.1   Farm and off-farm labour supply equations: males and females aged 12–19

	Males		Females	
	Coefficient	*Standard error*	*Coefficient*	*Standard error*
Farm				
Constant	-18.73**	10.58	0.97	9.29
Age	2.06*	0.38	0.25	0.30
Years of schooling	-0.40	0.47	-1.56*	0.37
Farm experience	3.72*	0.30	4.53*	0.26
Log of land holdings	0.27	0.49	-0.01	0.47
Log of farm assets	0.77*	0.32	0.42	0.32
Producer price index	-9.71**	6.06	-2.29	6.07
Hired wage	-0.30	0.23	-0.69*	0.23
Season dummy 2	-4.33*	2.13	-2.42	2.13
Season dummy 3	4.67**	2.42	2.89	2.22
Season dummy 4	1.70	2.17	-0.60	2.18
Predicted children	11.41*	3.52	2.50	3.21
Males 12–19	3.99	6.87	10.58	7.90
Females 12–19	-4.02	8.39	6.47	5.76
Males 20–59	34.54*	16.85	8.86	15.74
Females 20–59	-14.69**	9.02	13.18	8.40
Males 60 and over	13.40	14.90	-16.66	12.76
Females 60 and over	-5.78	17.26	11.81	12.57
Leisure males 12–19	-0.03	0.05	-0.08	0.06
Leisure females 12–19	0.03	0.06	-0.05	0.04
Leisure males 20–59	-0.32*	0.15	-0.09	0.14
Leisure females 20–59	0.10	0.07	-0.11**	0.06
Leisure males 60 and over	-0.06	0.12	0.14	0.10
Leisure females 60 and over	0.05	0.12	-0.07	0.09

continued on page 310

Table 11A.1   continued

| | Males | | Females | |
	Coefficient	Standard error	Coefficient	Standard error
Family consumption (/1000)	−3.43**	2.00	−0.52	1.79
Family consumption (/1000)*sch head	−0.20	2.33	−0.59*	0.27
Schooling of head	0.31	0.58	1.29*	0.53
Sigma 1	21.63*	0.56	20.45*	0.59
Off-farm				
Constant	−79.81*	19.42	−77.48*	12.42
Age	2.23*	1.09	1.60*	0.64
Years of schooling	1.02	1.24	1.04	0.73
Non-farm experience	13.28*	1.50	8.98*	0.80
Availability of electricity	−15.14*	6.45	8.91*	3.88
Log business assets	0.84	0.57	1.42	0.42
Sigma 2	33.33*	2.74	31.57*	1.67
Rho	−0.12**	0.07	−0.13**	0.08
$(b_{1i}^g + a_{ii}^g)/(b_{2i}^g + a_{ii}^g)$	−1.59*	0.45	1.17*	0.37
− Log likelihood	4941.88		5075.98	
Sample size	1153		1213	

* significant at 5 per cent level
** significant at 10 per cent level

Table 11A.2   Farm and off-farm labour supply equations: males and females aged 20–59

| | Males | | Females | |
	Coefficient	Standard error	Coefficient	Standard error
Farm				
Constant	110.95*	6.29	60.00*	8.34
Age	−0.47*	0.06	−0.54*	0.06
Years of schooling	−0.74*	0.20	−0.54*	0.23
Married	2.32*	1.12	−1.59	1.06
Farm experience	0.53*	0.51	1.03*	0.05
Log of land holdings	1.61*	0.29	−0.08	0.33
Log of farm assets	0.34*	0.16	0.50*	0.20
Producer price index	11.97*	3.75	−12.06*	4.14
Hired wage	0.17	0.13	−0.18	0.15
Season dummy 2	−2.54*	1.23	1.23	1.38
Season dummy 3	−2.73*	1.29	−4.68*	1.56
Season dummy 4	−3.00*	1.29	−1.88	1.51

Table 11A.2 continued

	Males		Females	
	Coefficient	Standard error	Coefficient	Standard error
Predicted children	1.55	2.16	5.20**	2.98
Males 12–19	9.03**	5.30	8.73	6.15
Females 12–19	4.18	4.91	10.66**	6.01
Males 20–59	–60.56**	4.17	–6.64	11.68
Females 20–59	1.07	6.23	–15.04*	5.07
Males 60 and over	–10.49	6.77	–8.79	9.23
Females 60 and over	1.48	9.83	–3.02	13.21
Leisure males 12–19	–0.07**	0.04	–0.07	0.04
Leisure females 12–19	–0.03	0.03	–0.08**	0.04
Leisure males 20–59	0.54*	0.04	0.03	0.10
Leisure females 20–59	–0.02	0.05	0.10*	0.04
Leisure males 60 and over	0.05	0.05	0.03	0.07
Leisure females 60 and over	0.00	0.06	0.02	0.09
Family consumption (/1000)	–4.24*	1.02	–2.05**	1.22
Family consumption (/1000)*sch head	–0.31*	0.12	–0.41*	0.17
Schooling of head	1.55*	0.33	1.05*	0.38
Sigma 1	19.28*	0.34	19.91*	0.40
Off-farm				
Constant	111.66*	12.11	–2.25	3.78
Age	–0.48*	0.09	–0.74*	0.08
Years of schooling	1.16*	0.32	1.28*	0.24
Married	3.91*	1.84	1.40	1.54
Non-farm experience	1.42*	1.34	1.74*	0.84
Availability of electricity	6.28*	1.95	7.87*	1.77
Log business assets	2.10*	0.22	2.39*	0.18
Sigma 2	26.20*	0.84	24.66*	0.62
Rho	0.45*	0.08	–0.12*	0.04
$(b_{1i}^g + a_{ii}^g)/b_{2i}^g + a_{ii}^g)$	1.30*	0.15	–0.05	0.13
– Log likelihood	11402.68		11446.35	
Sample size	1879		1978	

* significant at 5 per cent level
** significant at 10 per cent level

Table 11A.3   Farm and off-farm labour supply equations: males aged 60
and over

	Coefficient	Standard error
Farm		
Constant	121.14**	19.78
Age	−1.51*	0.18
Years of schooling	0.05	0.95
Married	0.69	2.69
Farm experience	7.09*	0.66
Log of land holdings	1.33**	0.75
Log of farm assets	0.62	0.50
Producer price index	−2.97	9.00
Hired wage	0.32	0.35
Season dummy 2	0.88	3.63
Season dummy 3	−6.14	4.15
Season dummy 4	−8.79*	3.77
Males 12–19	21.95	19.74
Females 12–19	−26.38	19.21
Males 20–59	16.78	43.57
Females 20–59	−12.04	15.05
Males 60 and over	−8.29	9.59
Females 60 and over	3.57	15.08
Leisure males 12–19	−0.14	0.14
Leisure females 12–19	0.19	0.13
Leisure males 20–59	−0.15	0.37
Leisure females 20–59	0.10	0.11
Leisure males 60 and over	0.21	0.13
Leisure females 60 and over	−0.02	0.10
Predicted children	−2.88	4.78
Family consumption (/1000)	−0.40	3.03
Family consumption (/1000)*sch head	−0.48	0.46
Schooling of head	0.20	1.13
Sigma 1	19.25*	0.89
Off-farm		
Constant	37.12	49.27
Age	−0.81**	0.47
Years of schooling	1.14	1.23
Married	2.01	6.44
Non-farm experience	12.74*	2.43
Availability of electricity	−10.15	8.80
Log business assets	3.40*	0.80
Males 12–19	6.62	24.68
Females 12–19	−13.34	29.76
Males 20–59	7.28	33.09
Females 20–59	−12.65	15.58
Males 60 and over	−14.34	25.62
Females 60 and over	1.68	11.83
Sigma 2	31.29*	3.35
Rho	−0.07	0.22
$(b_{1i}^g + a_{ii}^g)/(b_{2i}^g + a_{ii}^g)$	0.64	1.03
− Log likelihood	2007.64	
Sample size	390	

* significant at 5 per cent level
** significant at 10 per cent level

Table 11A.4 Farm and off-farm labour supply equations: females aged 60 and over

	Coefficient	Standard error
Farm		
Constant	93.15*	22.05
Age	-1.33*	0.27
Years of schooling	-0.15	0.91
Married	1.68	3.79
Farm experience	0.79*	0.07
Log of land holdings	-1.31	0.98
Log of farm assets	1.40*	0.47
Producer price index	8.47	9.73
Hired wage	-0.93*	0.42
Season dummy 2	-1.77	3.53
Season dummy 3	-10.55*	4.01
Season dummy 4	-8.28*	3.52
Males 12–19	50.42*	24.82
Females 12–19	16.16	21.03
Males 20–59	-40.25	38.02
Females 20–59	-9.22	22.60
Males 60 and over	-12.24	12.22
Females 60 and over	-4.60	6.67
Leisure males 12–19	-0.37*	0.18
Leisure females 12–19	-0.10	0.15
Leisure males 20–59	0.33	0.34
Leisure females 20–59	0.05	0.17
Leisure males 60 and over	0.05	0.09
Leisure females 60 and over	0.18**	0.12
Predicted children	-8.87	6.32
Family consumption (/1000)	-0.62	3.41
Family consumption (/1000)*sch head	0.00	0.50
Schooling of head	-0.29	0.89
Sigma 1	19.69*	0.91
Off-farm		
Constant	28.51	22.57
Age	-0.76*	0.30
Years of schooling	1.38	1.14
Married	3.49	4.99
Non-farm experience	1.12*	0.14
Availability of electricity	-0.68	5.66
Log business assets	2.56*	0.59
Sigma 2	22.00*	1.70
Rho	0.16	0.16
$(b_{1i}^g + a_{ii}^g)/(b_{2i}^g + a_{ii}^g)$	0.72*	0.36
− Log likelihood	1820.94	
Sample size	409	

* significant at 5 per cent level
** significant at 10 per cent level

Table 11A.5 Family consumption equation

	Coefficient	Standard error
Constant	2502.64*	584.94
Predicted leisure males 12–19	3.87	2.66
Predicted leisure females 12–19	2.30	2.32
Predicted leisure males 20–59	−11.14**	6.84
Predicted leisure females 20–59	7.42*	2.80
Predicted leisure males 60 and over	0.97	3.86
Predicted leisure females 60 and over	6.84*	3.45
Schooling head of household	52.98*	22.13
Leisure males 12–19*schooling head	0.02	0.07
Leisure females 12–19*schooling head	0.27*	0.07
Leisure males 20–59*schooling head	0.44*	0.13
Leisure females 20–59*schooling head	−0.10	0.10
Leisure males 60 and over*schooling head	−0.17	0.16
Leisure females 60 and over*schooling head	−0.06	0.14
Consumption price of aspirin	−2.46	2.75
Consumption price of cooking oil	0.08	0.23
Consumption price of noodles	−2.42*	0.55
Consumption price of potatoes	−1.44**	0.77
Dummy urban/Sierra	258.02	208.32
Dummy urban/Selva	1577.32*	320.73
Dummy rural/Costa	−92.65	205.50
Dummy rural/Sierra	−399.09*	190.60
Dummy rural/Selva	25.11	199.72
Predicted number of children	209.81**	126.07
Total males 12–19	−422.45	360.95
Total females 12–19	−381.85	333.72
Total males 20–59	1416.74**	771.48
Total females 20–59	−719.04**	372.92
Total males 60 and over	183.78	483.18
Total females 60 and over	−668.48	487.45
R^2		0.26
Adjusted R^2		0.24
Mean of dependent variable		1360.97
Sample size		1950

* significant at 5 per cent level
** significant at 10 per cent level

Table 11A.6   Mean values of explanatory variables in labour supply
equations

	Aged 12–19		Aged 20–59		Aged 60 and over	
	Males	*Females*	*Males*	*Females*	*Males*	*Females*
Farm hours	25.18	18.61	43.67	26.50	37.08	21.74
Off-farm hours	2.24	3.83	12.21	10.00	6.47	6.17
Age	13.72	14.01	37.56	37.05	68.91	69.33
Years of schooling	4.02	3.54	4.40	2.54	2.09	0.83
Farm experience	0.37	0.33	1.88	1.66	3.83	3.11
Non-farm experience	0.03	0.07	0.42	0.65	0.86	1.14
Schooling of head	2.98	2.97	3.26	3.10	2.47	2.06
Family consumption (/1000)	1.61	1.56	1.57	1.54	1.28	1.24
Log of land holdings	0.65	0.59	0.64	0.52	0.51	0.34
Log of farm assets	7.16	7.13	7.03	7.03	6.52	6.39
Log business assets	1.08	1.12	1.19	1.28	0.87	0.48
Producer price index	0.99	0.99	0.99	0.99	0.99	0.99
Hired wage	9.29	9.23	9.27	9.16	9.21	9.26
Availability of electricity	0.17	0.18	0.19	0.19	0.20	0.20
Predicted children	0.84	0.82	0.71	0.73	0.31	0.28
Males 12–19	1.84	0.79	0.73	0.76	0.38	0.33
Females 12–19	0.76	1.75	0.73	0.72	0.37	0.36
Males 20–59	1.11	1.13	1.46	1.11	0.53	0.65
Females 20–59	1.19	1.17	1.17	1.46	0.78	0.58
Males 60 and over	0.11	0.12	0.11	0.15	1.03	0.42
Females 60 and over	0.11	0.12	0.14	0.12	0.44	1.06
Leisure males 12–19	116.71	110.92	103.18	105.91	51.45	47.06
Leisure females 12–19	112.20	110.11	107.11	105.94	54.40	51.83
Leisure males 20–59	125.60	127.23	52.48	125.04	62.04	73.64
Leisure females 20–59	157.91	154.46	156.10	61.99	105.58	76.77
Leisure males 60 and over	13.69	14.37	13.90	19.03	0.00	51.48
Leisure females 60 and over	16.36	17.21	20.37	17.71	61.13	0.00

Notes

1. We would like to thank Menno Pradhan and David Zimmerman for their excellent assistance in this research project. This paper has benefited greatly from comments by Angus Deaton, James Heckman, Jim Hosek, Costas Meghir, Mark Pitt, T. Paul Schultz, Jacques van der Gaag, Wim Vijverberg, Finis Welch, and seminar participants at Rand, UCLA, Yale University, and the World Bank.

2. Rosenzweig (1978) develops a general equilibrium model of farm and off-farm labour markets in developing countries and empirically tests the impact of land reform on rural wages and wage differentials. Huffman and Lange (1989) explicitly consider the labour supply off the farm in their empirical models, but assume an interior solution for all but the off-farm work.

3. Barnum and Squire (1979) model farm production and off-farm labour supply, but assume independence of consumption and production decisions. Benjamin (1988) uses Indonesian household data to test for an implication of the hypothesis of independence between production and consumption decisions and, for that case, cannot reject the hypothesis of independence.

4. Kooreman and Kapteyn (1987) estimate a model allowing for multiple time uses, but require interior solutions.

5. Our two-step approach follows the general theory of two-step M estimation in Duncan (1987).

6. In addition to the usual identification conditions for simultaneous equation systems, there are logical consistency conditions that must be satisfied for a simultaneous model with mixed latent and observed variables (such as ours) to have a solution (Amemiya, 1974; Waldman, 1981; Maddala, 1983). In the general case, Amemiya showed that the condition is that every principal minor of the matrix of coefficients on the endogenous variables be positive.

7. Since our likelihood function is the same as in Amemiya and Maddala, we do not reproduce it here. Although for computational reasons Amemiya and others have suggested estimating the simultaneous Tobit model using various two-step procedures, current computer technology makes maximum likelihood estimation feasible even on microcomputers. To facilitate convergence, we transform the model by dividing each equation by its respective standard deviation of the error term. This transformation is analogous to that of Olsen (1978) for the single-equation Tobit model.

8. Allowing i's marginal return to depend not only on i's own hours worked but also on those of other family members means that it is not just the total hours of leisure of other family members that will affect i's labour supply. The hours of work of other family members on the farm will affect i's labour supply on the farm through the marginal return function and through its effect on the marginal utility of leisure. The hours of work off the farm of other family members will only influence i's labour supply through the marginal value of leisure. In this case, the hours on and off the farm would enter as separate endogenous variables, making it

much more likely that corners would be a problem and making the limited information approach less attractive. The estimation could still be done by full information maximum likelihood, integrating out the family-specific component.

9. For more information on the Peruvian survey, see Glewwe (1987). The Peruvian survey is part of a series of Living Standards surveys conducted in an increasing number of developing countries by the World Bank and the central statistical agencies. Surveys are currently in operation in the Ivory Coast, Mauritania, Ghana, and Jamaica. In Bolivia, Morocco, and Pakistan, surveys are in the advanced planning stages.

10. For further details on the construction of this variable, see Glewwe (1987).

11. Much of the off-farm work consists of work on a family-owned non-agricultural enterprise. However, in defining off-farm work we did not distinguish between off-farm work for others and for the family.

12. If the off-farm work is primarily as a self-employed business person, then the marginal return should also depend on the wage of hired workers, as was the case with self-employed agriculture. We do not have good measures of the wages and therefore do not include them in the analysis.

References

Amemiya, T. (1974) 'Multivariate Regression and Simultaneous Equation Models when the Dependent Variables are Truncated Normal', *Econometrica*, vol. 42, pp. 999–1012.

Ashenfelter, O. and Heckman, J. (1974) 'The Estimation of Income and Substitution Effects in a Model of Family Labor Supply', *Econometrica*, vol. 42, pp. 73–85.

Barnum, H. and Squire, L. (1979) 'An Econometric Application of the Theory of the Farm-Household', *Journal of Development Economics*, vol. 6, pp. 79–102.

Benjamin, D. (1988) 'Household Composition and Labor Demand: Testing for Rural Labor Market Efficiency', Industrial Relations Section Working Paper no 244, Princeton University, Princeton, NJ, USA.

Duncan, G. (1987) 'A Simplified Approach to M-Estimation with Applications to Two-Stage Estimators', *Journal of Econometrics*, vol. 34, pp. 373–89.

Glewwe, P. (1987) 'The Distribution of Welfare in Peru 1985–86', Living Standards Measurement Study Working Paper no 42, World Bank, Washington. DC.

Graham, J. and Green, C. (1984) 'Estimating the Parameters of a Household Production Function with Joint Products', *Review of Economics and Statistics*, vol. 66, pp. 277–83.

Gronau, R. (1977) 'Leisure, Home Production and Work: The Theory of the Allocation of Time', *Journal of Political Economy*, vol. 85, pp. 1099–1123.

Hausman, J. and Ruud, P. (1984) 'Family Labor Supply and Taxes', *American Economic Review*, vol. 74, pp. 242–8.

Huffman, W. E. and Lange, M. (1989) 'Off-farm Work Decisions of Husbands and Wives: Joint Decision Making', *Review of Economics and Statistics*, vol. 71, pp. 471–80.

Kooreman, P. and Kapteyn, A. (1987) 'A Disaggregated Analysis of the Allocation of Time within a Household', *Journal of Political Economy*, vol. 95, pp. 223–49.

Maddala, G. S. (1983) *Limited Dependent and Qualitative Variables in Econometrics* (Cambridge, England: Cambridge University Press).

Olsen, R. (1978) 'Note on the Uniqueness of the Maximum Likelihood Estimator of the Tobit Model', *Econometrica*, vol. 46, pp. 1211–15.

Pollak, R. A. and Wachter, M. (1975) 'The Relevance of the Household Production Function and Its Implications for the Allocation of Time', *Journal of Political Economy*, vol. 83, pp. 255–77.

Ransom, M. (1987) 'An Empirical Model of Discrete and Continuous Choice in Family Labor Supply', *Review of Economics and Statistics*, vol. 69, pp. 463–72.

Rosenzweig, M. (1978) 'Rural Wages, Labor Supply and Land Reform: A Theoretical and Empirical Analysis', *American Economic Review*, vol. 68, pp. 847–61.

Singh, I., Squire, L. and Strauss, J. (eds) (1986) *Agricultural Household Models: Extensions, Applications and Policy*, (Baltimore and London: Johns Hopkins University Press for the World Bank).

Waldman, D. (1981) 'An Economic Interpretation of Parameter Constraints in a Simultaneous Equations Model with Limited Dependent Variables', *International Economic Review*, vol. 22, pp. 731–9.

12 Survey Data on Expectations: What Have We Learnt?

G. S. Maddala[1]

UNIVERSITY OF FLORIDA

1 INTRODUCTION

Expectations play a major role in all economic activity. They are so ubiquitous in all economic modelling that it is not necessary to dwell on this issue at length. Early models of expectation were mostly extrapolative and the most popular model in the 1950s was the adaptive expectations model. Around 1960, Muth suggested that theories of expectation formation should be consistent with the economic model being considered and he said that, for lack of a better term, he would use the word 'rational' (Muth, 1961). In the 1970s, mainly with the impetus of Robert E. Lucas, Jr, the rational expectations model took off and now almost every paper published with the word 'expectations' in its title comes with a prefix 'rational'.

It is generally believed that there exists substantial evidence to suggest that the Muthian rational expectations hypothesis is at variance with survey evidence on expectations. The objectives of this paper are to:

1. examine whether the evidence really supports this conclusion;
2. evaluate the evidence on tests for rationality performed on survey data and to rationalise any apparent irrationality that exists;
3. examine what light survey data throw on how economic agents do form their expectations;
4. suggest ways of using survey data on expectations in econometric modelling;
5. examine the usefulness of survey data in the resolution of some theoretical controversies.

2 QUALITATIVE VERSUS QUANTITATIVE DATA

2.1 Sources of Survey Data on Expectations

There are several sources of survey data on expectations. A majority of the data sets are qualitative but some are quantitative and others are a mixture of qualitative and quantitative data. In the case of qualitative data, respondents are asked whether they expect a variable (rate of inflation, GNP, interest rates, etc.) to go up, go down or stay the same. In the case of mixed qualitative–quantitative data, only those who answered that the variable would change are asked to give a quantitative estimate. The usual argument in favour of asking a qualitative question is that respondents are usually busy and are not likely to give a quantitative estimate. This is particularly the case when information is sought on a large number of variables as in the case of the business test data analysed by Koenig and Nerlove (1986).[2]

2.2 Quantitative Estimates from Qualitative Data

There have been two approaches to the analysis of qualitative data. One is to analyse them as they are and the other is to construct quantitative data from them and then analyse the quantitative data. Koenig *et al.* (1985) and Koenig and Nerlove (1986) are illustrations of the direct use of qualitative data. These authors use the log linear model.

A majority of studies, however, convert the qualitative responses to quantitative data. By far the most commonly used method is that due to Knöbl (1974) and Carlson and Parkin (1975). The Carlson–Parkin method computes estimators of the sample mean and variance of the distribution of expectations. This method rests on the assumption that respondents answer 'no change' if the change they perceive is below a certain threshold, δ. Given the proportions of the respondents in the categories: 'up', 'down' and 'stay the same', and given an assumption about the distribution of the expectations, we can obtain the mean μ and variance σ^2 of the distribution of expectations provided we have an estimate of δ. Carlson and Parkin assumed expectations to be normally distributed though Carlson (1977) found price expectations to be non-normal. Non-normal distributions can be used as shown by Batchelor (1981). The main problem is getting an estimate of δ. Knöbl (1974) assumed a value of $\delta = 2.0$. Carlson and Parkin (1975) suggest estimating δ by assuming long-term unbiasedness. This method has been criticised on the grounds that it biases rationality tests on survey data towards non-rejection. Batchelor (1982) chooses the threshold δ to minimise the sum of squared expectations errors.

Apart from these differences in the methods of estimating the threshold of perception δ, the idea that those who answer 'same' do so because they cannot perceive the difference is not very appealing. An alternative explanation for the 'stay the same' category is that the individual has chosen not to make any investment in price level information and is using the costless predictor of 'no change'. Or else the individual has invested in a costly predictor and the prediction calls for no price change.

A model that studies the determinants of information acquisition is that by Fishe and Idson (1989). They assume that information on inflation is costly to acquire, that individuals vary with respect to their incentives to acquire information, and that the quantity of information acquired is a function of factors that affect the expected return to information investment (age, education and income of the respondent). To the extent that these factors vary across individuals, a given survey will include forecasts made from different sets of information. Also, the variance of an individual's forecast is expected to vary inversely with the amount of information acquired. Fishe and Idson observe that the survey by the Survey Research Center of the University of Michigan (SRC) asks the direction question first and the quantitative question next. Someone who responds 'don't know' to the direction question has presumably acquired less information than someone who responds 'don't know' to the quantitative question. Using the SRC data from 24 monthly surveys during 1978 and 1979, they find evidence in favour of the differential information hypothesis. Fishe and Idson find that the more the education and income of an individual, the lower the variance of that individual's inflationary expectation.[3]

An alternative method of quantifying the qualitative responses is that used by Pesaran (1988, ch. 8). Suppose we have the proportions A_t, B_t and C_t respectively in the categories 'down,' 'same' and 'up' for the perceptions of the past inflation rate; and A_t^*, B_t^* and C_t^* in the same categories for expectations about the future inflation rate. Pesaran suggests regressing the observed inflation rate p_t on A_t and C_t (we omit the 'stay the same' category, B_t) and using the estimated regression coefficients to get the predicted inflation rate from A_t^* and C_t^*. Thus, if the regression equation is

$$p_t = \alpha A_t + \beta C_t + \varepsilon_t$$

Pesaran suggests using the estimates $\hat{\alpha}$ and $\hat{\beta}$ of the regression coefficients to get estimates of the predicted inflation rate p_t^*. Thus, $\hat{p}_t^* = \hat{\alpha} A_t^* + \hat{\beta} C_t^*$.

The reliability of this method is not known. It can be checked only if we have continuous data for both the perceptions of inflation and expectations of inflation. This can perhaps be done with the data for Sweden analysed by Jonung (1981).

2.3 Mixed Qualitative–Quantitative Data

There are some surveys where it is customary to get quantitative estimates of expectations only from those respondents whose answer to the qualitative question indicated a change. In the SRC survey, quantitative estimates were obtained only for those who indicated that prices would go up, and only from the second quarter of 1966.

The SRC mixed qualitative–quantitative data were analysed by de Menil and Bhalla (1975) and Juster and Comment (1978). They calculated the price expectation series as a weighted average of the answers to the quantitative question with zero substituted for those who expected the prices to stay the same or go down.

Fishe and Lahiri (1981) argue that the procedure of assigning a price expectation value of zero to the 'stay the same' or 'go down' categories used by de Menil and Bhalla is arbitrary. They suggest the use of limited dependent variable models to estimate the mean μ_t and variance σ_t^2 of the expectation distribution, as well as δ_t the threshold value of perceptibility. The maximum likelihood procedure is described in Maddala *et al.* (1983, pp. 279–80) and estimates are presented for the expected rate of inflation (μ_t), uncertainty (σ_t) and perceptibility (δ_t).[4]

This procedure produces improved price expectations series compared with the procedures used by de Menil and Bhalla and Juster and Comment. This can be seen from the mean squared error of forecasts from the different procedures, presented in Fishe and Lahiri (1981, p. 100). The Fishe–Lahiri series generated from the SRC data have smaller mean squared forecast errors than the de Menil–Bhalla series and the Livingston series in forecasting the actual rate of inflation. In fact, the Livingston series performed the worst, thus suggesting that laymen are better than experts, or that a larger sample of laymen is better than a small sample of experts.

The data by Visco (1984) are qualitative but since the limits for the different categories are specified, one can compute the mean and variance of the distribution of expectations once the underlying distribution is specified. Visco considers the uniform and normal distributions.

2.4 Adequacy of the Carlson–Parkin Technique

The mixed qualitative–quantitative data sets have also been used to test the adequacy of the Carlson–Parkin approach of generating quantitative data from qualitative responses. Defris and Williams (1979) use the University of Melbourne survey data to compare the quantitative estimates obtained from the quantitative responses, with quantitative estimates obtained from the purely qualitative questions, using the Carlson–Parkin method. They find the latter method unsatisfactory because it gives very erratic results. Batchelor (1986) makes a similar comparison using the SRC data, though it is not clear whether he obtained the estimates from the truncated quantitative data using the de Menil–Bhalla procedure which ignores the truncation or the Fishe–Lahiri procedure which takes truncation into account. In any case, he found the performance of the Carlson–Parkin procedure not very satisfactory. Batchelor concludes that it is always best to get quantitative responses in surveys and if this is not possible and one has to use the Carlson–Parkin method, it should be refined to allow for non-normality. An earlier paper by Batchelor (1981) uses the Carlson–Parkin method using skewed stable distributions rather the normal distribution, and finds that this eliminates symptoms of irrationality previously found in survey-based measures of expectations.

3 TESTS FOR RATIONALITY

There is an enormous literature on tests of rationality (in the Muthian sense) of survey data. The predominant, if not universal, conclusion is that survey expectations are irrational. Some argue that this conclusion is due to the use of inappropriate data, wrong information sets and faulty statistical procedures of analysis. This point is discussed in the next section. The test procedures used run as follows.

If y_t^* is the expected value of y_t, then rationality implies that the forecast error $(y_t - y_t^*)$ is uncorrelated with variables in the information set I_{t-1} when forecasts are formed. It is customary to start with a test of unbiasedness by estimating the equation $y_t = \beta_0 + \beta_1 y_t^* + \varepsilon_t$ and testing the hypothesis $\beta_0 = 0, \beta_1 = 1$. Further, since y_{t-1} is in the information set, the following equation can be estimated:

$$y_t - y_t^* = \alpha_0 + \alpha_1 y_{t-1} + \varepsilon_t$$

Rationality implies that $\alpha_0 = 0$ and $\alpha_1 = 0$. This is a test for efficiency. Another alternative equation is:

$$y_t - y_t^* = \alpha_0 + \alpha_1(y_{t-1} - y_{t-1}^*) + \varepsilon_t$$

Again rationality implies that $\alpha_0 = 0$ and $\alpha_1 = 0$. This is a test for no serial correlation. If the forecast errors exhibit a significant non-zero mean and serial correlation (significant α_1) then this implies that the information contained in past forecast errors was not fully utilised in forming expectations about the future. Tests based on y_{t-1} and $(y_{t-1} - y_{t-1}^*)$ are weak tests for rationality. The strong version says that the forecast error $y_t - y_t^*$ is uncorrelated with all the variables known to the forecaster.

Also, since $y_t = y_t^* + \varepsilon_t$ where ε_t and y_t^* are independent, we have $\text{Var}(y_t) > \text{Var}(y_t^*)$. Lovell (1986) considers these two tests:

(i) tests based on y_{t-1}, and
(ii) tests based on $\text{Var}(y_t) > \text{Var}(y_t^*)$.

He examines the evidence from a number of surveys on sales and inventory expectations, price expectations, wage expectations, data revisions and so on, and argues that in a majority of cases the tests of rationality reject the hypothesis of rationality.

One problem of using an incomplete information set is the following. If we have two sets of variables z_{1t} and z_{2t} in the information set I_{t-1}, so that we should be estimating

$$y_t - y_t^* = \beta_1 z_{1t} + \beta_2 z_{2t} + \varepsilon_t$$

and we mistakenly omit z_{2t} and test $\beta_1 = 0$, we can mistakenly accept the hypothesis of rationality. This can happen, for instance if $\beta_1 = 0$, $\beta_2 \neq 0$ but z_1 and z_2 are uncorrelated.

The question of what variables should be included in the information set I_{t-1} actually depends on costs and benefits. It is true that past values of the variable being forecast are readily available and should be in the information set. But the same cannot be said of other variables. Agents with economically rational expectations will set the marginal cost equal to the marginal benefit of acquiring information. In practice, however, since these costs and benefits are difficult to observe, it is hard to say what the information set I_{t-1} ought to be. The cost–benefit argument, however, might explain why the Livingston price expectations data fail tests of rationality. Applied to this data set, it implies that most of the respondents must have had little incentive to produce good forecasts. The respondents have no risk of loss of reputation since individual forecasts are not published and moreover, those working in government, universities and financial institutions are too busy to give much thought to the forecasts. Hafer and Resler (1982) found that it was economists employed in non-financial businesses, who were closest to the price-setting process, who provided 'rational' forecasts of the Consumer Price Index.

Figlewski and Wachtel (1983) point out another source of bias in tests for rationality, this one arising from aggregation over individuals. Thus, if only the mean (or median) response of a number of individuals is considered, the rationality of the mean response may be unrelated to the rationality of individual responses. When Figlewski and Wachtel (1981) analyse the individual forecasts from the Livingston data, they do reject rationality.

Visco (1984, pp. 156–9) also considers the implications of aggregation on using the mean of the expectational distribution for tests of rationality. Unlike Figlewski and Wachtel, he does not have individual data. The categorical data can yield only the mean and variance. He, therefore, makes an assumption of the relationship between the deviations of the individual expectations from the group mean, and the standard deviation σ_t of the distribution of expectations and derives the equation

$$p_t = \alpha + \beta p_t^e + \delta\sigma_t + e_t$$

We test the hypothesis $\alpha = 0$ and $\beta = 0$ but we do this after adding σ_t to the equation.

Saunders (1981) performs tests of rationality with Australian producers' price expectations. When he performs tests with data at the individual firm level, he rejects the hypothesis of rationality. However, when he performs the tests with time series data based on averages for each period, he does not reject the hypothesis of rationality. Urich and Wachtel (1984) also apply tests of rationality to money supply expectations using aggregated and disaggregated data. If the usual and erroneous procedure is applied to survey forecasts, which is to use the mean of the forecasts for each survey, the data seem to support the rationality hypothesis. However, when the same set of tests are applied to the disaggregated (individual level) data the hypothesis of rationality is soundly rejected.

The preceding tests are all tests for what might be called 'mean rationality'. Although rational expectations models have argued that economic agents should condition their forecasts on the basis of the entire information set available to them, such an argument has not often been applied in the context of agents' expectations about the variability of the economic processes. The ARCH model due to Engle (1983) is one approach that has been followed. But again, like the rational expectation hypothesis, this is an assumption that is imposed on the model and the ARCH effect could be a consequence of several different sources of misspecification such as omission of lagged variables, assumption of constancy of the coefficients in the presence of parameter variation, and so on. Survey data provide a source for testing the validity of the ARCH specification. Taylor (1989) for instance finds the evidence in favour of the ARCH effect very weak. Of course, there is the question of how measures of uncertainty should be constructed from the survey data and whether cross-forecaster variation, a measure often used, is an adequate measure of forecasting uncertainty. The ASA–NBER surveys enable us to construct measures of forecasters' uncertainty. These measures, used by Zarnowitz and Lambros (1987) and Lahiri *et al.* (1988) can be used to test variance rationality as well as appropriateness of the ARCH specification.

4 RATIONALISING THE IRRATIONALITY

4.1 Are Forecasters Irrational?

The evidence discussed in the previous section has been interpreted by some investigators as indicating irrationality (Pearce, 1979; Friedman, 1980) or that the survey data are somehow wrong or irrelevant (Pesando, 1975). There have been, however, some arguments advanced to show that the failure of survey data on expectations to pass the tests for rationality outlined in the previous section need not imply that forecasters are irrational. The arguments advanced are theoretical as well as statistical.

4.2 Theoretical Arguments

Grossman (1975, p. 264) showed that because of non-linearities in the underlying model, the rational expectations hypothesis does not imply that the anticipated value of a variable is equal to its mathematical expectation in all circumstances. Stegman, (1985), Visco (1984, pp. 133–4) and Zellner (1986) argue that when costs of forecast errors are asymmetric, a biased forecast is rational. Zarnowitz (1985) reviews several survey forecasts on inflation and real GNP growth. He finds that almost all forecasters underestimated inflation and overestimated real GNP growth. Zellner argues that this is consistent with the asymmetric loss function he considers. Of course, in order to make sense of such inferences, one needs to find a justification for the forecasters' loss functions being asymmetric.

Leonard (1982, p. 160) explains the downward bias he observes in wage forecasts by arguing that it may be desirable behaviour on the firms' part if firms find it less costly to raise wages initially set too low and hire additional workers, than to lower wages set too high and fire extra workers. In this case the source of the asymmetry in the loss function is easy to see. The same cannot, perhaps, be said about inflation forecasts and GNP forecasts. On the other hand, the asymmetry in the loss function regarding producers' expectations about selling prices as in Saunders' (1981) study can be given an easy interpretation.

Cukierman (1986) gives another justification for the observed bias in the forecasts. He argues that the bias can arise from the inability of economic agents to sort out immediately the permanent and transitory components of any economic shocks. In the presence of the permanent–transitory confusion, slow learning is optimal and therefore rational. Thus, the simple rationality tests discussed in the previous section would lead to the acceptance of the rationality hypothesis during tranquil periods and rejection when large permanent changes (like the oil-price shocks of the 1970s) occur. Cukierman observes that this is consistent with the findings of Visco (1984) who rejected the rationality of expectations only for the turbulent period of the 1970s.

A similar argument is made by Lewis (1989). She demonstrates how forecast errors can be systematic when the market participants rationally learn the true process that generates the fundamentals. During the early 1980s, the survey data show systematic underprediction of the strength of the US dollar. Lewis explains this by arguing that following the tightening of the US money market, agents did not immediately believe that the change would persist but instead learned about the shift rationally.

4.3 Statistical Arguments

The statistical arguments are that tests for rationality of survey data have been based on inappropriate data sets, information sets or estimation methods. For instance, it has often been argued that the respondents in the Livingston surveys had no incentive to give well thought out answers and, thus, this is the wrong data set to discuss rationality of survey data. As noted by Hafer and Resler (1982) only those respondents closest to the price setting process provided 'rational' forecasts of the Consumer Price Index. Keane and Runkle (1989) argue that tests of rationality based on the Livingston data are not appropriate and suggest the use of the ASA–NBER survey data. The respondents in this survey have an incentive to do careful analysis because they sell in the market the same forecasts which they report to the survey.

The next argument is that of inappropriate information sets used in tests for rationality. It is important to examine what data sets the respondents are expected to have. Keane and Runkle (1989) point out that previous studies of price forecast rationality ran tests using the revised data on actual prices. This is unfair because the forecasters cannot be expected to have access to the revised data for the previous period. Hence, Keane and Runkle apply tests for rationality using the unrevised data to which the forecasters are expected to have access. Zarnowitz (1985) also argued that the use of revised data could affect inferences on rationality.

The next argument is that of inappropriate statistical methods. If y_t and y_t^e are non-stationary and are characterised by unit root processes, the tests of rationality discussed in Section 3 would lead to an incorrect finding of bias when such bias does not exist. If it can be shown that the actual series has a unit root, then so should the forecast series under the assumptions of rational expectations. Furthermore, $y_t - y_t^e$ should be a random process and should not have a unit root, that is y_t and y_t^e should be cointegrated with a cointegrating factor of 1. The proper test in this case is a test for cointegration as outlined in Granger (1986) and Engle and Granger (1987) along with a test for randomness of the errors. Lahiri and Chun (1989) apply such tests on the ASA–NBER data and conclude that the tests do not reject the hypothesis of rationality. Note that the test is based on the hypothesis that y_t and y_t^e are *not* cointegrated, that is, $y_t - y_t^e$ has a unit root. A rejection of this hypothesis implies rationality. For the Livingston data, Lahiri and Chun find that this hypothesis is not rejected. Thus, the Livingston data fail the test of rationality even with the cointegration test. Similar tests for rationality based on cointegration have been applied by Hafer and Hein (1989), Hakkio and Rush (1989), and Liu (1989).

Keane and Runkle (1989) give another reason why the statistical procedures are inappropriate. They argue that previous studies assumed that errors are uncorrelated across forecaster and used the ordinary least squares (OLS) method. They assume that errors are correlated across forecasters and use the generalised method of moments (GMM) estimator. They find that the hypothesis of rationality is not rejected when this method (the correct one in their opinion) is used. Thus, if the correct data set, information set, and estimation method are used, one does not reject the hypothesis of rationality.

5 EVIDENCE ON EXPECTATION FORMATION

One other important point which survey data can throw light on is on how economic agents form expectations. This can be inferred by fitting different models of expectations to the observed data. Another alternative is to ask the respondents how they do form their expectations. The latter approach has been followed by Allen and Taylor (1989). Frankel and Froot (1986) explain exchange rate dynamics by assuming that some traders are chartists and form expectations by using technical analysis and that others are fundamentalists and form expectations by using fundamental economic analysis.

In an attempt to ascertain the influence of chartism on traders in the foreign exchange market, Allen and Taylor (1989) conducted a questionnaire survey of chief foreign exchange dealers in the London market. Their survey showed that almost all dealers regarded chartism and fundamentals as complementary rather than competitive as assumed by Frankel and Froot. Chartism appears to be most used for forecasting over short horizons (intra-day to one week) given the lack of economic data at that frequency. For longer forecasting horizons (one month to one year) the weight given to fundamentals increases. For one year forecasts 30 per cent of the respondents relied on pure fundamentals and 85 per cent judged fundamentals to be more important than charts. The Allen and Taylor study is an example of survey data being used to get an idea of how expectations are formed by asking respondents directly how they do form their expectations. The issue of chartism versus fundamentals cannot really be disentangled from the observed data.

In almost all other studies, the process of expectation formation is inferred by fitting alternative models of expectation to the survey data. Carlson and Parkin (1975, p. 132) suggest a general error learning model that relates changes in expectations to past errors. Figlewski and Wachtel (1981) estimate both the adaptive regression model and the regressive expectations model for the Livingston data. The regressive expectations model assumes that inflation rates return to their normal level. Figlewski and Wachtel did not find the regressive model to be satisfactory for the Livingston date. They find the adaptive regression model more appropriate but they find that there are substantial differences in the adaptation coefficients between different individuals and over time.

Urich and Wachtel (1984) estimate the adaptive, extrapolative and regressive expectations models for the data on expectations about weekly money supply announcements. Their results indicate that the regressive and adaptive models dominate the extrapolative. They settle on a model that includes both the adaptive and regressive elements.

Mullineaux (1980) uses the Livingston price expectations data to study whether money growth rates are used in forming expectations about inflation. He uses lagged inflation rates and lagged money supply growth as explanatory variables. He finds the latter variables significant, but finds the unemployment rate to be not significant when it is added to the equation.

Fishe and Lahiri (1981) use changes in the actual price level, changes in money supply and changes in the unemployment rate as explanatory variables to explain the price expectations data that they generate from the University of Michigan surveys. They find that the unemployment rate is not as important as the other variables.

These studies focused on how the forecasts were related to economic variables. If the estimated coefficients are significant, this is interpreted as indicating that the forecasters used these variables in their forecasting procedure. Caskey (1985) asks a different type of question. Using a Bayesian learning model he tries to explain why the Livingston group forecast as it did. He starts with the assumption that each member of the Livingston group had some prior notions about inflation and that the panel followed Bayes's Rule in updating their beliefs. Caskey finds that the Livingston forecasts are consistent with optimal forecasting behaviour. However, the method of estimation he uses is to choose the values of the parameters of the Livingston group's prior distribution such that when this prior is updated each period, the forecast series resembles the Livingston series. It is a curious example of estimating the prior distribution from the data. What this exercise shows is that one can find a prior distribution that will show that the Livingston group used the available information efficiently.

The predominant concern with many analyses using the price expectations data has been whether variables relating to monetary and fiscal policy play a major role in determining expectations about inflation after including lagged values of the inflation rate. The results using survey data generally indicate that monetary variables are significant and variables related to fiscal policy are not. By contrast, in the area of foreign exchange rate expectations, the predominant concern has been whether exchange rate expectations have a de-stabilising effect on the currency markets.

Frankel and Froot (1987) investigate different models of expectations using survey data from Money Market Services (MMS), the *Economist*, and the Amex Bank Review. Define S_t as the log of the spot exchange rate at time t, and S^*_{t+1} as the log of the expected spot exchange rate at time $(t+1)$, the expectation being formed at time t. Frankel and Froot consider the following models:

(i)   Static expectations: $S^*_{t+1} = S_t$
(ii) Distributed lag: $S^*_{t+1} = (1-\beta)S_t + \beta S_{t-1}$ $0 < \beta < 1$
(iii) Adaptive expectations: $\Delta S^*_{t+1} = \gamma(S_t - S^*_t)$ $0 < \gamma < 1$
(iv) Regressive expectations: $S^*_{t+1} = (1-\alpha)S_t + \alpha S^n_t$ $0 < \alpha < 1$
      where S^n_t is the 'normal' or 'long-run equilibrium' exchange rate for time t.
(v)   Bandwagon expectation: $\Delta S^*_{t+1} = \theta \Delta S_t$ $\theta > 0$.
(vi) Adaptive bandwagon: $\Delta S^*_{t+1} = \lambda(S^*_t - S_t) + \alpha \Delta S_t$.

The bandwagon expectations model is the only one that results in destabilising the currency markets (provided the restrictions on β, γ, α

in the other models are valid). The bandwagon model implies that if the currency has been depreciating (appreciating), investors expect that it will continue to depreciate (appreciate). The general conclusion they reach from the results they present is that the static expectations or 'random walk' model and the bandwagon expectations model are rejected.

The MMS data refer to the medians of the responses reported in each time period. Tests of rationality could be subject to aggregation biases as we noted earlier. Also, even if some model like the adaptive expectations model is estimated, as Figlewski and Wachtel note, the adaptation coefficients can differ across individuals and may change over time. Ito (1988), therefore, considers micro survey data on foreign exchange rates collected by the Japan Centre for International Finance (JCIF) in Tokyo. The tests for rationality which he performs at the individual level soundly reject rationality of the survey data. However, Ito does not investigate the issue of alternative models of expectations.

6   USING SURVEY DATA IN ECONOMETRIC MODELS

6.1   Using Survey Measures of Expectations

Given the predominant evidence that survey expectations are biased, what can we do with these survey data on expectations? Of course, the natural tendency is to say 'ignore the data and do no more surveys'. However, a more reasonable approach is to devise methods of using the survey data which take account of these shortcomings. Suppose that we are considering expectations about inflation. (The arguments would be similar for expectations about other variables.) The unobserved expected inflation occurs as an explanatory variable in the interest rate equation, the demand for money equation, the wage equation and so on. The survey measure of expectation can also be viewed as being dependent on this unobserved variable. Thus, we have one more indicator for the unobserved expected rate of inflation. The use of such multiple indicator-multiple cause (MIMIC) models is illustrated in Lahiri and Zaporowski (1987).

6.2   Using Survey Measures of Dispersion

Survey data give two measures on expectations: the mean and the variance of the distribution of expectations. One of the uses of the measures of dispersion has been in studies relating inflation uncertainty to economic activity. That inflation uncertainty has a detrimental effect on economic activity has been suggested by many economists. The reasoning is that the uncertainty will lead economic agents to make erroneous decisions regarding resource allocations. Though this proposition is theoretically sound, one has to answer the questions of how exactly to define inflation uncertainty, how to measure it and how to incorporate it into an empirical investigation of macro models.

One common practice involves taking the dispersion of predictions at a point of time as a proxy for uncertainty. This technique has been used on the Livingston forecasts by Bomberger and Frazer (1981), Cukierman and Wachtel (1982), and on the Michigan SRC data by Maddala *et al.* (1983). Hasbrouck (1984) uses the cross-forecaster dispersion of economic activity forecasts as a proxy for real uncertainty and finds it to be a significant determinant of stock returns.

There are two major problems with this approach. The first is about the use of forecaster discord for forecast uncertainty. The second is the definition of variability itself. What is relevant is not the variance of the inflation rate itself but the variance of the unanticipated part. Cukierman and Wachtel (1982) argue that a natural measure of inflation uncertainty is the variance of the forecast error of the inflation rate, which can be proxied by computing the mean-squared forecast error of inflation over individual respondents to the survey. They argue that all the measures commonly used for inflation uncertainty are positively correlated. This does not, however, mean that the results obtained from the use of the different measures will be the same.

Evidence on forecaster discord and inflation uncertainty is available from the ASA–NBER survey data. In contrast to the other expected inflation surveys, such as the Livingston survey, the respondents to the ASA–NBER survey are also asked to assign a probability of outcome to various ranges of annual percentage change in the implicit price deflator (IPD). For each respondent, the mean and variance of the probability distribution of forecasts can be computed. The mean of the means of these distributions represents the average expected rate of change in the IPD perceived by the individuals surveyed. The mean of the variances (or standard deviations) of these distributions represents the average level of uncertainty perceived by the respondents. Zarnowitz and Lambros (1987) have argued that this variance represents a more explicit measure of inflation uncertainty. They also report that the forecaster discord measure often used is substantially smaller than this measure of uncertainty. Lahiri, Teigland and Zaporowski (1988) find that though there is a similarity in the movement of the two measures, there are periods when they moved in opposite directions. For instance, in 1973 a very high level of disagreement among forecasters was accompanied by very low uncertainty (mean of the variances of the probability distributions). Exactly the opposite situation prevailed during 1983. Lahiri *et al.* estimate a reduced form interest rate equation with inflation uncertainty computed from the ASA–NBER survey and find the coefficient of expected inflation to be substantially below 1. Estimation of the same equation using forecaster discord usually produced higher estimates.

An alternative method of estimating the variance of inflation is the ARCH model suggested by Engle (1983). If p_t is the inflation rate at time t, the ARCH model specifies:

$$p_t|x_t \sim N(x_t\beta,h_t)$$

$$h_t = \alpha_0 + \alpha_1\varepsilon_{t-1}^2 + \ldots + \alpha_p\varepsilon_{t-p}^2$$

$$\varepsilon^t = p_t - x_t\beta$$

Engle reports that the ARCH variances are larger than the Livingston variances. Earlier, we noted that the measures of uncertainty (the means of the variances of the individuals' probability distributions) from the ASA–NBER data were also higher than the measures of forecaster discord. A comparison of this measure of uncertainty with the measures derived from the ARCH model for the ASA–NBER data shows that the average variance is roughly the same but the time pattern is different. It thus appears that the results from the survey data are at variance with those given by the ARCH model.

When it comes to the use of the Livingston surveys, the use of forecaster discord becomes more problematic. The discord may arise as a purely methodological artifact. The Livingston respondents are polled during a period of several weeks. If significant information arrives during this period, the predictions of early and late respondents will differ for reasons that have no direct relationship to forecast uncertainty. Similar problems arise with any surveys where respondents are polled over a length of time.

7 SURVEY DATA IN FOREIGN EXCHANGE MARKETS

There are many surveys on exchange rates: the MMS, Amex and *Economist* surveys analysed by Frankel and Froot (1987), the Japan Centre for International Finance (JCIF) survey used by Ito (1988) and the Godwins survey used by Taylor (1989). Dominguez (1986) shows that the MMS data fail the standard tests for rationality (unbiasedness, efficiency, no serial correlation in errors, and so on). However, it is questionable whether these tests are appropriate. If we denote the spot rate by S_t and the expected rate by S_t^e, then it can be shown that both S_t and S_t^e are non-stationary, in fact they can be shown to be $I(1)$, that is integrated to order 1. If this is the case, the proper test for the rational expectations hypothesis should be equivalent to a test for cointegration with a cointegrating factor of 1. We have to test the hypothesis that $S_t - S_t^e$ is not $I(1)$. In addition, $S_t - S_t^e$ should be a white noise. Liu (1989) performed the cointegration tests with the exchange rates in the level and log form using the MMS weekly data on exchange rate expectations. He finds that for all the four currencies: British pound, Deutsche Mark, Swiss franc, and Japanese yen, the hypothesis that $S_t - S_t^e$ is *not* cointegrated is convincingly rejected. In addition, the Q-statistics to test serial correlation were not significant. Thus, the cointegration tests do not reject the hypothesis of rationality.

The surveys investigated by Dominguez and Frankel and Froot have only the median responses reported. These data mask investigators' heterogeneous preferences. Focusing on the median misses the most interesting questions such as whether the differences are temporary or permanent and whether the rationality hypothesis is more likely to be rejected with data on individuals. The micro data analysed by Ito (1988) show substantial 'individual effects', that is, heterogeneity that persists over time. The rational expectations hypothesis is rejected at the individual level. However, Ito uses the conventional tests described earlier in Section 3, and not those based on cointegration. Finally, the market participants appear to have a 'bandwagon' expectation in the short run but a stabilising one in the long run.

Survey data, particularly the micro data, have been useful in throwing light on the process of expectation formation. The general conclusion that emerges is that the shorter the forecast horizon, then the more expectations are extrapolative of recent price trends – that is, chartism plays a major role. For longer time horizons market fundamentals play a major role. A regressive or return to 'normal' model of expectations applies. Another conclusion that emerges is that the bandwagon expectations model is not a valid representation. The absence of bandwagon effects implies that expectations in the foreign exchange market are not destabilising.

Yet another issue where survey data have been useful is in analysing the relationship between forward rates and future spot rates in the foreign exchange market. There is substantial evidence that the forward foreign exchange rate is a biased predictor of the future spot exchange rate. Though everyone agrees about the existence of the bias, there is considerable disagreement on whether the bias is evidence of a risk premium or a violation of rational expectations. Some assume risk-neutrality and attribute the bias to non-rationality of expectations. Others, like Diebold and Pauly (1988), attribute the bias to risk premiums varying over time. Using survey data it is possible to appropriate the blame for the non-optimality of the forward rate as a predictor of the spot rate between failure of the assumption of risk-neutrality and failure of the assumption of rational expectations.

Froot and Frankel (1989) estimate the effect of the failure of the two assumptions of risk-neutrality and rational expectations, using the data from the MMS, Amex and *Economist* surveys. They conclude that the bias is mostly attributable to expectational errors rather than to a risk premium. They reject the hypothesis that all the bias in the forward rate is due to a risk premium, but they cannot reject the hypothesis that all the bias is attributable to systematic expectational errors. However, the analysis by Liu (1989) based on weekly MMS data does not reject the hypothesis of rationality of expectations and attributes the bias to risk premium. Thus, an analysis of weekly data and tests based on cointegration give conclusions opposite to those arrived at by Froot and Frankel.

Taylor (1989) makes a similar study using the data collected by Godwins in London. However, the data are qualitative (up, stay the same, down categories), and Taylor uses the Carlson–Parkin technique to generate the quantitative data. As noted earlier, there are some problems with such conversion of qualitative to quantitative data. Taylor, however, arrives at the conclusion that it is the risk premium which is primarily responsible for the failure of the forward rate to act as an optimal predictor of the future spot rate.

The fact that the data used by Taylor are qualitative and those by Frankel and Froot are quantitative, is a merit of the latter data.

However, there are other differences which suggest that the data used by Taylor are perhaps more appropriate for the analysis. The data used by Frankel and Froot are means (or medians) of the individual responses. Moreover, the Amex surveys were conducted by mail over a period up to a month and as with the Livingston survey, it is difficult to give an exact date, and to specify the associated information set, for the mean response. In both the Amex and MMS surveys it is not clear that the same set of respondents was used over time. Another problem is that since the data collected by the *Economist* or MMS surveys refer to currency traders who are interested in short-term trading, the respondents may not devote too much effort to long-term expectations. Taylor's study is based on data from the same set of financial institutions over the entire period. Also, the typical survey respondent is a manager of large, medium- to long-term investment portfolios, and hence has an incentive to produce good forecasts.

The discrepancy between the results of Froot and Frankel (1989) and Taylor (1989) suggests that it is very important to pay attention to who will be surveyed and to whether the data collected are qualitative or quantitative. A further issue relates to the analysis of median responses as analysed by Froot and Frankel *versus* individual data. The median responses mask important information on heterogeneity of expectations.

8 SURVEY DATA ON INTEREST RATES

Survey data have been useful in resolving some controversies in the term structure of interest rates. Tests of the expectations theory of the term structure have led to a rejection of that theory. However, the literature does not test the expectations hypothesis in isolation. It examines the joint hypothesis that the investor's expectations conform with the expectations theory, and that those expectations are rational in the sense of Muth. Survey data enable us to separate these two hypotheses (see Froot, 1989). Froot uses the Goldsmith–Nagan data which give the mean of the survey responses for the different periods. The Blue Chip Financial Forecasts (BCFF) conducted by Bob Eggert give individual forecasts of over forty professionals working in the major financial institutions. Batchelor (1988) uses these data to develop a theory of term structure based on investors' uncertainty about expectations. He uses the forecaster discord as a measure of uncertainty (the way forecaster discord was used to measure inflation uncertainty). This issue has been discussed earlier in Section 6.2.

The Goldsmith–Nagan survey data have been used by Hafer and Hein (1989) to compare survey forecasts with forecasts implied by the futures markets.[5] They conclude that the survey forecasts are unbiased predictors of future rates, but find that there is little difference in the forecasting accuracy of the two.

9   USE OF SURVEY DATA TO STUDY DISEQUILIBRIUM DYNAMICS

One of the most important contributions of survey data has been on the issue of the response of economic agents to disturbances in the markets. This issue is central to the debate on appropriate macroeconomic policies. There are two schools of thought: the disequilibrium macroeconomic theorists and new classical equilibrium macroeconomists. The former group argues that prices are inflexible in the short run and that it is quantities rather than prices which adjust to economic shocks. The latter school believes in instantaneous adjustment of prices. The Munich business test data for German firms gathered by the IFO institute and the INSEE data for French firms have been used to throw light on this issue. The methodology used is that of log linear models. Koenig and Nerlove (1986) carry out an elaborate study of both the French and German data and find support for the disequilibrium macroeconomic view for French firms.

A detailed discussion of these models would make this paper much longer. Furthermore, we have not discussed at any length the use of survey data in macro models either. A detailed discussion of the use of survey data in micro and macro models has been omitted.

10   CONCLUSIONS

1. Considerable attention has been devoted to the so-called tests of rationality of survey data. However, the failure of the tests for rationality does not mean that survey data are not useful. There is evidence in some cases, especially with price expectations data and foreign exchange expectations data that inappropriate data

sets, information sets and estimation methods account for the rejection of the rationality hypothesis.

2. The survey data suggest that there are considerable lags in perceptions, considerable uncertainty about how the economic system operates and considerable lags in price adjustment to signals that are often inconsistent. There is also a confusion between the permanent and transitory components when the economic system is subjected to large shocks. These several factors produce the biases in the survey data that are observed. These findings have important implications for the modelling of expectations and also the design of macroeconomic policies.

3. Another finding which has important implications for macroeconomic policy is that by Koenig and Nerlove (1986) and others using the data on French and German firms who found substantial evidence in favour of the disequilibrium hypothesis which postulates that in the short run it is quantities rather than prices which respond to exogenous shocks.

4. Too much attention has been devoted to tests of rationality and not much to the question of how survey data can be used effectively in econometric modelling. Exceptions are the work by Lahiri and Zaporowski (1987), the work on risk premia in the foreign exchange market by Froot and Frankel (1989) and Taylor (1989), and the work on inflation uncertainty and economic activity.

5. Uncertainty over expectations plays a crucial role in many econometric models. There is considerable dispute on how this should be measured. One common measure is the variance of cross-respondent expectations from the survey data. However, this has been found to be unsatisfactory. There are some data sets where data on the uncertainty of forecasts are obtained from the respondents themselves. These data should be used more often.

6. Qualitative data have been very often converted to quantitative data using the Carlson–Parkin method. However, where quantitative data have been available, a comparison of the results, using the quantitative data with those yielded by the use of the Carlson–Parkin method on the corresponding qualitative data, reveals serious deficiencies with the Carlson–Parkin method. If the method is to be used, it appears that it is better to use it assuming a stable non-normal distribution rather than the normal distribution. The adequacy of the regression method suggested by Pesaran has not been investigated and, in any case, it is not a

method that can be applied unless one has data on perceptions of the past as well as expectations about the future. Since such data are not usually available (except from Swedish surveys) the Pesaran method is not of much use. In any case, its adequacy has not been checked in the way it has been done for the Carlson–Parkin method.

7. There is substantial evidence on the non-normality of the distribution of expectations. Hence, non-normal distributions should be used whenever feasible.

8. Not much can be done about the deficiencies of the data that have been collected already. But in future, it would be better if data were to be collected on a quantitative scale. Respondents can be asked to give different point estimates with associated probabilities. This would enable us to construct measures of uncertainty associated with forecasts. Furthermore, it is important to pay attention to the question of whose expectations are relevant for the problem at hand. More attention should be given to who is being surveyed. The Livingston data illustrate this problem. Many respondents in the survey have been found to have no incentive to invest in information and to give considered forecasts. Paradoxically enough, these are precisely the data that have been most analysed. In my view too many papers have been based on these data.

9. Survey data can be useful in resolving the issue of whether the forward exchange rate is a biased predictor of the future spot rate either because expectations are not rational or because of the risk premium. However, the conclusions seem to differ depending on what data set is used and how the tests for rationality are performed (cointegration tests *versus* the conventional tests).

10. Survey data on interest rates have been useful in throwing new light on the expectations hypothesis of the term structure, and on the forecasting accuracy of survey expectations and the implied forecasts derived from the futures markets.

11. Survey data in which only the mean or median response is reported are not as useful as the micro data. Heterogeneity of expectations is an important factor on which survey data can throw light. In future, since the individual data are collected anyway, it would be more useful if these data were to be made available to researchers.

Notes

1. I would like to acknowledge helpful comments from William Bomberger, R. P. H. Fishe, Kajal Lahiri, and Peter Liu on an earlier draft, and from Angus Deaton, Jacques Van der Gaag, Marc Nerlove and Paul Taubman at the meetings in Athens.
2. This point was specially emphasised by Marc Nerlove.
3. Van der Gaag pointed out that this procedure rests on the normality assumption and there is considerable evidence which suggests that price expectations are not normally distributed. However, the evidence in the Fishe–Idson paper is so strong that the conclusions are not likely to change if some non-normal distributions are considered (this is feasible but computationally very costly).
4. One drawback of this procedure is that it depends on the normality of the distribution of expectations. This assumption, however, can be relaxed.
5. Paul Taubman raised the question of the relationship between survey forecasts and futures markets when this paper was presented in Athens. The Hafer and Hein study on interest rates is quoted here for that purpose. I have been studying a similar comparison with data on the foreign exchange market but the results are not ready yet.

References

Allen, H. and Taylor, M. P. (1989) 'Charts and Fundamentals in the Foreign Exchange Market', discussion paper no 40, Bank of England.

Batchelor, R. A. (1981) 'Aggregate Expectations Under the Stable Laws', *Journal of Econometrics*, vol. 16, pp. 199–210.

Batchelor, R. A. (1982) 'Expectations, Output and Inflation: The European Experience', *European Economic Review*, vol. 17, pp. 1–25.

Batchelor, R. A. (1986) 'Quantitative and Qualitative Measures of Inflation Expectations', *Oxford Bulletin of Economics and Statistics*, vol. 48, pp. 99–120.

Batchelor, R. A. (1988) 'A Weakly-Held Expectations Theory of the term Premia in US Treasury Bills', manuscript, City University Business School, London.

Bomberger, W. A. and Frazer, W. J., Jr (1981) 'Interest Rates, Uncertainty and the Livingston Data', *Journal of Finance*, vol. 36, pp. 661–75.

Carlson, J. A. (1977) 'Are Price Expectations Normally Distributed?' *Journal of American Statistical Association*, vol. 70, pp. 749–54.

Carlson, J. A. and Parkin, M. (1975) 'Inflation Expectations', *Economica*, vol. 42, pp. 123–38.

Caskey, J. (1985) 'Modelling the Formation of Price Expectations: A Bayesian Approach', *American Economic Review*, vol. 75, no 4, pp. 768–76.

Cukierman, A. (1986) 'Measuring Inflationary Expectations: A Review Essay', *Journal of Monetary Economics*, vol. 17, pp. 315–24.

Cukierman, A. and Wachtel, P. (1982) 'Inflationary Expectations: Reply and Further Thoughts on Inflation Uncertainty', *American Economic Review*, vol. 72, no 3, pp. 508–12.

Defris, L. V. and Williams, R. A. (1979) 'Quantitative versus Qualitative Measures of Price Expectations: The Evidence from Australian Consumer Surveys', *Economics Letters*, vol. 2, pp. 169–73.

de Menil, G. and Bhalla, S. S. (1975) 'Direct Measurement of Popular Price Expectations', *American Economic Review*, vol. 65, pp. 169–80.

Diebold, F. X. and Pauly, P. (1988) 'Endogenous Risk in a Rational Expectations Portfolio-Balance Model of the Deutschemark/Dollar rate', *European Economic Review*, vol. 32, pp. 27–54.

Dominguez, K. M. (1986) 'Are Foreign Exchange Forecasts Rational?' *Economics Letters*, vol. 21, pp. 277–81.

Engle, R. F. (1983) 'Estimates of the Variance of US Inflation Based upon the ARCH Model', *Journal of Money, Credit and Banking*, vol. 15, pp. 286–301.

Engle, R. F. and Granger, C. W. J. (1987) 'Co-integration and Error Correction: Representation, Estimation and Testing', *Econometrica*, vol. 55, pp. 251–76.

Figlewski, S. and Wachtel, P. (1981) 'The Formation of Inflationary Expectations', *Review of Economics and Statistics*, vol. 63, pp. 1–10.

Figlewski, S. and Wachtel, P. (1983) 'Rational Expectations, Informational Efficiency and Tests Using Survey Data: A Reply', *Review of Economics and Statistics*, vol. 65, pp. 529–31.

Fishe, R. P. H. and Idson, T. L. (1989) 'Information-Induced Heteroskedasticity in Price Expectations Data', manuscript, University of Miami, Florida.

Fishe, R. P. H. and Lahiri, K. (1981) 'On the Estimation of Inflationary Expectations from Qualitative Responses', *Journal of Econometrics*, vol. 16, pp. 89–102.

Frankel, J. A. and Froot, K. A. (1986) 'Understanding the US Dollar in the Eighties: The Expectations of Chartists and Fundamentalists', *Economic Record*, vol. 62 (supplementary issue) pp. 24–38.

Frankel, J. A. and Froot, K. A. (1987) 'Using Survey Data to Test Standard Propositions Regarding Exchange Rate Expectations', *American Economic Review*, vol. 77, pp. 133–53.

Friedman, B. M. (1980) 'Survey Evidence on the Rationality of Interest Rate Expectations', *Journal of Monetary Economics*, vol. 6, pp. 453–65.

Froot, K. A. (1989) 'New Hope for the Expectations Hypothesis of the Term Structure of Interest Rates', *Journal of Finance*, vol. 44, pp. 283–305.

Froot, K. A. and Frankel, J. A. (1989) 'Forward Discount Bias: Is it an Exchange Risk Premium?' *Quarterly Journal of Economics*, vol. 104, pp. 139–61.

Granger, C. W. J. (1986) 'Developments in the Study of Co-integrated Economic Variables', *Oxford Bulletin of Economics and Statistics*, vol. 48, pp. 213–28.

Grossman, S. (1975) 'Rational Expectations and the Econometric Modelling of Markets Subject to Uncertainty: A Bayesian Approach', *Journal of Econometrics*, vol. 3, pp. 255–72.

Hafer, R. W. and Hein, S. E. (1989) 'Comparing Futures and Survey Forecasts of Near Term Treasury Bill Rates', *Federal Reserve Bank of St Louis Review*, May–June, pp. 33–42.

Maddala: Survey of Information on Expectations   343

Hafer, R. W. and Resler, D. H. (1982) 'On the Rationality of Inflation Forecasts: A New Look at the Livingston Data', *Southern Economic Journal*, vol. 48, pp. 1049–56.

Hakkio, C. S. and Rush, M. (1989) 'Market Efficiency and Cointegration: An Application to the Sterling and Deutschemark Exchange Markets', *Journal of International Money and Finance*, vol. 8, pp. 75–88.

Hasbrouck, J. (1984) 'Stock Returns, Inflation and Economic Activity: The Survey Evidence', *Journal of Finance*, vol. 39, pp. 1293–310.

Ito, T. (1988) 'Foreign Exchange Rate Expectations: Micro Survey Data', NBER Working paper no 2679.

Jonung, L. (1981) 'Perceived and Expected Rates of Inflation in Sweden', *American Economic Review*, vol. 71, pp. 961–8.

Juster, T. and Comment, R. (1978) 'A Note on the Measurement of Price Expectations', mimeo, University of Michigan, Ann Arbor, Michigan.

Keane, M. P. and Runkle, D. E. (1989) 'Are Economic Forecasts Rational?' *Federal Reserve Bank of Minneapolis Quarterly Review*, Spring, 1989, pp. 26–33.

Knöbl, A. (1974) 'Price Expectations and Actual Price Behaviour in Germany', *International Monetary Fund Staff Papers*, vol. 21, pp. 83–100.

Koenig, H. and Nerlove, M. (1986) 'Price Flexibility, Inventory Behavior and Production Responses', in Heller, W., Starr, R. M. and Starrett, D. A. (eds) *Equilibrium Analysis, Essays in Honor of K. J. Arrow, Vol. II* (Cambridge, UK: Cambridge University Press) pp. 179–218.

Koenig, H., Nerlove, M. and Oudiz, G. (1985) 'On the Formation of Price Expectations: An Analysis of Business Test Data of Log-Linear Probability Models', *European Economic Review*, vol. 29, pp. 103–38.

Lahiri, K. and Chun, T. S. (1989) 'Some Tests for Unbiasedness in the Long Run Using Survey Data', *International Economic Journal*, vol. 3, pp. 27–42.

Lahiri, K., Teigland, C. and Zaporowski, M. (1988) 'Interest Rates and the Probability Distribution of Price Forecasts', *Journal of Money, Credit and Banking*, vol. 20, pp. 233–48.

Lahiri, K. and Zaporowski, M. (1987) 'More Flexible Use of Survey Data on Expectations in Macroeconomic Models', *Journal of Business and Economic Statistics*, vol. 5, no 1, pp. 69–76.

Leonard, J. S. (1982) 'Wage Expectations in the Labor Market: Survey Evidence on Rationality', *Review of Economics and Statistics*, vol. 64, no 1, pp. 157–61.

Lewis, K. K. (1989) 'Changing Beliefs and Systematic Rational Forecast Errors With Evidence from Foreign Exchange', *American Economic Review*, vol. 79, pp. 621–36.

Liu, P. C. (1989) 'The Dynamics of Nominal Exchange Rates', unpublished Ph.D. dissertation, University of Florida, Gainesville, Florida.

Lovell, M. C. (1986) 'Tests of the Rational Expectations Hypothesis', *American Economic Review*, vol. 76, pp. 110–24.

Maddala, G. S., Fishe, R. P. H. and Lahiri, K. (1983) 'A Time–Series Analysis of Popular Expectations Data', in Zellner, A. (ed.) *Economic Applications of Time–Series Analysis* (Washington, DC: US Census Bureau) pp. 278–89.

Mullineaux, D. J. (1980) 'Inflation Expectations and Money Growth in the US', *American Economic Review*, vol. 70, pp. 149–61.

Muth, J. F. (1961) 'Rational Expectations and the Theory of Price Movements', *Econometrica*, vol. 29, pp. 315–35.

Pearce, D. K. (1979) 'Comparing Survey and Rational Measures of Expected Inflation: Forecast Performance and Interest Rate Effects', *Journal of Money, Credit and Banking*, vol. 11, pp. 447–56.

Pesando, J. E. (1975) 'A Note on the Rationality of Livingston Price Expectations', *Journal of Political Economy*, vol. 83, pp. 849–58.

Pesaran, M. H. (1988) *Limits to Rational Expectations* (Oxford: Basil Blackwell).

Saunders, P. (1981) 'The Formation of Producers' Price Expectations in Australia', *Economic Record*, vol. 57, pp. 368–78.

Stegman, T. (1985) 'On the Rationality of the Rational Expectations Hypothesis', *Australian Economic Papers*, vol. 24, pp. 350–5.

Taylor, M. P. (1989) 'Expectations, Risk and Uncertainty in the Foreign Exchange Market: Some Results Based on Survey Data', *Manchester School*, vol. 57, no 2, pp. 142–53.

Urich, T. and Wachtel, P. (1984) 'The Structure of Expectations of the Weekly Money Supply Announcement', *Journal of Monetary Economics*, vol. 13, pp. 183–94.

Visco, I. (1984) *Price Expectations in Rising Inflation* (Amsterdam: North Holland).

Zarnowitz, V. (1985) 'Rational Expectations and Macroeconomic Forecasts', *Journal of Business and Economic Statistics*, vol. 3, pp. 293–311.

Zarnowitz, V. and Lambros, L. A. (1987) 'Consensus and Uncertainty in Economic Prediction', *Journal of Political Economy*, vol. 95, no 5, pp. 591–621.

Zellner, A. (1986) 'Biased Predictors, Rationality and the Evaluation of Forecasts', *Economics Letters*, vol. 21, pp. 45–8.